Temperament

Individual Differences
at the Interface of
Biology and Behavior

Temperament

Individual Differences

at the Interface of

Biology and Behavior

1994

John E. Bates & Theodore D. Wachs

American Psychological Association
Washington, D.C.

Published by
American Psychological Association
750 First Street, NE
Washington, DC 20002

Copies may be ordered from
APA Order Department
P.O. Box 2710
Hyattsville, MD 20784

In the UK and Europe, copies may be ordered from
American Psychological Association
3 Henrietta Street
Covent Garden, London
WC2E 8LU England

Typeset in Century Book by Techna Type, Inc., York, PA

Printer: Quinn-Woodbine, Inc., Woodbine, NJ
Cover and Jacket Designer: RCW Communication Design, Inc., Falls Church, VA
Jacket Illustrator: Elizabeth Wolf, Washington, DC
Technical/Production Editor: Mark A. Meschter

Library of Congress Cataloging-in-Publication Data
Temperament : individual differences at the interface of biology and
    behavior / edited by John E. Bates and Theodore D. Wachs.
        p.   cm.
    Includes bibliographical references and index.
    ISBN 1-55798-222-8
    1. Temperament. 2. Temperament—Physiological aspects.
    3. Temperament in children—Physiological aspects.
    4. Temperament in children. 5. Individual differences in children.
    I. Bates, John E., 1945–   . II. Wachs, Theodore D., 1941–   .
    [DNLM: 1. Temperament—physiology.   2. Behavior—physiology.
    3. Individuality.   BF 798 T2815 1994]
    BF798.T444   1994
    155.2′6—dc20
    DNLM/DLC
    for Library of Congress   93-47187
                                                                        CIP

British Library Cataloguing-in-Publication Data
A CIP record is available from the British Library

Printed in the United States of America
First Edition

APA Science Volumes

Best Methods for the Analysis of Change: Recent Advances,
Unanswered Questions, Future Directions
Cardiovascular Reactivity to Psychological Stress and Disease
The Challenge in Mathematics and Science Education: Psychology's
Response
Cognition: Conceptual and Methodological Issues
Cognitive Bases of Musical Communication
Conceptualization and Measurement of Organism–Environment
Interaction
Developmental Psychoacoustics
Emotion and Culture
Hostility, Coping, and Health
Organ Donation and Transplantation: Psychological and Behavioral
Factors
The Perception of Structure
Perspectives on Socially Shared Cognition
Psychological Testing of Hispanics
Researching Community Psychology: Issues of Theory and Methods
Sleep and Cognition
Studying Lives Through Time: Personality and Development
The Suggestibility of Children's Recollections: Implications for
Eyewitness Testimony
Taste, Experience, and Feeding
Temperament: Individual Differences at the Interface of Biology and
Behavior
Through the Looking Glass: Issues of Psychological Well-Being in
Captive Nonhuman Primates

A PA expects to publish volumes on the following conference topics:

Changing Ecological Approaches to Development: Organism–Environment Mutualities

Converging Operations in the Study of Visual Selective Attention

The Psychology of Industrial Relations

Measuring Changes in Patients Following Psychological and Pharmacological Interventions

Perspectives on the Ecology of Human Development

Sleep Onset: Normal and Abnormal Processes

Stereotypes: Brain–Behavior Relationships

Women's Psychological and Physical Health

As part of its continuing and expanding commitment to enhance the dissemination of scientific psychological knowledge, the Science Directorate of APA established a Scientific Conferences Program. A series of volumes resulting from these conferences is jointly produced by the Science Directorate and the Office of Communications. A call for proposals is issued several times annually by the Science Directorate, which, collaboratively with the APA Board of Scientific Affairs, evaluates the proposals and selects several conferences for funding. This important effort has resulted in an exceptional series of meetings and scholarly volumes, each of which individually has contributed to the dissemination of research and dialogue in these topical areas.

The APA Science Directorate's conferences funding program has supported 29 conferences since its inception in 1988. To date, 21 volumes resulting from conferences have been published.

William C. Howell, PhD
Executive Director

Virginia E. Holt
Assistant Executive Director

Contents

Part Three: Implications of Biological Models of Temperament

Contributors

John E. Bates, Department of Psychology, Indiana University

Susan D. Calkins, Institute for Child Study, University of Maryland

Douglas Derryberry, Department of Psychology, Oregon State University

Warren O. Eaton, Department of Psychology, University of Manitoba, Winnipeg, Manitoba, Canada

Robert N. Emde, University of Colorado Medical School, Denver, Colorado

Nathan A. Fox, Institute for Child Study, University of Maryland

Megan R. Gunnar, Institute of Child Development, University of Minnesota

Beverly King, Department of Psychological Science, Purdue University

Charles A. Nelson, Institute of Child Development, University of Minnesota

Robert Plomin, Center for Developmental and Health Genetics, Pennsylvania State University

Michael I. Posner, Department of Psychology, University of Oregon

Mary K. Rothbart, Department of Psychology, University of Oregon

Kimberly J. Saudino, Center for Developmental and Health Genetics, Pennsylvania State University

Joseph E. Steinmetz, Department of Psychology, Indiana University

Jan Strelau, Faculty of Psychology, University of Warsaw, Warsaw, Poland

Theodore D. Wachs, Department of Psychological Science, Purdue University

Marvin Zuckerman, Department of Psychology, University of Delaware

Preface

B oth basic and clinical scientists, especially those interested in child development, have become increasingly interested in temperament. Part of this appeal has to do with the fact that temperament can be viewed at both a biological and a behavioral level. The main appeal of the concepts of temperament is that they theoretically represent fundamental, biological processes. This has made temperament especially important in the scientific movement toward understanding children's development as a systemic process, with contributions not only from the environment but also from characteristics of the individual child. Although temperament is theoretically at the interface of biology and behavior, for the most part, research on temperament focuses on behavioral rather than biological processes.

This book grew initially out of our curiosity about how temperament is rooted in biology. Like many other researchers, both of us have studied temperament primarily as a behavioral variable, viewing the assumed biological basis as a black box. In large part, this reflects our lack of understanding about the biological basis of behavior in general and temperament in particular. Although a number of book chapters and articles have appeared in the past few years that include some information about the biological bases of temperament, few of them have focused sharply on this question. We felt, even as behaviorally oriented researchers, that a sharper focus was needed.

Our search for a better developed understanding of the biological roots of temperament first took the form of a conference that we organized. We had been tapped to take our turn as organizers of the Ninth Occasional Temperament Conference, a loosely organized but remarkably persistent and regular group of developmentally oriented researchers that has been meeting about every 2nd year since the late 1970s. We decided on a biological focus. This conference was held from October 29–31, 1992, in Bloomington, Indiana.

The main discussions of the conference focused on the topics that are presented in this book in the form of chapters. We felt that the sharp focus that we had sought was realized in these presentations and in the dialogue that ensued. An opening in the conference's schedule allowed Hill Goldsmith (a noted behavioral geneticist) to extemporaneously organize a very interesting panel discussion on quantitative genetics approaches. Other participants in this discussion included Adam Matheny, Dick Rose, Julia Braungart, and Bob Emde. In addition to the main discussions, posters were presented by a number of other noted researchers, including C. Stifter, J. Cameron, D. Rice, R. Hansen, D. Rosen, W. Carey, L. Weissbluth, M. Weissbluth, B. Schraeder, A. Sanson, M. Prior, D. Smart, F. Oberklaid, S. McClowry, G. Mettetal, R. Thomas, C. Ratekin, A. Slotboom, E. Elphick, M. Trudel, A. Legendre, F. Sinclair, J. Naud, Pai Chih Kao, J. Worobey, G. Kochanska, and K. Murray. These researchers and others (e.g., Stella Chess, Alex Thomas, Chuck Halverson, and Roy Martin) contributed greatly to the intellectual stimulation of the meeting.

With the conference as a springboard, the next step in our search was the present book. Some of the biologically oriented researchers who participated at the conference were asked to contribute chapters on their specialty areas. They were asked not merely to summarize their knowledge on the biological roots of temperament but to bridge the apparent gap between behavioral and biological researchers. We feel that the chapter authors succeeded in this mission. Behaviorally oriented readers of this book will gain a greater appreciation of the beautiful details of the biological roots of individual differences in development. Biologically oriented readers will gain a greater appreciation of how individual differences in behavior might result from complex interactions between biological and nonbiological processes.

An effort such as this owes much to the contributions of others. The contribution of an edited collection such as this one is directly related to the effort and skill of the chapter authors. We were exceedingly fortunate to have the collaboration of authors of such high quality. They are an eminent group of scholars who have definitely provided the educational process we sought when we started this project. We are grateful to them for sharing their expertise in such interesting writing and for their gracious responses to our editorial efforts.

The American Psychological Association (APA) Science Directorate awarded us a grant for organizing the conference. The editors are grateful not only to APA for their financial support of the conference but also to the Dean of Research at Indiana University and the Dean of Liberal Arts at Purdue University for providing matching funds. We also wish to thank our respective departmental chairpersons, Margaret Intons-Peterson (Indiana University) and Gerald Gruen (Purdue University) for their support and encouragement. Thanks are also due to a number of colleagues and students, who helped greatly in the preparations for and logistics of the conference, and to Liz Feitl, who provided secretarial–organizational help in getting the preparations for the conference underway. We also are especially grateful to Lana Fish, who handled the major part of the conference arrangements in her typical outstanding way.

The conference and the editing of this book have been both challenging and stimulating for us. We hope that the readers of this book will find some of the same challenges and rewards.

John E. Bates
Theodore D. Wachs

CHAPTER 1

Introduction

John E. Bates

Interest in the topic of temperament has grown at an increasing rate over the past 25 years, especially in the context of child development (Bates, 1989b). Temperament terms frequently appear in models of child development and social adjustment. Among the empirical advances in the area are the covariations found between temperament and other dimensions, including behavior problems (Bates, 1987, 1989a); attachment (Belsky & Rovine, 1987; Goldsmith & Alansky, 1987); maternal depression (Cutrona & Troutman, 1986); parent–child relations (Crockenberg, 1986); and children's behavior in laboratory learning situations (Wachs, Morrow, & Slabach, 1990), during IQ testing (Bathurst & Gottfried, 1987), at home (Sanson, Prior, & Oberklaid, 1985), and in the classroom (Pullis, 1985). Despite this empirical progress, however, there is still considerable uncertainty about the meaning of the empirical results. Do operational measures reflect influences from core, inborn factors in the child—as model testers have hoped—or alternatively, are they indexes of the current environment, the accumulated experience of the child, or informants' cognitive–perceptual construal processes?

Concepts of Temperament

Conceptually, temperament encompasses multiple levels (Bates, 1989b). At the most observable level, dimensions of temperament are defined in terms of patterns of behavior, with questions of the developmental origins of the behavior set aside. For example, one could define a dimension of temperament as the behavior pattern of negative emotionality. At this level of definition, one is not concerned with origins—whether from constitutional factors, environmental–experiential factors, or both. In contrast, at a deeper level, dimensions of temperament are explicitly defined as behavior patterns that develop from biological characteristics. The developmental process by which constitutional factors produce temperament, including genes and neural structure and function, has to include repeated organism–environment transactions (Wachs, 1992). Indeed, it is becoming very difficult to think of biological influences, from the level of the DNA codes on up, as operating independently of the environment (Gottlieb, 1992; Hinde, 1992).

There is nearly universal agreement among temperament researchers that the individual differences that are called temperament have developmentally early, biological roots (Goldsmith et al., 1987). In fact, a very big part of the conceptual appeal of temperament concepts is their assumed inborn, biological basis, even if it is also generally agreed that temperament characteristics may shift over time to some degree. Researchers and clinicians are more and more often searching for improved ways to describe how biological and environmental factors interact to produce individual adaptations (Lazarus, 1991; Wachs & Plomin, 1991). Nevertheless, until now, the major research emphasis has been on temperament at the behavioral level. Only recently has emphasis been given to empirical and theoretical explorations of the biological roots of temperament.

This book brings together leading examples of the recent research on the biological origins of temperament-relevant behavior. The book was intended to be useful not only for behaviorally oriented researchers who have found it difficult to keep up with the exciting developments in neuroscience, but also for biologically oriented researchers who might gain a greater appreciation for how their skills and knowledge might be creatively applied to the socially and scientifically important questions emerging from research on human individual differences. The chapters presented here describe advances in the description and understanding of the brain processes associated with temperamentlike behavioral events and more molar individual difference patterns. At the same time, they suggest alternatives to the traditional ways in which one thinks about and designs research on temperament.

Aside from its biological basis, another part of the conceptualization of temperament is the idea that the dimensions of temperament appear relatively early in life and are core factors in a stable personality (Buss & Plomin, 1984). For this reason, temperament researchers have been particularly interested in measures of temperament in the earliest years of childhood and in questions about the stability or instability of temperament across development (e.g., Thomas & Chess, 1977). With careful attention to covariance between biological factors and temperamental behavior, it may be possible to understand not only the genetic and neural roots of early appearing traits but also how later appearing traits can fit the definition of temperament. For example, even though it is assumed to be at least partly due to inherited traits (see Eaton, chapter 10 in this book; Plomin & Saudino, chapter 6 in this book), activity level may not become a stable individual difference until children have reached a certain level of physical mobility (Rothbart, 1989). It might be thought that any instability in a temperamentlike trait would reflect environmental forces. However, there appears to be evidence that continuity and change themselves are partly due to inherited characteristics (Eaton, chapter 10).

In defining temperament, it is important to remember that the term *temperament* is a rubric—an umbrella that covers more specific concepts (Goldsmith & Rieser-Danner, 1986). There is less agreement on what specific variables ought to be included as part of temperament than on what the most abstract definition of temperament ought to be. However, there is considerable agreement that temperament refers to characteristic patterns of emotional reactions, including sensitivity and intensity of reaction (Goldsmith & Campos, 1982; Strelau, 1983; Thomas & Chess, 1977) and emotional self-regulation (Rothbart, 1989), as well as referring to activity (Buss, 1989; Eaton, 1983) and sociability (Buss & Plomin, 1984). There has recently been some notable progress in organizing the concepts of temperament and personality from a "top-down" perspective (Zuckerman, 1991). There are thousands of potential adjectives to describe individual behavioral differences, and hundreds of higher order collections of these descriptors have been incorporated into personality and temperament scales. Several decades of empirical research on these ratings of personality show that the scales and descriptors fall rather consistently into a small number of higher order factors (e.g., see Goldberg, 1993). The two dimensions that have been of most interest in recent studies of biological substrates of temperament are *negative emotionality*, which includes variables such as fearfulness, anxiety/tension, inhibition, and dysphoria, and *positive emotionality*, which includes enthusiasm, excitement, and happiness. Zuckerman (1991; chapter 9 in this book) makes a good case for a third dimension—*impulsive, unsocialized sensation seeking*, which is a stable, early appearing trait that appears to be separate from positive and negative emotionality.

Child temperament researchers have developed temperament scale analogues for each of the three, second-order dimensions of personality. For example, negative mood (Thomas & Chess, 1977) and difficultness (Bates, 1980) at least roughly represent the negative emotionality dimension, whereas sociability and activity level (Buss & Plomin, 1984) pertain to positive emotionality. Resistance to control (Bates & Bayles, 1984) may represent the impulsive sensation-seeking dimension. The reduced dimension systems of description are actually proving to be powerful tools for organizing knowledge about biological processes in behavioral adaptation. Gray (1991), for example, described two systems: (a) a behavioral inhibition system, which is relevant to the second-order construct of negative emotionality, with its roots in the septohippocampal system, and (b) a behavioral approach system, which is relevant to positive emotionality, with its roots in a variety of structures including the caudate, the accumbens, and the prefrontal cortex, in addition to the septohippocampal system. However, there is no certainty that dimensions of temperament are truly homologous to the second-order dimensions of personality; nor is there certainty that the full range of temperament variables would be well described in only a three-dimensional space (Halverson, Kohnstamm, & Martin, in press).

Preview of the Book

This book was designed to function in some way as a bridge between the "top-down" approach, in which behaviorally oriented researchers start with key behavior patterns and look for associated neural processes, and the "bottom-up" approach, in which biologically oriented researchers start from known biological events and try to predict the behavioral patterns that are associated with them. Both approaches are necessary and should inform each other (Zuckerman, 1991). The authors of the chapters have bridged these two approaches in a number of interesting ways. The first two substantive chapters provide an orientation to neural processes and brain development that are of likely relevance to temperament. In chapter 2, Steinmetz explains the basic but complex neural anatomy and information processing that are relevant to emotional behavior and, by extension, to temperament. He gives as much detail as one would want in a source such as this, yet he manages to keep clear sight of the broader question of which brain systems are likely to be involved in organizing the behavioral patterns that are related to temperament. Along with Gray (1991), Steinmetz focuses mostly on the behavioral patterns of inhibition to novelty or conditioned signals of threat, approach to signals of reward, and defensive aggression and flight to signals of unconditioned threat. Steinmetz emphasizes that temperament and learning are in dynamic interaction over the course of development. This emphasis points toward a more biologically advanced version of the organism–environment fit concepts that have been widely used since the 1970s, most notably the goodness-of-fit concept of Thomas and Chess (1977). Steinmetz outlines a within-subjects research paradigm for contrasting the neural processes of aversive versus appetitive conditioning—two kinds of learning that are likely to be involved in the development of temperament behavioral patterns.

In chapter 3, Nelson complements Steinmetz's review with his own brief, lucid review of the neurobiology, with an emphasis on the development of the systems that are relevant to emotion and temperament. Nelson concentrates on the striatum, which is important for organizing motor responses; the hippocampus, which is important in memory and detection of novelty; the inferior temporal region TE, which is involved in explicit long-term memory; the amygdala, a memory area that organizes emotional reactions in social situations; and areas of the prefrontal cortex, which hold "on-line" the sensory and emotional associations that are formed in the limbic systems (including the amygdala and hypothalamus) while formulating behavioral responses. Nelson discusses the development of these systems in the context of the overall development of the nervous system. If one is to understand temperament, then one needs to understand the development of the neural systems that underlie emotional or temperament-relevant behaviors. Nelson suggests ways in which some of the instability of individual differences in temperament in infancy may pertain to the developmental process of the nervous system. For example, although the basic emotional expressions of response to novelty are available early in infancy, the sustained, situationally appropriate action patterns in response to novelty become available only late in the 2nd year of human development.

In chapter 4, Rothbart, Derryberry, and Posner continue and expand on the theme of development of temperament. This chapter places more emphasis on definition of behavioral traits than did the first two chapters, but it still describes neural systems in some detail. From a developmental perspective, Rothbart et al. review the reduced-dimension, Big Five–type dimensions of personality in relation both to childhood temperament and underlying neural systems. One thing that is distinctive about the perspective of Rothbart et al. is their emphasis on the role of attention. They do not deny the importance of fear in regulating approach and aggressive behaviors, but they also argue that attentional abilities and tendencies come to assume an important function in regulating emotion and behavior. Rothbart et al. detail two different attentional systems in the brain: the posterior network, which is involved in orientation to sensory stimuli, and the anterior network, which takes information from the limbic system and is involved not only in awareness of events but also in the integration of emotional experience and behavioral expression. They also discuss the role of positive social orientation in controlling the experience of situations and the expression of emotional and behavioral responses. This variable is in the Big Five models of personality as agreeableness, and Rothbart et al. make a detailed argument for it having specific neural underpinnings and being temperamental in nature, (although heavily influenced by experience). In addition, Rothbart et al. provide some advanced lessons on the biological conceptions of temperament, for example, pointing out the somewhat subtle but interesting neural and behavioral differences between the behavioral approach-type systems of Gray (1991), Depue and Iacono (1989), and Panksepp (1986).

Strelau, in chapter 5, bypasses the Big Five dimensions and looks for a single unifying theme in temperament. He begins by reviewing the history of the concept of arousal as related to both temperament measures and psychophysiological systems. Strelau argues that a fundamental aspect of many of the very large number of temperament and personality dimensions, such as extraversion, neuroticism, sensation seeking, and behavioral inhibition, is that they all involve the more general construct of arousability. Strelau does not state that the different dimensions are all equivalent at either the psychological or the physiological level, but he argues that the individual differences in the different psychological and brain systems all share the phenomenon of arousability. This theoretical essay is a logical extension of Strelau's earlier research (e.g., 1983), which bridges both Eastern European and Western notions of temperament. It points the way toward an interesting, biologically informed, conceptual integration.

Chapter 6 by Plomin and Saudino, which is on the role of genetics in temperament, is as oriented toward methodology as Strelau's chapter is oriented toward theory. Plomin and Saudino quickly pass over the more traditional genetic analyses that measure the degree of heritability of a trait. Rather, they first review the important new quantitative genetics methods such as multivariate genetic analysis and genetic analysis of age-to-age change and continuity. They then focus on the fast-developing, futuristic field of molecular genetics. Their chapter provides an introduction to the terminology and research strategies for identifying the particular genes that combine to code for temperament and other behavior patterns. For example, one way of searching for quantitative trait loci— the multiple genes that affect a given trait in varied degrees—involves the use of recombinant inbred strains of mice. The method has identified a number of markers of genes affecting the trait of activity level. For example, on Chromosome 14, there appear to be activity-related genes somewhere in the vicinity of five different markers. Some of the regions appear to correspond to human chromosome regions, which makes them likely starting points in the search for markers of human activity differences. Another research strategy involves what is called allelic association. Plomin and Saudino present an exciting preliminary finding with this approach: They compared nine children who were rated by their mothers as being highly active with another nine children who were rated as being very low in activity. They found that the high-activity children more frequently had a particular gene that codes for tyrosinase, an enzyme that is involved in the production of a particular protein. Replication of this finding will be crucial. The number of genes affecting activity level is likely to be large, but locating even one gene will be very advantageous.

The next three chapters consider relatively focused topics concerning temperament differences in adaptation. Each of the chapters pertains to the behavioral distinction of approach versus withdrawal (or inhibition) in response to novelty, a distinction that appears to stem from two related but fundamentally separate systems. In chapter 7, Gunnar analyzes the role of temperament in children's coping with stress, placing temperament in the context of a theoretically rich and empirically supported model of coping. Besides temperament, other elements of Gunnar's model include the objective characteristics of the situation, the child's prior experiences, and the child's current emotional state, which only partly depends on temperament. All of these elements influence the child's initial appraisal of the situation as potentially pleasurable versus threatening. From this appraisal come explorative, inhibitive, or other coping responses, with each having different psychophysiological consequences. Cortisol is the end product of the coping-with-threat branch, which is derived from the hypothalamic–pituitary–adrenocortical system, the activation of which is which is typically experienced as distressing. Gunnar does not look at stress as a disembodied stimulus; she describes it as being intimately related to the demands and supports of social situations in active transaction with the child. She considers the differences between adaptation early in the preschool year and later in the year. She considers the role of the child's felt security (as indexed by attachment classifications), as well as the way in which supportive caregivers manage possible threats for the child. Outgoing children show higher cortisol levels than do inhibited children early in the school year, which probably reflects the likelihood that their active exploration occasionally produces stress (e.g., conflict with a peer). However, the outgoing children then show lower cortisol levels later in the year, when they presumably have mastered the environment, at least in relation to the mastery of the shy children, who are now being urged to increase their explorations and thus experience the stress that exploration and mastery may sometimes bring.

The biological roots of inhibition versus approach in response to novelty are also considered, from a different perspective, by Calkins and Fox in chapter 8. Calkins and Fox assess behavioral inhibition at age 4 months by an index of high motor activity and negative affect in response to a series of novel stimuli. This index predicts asymmetry in activation of the brain in response to stresses at 9 months and greater fearfulness at age 14 months. Asymmetry in cortical activation appears to reflect an underlying organization in the systems that control approach and inhibition. In general, Calkins and Fox point out, when approach is elicited, there is more left frontal cortex activation than there is right frontal cortex activation; and when withdrawal is elicited, there is more right activation than left activation. These events are related to events in the limbic system, as detailed in the chapters by Steinmetz, Nelson, and Rothbart et al. (chapters 2, 3, and 4, respectively). Calkins and Fox share the perspective of Gunnar (chapter 7) that the biological predispositions of the child act only in interaction with environmental and self-generated sources of regulation of emotion and behavior. In keeping with this perspective, they pose questions about developmental continuity and change as related to environmental pressures, temperamentlike characteristics other than inhibition (tendency to become frustrated), and attachment security.

Both Gunnar's and Calkins and Fox's chapters consider both inhibition and outgoingness in children. In chapter 9, Zuckerman considers traits that reflect the disinhibition dimension of impulsive unsocialized sensation seeking in adults and children. Taking a top-down perspective, Zuckerman summarizes the extensive literature on the behavioral, demographic, psychopathological, and conditioning correlates of impulsive sensation seeking, thereby demonstrating the conceptual coherence of the dimension. At its positive extreme, sensation seeking is associated with disorders such as the psychopathic personality. However, at more normal levels, it is clear that there are important functions for the dimension, including (a) the ability to attend sharply to signals of possible reward and ignore distractors like punishment and (b) continued cortical responding to intense stimuli rather than cortical inhibition. Zuckerman then reviews the extensive evidence on biological factors in the dimension, considering psychophysiological responses to signals of reward and punishment, augmentation versus reduction of cortical evoked potentials, psychopharmacological correlates of sensation seeking (with special attention to monoamine oxidase, dopamine, and serotonin), experimental psychopharmacological evidence, the effects of hormones (with special attention to gonadal hormones), and genetics.

The last three chapters of this book consider the implications of the biological–behavioral research trends that are exemplified in the preceding chapters. Eaton, in chapter 10, considers methodological implications of the imminent uniting of behavioral and biological traditions in temperament research. He uses a number of examples from his research on children's activity differences. Eaton first addresses the problem of how to narrow one's search amongst the thousands of possible linkages between temperament variables and biological characteristics. He recommends starting with behavior traits with practical importance, such as difficult temperament and coping with stress. He also recommends an alertness to serendipitous advances in measurement that could be capitalized on. One example is ultrasound technology, which was not developed to aid behavioral researchers but which Eaton has used to objectively measure individual differences in fetal activity. One methodological bonus of this capitalization on technology is that the objective measure turned out to correspond well to expectant mothers' reports of the phenomenon. Eaton goes on to make other methodological suggestions. One powerfully presented suggestion is to be mindful of the likelihood that even substantively important effects are likely to involve small correlations or small differences between group means. Modest effect sizes imply the need to use larger samples than are used in many studies. A corollary is to develop both biological and behavioral measures that can be collected on many subjects. Similarly, there is also a need to improve the reliability of measures through aggregation of measurements, not only in the typical context of behavioral measurement but also in the context of biological measurement, as Gunnar (chapter 7) did in averaging across daily cortisol samples. Eaton also reminds us of the importance of maintaining a developmental perspective to avoid being misled by cross-sectional data on temperament and its biological underpinnings. As a case in point, he cites the study by Saudino and Eaton (1993), which found that activity levels of monozygotic twins were more concordant than those of dizygotic twins at both 7 and 36 months of age. Longitudinal data showed that there was an overall increase in activity between the two ages, with the increases more similar for monozygotic twins than for dizygotic twins. However, the stability of activity across these ages was very low, which suggests different genetic processes operating at the two different points in development.

The practical applications of the trends in temperament research are considered by Bates, Wachs, and Emde in chapter 11. This chapter responds to the trends shown in this book in the following ways: (a) by focusing on the dimensions of temperament that have the best conceptual convergence with the dimensions of the Big Three personality system (positive affectivity, negative affectivity, and constraint vs. impulsiveness), which have relevance to socially important child outcomes and which are supported by reasonably detailed empirical data on physiological and genetic aspects, and (b) by extrapolating from current applications and the research trends to possible ways of making use of an improved description of biological differences in relation to overt behavioral differences. Bates et al. review current practice innovations and present in their future applications section a few ideas that may deserve applied development. One example is the assessment of congruence between vocal and other behavioral displays of a young child's distress and psychophysiological stress by-products (e.g., cortisol assays). Bates et al. predict that this will yield diagnostic information that will provide a firmer basis for antianxiety versus behavior-suppression treatments in younger children than the current behavioral distinctions between internalizing versus externalizing distinctions now provide. However, at the same time, they are quite cautious in their projections because of the early stage of temperament research and the general lack of empirical evaluation of existing ways of using temperament.

Finally, in chapter 12, Wachs and King critically summarize the research trends found in the preceding chapters of this book. They argue that the future of temperament research does not belong only to the biologically oriented investigators but also to those who are firmly rooted in behavioral approaches and who can synergistically learn from and contribute to biological explorations. They highlight the major brain systems that have been implicated in temperament and point to further issues, such as the need for more specificity about the neurochemical processes that are associated with temperament, the need for conceptually organizing the immense complexity of multiple brain systems that interact with each other, and the need for more precisely defined behavioral systems onto which biological systems may be mapped. Wachs and King highlight a number of key issues common to a number of the book's chapters, such as a developmental perspective and the importance of environmental contexts in understanding psychobiological events. The latter issue launches an illuminating summary of the ways in which it is possible to conceptualize the interactions between the individual and the environment.

References

Bates, J. E. (1980). The concept of difficult temperament. *Merrill-Palmer Quarterly, 26,* 299–319.

Bates, J. E. (1987). Temperament in infancy. In J. D. Osofsky (Ed.), *Handbook of infant development* (2nd ed., pp. 1101–1149). New York: Wiley.

Bates, J. E. (1989a). Applications of temperament concepts. In G. A. Kohnstamm, J. E.

Bates, & M. K. Rothbart (Eds.), *Temperament in childhood* (pp. 321–355). New York: Wiley.

Bates, J. E. (1989b). Concepts and measures of temperament. In G. A. Kohnstamm, J. E. Bates, & M. K. Rothbart (Eds.), *Temperament in childhood* (pp. 3–26). New York: Wiley.

Bates, J. E., & Bayles, K. (1984). Objective and subjective components in mothers' perceptions of their children from age 6 months to 3 years. *Merrill-Palmer Quarterly, 30,* 111–130.

Bathurst, K., & Gottfried, A. (1987). Untestable subjects in child development research: Developmental implications. *Child Development, 58,* 1135–1144.

Belsky, J., & Rovine, M. (1987). Temperament and attachment security in the strange situation: An empirical rapproachment. *Child Development, 58,* 787–795.

Buss, A. (1989). Temperaments as personality traits. In G. A. Kohnstamm, J. E. Bates, & M. K. Rothbart (Eds.), *Temperament in childhood* (pp. 49–58). New York: Wiley.

Buss, A., & Plomin, R. (1984). *Temperament: Early developing personality traits.* Hillsdale, NJ: Erlbaum.

Crockenberg, S. B. (1986). Are temperamental differences in babies associated with predictable differences in caregiving? In J. Lerner & R. Lerner (Eds.), *Temperament and psychosocial interaction in children.* San Francisco: Jossey-Bass.

Cutrona, C. E., & Troutman, B. (1986). Social support, infant temperament and parenting self-efficacy. *Child Development, 57,* 1507–1518.

Depue, R. A., & Iacono, W. G. (1989). Neurobehavioral aspects of affective disorders. *Annual Review of Psychology, 40,* 457–492.

Eaton, W. O. (1983). Measuring activity level with actometers: Reliability, validity, and arm length. *Child Development, 54,* 720–726.

Goldberg, L. (1993). The structure of phenotypic personality traits. *American Psychologist, 48,* 26–34.

Goldsmith, H. H., & Alansky, J. A. (1987). Maternal and infant temperamental predictors of attachment: A meta-analytic review. *Journal of Consulting and Clinical Psychology, 55,* 805–816.

Goldsmith, H. H., Buss, A., Plomin, R., Rothbart, M. K., Thomas, A., Chess, S., Hinde, R. A., & McCall, R. B. (1987). What is temperament? Four approaches. *Child Development, 58,* 505–529.

Goldsmith, H. H., & Campos, J. J. (1982). Toward a theory of infant temperament. In R. N. Emde & R. J. Harmon (Eds.), *The development of attachment and affiliative systems* (pp. 161–193). New York: Plenum.

Goldsmith, H. H., & Rieser-Danner, L. (1986). Variation among temperament theories and validation studies of temperament assessment. In G. A. Kohnstamm (Ed.), *Temperament discussed* (pp. 1–10). Lisse, The Netherlands: Swets & Zeitlinger.

Gottlieb, G. (1992). *Individual development and evolution: The genesis of novel behavior.* New York: Oxford University Press.

Gray, J. A. (1991). The neuropsychology of temperament. In J. Strelau & A. Angleitner (Eds.), *Explorations in temperament* (pp. 105–128). New York: Plenum.

Halverson, C. F., Kohnstamm, G. A., & Martin, R. P. (in press). *The developing structure of temperament and personality from infancy to adulthood.* Hillsdale, NJ: Erlbaum.

Hinde, R. A. (1992). Developmental psychology in the context of other behavioral sciences. *Developmental Psychology, 28,* 1018–1029.

Lazarus, R. S. (1991). *Emotion and adaptation.* New York: Oxford University Press.

Panksepp, J. (1986). The psychobiology of prosocial behaviors: Separation distress, play, and altruism. In C. Zahn-Waxler, E. M. Cummings, & R. Iannotti (Eds.), *Altruism and aggression: Biological and social origins* (pp. 19–57). Cambridge, UK: Cambridge University Press.

Pullis, M. (1985). LD students' temperament characteristics and their impact on decisions by resource and mainstream teachers. *Learning Disability Quarterly, 8,* 109–121.

Rothbart, M. K. (1989). Temperament and development. In G. A. Kohnstamm, J. E. Bates, & M. K. Rothbart (Eds.), *Temperament in childhood* (pp. 187–247). New York: Wiley.

Sanson, A., Prior, M., & Oberklaid, F. (1985). Normative data on temperament in Australian children. *Australian Journal of Psychology, 37,* 185–195.

Saudino, K. J., & Eaton, W. O. (1993). *Genetic influences on activity level: II. An analysis of continuity and change from infancy to early childhood.* Manuscript submitted for publication.

Strelau, J. (1983). *Temperament, personality, activity.* San Diego, CA: Academic Press.

Thomas, A., & Chess, S. (1977). *Temperament and development.* New York: Brunner/Mazel.

Wachs, T. D. (1992). *The nature of nurture.* Newbury Park, CA: Sage.

Wachs, T. D., Morrow, J., & Slabach, E. (1990). Intra-individual variability in infant visual recognition performance: Temperamental and environmental correlates. *Infant Behavior and Development, 13,* 401–407.

Wachs, T. D., & Plomin, R. (1991). *Conceptualization and measurement of organism–environment interaction.* Washington, DC: American Psychological Association.

Zuckerman, M. (1991). Biotypes for basic personality dimensions? "The Twilight Zone" between genotype and social phenotype. In J. Strelau & A. Angleitner (Eds.), *Explorations in temperament* (pp. 129–146). New York: Plenum.

PART ONE

Basic Biological
and Theoretical
Perspectives

CHAPTER 2

Brain Substrates of Emotion and Temperament

Joseph E. Steinmetz

O ver the past several years, a number of researchers who have been interested in understanding how the brain initiates and guides behavioral and psychological functions have made great progress in defining the neural substrates of a number of processes. For example, details about the role of the premotor and motor areas of the neocortex in the planning and execution of movement have been delineated (di Pellegrino & Wise, 1991; Georgopoulos, Schwartz, & Kettner, 1986; Ojakangas & Ebner, 1991); the basic neural systems that are involved in sensation, simple perception, attention, and memory are beginning to be defined (Kaas, 1991; Livingston & Hubel, 1988; Mishkin, Ungerleider, & Macko, 1983; Posner, Inhoff, Freidrich, & Cohen, 1987; Squire, 1987); and the brain areas and systems that

I thank Sheree Logue, Daniel Miller, Elizabeth Klamo, and Predrag Sorgich for their efforts and contributions made in the development of the rat-signaled barpressing procedures. I also acknowledge John E. Bates for introducing me to the temperament research area. Portions of the research described in this chapter were supported by National Institute of Mental Health grant MH 44052 and by funds from the Center for the Integrated Study of Animal Behavior at Indiana University.

are involved in several forms of simple learning and memory, such as classical or instrumental conditioning, have been studied (Steinmetz & Thompson, 1991). In spite of these advances, however, knowledge of the brain systems and processes that are involved in more complex behavioral or psychological phenomena is rather scant. This is not surprising in light of the fact that several years of experimentation have been necessary to define and study nervous system correlates of the simplest forms of behavior. It is reasonable to assume that as the behavioral and psychological functions become more and more complex, the brain processes that underlie these functions become equally complex.

Temperament is an example of a complex behavioral or psychological process. It can be defined as

> biologically rooted individual differences in behavioral tendencies that are present early in life and are relatively stable across various kinds of situations and over the course of time. Furthermore, there is general agreement that temperament is manifest largely in the context of social interaction. (p. 4, Bates, 1989)

Because brain activity, to some extent, underlies all behavioral and psychological processes, it is reasonable to assume that at least some of the "biologically rooted individual differences" that form the basis of temperament are attributable to individual differences in neural function. This fact makes the study of the neural substrates of temperament doubly difficult. Not only must one study how regions of the nervous system generate and maintain a highly complex psychological phenomenon, but one must also study factors that lead to individual differences in activity of these nervous system areas.

One way of conceptualizing the neurobiology of temperament is shown, in very general terms, in Figure 1. At the core of this system is a set of temperament-related brain structures that are responsible for generating and maintaining temperament-related behavioral patterns. Activity in these brain structures is triggered by appropriate stimuli in the environment. One may assume that the stimuli that trigger activity in temperament-related brain structures can be either quite specific, such as single objects in the environment, or quite complex, such as might be expected during social interaction in which the entire context of the

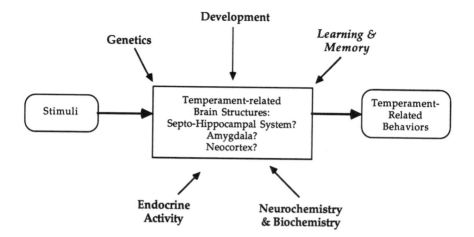

FIGURE 1. A schematic representation of how behaviors related to emotions or temperament might be generated. Several factors that might influence activity in temperament-related brain structures are also shown.

experience might be necessary to activate the temperament-related brain structures. Activity in such structures reliably generates individualized patterns of behavior or constellations of behaviors that are recognized as indicators of temperament. These behaviors include the overt displays of temperament that are typically recorded by researchers who are interested in defining and studying temperament behavior. These behaviors are typically measured by obtaining parental reports through questionnaires and interviews, observing behavior in naturalistic settings such as the home, observing behavior in laboratory situations, or measuring psychophysiological responses (Bates, 1989).

Assuming that one can locate the brain structures or systems that encode, initiate, and maintain the behavioral patterns that are related to temperament, it seems crucial that a number of potential influences on activity in these structures be studied in hopes of determining how these factors might contribute to individual differences noted in the display of temperament. Some of these influences are shown in Figure 1. *Genetics* refers to gene effects that might contribute to differences in basic neural structure or neural connectivity that are seen when individual brains are compared. *Development* includes all variations in developmental processes, from conception onward, that could promote individual differences in neural structure or connectivity. *Endocrine activity* refers to the effects of circulating hormones on the activity in temperament-related structures. *Neurochemistry* and *biochemistry* include chemical influences that determine activity within the neurons of temperament-related structures as well as influences on synaptic interactions between neurons. Finally, *learning* and *memory* refer generally to the influence that previous experience has on activity in the temperament-related brain systems.

In this very simple model of the neurobiology of temperament, the just-listed factors (as well as possibly other factors) could all potentially influence activity in the brain regions that are involved in the encoding of temperament. To advance the understanding of how brain activity is involved in temperament, therefore, it seems necessary to assess the contributions, if any, that each of these factors might make in determining temperament-related behavior. As just pointed out, the study of the neurobiology of temperament could be regarded as a two-step process. First, the structures that are involved in the encoding of temperament (i.e., generating temperament-related behaviors) must be identified. Second, once the structures have been identified, factors that could contribute to individual differences in activity in the structures must be evaluated to determine what influences account for the individual differences in the behavioral patterns of temperament.

This chapter addresses two issues. The first is which brain structures and systems are likely to be involved in the encoding of temperament. The second is how to develop a paradigm for evaluating the origins of temperament-related behavior, and toward this, the chapter describes a new adaptation of an animal learning paradigm. I hope that this presentation provides a useful framework for understanding the neurobiology of temperament.

Neural Structures and Systems Likely Involved in Temperament

Because temperament appears to reflect individual differences in the patterns of emotion that are displayed, it seems likely that the brain systems that are involved in emotion would also be centrally involved in the encoding of temperament. The core of this emotional system is the limbic system, which includes the septohippocampal system, the limbic cortex, the hypothalamus, and the amygdala. Other brain areas of interest include the autonomic nervous system and the effector systems (e.g., the basal ganglia), which likely guide emotion-related movements as well as brain stem areas that are involved in "arousal" or vigilance. The following sections describe the structure, function, and interconnections of these brain systems.

Overview

Over the years, the limbic system has been implicated in a number of brain functions including olfactory processing, memory, and emotion. MacLean (1955) used the term *limbic system* to designate a brain region composed of a ring of tissue comprising the medial wall of each cerebral cortex (i.e., the limbic lobe) together with a number of subcortical brain regions that are centrally involved in the generation and expression of emotions. His definition of the limbic system included the olfactory cortex, the hippocampal formation, the cingulate and subcallosal gyri (all cortical regions), and several subcortical areas including the septum, amygdala, hypothalamus, epithalamus, anterior thalamic nuclei, and a small portion of the basal ganglia. The brain regions that make up the limbic system are highly interconnected and capable of accessing much information including activity in nearly all regions of the neocortex as well as information about neuroendocrine and autonomic activities. In part because the limbic system communicates with these neocortical areas as well as endocrine and autonomic brain areas, it has long been considered the primary system involved in integrating and processing emotions.

The Septohippocampal System

Papez (1937) was among the first to recognize that portions of the limbic system were involved in emotions. Papez believed that the neural substrate of emotion was based on a successive loop of structures that included the hippocampus, the mammillary body, the anterior thalamic nuclei, and the cingulate gyrus. These structures, along with other portions of the septohippocampal system that comprise the *Papez circuit*, are shown in Figure 2. Each of these structures seems to play a role in processing emotions. The hippocampus has been implicated in learning, memory, and timing functions, whereas the mammillary bodies may provide an important link between the hypothalamus and other parts of the limbic system. The anterior thalamic nuclei provide a link between other brain regions and the limbic system. The cingulate gyrus has efferent projections to a number of areas including neocortical association areas, the basal ganglia, and areas that are linked indirectly to the cerebellum. The links with the basal ganglia and the cerebellum are potential routes for limbic system communication with portions of the motor system, which thus provides a means for generating the overt behaviors that are associated with emotions.

To this basic framework of limbic system structures, a number of other interconnections have been added over the years, and the central neural network that is thought to be involved in emotions has been refined somewhat (e.g., Smith & DeVito, 1984). For example, it is now known that the hippocampus proper does not project to the mammillary bodies and does not receive projections from the cingulate gyrus. Rather, a cortical area known as the subicular complex projects to the mammillary body and the anterior thalamic nuclei, and the cingulate gyrus projects back to the subicular area. A number of other neural pathways interact with this closed loop. The subiculum projects also to the entorhinal area and bidirectionally connects with several neocortical association areas. The entorhinal area has efferent projections to the hippocampus proper, which marks the beginning of the well-studied *hippocampal trisynaptic circuit* (i.e., projections from the entorhinal cortex to the dentate gyrus to Ammon's horn of the hippocampus, which then project back to the entorhinal area). The subiculum seems to play a central role in limbic system function: It communicates with the neocortex, provides input to the hippocampal trisynaptic circuit, and is also part of a loop of processing through the mammillary bodies and cingulate gyrus.

The involvement of the hippocampal trisynaptic circuit in learning and memory has often been examined, including studies of long-term potentiation (Bekkers & Stevens, 1990; Swanson, Teyler, & Thompson,

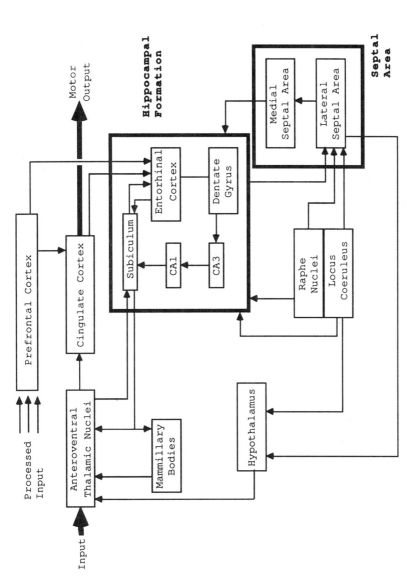

FIGURE 2. A schematic representation of the major components of the septohippocampal system as well as the major brain areas interconnected with this system.

1982) and spatial learning (Eichenbaum, Stewart, & Morris; 1990; Morris, Garrud, Rawlins, & O'Keefe, 1982). Interestingly, the hippocampal trisynaptic circuit has only one major subcortical output. Cells in Ammon's horn project to the lateral septal nucleus. The lateral septal nucleus then projects to the medial septal–diagonal band nuclear complex, which in turn projects to the entire hippocampal formation. The medial septal–diagonal band area is the major source of acetylcholine for the hippocampus as well as neocortical brain areas. Acetylcholine is a neurotransmitter thought to be involved in learning, memory, and cognition as well as several other brain processes. In addition to participating in this closed hippocampal loop, the medial and lateral septal areas receive inputs from the hypothalamus and brain stem.

As can be seen in Figure 2, a common occurrence throughout the septohippocampal system is the presence of information processing in a variety of closed loops. Each of these loops seems to serve a specific function that is associated with limbic system activity such as timing (septal loops), response processing (cingulate gyrus loop), processing of sensory stimuli (trisynaptic loop), and so on. The loop structure that is associated with the septohippocampal system provides a sophisticated circuitry for information processing such as the processing that is necessary for generating emotional responses. Indeed, the neural processes that are involved in generating and regulating emotional responses require the integration of much information such as assessing the organism's internal and external environments, matching present experiences with past experiences, and selecting responses (both autonomic and somatic) that are appropriate for the situation. A relatively complicated circuitry, such as the limbic system with its variety of structures and interconnections, is likely at the heart of generating and regulating emotional states.

The Amygdala

Another major component of the limbic system is the amygdaloid complex, which is defined as a complex of nuclei and specialized cortical areas that are located in primates within the rostromedial portion of the temporal lobe. The complex is typically divided into four major areas: the periamygdaloid cortex, the corticomedial nuclei, the central nuclei, and the basolateral nuclei. This structure has been implicated in a variety of functions including the integration and control of emotional and autonomic behavior, involvement in primate reproductive and feeding behaviors (especially "cognitive" aspects), and memory processes. The emotional aspects of amygdaloid function were first detailed by Kluver and Bucy (1939), who described a constellation of changes in emotion-related behaviors in monkeys after amygdaloid lesions. Since these observations, interest in studying the involvement of the amygdala in emotions and emotion-related behavior has remained.

Figure 3 shows the major patterns of connectivity between the amygdala and a variety of other brain regions. Several cortical connections can be seen including the olfactory cortex, the entorhinal cortex, the hippocampus, the temporal cortex, the insular cortex, and the orbital and medial prefrontal cortices. The mediodorsal thalamic nuclei, which provide a link between the hypothalamus and the prefrontal cortex, and the midline thalamic nuclei, which provide a link between the brain stem and the hypothalamus, are both innervated by amygdaloid projections. Furthermore, amygdaloid projections to the nucleus accumbens and the striatum (both considered parts of the basal ganglia) are also present. These projections may be an important part of the limbic system because they could provide a type of "effector" system for behavior or regions of sensorimotor integration that are important for motor and cognitive function. A number of descending projections from the amygdala can also be described, including projections from the amygdala to the hypothalamus as well as projections to the substantia nigra and the ventral tegmental area, two brain stem areas that supply dopamine to the striatum and the neocortex. Dopamine is a major neurotransmitter that has been implicated in a variety of brain processes including reward and reinforcement.

The general pattern of connectivity in many areas of the amygdala involves bidirectional (i.e., reciprocal) innervation: Many regions of the amygdala project out to brain structures that in turn project back to the amygdala. The three nuclear regions of the amygdala, in general, contact different brain structures. The corticomedial nuclei receive massive input from the olfactory bulb and the cortex, the basolateral region shares bidirectional connections with large portions of the neocortex, and the central nucleus projects largely to the hypothalamus and parasympathetic nuclei of the brain stem. Many projections between the hippocampus and

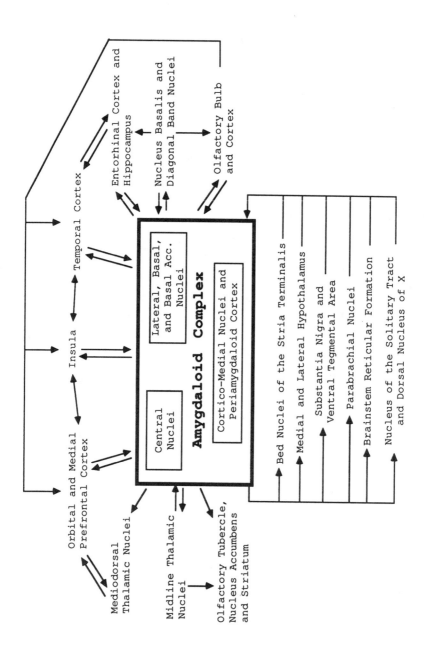

FIGURE 3. A schematic representation of neural connectivity involving the amygdaloid complex. From *Encyclopedia of Neuroscience* (Vol. 1, p. 41) edited G. Adelman, 1987, Boston: Birkhauser. Copyright 1987 by Birkhauser. Adapted by permission.

the amygdala have also been located, which thus provides a communication link between the septohippocampal and amygdaloid regions of the limbic system.

The Hypothalamus and Other Influences on Limbic System Structures

The hypothalamus is located in the ventral portion of the diencephalon adjacent to the brain's ventricular system. It has two major subdivisions: a nuclear area that is located medially and a fiber-rich area that is located laterally. Most of these fibers compose the medial forebrain bundle, which contains ascending fibers from the brain stem reticular formation and descending fibers from basal portions of the forebrain. The medially positioned hypothalamic nuclei receive input mainly from the medial forebrain bundle. As noted earlier, there are direct projections from the hippocampus to the hypothalamic nuclei as well as direct projections from the amygdala.

A variety of functions have been described for the hypothalamus. First, this structure produces a series of hormones that regulate production and secretion of hormones in the anterior pituitary (e.g., thyroid-stimulating hormone and growth hormone). Second, the hypothalamus regulates water balance through osmoreceptors that appear to sample serum osmolality. Third, the hypothalamus regulates autonomic function by regulating or controlling both sympathetic and parasympathetic regions of the brain stem. Fourth, hypothalamic activity is involved in reinforcement mechanisms, that is, those mechanisms that are involved in increasing or decreasing the probability that certain behaviors will occur. Fifth, feeding and drinking behaviors involve hypothalamic function, possibly through the regulation of ingestive behaviors. Sixth, reproductive behavior is dependent to a degree on hypothalamic activity in that the production and maintenance of reproductive hormones are regulated by the hypothalamus. Finally, the regulation of biological rhythms is largely dependent on hypothalamic function.

A number of these hypothalamic functions, such as autonomic regulation, reinforcement, and endocrine modulation, are associated with emotions and emotion-related behaviors. As such, the hypothalamus seems to be a key portion of the neural substrates of emotions. Central to this involvement is the general position and role of the hypothalamus in brain function: This brain structure serves as the key interface between the nervous system and other physiological systems such as the cardio-vascular and endocrine systems. Indeed, many—if not all—physiological manifestations of emotional experience are dependent on hypothalamic activity.

Two other brain projection systems should be noted: the raphe nuclei and the locus coeruleus (see Figure 2). These two brain areas are located in the medulla and pontine brain stem, respectively. Most of the neurons in the raphe nuclei contain serotonin and project rather diffusely to the forebrain, including the septohippocampal system. The locus coeruleus contains about half of the brain's norepinephrine neurons and also projects rather diffusely throughout the forebrain, although termination patterns of individual neurons in the various regions of the forebrain are rather well defined. Studies of the activity of raphe nuclei and locus coeruleus neurons have shown that these areas encode different aspects of sleep/waking states: Neurons of the raphe nuclei become active with sleep onset, whereas neurons of the locus coeruleus are most active during awake states, with activity levels being related to levels of arousal or attention. It seems likely that together these brain regions could determine, to some extent, the general arousal level of forebrain neurons and contribute to processes like stimulus selection and vigilance. This arousal-related function would seem important for brain areas that are involved in processing information related to emotions, such as the septohippocampal system, which is innervated extensively by the raphe nuclei and the locus coeruleus.

Why Is the Limbic System Likely to Be Centrally Involved in Emotions and Temperament?

The most compelling reasons for suspecting that the limbic system is the core system involved in the encoding of emotions and temperament lie in the patterns of connectivity that exist for the system. The septohippocampal system and the amygdala are directly and strongly interconnected, and both project to association areas in the neocortex, to the brain stem and hypothalamus, and to somatomotor systems that are likely involved in generating behaviors. In addition, neural activity in the neocortex, brain stem, and hypothalamus project back to the limbic system, which thus provides important feedback from the target structures. Thus, the limbic system can be thought of as a set of highly interconnected structures that serve as an interface between the hypothalamus, brain stem, and neocortical areas. In short, the limbic system has all of the connections that are necessary to bidirectionally mix the cognitive aspects of emotions (i.e., via neocortical connections) with the more autonomic, physiological, or motor aspects of emotion (i.e., via hypothalamic and brain stem connections).

Gray's Model of the Neuropsychology of Temperament

Borrowing from studies of animal learning and behavior, neuropsychology, psychopharmacology, and neuroscience, Gray (1991) presented a rather detailed model concerning the neural substrates of emotion and temperament that involve many of the brain systems described in the preceding sections. This model assumes initially that there are three fundamental emotional systems. Furthermore, each of these emotional systems is thought to respond to subsets of reinforcing events with specific types of behavior and be mediated by a separate set of interacting brain structures that process specific types of information. Gray called these systems the *behavioral inhibition system* (BIS), the *fight–flight system* (FFS), and the *behavioral approach system* (BAS). Furthermore, Gray believed that the individual differences in the functioning of these three emotion systems underlie human temperament as conventionally measured. I present this model because it serves as an excellent example of how the previously presented brain systems might interact to determine emotion- or temperament-related behavior.

Activity in the BIS is elicited by conditioned stimuli that are associated with punishment, stimuli that are associated by the omission or termination of reward, or by novel stimuli. These stimuli cause an interruption of ongoing behavior (i.e., behavioral inhibition), an increase in arousal, and an increase in attention. Neurally, the BIS is thought to involve activity in the septohippocampal system, which was described earlier. In Gray's (1991) model, the septohippocampal system is thought of as a *comparator* or "a system which, moment to moment, predicts the next likely event and compares this prediction to the actual event" (p. 112, Gray, 1991). In this system, if there is a mismatch between what is predicted (as determined by assessing a number of factors such as current motor state and memories for past events) and what is actually encountered, then the BIS outputs are activated to halt behavior. The core of the comparator function is thought to be the subicular area, which receives input indirectly from cortical sensory association areas, receives predictions from and generates the next prediction in the Papez circuit, and interfaces with motor programming systems. The prefrontal cortex provides the comparator system with information about the ongoing motor program, whereas interactions within the ascending systems from the raphe nuclei and the locus coeruleus might alert the whole system to threat. Timing functions, which are necessary for determining the rate at which the comparator operates, are thought to originate in the operations of the septal area.

The FFS responds to unconditioned aversive stimuli with defensive aggression or escape behavior. Gray (1991) identified at least three levels of the nervous system that have structures that could potentially encode the FFS. These levels include the amygdala, the medial hypothalamus, and the central gray. More specifically, the amygdala inhibits the medial hypothalamus, which inhibits the final output pathway in the central gray. Thus fight–flight is thought to be mediated through the amygdaloid inhibition of a brain area that normally inhibits a behavioral output pathway.

According to Gray (1991), the BAS is a positive feedback system that is activated by stimuli associated with reward or the termination or omission of punishment. He further postulated that the BAS is activated to a degree that is proportional to the spatiotemporal proximity of the eliciting stimuli to the unconditioned appetitive stimulus with which they are associated. This arrangement creates a system that guides an organism to the goals it needs to attain for survival. The key neural systems that are thought to underlie the BAS include the basal ganglia, the dopaminergic fibers that ascend from the midbrain to innervate the basal ganglia, the thalamic nuclei associated with basal ganglia function, and neocortical areas closely linked to the basal ganglia. More specifically, this neural system is actually composed of two interrelated subsystems that can be referred to as the *caudate motor system* and the *accumbens motor system* (see Figure 4). The caudate motor system includes nonlimbic cortex (e.g., the association cortex), the caudate–putamen, and the dorsal globus pallidus (i.e., portions of the basal ganglia), the ventral anterior and ventral lateral nuclei of the thalamus, and the ascending dopaminergic pathway from the substantia nigra. The accumbens motor system includes limbic cortex (i.e., the cingulate and prefrontal cortices), the nucleus accumbens and the ventral globus pallidus (i.e., portions of the basal ganglia), the dorsomedial thalamic nucleus, and the ascending dopaminergic projections from a midbrain area called A10. The nucleus accumbens portion of the basal ganglia receives input from the two "emotional" brain systems described earlier: the amygdala and the septohippocampal system.

Inspection of Figure 4 reveals the nature of the caudate and accumbens systems that underlie the BAS. Both systems are composed of at least three interacting feedback loops. Gray (1991) proposed that the patterns of excitation and inhibition produced by activity in these loops account for specific operational features of the BAS. Because the caudate system is connected with the sensory and motor cortices, it is assumed that this system encodes the specific content of each step in a motor program (e.g., the next word that is to be spoken in a sentence). The accumbens system, on the other hand, has been hypothesized to permit switching from one step to the next in a motor program. Gray suggested that establishing the step sequence that comprises a motor program and also the orderly running of the program is directed by amygdaloid projections that terminate in the nucleus accumbens. These projections carry information about cue–reinforcement associations. As already described, the septohippocampal system checks whether the outcome of a particular motor step matches the expected outcome. Any information regarding a mismatch in actual and expected outcomes is projected to the nucleus accumbens via fibers that originate in the subiculum. The role of the

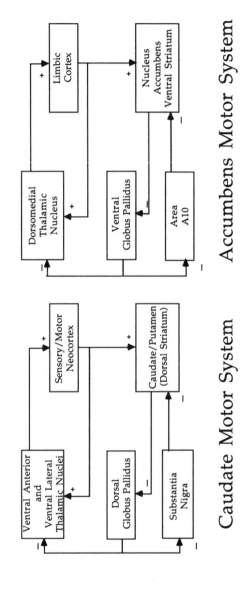

Caudate Motor System   Accumbens Motor System

FIGURE 4. Schematic representations of the caudate motor system and the accumbens motor system. Excitatory projections are indicated by a plus sign; inhibitory connections are denoted by a minus sign.

prefrontal cortex is thought to be in coordinating the activities of the basal caudate, accumbens, and septohippocampal systems. Gray assumed that maintenance of activity in the striatal, thalamic, and cortical neurons involved in a motor step is due to reverberatory activity in the loops that make up the caudate and accumbens systems, and by lateral inhibition present in the striatum. These patterns of reverberatory activity are periodically interrupted by activity in dopaminergic inputs to the striatum. The duration of a step in the motor program corresponds to the joint operation of the loops that make up the caudate and accumbens systems. Finally, timing in the BAS is coordinated between the septohippocampal monitoring system and the basal ganglia motor programming system.

Gray (1991) neurologically defined temperament in the context of activity in the BIS, the FFS, and the BAS. He wrote the following:

> It is assumed that temperament reflects individual differences in predispositions toward particular kinds of emotion. We may now rephrase that assumption thus: temperament reflects parameter values (Gray, 1967) that determine, for a particular individual, the operating characteristics of our three emotion systems, alone and in interaction with one another. A further basic assumption is that the major dimensions of personality, as measured by such multivariate statistical techniques as factor analysis (e.g., Eysenck & Eysenck, 1985; Zuckerman, Kuhlman, & Camac, 1988) are created by individual differences in such parameter values. (p. 23, Gray, 1991)

In this hypothesized system, individual differences in the various dimensions of personality are produced by differences in the relative activity within and interactions between the three postulated fundamental emotional systems. Gray used current understanding of the three emotional systems to predict likely structures of human personality; that is, he predicted dimensions of personality that correspond to individual differences in the function of the three emotional systems. For example, individual differences in the intensity of BIS function might correspond to trait anxiety with the high pole corresponding to high-trait anxiety. Individual differences in FFS function might encode the range of aggressive–defensive behaviors. Individual differences in the functioning of the BAS could correspond to the ranges seen in the tendency to show behavior that is motivated by positive reinforcement and the accompanying plea-surable emotions.

Using data about brain systems that are known to be involved in emotions, learning, memory, and motor behavior, Gray (1991) developed a rather comprehensive model of how the brain might encode the complex phenomenon known as temperament. Above all, Gray's model provides a useful framework for future experiments in that it makes concrete predictions about how individual differences in personality dimensions might be explained by activity in specific brain systems.

The Influence of Learning and Memory on Temperament-Related Behaviors

When studying the psychological phenomenon of temperament, it is im-portant to make sure that the individual differences in observed behavior are indeed related to the major factors purported to be associated with temperament (i.e., genetic factors) and not due to factors related to other psychological functions. Typically, an individual's temperament or emo-tion is assessed by directly observing behaviors or patterns of behavior such as evaluating an individual's oral or written replies to a series of questions, collecting parental reports of a child's activities, or by directly observing an individual either at home or in the laboratory. Past expe-rience has a major influence on the behaviors that are displayed during these subsequent observation periods. In other words, it is likely that behaviors that are used to assess temperament or emotion are influenced substantially by learning and memory processes. Thus, to study temper-ament or emotion, it seems important that the individual differences in learning and memory be systematically studied and potentially accounted for before the individual differences observed in behavior are attributed to factors related to temperament. This assumes, of course, that learning and memory processes are separable from temperament-related pro-cesses. It seems just as likely that learning and memory processes (i.e., the influence of past experience) accounts for some of the individual differences attributed to temperament and that learning and memory actually determine, to some extent, the patterns of behavior associated with individual temperaments, even if the deepest roots of the individual differences in the patterns are in genetic differences.

It is fascinating to note that most of the neural structures described in the preceding sections that are likely to play major roles in determining patterns of emotion or temperament are also involved in learning and memory processing. In fact, many of these structures have been studied more extensively for their participation in learning and memory phenomena. The hippocampus, for example, has long been implicated in learning and memory. Anterograde amnesias that have been observed after hippocampal removal have been well documented, which thus suggests that this structure plays some role in the formation or storage of new memories (Squire, 1987). The memorylike phenomenon known as long-term potentiation has been observed in the hippocampus by a number of researchers (Swanson et al., 1987; Teyler, 1991). Recording and lesion experiments have shown that the septohippocampal system encodes the learning of temporal and spatial learning tasks such as Pavlovian conditioning and maze learning (Eichenbaum et al., 1990; Morris et al., 1982; Sears & Steinmetz, 1990). The amygdala has also been shown to play a role in learning and memory including emotional memory processing (Farb, Aoki, Milner, Kaneko, & LeDoux, 1992), fear learning (Davis, 1992; Grillon, Ameli, Woods, Merikangas, & Davis, 1991; LeDoux, Cicchetti, Xagoraris, & Romanski, 1990), and autonomic learning such as Pavlovian heart rate conditioning (Applegate, Frysinger, Kapp, & Gallagher, 1982; McCabe, Gentile, Markgraf, Teich, & Schneiderman, 1992). The basal ganglia have been shown to encode certain aspects of learning, especially those aspects that involve the integration of somatosensory information and motor output (Aldridge, Jaeger, & Gilman, 1991; Gardiner & Kitai, 1992). It is likely that the cerebellum—a potential component of the motor system that is involved in the expression of emotions and temperament—is also involved in the production of learned responses, especially those involving quick, discrete movements (for a review see Steinmetz & Thompson, 1991). Finally, the neocortical areas described earlier have also been implicated in memory. The prefrontal cortex, for example, is known to be involved in behavioral situations that require working memory processes or certain aspects of visual memory and aspects of cognition (Fuster, 1980; Goldman-Rakic, 1988; Passingham, 1985).

It also should be noted that not only is it possible that learning and memory may affect the display of emotions or temperament, but that emotions and temperament may affect the processes of learning and memory. The effects of emotions on acquisition and recall of simple and complex learning and memory have been studied extensively. In the animal and human literature, the strong influence that fear, stress, or anxiety has on learning and memory has been well documented (e.g., Davis, 1992; Klein, 1987; Mowrer, 1939; Rescorla & Solomon, 1967). The phenomenon known as "flashbulb" memory may serve as another example of how emotions can affect memory formation (Brown & Kulik, 1979). These memories are particularly vivid recollections that form in conjunction with a rather strong emotional or stressful event. The formation of these memories may be related to the presence of circulating hormones or other physiological by-products of the emotional state that were present at the time the memories were formed (Squire, 1987). Similar to the powerful effects that fear has on learning and memory, flashbulb memories illustrate the point that emotions can greatly affect the processes of learning and memory. Again, these data support the idea that memory and emotions or temperament are somewhat interrelated.

Given the observations that the same or similar neural structures are involved in a variety of processes related to learning and memory and processes related to emotions or temperament and that emotional experiences can affect learning and memory, it seems likely that there might be a relationship between memory and temperament processes during the generation of behavior thought to reflect temperament. This potential relationship certainly seems worthy of further study. Several questions concerning this relationship can be asked, including: (a) What aspects of memory and temperament are encoded by the variety of structures described earlier? (b) Are the same neurons within each structure used to encode memory and temperament or emotion, or do separate populations of neurons participate in the respective processes? (c) How do the various structures interact during memory and temperament processing to produce the memory- or temperament-related behaviors that are observed; that is, even though similar structures seem to encode memory and temperament, are there differences at the systems level in how these structures interact to produce the respective phenomena? It seems necessary to explore these issues, as well as a variety of other issues, to further the understanding of the neural substrates of temperament.

An Experimental Approach for Evaluating the Effects of Learning and Memory on Temperament

One line of research that my colleagues and I have recently begun in my laboratory is an examination of similarities and/or differences in how the brain encodes appetitive and aversive learning. Appetitive learning refers to any learning situation that involves using a reward or positive reinforcement to increase or decrease the frequency of a behavior that is being monitored, whereas aversive learning refers to any learning situation that involves use of punishment or a noxious stimulus to increase or decrease the frequency of a behavior that is under observation. One goal of this research is to develop a standard series of nonhuman animal conditioning procedures that attempt to equalize as closely as possible appetitive and aversive training. I believe that if the appetitive and aversive training situations are made as similar as possible, then differences in conditioning-related behaviors (as well as neural function) that are potentially attributed to a number of extraneous factors such as training context, stimuli, and response requirements can be eliminated or reduced. These procedures should therefore allow researchers to assess those differences in behavior and neural activity that are attributed primarily to the consequence of the learning (i.e., appetitive vs. aversive). This conditioning procedure is described in the following paragraphs.

What applicability might this line of research have for studies of the neurobiology of temperament? I believe that contributions made by learning and memory processes to temperament-related behaviors might be assessed by exposing subjects to various amounts of appetitive and/or aversive training during specific portions of their life span. In essence, these procedures set up consequent situations that can be characterized as simple approach or avoidance. Moreover, any animal model of temperament that might be established by these procedures should facilitate the study of the neural substrates of memory, emotion, and temperament via future recording, lesion, and anatomy experiments. I describe these conditioning procedures as well as some preliminary results concerning brain regions that encode appetitive and aversive learning; I then speculate about how these procedures could be used to assess the influence of learning and memory on temperament-related behaviors.

We chose a signaled barpressing task in rats as a standard preparation for studying appetitive and aversive learning. Figure 5 provides a schematic overview of these training procedures. In the typical appetitive situation, a rat is placed in a standard operant conditioning chamber, and a 3-s tone (2 kHz, 85 dB) is presented. The task is quite simple. If the rat

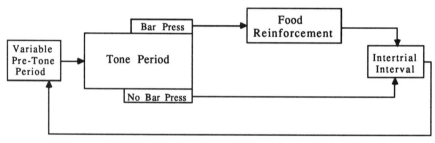

Signaled Appetitive Conditioning

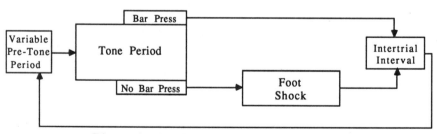

Signaled Aversive Conditioning

FIGURE 5.   Schematic representations of the appetitive and aversive signaled barpressing tasks. Typically the tone period is 1–5 s, the intertrial interval is 10–15 s, and the variable pretone period ranges from 1–8 s.

presses a response bar that is present in the chamber during the 3-s tone, then a food pellet is delivered to a food tray next to the bar and the tone is terminated. If that rat fails to press the bar, then no food is delivered on that trial. A 10–15-s intertrial interval is then allowed to elapse before the next trial is delivered. To decrease the number of barpresses made during the intertrial interval (and thus the opportunity for the rat to rapidly or continuously press the bar for food reward instead of waiting for the tone signal), a random 1–8-s pretone period is inserted before the onset of the subsequent trial. If the rat presses the bar during this pretone period, then the intertrial interval is reset and the trial is not presented; that is, the rat must withhold barpressing during the nontone periods. Control rats are treated identically to "tone" rats except that no tone is presented. Any food pellets that the control rats receive are due to random barpresses made during the 3-s period when the tone is normally on. In the typical aversive learning situation, the rats are placed in the same chamber as used for the appetitive training and presented the same 3-s tone (2 kHz, 85 dB). A barpress made during the tone period allows the rat to avoid a mild electric footshock (400 µA) that is delivered via a floor grid. Failure to press the bar during the tone period results in a 3-s pulsed footshock (250 ms on, 750 ms off), which can be terminated (i.e., escaped) by pressing the bar. All intertrial intervals and pretone requirements, as described for the appetitive situation, are used in the aversive situation.

Several points can be made concerning the similarities of these two procedures. First, within-subjects designs are typically used. The same rat can be conditioned in the appetitive and aversive tasks in either order of conditioning task presentation. Second, because conditioning involves the same chamber, the general context (i.e., environment) of the conditioning tasks is equalized. Third, the same signal is used to induce the barpress response (e.g., 2 kHz, 85 dB). Fourth, the same barpress response is required to either gain the food pellet or avoid the footshock. Fifth, the timing and trial requirements such as intertrial interval, interstimulus interval, and number of trials per day can be set equal. In short, I believe that equalizing the factors listed here eliminates some sources of variation that influence the rate, degree, and manner in which appetitive and aversive responses are learned and remembered. This has already proven valuable for studying the neural structures that are involved in the encoding of these forms of learning (see the following discussion).

The behavioral results of this paradigm have shown that rats can learn both tasks within a reasonable number of training sessions. By systematically varying a variety of training parameters, however, several differences in the rate and manner in which the tasks are learned have been noted. For optimal (i.e., most rapid and robust) learning of the appetitive task, 1–3-s tones appear to be best, with 100 trials per session presented. Optimal learning of the aversive task seems to be produced with 300 trials per session of 3–5-s tones. Even though barpress responses are made during both procedures, the manner in which the barpresses are executed differs for the two procedures. During appetitive training, the rats appear to press the bar very early in the trial period; whereas during aversive training, the rats delay avoidance responding to just before shock onset. Also during aversive training, the rats show a strong freeze response that may be related to conditioned fear (e.g., Davis, 1992). This freezing response is followed by a rather stereotypical pattern of barpressing behavior during the latter portion of the tone period. The preliminary data also show differences in autonomic learning during the two training procedures. These initial findings are encouraging because they indicate that different brain systems or different portions of the same brain systems are likely to be engaged during these similar appetitive and aversive learning situations.

Some preliminary data concerning the brain substrates of these two learning situations have been collected. For example, using a within-subjects design, my colleagues and I have shown that bilateral ibotenic acid lesions of the deep cerebellar nuclei prevent acquisition of the aversive task (both avoidance and escape responding) without affecting acquisition of the appetitive task (Steinmetz, Logue, & Miller, 1993). At the very least, these data indicate that the cerebellum may participate in the generation of motor responses that are used during the aversive conditioning tasks but not during the appetitive task. The aversive deficit, however, cannot simply be a motor deficit because normal robust barpressing was observed during the appetitive task. My colleagues and I have also begun analyzing the participation of the hippocampus in these learning tasks (Logue, Klamo, Miller, & Steinmetz, 1992). Ibotenic acid lesions of the hippocampus do not affect postlesion performance of the appetitive or aversive tasks if the training is given before the lesion. If the lesions are made before training, however, then effects can be discerned. Specifically, the lesions facilitate the learning of the appetitive task in that the lesioned rats learn the task at a rate 2–4 times faster than that for the nonlesioned rats. Lesions also seem to facilitate learning of the avoidance response. These hippocampal data imply that the limbic system may participate in some fashion in the acquisition of both appetitive and aversive responses. The precise role of the hippocampus in the acquisition processes must still be delineated, however.

To date, the behavioral and neural data have been encouraging in that the training procedures seem powerful enough to allow researchers to study similarities and differences in the behavioral processes and neural substrates that underlie this simple form of learning. Of central importance to the present discussion is how these procedures might be used to study emotional processes and temperament. I believe that exposing animals to one or both of these procedures may allow researchers to study interactions between learning and memory processes and temperament processes. More specifically, a number of manipulations of these barpressing tasks could be used to assess the influence of learning and memory on emotional or temperamental states of the animals as well as the neural substrates of these phenomena. These experiments could include: (a) varying the order of appetitive and aversive training and observing the rates of somatic (i.e., barpress) and autonomic (e.g., heart rate) learning; (b) varying the amounts of appetitive and aversive training and observing the rates and patterns of somatic and autonomic learning; (c) varying the context in which the appetitive and aversive training take place while recording somatic and autonomic responding; (d) assessing the effects of systematic lesions of the septohippocampal, amygdaloid, striatal, and hypothalamic systems on somatic and autonomic responding during appetitive and aversive training; (e) performing electrophysiological analyses of activity in the septohippocampal, amygdaloid, striatal, and hypothalamic systems during appetitive and aversive training; (f) assessing developmental effects on acquisition and performance of the appetitive and aversive tasks; (g) using rats of different strains or with systematically varied life histories (e.g., handled vs. nonhandled); and (h) developing signaled learning tasks for humans that parallel the rat experiments in hopes of altering, at least in the short-term, experience with appetitive and aversive learning.

The goal of all of the just-listed manipulations is to alter, in a systematic fashion, exposure to appetitive and/or aversive learning experience at some point during the life span. The expectation is that if learning and memory of these training procedures affect behaviors used to measure temperament, then rather precise relationships between the training experiences and subsequent temperament measurements should be produced. Varying the context of the learning and testing would seem very important for making these assessments. Measurements of reactivity to stimuli, patterns of autonomic responding, performance in transfer of training paradigms, and patterns of electroencephalographic or evoked potentials—as well as a variety of standard procedures that assess emotionality in animals—might serve as baseline measurements of the temperament of the rats before and after the training experience. A lack of change in these measurements might indicate that the appetitive and/or aversive experiences did little to influence the emotionality or temperament of the rat. Conversely, changes in these measurements as a result of training might indicate that the learning and memory of these experiences affected the temperament measurements. Also of central importance is the concomitant analysis of the activity of brain structures and systems that are involved in the training and testing procedures. Coupled with the behavioral manipulations, lesion, recording, anatomical, and pharmacological experiments should advance the understanding of the neural substrates of temperament and the interactions between experience and temperament.

Conclusion

In this chapter, I summarized the neural structures and systems that are likely to be involved in the encoding of emotions and temperament. These systems include the septohippocampal system, the amygdala, the basal ganglia, and the neocortex. I also presented Gray's (1991) rather specific and well-detailed model that describes how several of these systems might interact to produce the individual differences that are the hallmark of temperament. Finally, I discussed the potential influences of learning and memory on temperament and presented a series of appetitive and aversive training techniques as a possible method for evaluating the effects of learning and memory on temperament as well as for assessing the function of brain structures and systems that are thought to encode temperament.

One final point deserves emphasis. Although researchers have identified specific structures that seem to be involved in generating and maintaining temperament-related behaviors, all evidence to date suggests that these structures are highly interrelated and act as a rather intricate and integrated system. One needs only to identify the number of loops and reciprocally innervated structures present in each of these brain areas to gain an appreciation for the number of possible ways that these structures can communicate with each other. Given this wealth of connectivity, it is not surprising that great individual differences in certain behavioral patterns and psychological function, such as temperament, are observed. Moreover, because a great number of factors can influence the overall function of this neural system—factors like genetics, developmental processes, biochemistry, neurochemistry, and learning and memory—the individual differences in behavior become more and more likely. Indeed, it appears that future advancements in the understanding of the neurobiology of temperament will depend, in part, on assessing the contributions that each of these factors make in producing behaviors that are associated with temperament and emotion.

References

Adelman, G. (Ed.). (1987). *Encyclopedia of neuroscience*. Boston: Birkhauser.

Aldridge, J. W., Jaeger, D., & Gilman, S. (1991). A comparison of single unit activity in primate caudate nucleus and putamen in a sensory cued motor task. In G. Bernardi, M. B. Carpenter, G. Di Chiara, M. Morelli, & P. Stanzione (Eds.), *The basal ganglia III* (pp. 303–312). New York: Plenum.

Applegate, C. G., Frysinger, R. C., Kapp, B. S., & Gallagher, M. (1982). Multiple unit activity recorded from amygdala central nucleus during Pavlovian heart rate conditioning in rabbit. *Brain Research, 238*, 457–462.

Bates, J. E. (1989). Concepts and measurements of temperament. In G. A. Kohnstamm, J. E. Bates, & M. K. Rothbart (Eds.), *Temperament in childhood* (pp. 3–26). New York: Wiley.

Bekkers, J. M., & Stevens, C. F. (1990). Presynaptic mechanism for long-term potentiation in the hippocampus. *Nature, 346,* 724–729.

Brown, R., & Kulik, J. (1977). Flashbulb memories. *Cognition, 5,* 73–99.

Davis, M. (1992). The role of the amygdala in fear-potentiated startle: Implications for animal models of anxiety. *Trends in Pharmacological Sciences, 13,* 35–41.

di Pellegrino, G., & Wise, S. P. (1991). A neurophysiological comparison of three distinct regions of the primate frontal lobe. *Brain, 114,* 951–978.

Eichenbaum, H., Stewart, C., & Morris, R. G. M. (1990). Hippocampal representation in place learning. *Journal of Neuroscience, 10,* 3531–3542.

Eysenck, H. J., & Eysenck, M. W. (1985). *Personality and individual differences: A natural science approach.* New York: Plenum.

Farb, C., Aoki, C., Milner, T., Kaneko, T., & LeDoux, J. (1992). Glutamate immunoreactive terminals in the lateral amygdaloid nucleus: A possible substrate for emotional memory. *Brain Research, 593,* 145–158.

Fuster, J. M. (1980). *The prefrontal cortex: Anatomy, physiology and neuropsychology of the frontal lobe.* New York: Raven Press.

Gardiner, T. W., & Kitai, S. T. (1992). Single-unit activity in the globus pallidus and neostriatum of the rat during performance of a trained head movement. *Experimental Brain Research, 88,* 517–530.

Georgopoulos, A. P., Schwartz, A. B., & Kettner, R. E. (1986). Neuronal population coding of movement direction. *Science, 233,* 1416–1419.

Goldman-Rakic, P. S. (1988). Topography of cognition: Parallel distributed networks in primate association cortex. *Annual Review of Neuroscience, 11,* 137–156.

Gray, J. A. (1967). Disappointment and drugs in the rat. *Advancement of Science, 23,* 595–605.

Gray, J. A. (1991). The neuropsychology of temperament. In J. Strelau & A. Angleitner (Eds.), *Explorations in temperament: International perspectives on theory and measurement* (pp. 105–128). New York: Plenum.

Grillon, C., Ameli, R., Woods, S. W., Merikangas, K., & Davis, M. (1991). Fear-potentiated startle in humans: Effects of anticipatory anxiety on the acoustic blink reflex. *Psychophysiology, 28,* 588–595.

Kaas, J. H. (1991). Plasticity of sensory and motor maps in adult mammals. *Annual Review of Neuroscience, 14,* 137–167.

Klein, D. F. (Ed.). (1987). *Anxiety.* Basel, Switzerland: Karger.

Kluver, H., & Bucy, P. C. (1939). Preliminary analysis of the temporal lobes in monkeys. *Archives of Neurology and Psychiatry, 42,* 979–1000.

LeDoux, J. E., Cicchetti, P., Xagoraris, A., & Romanski, L. M. (1990). The lateral amygdaloid nucleus: Sensory interface of the amygdala in fear conditioning. *Journal of Neuroscience, 10*, 1062–1069.

Livingston, M., & Hubel, D. (1988). Segregation of form, color, movement and depth: Anatomy, physiology, and perception. *Science, 240*, 740–749.

Logue, S. F., Klamo, E. M., Miller, D. P., & Steinmetz, J. E. (1992). Ibotenic acid lesions of the hippocampus facilitate acquisition of an appetitive signalled bar-pressing task. *Society for Neuroscience Abstracts, 18*, 1058.

MacLean, P. D. (1955). The limbic system ("visceral brain") and emotional behavior. *Archives of Neurology and Psychiatry, 73*, 130–134.

McCabe, P. M., Gentile, C. G., Markgraf, C. G., Teich, A. H., & Schneiderman, N. (1992). Ibotenic acid lesions in the amygdaloid central nucleus but not in the lateral subthalamic area prevent the acquisition of differential Pavlovian conditioning of bradycardia in rabbits. *Brain Research, 580*, 155–163.

Mishkin, M., Ungerleider, L. G., & Macko, K. A. (1983). Object vision and spatial vision: Two cortical pathways. *Trends in Neurosciences, 6*, 414–417.

Morris, R. G. M., Garrud, P., Rawlins, J. N. P., & O'Keefe, J. (1982). Place navigation impaired in rats with hippocampal lesions. *Nature, 297*, 681–683.

Mowrer, O. H. (1939). A stimulus–response analysis of anxiety and its role as a reinforcing agent. *Psychological Review, 46*, 553–565.

Ojakangas, C. L., & Ebner, T. J. (1991). Scaling the metrics of visually guided arm movements during motor learning in primates. *Experimental Brain Research, 85*, 314–323.

Papez, J. W. (1937). A proposed mechanism of emotion. *Archives of Neurology and Psychiatry, 38*, 725–744.

Passingham, R. E. (1985). Memory of monkeys (*Macaca mulatta*) with lesions in prefrontal cortex. *Behavioral Neuroscience, 99*, 3–21.

Posner, M. I., Inhoff, A. W., Freidrich, F. J., & Cohen, A. (1987). Isolating attentional systems: A cognitive–anatomical analysis. *Psychobiology, 15*, 107–121.

Rescorla, R. A., & Solomon, R. L. (1967). Two-process learning theory: Relationships between Pavlovian conditioning and instrumental learning. *Psychological Review, 74*, 151–182.

Sears, L. L., & Steinmetz, J. E. (1990). Acquisition of classically conditioned-related activity in the hippocampus is affected by lesions of the cerebellar interpositus nucleus. *Behavioral Neuroscience, 104*, 681–692.

Smith, O., & DeVito, J. (1984). Central neural integration for the control of autonomic responses associated with emotion. *Annual Review of Neuroscience, 7*, 43–65.

Squire, L. R. (1987). *Memory and brain.* New York: Oxford University Press.

Steinmetz, J. E., Logue, S. F., & Miller, D. P. (1993). Using signaled barpressing tasks to study the neural substrates of appetitive and aversive learning in rats: Behavioral manipulations and cerebellar lesions. *Behavioral Neuroscience, 107*, 941–954.

Steinmetz, J. E., & Thompson, R. F. (1991). Brain substrates of aversive classical conditioning. In J. Madden IV (Ed.), *Neurobiology of learning, emotion and affect* (pp. 97–120). New York: Raven Press.

Swanson, L. W., Teyler, T. J., & Thompson, R. F. (1982). Hippocampal long-term potentiation: Mechanisms and implications for memory. *Neurosciences Research Program Bulletin, 20*, 617–765.

Teyler, T. J. (1991). Memory: Electrophysiological analogs. In J. L. Martinez & R. P. Kesner (Eds.), *Learning and memory: A biological view* (pp. 299–358). San Diego, CA: Academic Press.

Zuckerman, M., Kuhlman, D. M., & Camac, C. (1988). What lies beyond E and N? Factor analysis of scales believed to measure basic dimensions of personality. *Journal of Personality and Social Psychology, 54*, 96–107.

CHAPTER 3

Neural Bases of
Infant Temperament

Charles A. Nelson

W hen asked as a cognitive neuroscientist where temperament traits reside in the brain, I am immediately reminded of the story of phrenology, one of Franz Joseph Gall's (1758–1828) least distinguished contributions to the brain sciences. Gall felt that all human intellectual, moral, and psychological traits (see Figure 1) were (a) innate and (b) localizable in the brain. With regard to the latter, Gall speculated further that one could infer the location of such traits by examining corresponding bumps on the surface of the scalp (for an excellent discussion of this proposal see Thompson & Robinson, 1979).

Although Gall was clearly wrong about the significance of such bumps, he is to be credited for raising the possibility that brain functions can, in fact, be localized. However, applying this principal to temperament is a bit more challenging than applying it to perceptual or cognitive abilities, which have long been the domains of neuropsychologists and neurologists. Many of the behavioral traits that are thought to reflect tem-

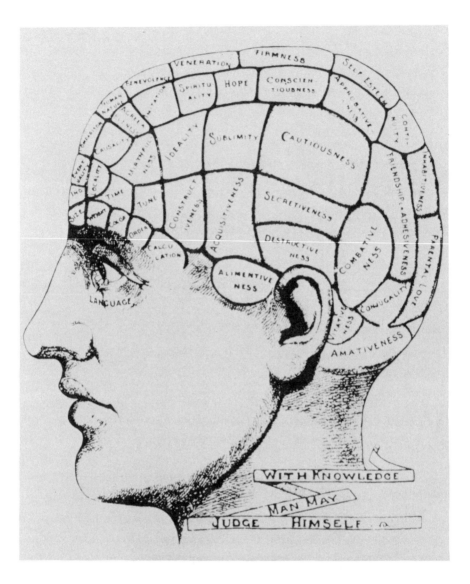

FIGURE 1. According to Gall, all psychological traits could be localized in the brain. Furthermore, Gall claimed that the location of these traits could be inferred by corresponding bumps on the surface of the skull. From *Neurophilosophy: Toward a Unified Science of Mind–Brain (p. 158) by P. S. Churchland, 1986, Cambridge, MA: MIT Press. Copyright 1986 by MIT Press. Adapted by permission.*

perament are considerably more amorphous than the cognitive abilities that I study in my current research program (e.g., memory). This is not because such traits are poorly defined but rather because they are simply less tangible than are cognitive traits from a measurement perspective and perhaps even from a definitional perspective. Furthermore, although I firmly believe that the brain is the source of all behavior and that the development of all behavior is predicated on changes in the brain (e.g., formation of dendritic spines; synapse formation), this is not tantamount to saying that one can "localize" all behavior in the brain: It is simply not the case that things are located in the brain much the way bread is located in the pantry or that vegetables are located in the refrigerator. Although there are established relations between structure and function (e.g., the amygdala plays an important role in emotion), the brain is an intricate series of interconnected circuits and systems. Accordingly, attempting to isolate to one part of the brain something like "behavioral inhibition" is likely to be unproductive.

Be that as it may, when discussing temperament in this chapter, I apply the same argument I have made previously about the recognition of emotion (cf. Nelson, 1987, 1993c) and the ontogeny of memory (cf. Nelson, 1993b): Namely, that behaviors that may have been selected for through evolution, to the point that they now appear ubiquitous in the species in one form or another, are likely to have some neural bases (for an excellent discussion of this point in the context of memory see Sherry & Schacter, 1987). Whether these traits and their corresponding neural underpinnings reflect experience-expectant or experience-dependent learning (e.g., Greenough & Black, 1992) is unknown. Nevertheless, many of the same traits of temperament that I view as impossibly complex and entangled with things like culture and language appear also to be constitutionally based (cf. Buss & Plomin, 1984), and thus should, in theory, have some place in the brain. It is my goal in this chapter to demonstrate the veracity of this proposal.

I limit my discussion to behaviors that have variously been described as *behavioral approach* versus *behavioral withdrawal* or the *behavioral facilitation system* versus the *behavioral inhibition system*. I also address the neural bases of *positive affect* versus *negative affect*, as well

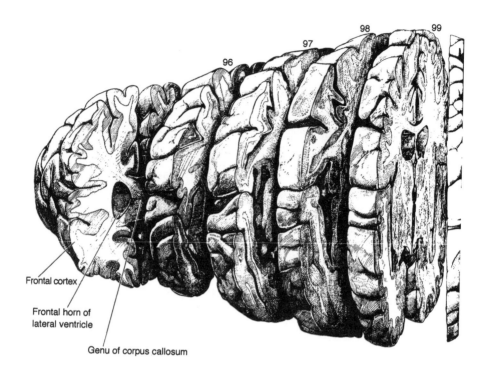

FIGURE 2. An atlas of the human brain composed of frontal cross sections (i.e., sections made perpendicular to the long axis of the forebrain). The left-most portion of the figure represents the front (e.g., frontal lobe), whereas the right-most portion represents the back (e.g., occipital lobe). Figures

as infants' reactivity to novelty. I have selected these traits from a far longer list primarily because most temperament researchers seem to agree that these traits do, indeed, reflect some aspect of temperament, and because I consider speculation about the brain bases of these traits to be a tractable enterprise. I hasten to add, however, that establishing links between brain and temperament in the context of development is actually a secondary goal. My primary goal is to introduce some key concepts in neuroanatomy and neurobiology to the behavioral scientist who studies temperament and to provide a tutorial on the development of those brain regions that may underlie temperament. (A tutorial on "mature" structure–function relations is provided by Steinmetz in chapter 2 of this book.)

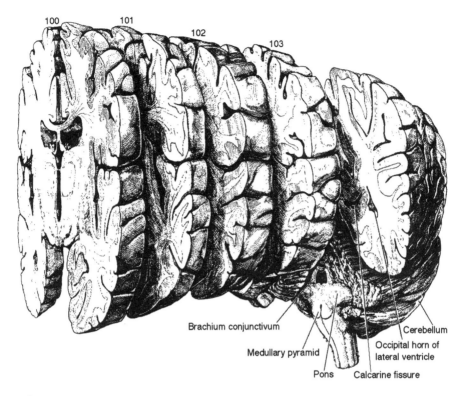

Brachium conjunctivum

Medullary pyramid

Pons   Calcarine fissure

Cerebellum

Occipital horn of
lateral ventricle

FIGURE 2.   (*continued*) 3–5 represent three different cross-sections of this atlas. From *Fundamental Neuroanatomy* (pp. 244–245) by W. J. H. Nauta and M. Feirtag, 1986, New York: Freeman. Copyright 1986 by Freeman. Adapted by permission.

It is only after providing this overview that I shamelessly approach the topic of brain–temperament relations.

Behavioral Approach System

The behavioral approach (cf. Gray, 1982, 1990, 1991), or *behavioral activation* (Fowles, 1980), system refers formally to an emotional system that has evolved to motivate forward locomotion and search behavior toward stimuli construed as positive, but that may not initially be within close proximity. It appears to be a generalized emotional system that is activated by a host of stimuli associated with pleasurable engagement with the environment. As a result, such behaviors are also likely to correlate with positive emotionality on the part of the individual.

Many investigators have speculated about the neurobiological bases of this system, and the account that follows represents a compilation of these views (for details see Collins, 1991; Collins & Depue, 1992; Gray, 1990; Rolls, 1990).

The orbitoprefrontal cortex (OFC; see Figures 2 and 3), which is thought by many to be the administrator of the basolimbic forebrain circuitry, receives multimodal, integrated sensory information from distal uni- and multisensory cortices; it also receives emotional associations formed by the amygdala. The OFC is thought to hold these associations "on-line" in representational memory and then dictate how the organism should behave (see Goldman-Rakic, 1987). For example, through its efferent ("outgoing") projections, the OFC may initiate or inhibit motor, autonomic, and neurohumoral responses to specific sensory events. Through its connectivity with a variety of subcortical structures (e.g., the thalamus), the OFC may facilitate the selection and initiation of appropriate behavioral responses. Within the OFC also lie cortical nodes of neural networks that are devoted to emotional expressions. Finally, through its direct projection to dopamine-rich cells in ventral tegmental areas, the OFC likely influences the affective patterning of motor responses to stimulus events. Through this complex array of connections, the OFC regulates the adaptation of emotional behavior across environmental contexts.

One bit of evidence that supports the just-described roles of the OFC concerns the consequences of damaging this structure. Damage to the OFC results in an impaired ability to modulate instrumental behaviors with respect to reward contingencies, which is demonstrated in animals by enhanced responding to nonreward, reduced reward, and rewarding but task-irrelevant (i.e., novel) events (cf. Collins & Depue, 1992). In humans, lesions of the OFC result in the inability to generate and sustain appropriate social affect; such patients are also insensitive to the emotional well-being of others (cf. Stuss & Benson, 1984, 1986).

Let me now briefly elaborate on how this system is thought to work. Upon the detection of some incentive stimulus (i.e., something to promote approach behavior), information regarding the appetitive features of this stimulus are transmitted by the amygdala (see Figure 4) and the temporal

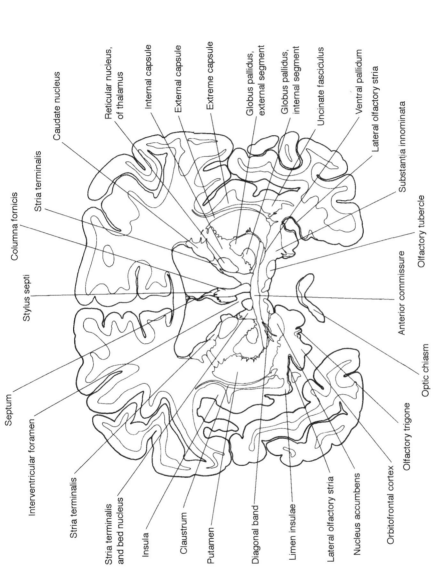

FIGURE 3. In the lower left portion of this figure, the orbitoprefrontal cortex is illustrated in this coronal section (section 97 from Figure 2). Several striatal structures are also illustrated (e.g., putamen, globus pallidus). From *Fundamental Neuroanatomy* (p. 249) by W. J. H. Nauta and M. Feirtag. 1986. New York: Freeman. Copyright 1986 by Freeman. Adapted by permission.

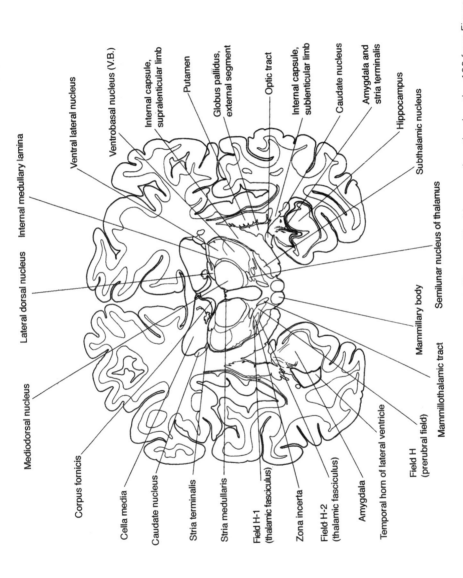

FIGURE 4. In the lower left portion of this figure, the amygdala is illustrated in this coronal section (section 100 from Figure 2), whereas another limbic structure—the hippocampus—is illustrated in the lower right. From *Fundamental Neuroanatomy* (p. 255) by W. J. H. Nauta and M. Feirtag, New York: Freeman. Copyright 1986 by Freeman. Adapted by permission.

pole (i.e., the tip of the temporal lobe) to the OFC. The OFC encodes this information, augmented in part by input from the hippocampus (see Figure 4) and hippocampal formation regarding similar stimuli that have been experienced in the past. To activate some appropriate motor response, the OFC transmits information related to the initiation or alteration of locomotor activity to the ventral striatum. Striatal efferents then activate the ventral pallidum (see Figure 3), which integrates body movements through motor cortices (these former structures comprise a portion of the striatum in general; see later section).

This description is by necessity brief, and the reader is encouraged to consult more detailed descriptions (e.g., Collins & Depue, 1992; Fowles, 1980; Gray, 1990). Rather than describe in detail the numerous other structures that are thought to be involved in this general circuitry, I initially focus attention on the amygdala. I do so primarily because it is this structure that appears to play important roles in many aspects of temperament and emotion in general.

The amygdala, a subcortical region, lies in the anterior (forward) part of the temporal lobe (see Figure 4). It is thought to play several important roles in the context of emotion (for a discussion see Rolls, 1990). It is known, for example, to play a critical role in stimulus–reinforcement conditioning, and it appears to mediate the formation of emotional associations that are attached to central representations of stimulus events (Aggleton & Mishkin, 1986; Jones & Mishkin, 1972). The amygdala may also generate subjective emotional experience during the process of associative recall. Thus, one can think of the amygdala as the organ that formulates and perhaps makes attributions about the emotional significance of some stimulus or event, be these events exogenous or endogenous. It is, in other words, the organ that permits humans to "have" an emotional experience. In contrast, the OFC appears to be the organ that regulates how (and whether) one acts on this experience.

Bilateral removal of the amygdala in the adult monkey results in the lack of fear to stimuli that should produce fear, anger, or withdrawal (Jones & Mishkin, 1972). In the infant monkey, similar ablation results in a complete lack of social contact with peers, extreme submissiveness, and blank or unexpressive faces (Bachevalier, 1991).[1] Important in the context of temperament, the amygdalectomized animal shows severe deficits in maternal and social–affiliative behavior (Kling, 1986; Kling & Steklis, 1976). I hasten to add, however, that similar behavioral effects are produced when afferent ("in coming") inputs to the amygdala are cut and when the temporal pole is lesioned. It is unclear whether behavioral effects that are caused by temporal pole lesions are due to the disconnection of the temporal pole from the amygdala or to the fact that object and event recognition are impaired and the animal thus fails to recognize stimuli, be they social or nonsocial in nature.

When the amygdala and the OFC are considered together, it appears that the former is responsible for the emotional tone attributed to ongoing events in the environment (and perhaps internal events as well), whereas the OFC directs the organism to respond to these events. In the present context, the OFC appears to direct the organism to approach such events.

The OFC and the amygdala are, of course, not the only structures in this circuit. Another is the hippocampus (and hippocampal formation in general)—the structure that provides information to the organism as to whether the stimulus or event then occupying the animal's attention has been experienced before (i.e., is it familiar) or is novel. I discuss this topic further in the review of the behavioral inhibition system (also see Steinmetz, chapter 2 in this book).

In summary (and in very general terms), the amygdala appears to be the site at which emotions are formed and emotional associations are made, whereas the OFC appears to use this information in determining and directing the course of action. In the context of the behavioral facilitation system, the emotion that is experienced is presumably positive in tone, and the behavior that is then initiated is approach.

Behavioral Inhibition System

The emotional counterweight to the behavioral approach system—the behavioral inhibition system—is a system that is concerned with halting behavior or withdrawing from or avoiding certain situations. Thus, neg-

---

[1]Note that in the research conducted with infant monkeys, the hippocampus is also removed along with the amygdala.

ative affect (such as anxiety or perhaps in the adult, depression or dysphoria) should correspond with behavioral inhibition. According to Gray (e.g., 1982), the eliciting events are conditioned stimuli that are associated with punishment, the omission or termination of reward, or novel stimuli. In general, high levels of novelty and intensity should produce behavioral inhibition, an increment in arousal, and increased attention. With continued stimulation, habituation should occur, and eventually, no response should be elicited.

The behavioral inhibition system depends on a comparator process (cf. Gray, 1982, 1990, 1991). On a moment-by-moment basis, the comparator evaluates the event that has just occurred and predicts the next event that is likely to occur. It is in some respects, then, a match–mismatch detector.

Some of the key functions of the comparator include (a) receiving information and describing the current state of the perceptual world, (b) using this stored information to describe past regularities that allow the organism to compare past events to present events, (c) using these sources of information to make predictions about the next (expected) event and then deciding whether there is a match or a mismatch, and (d) bringing the system to a halt if there is a mismatch (for an excellent summary of these and other functions see Collins, 1991; Collins & Depue, 1992).

The key to this behavioral system can be found in the hippocampal formation and its surrounding structures (notably the septal and entorhinal areas, the dentate gyrus, the hippocampus, the subiculum, and the presubiculum; see Figure 5), the prefrontal cortex (including the OFC; see Figure 3), and portions of the motor system. Let me put these structures in some functional context.

First and foremost, the comparator process depends on the hippocampal formation. In Gray's (1991) model, the subiculum plays a particularly important role (a portion of the subiculum, the presubiculum, is illustrated in Figure 5) because it is this area that receives inputs from the entorhinal cortex, which itself is a recipient of input from all cortical sensory association areas. A second and related function of the comparator, of course, is the ability to make predictions about future events.

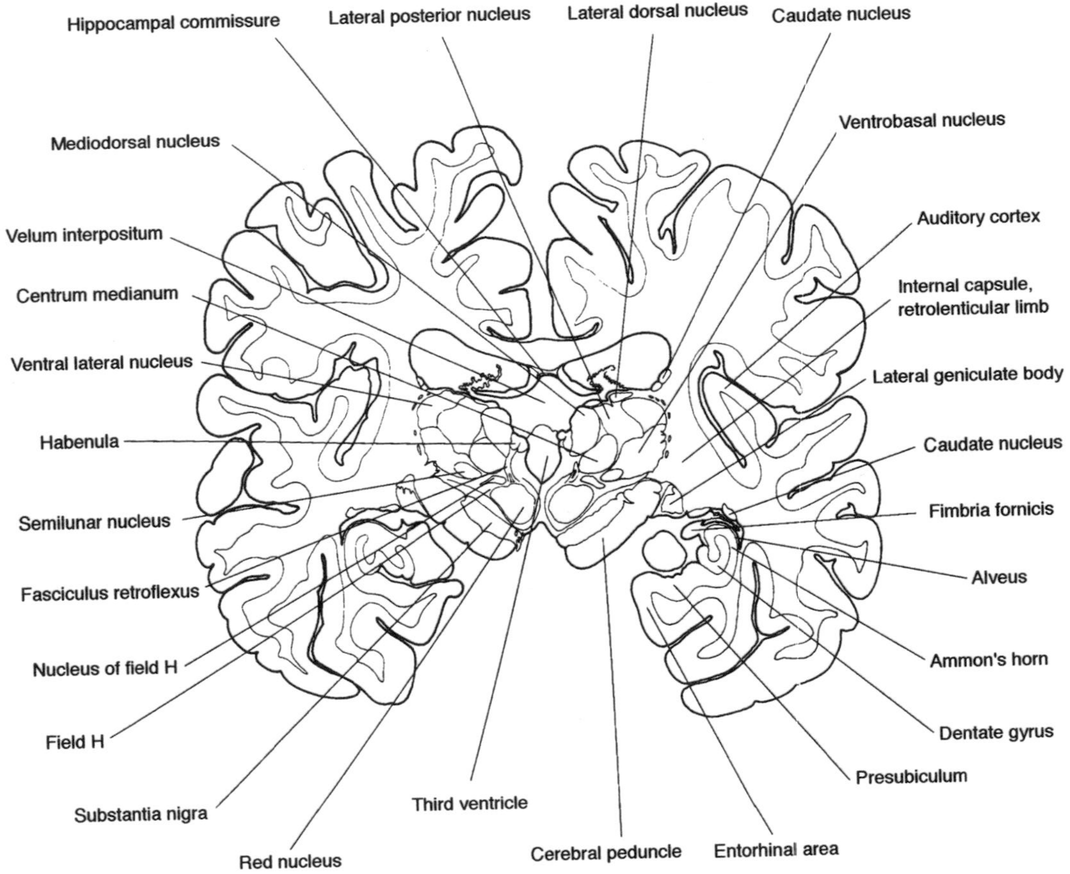

FIGURE 5. The various structures that comprise the hippocampal formation and surrounding cortex (entorhinal area, presubiculum, dentate gyrus, and hippocampus proper [Ammon's horn]) are illustrated in this coronal section in the lower right hand portion of the figure (section 102 from Figure 2). From *Fundamental Neuroanatomy* (p. 259) by W. J. H. Nauta and M.

This, according to Gray (1991), depends on the *Papez circuit*, which is the circuit that extends from the subiculum to the mammillary bodies of the hypothalamus (see Figure 4), the anteroventral thalamus, the cingulate cortex, and back to the subiculum (for detailed descriptions of this circuit see Kandel & Schwartz, 1985; LeDoux, 1986). Third, the ability to act on the information that is derived from the comparator depends on the motor circuitry. Finally, the prefrontal cortex is allotted the role of providing the comparator system with information concerning current motor programs (via its projections to the entorhinal and cingulate cortices).

On the basis of the foregoing descriptions of both the neuroanatomy and behavioral profiles of the behavioral inhibition system, one would predict that negative affect, such as anxiety or depression, should correlate with individuals who are behaviorally inhibited. Support for this claim has recently been found in neuroimaging studies using positron emission tomography (PET). For example, Raichle and colleagues (e.g., Reiman, Raichle, Butler, Herscovitch, & Robins, 1984) reported that patients with panic disorder differed from normals only in the hyperactivation noted in the entorhinal cortex and the subiculum. More recently, Reiman, Fusselman, Fox, and Raichle (1989) reported that under conditions of anticipatory anxiety (anticipation of a shock), normal individuals showed bilateral activation of the temporal poles. These results bode well with respect to related data: for example, stimulation of the temporal pole influences the autonomic functions that are associated with an anxious state (Kaada, 1960). In addition, stimulation of the temporal pole in nonhuman primates produces behavioral inhibition (Kaada, 1960), and bilateral lesions of this region in nonhuman primates attenuates the expression of fear in response to normally threatening situations (Penfield & Jasper, 1954).

In terms of other aspects of negative affect, when a dysphoric state is induced in normal individuals, activation is observed bilaterally in the OFC regions of women and is observed in the left OFC of men (Pardo, Pardo, & Raichle, 1993). When a group of depressed individuals is examined (in relation to normal controls), one observes left OFC hyperactivation, left amygdaloid activation, and bilateral caudate activation (Drevets et al., 1992). Interestingly, during remission, these same depressed individuals show normal activity of the frontal regions but continue to show left amygdaloid hyperactivation (Drevets et al., 1992). This latter finding has been interpreted to suggest that the amygdaloid activation may reflect a trait marker, whereas the frontal activation reflects a state marker (cf. Drevets et al., 1992).

In summary, there is ample evidence to support the functional link between the experience and expression of negative affect and the neural circuitry that is involved in the behavioral inhibition system (e.g., amygdala, hippocampus, related temporal lobe structures, and OFC). Having established this link, the question most germane to this chapter concerns when these structures develop. Before describing the development of these specific structures, however, I provide an overview of brain development in general.

A Primer on Human Central Nervous System Development

Several weeks after conception, the human embryo begins to divide into three layers. The outer layer—the *ectoderm*—becomes the skin, sense organs, and, most important, the nervous system. By approximately Embryonic Day 18, the dorsal ("toward the back") side of the ectoderm begins to thicken and form a pear-shaped neural plate. In the center of this structure a longitudinal neural groove begins to appear (see Figure 6). This groove deepens and then gradually folds over onto itself. This process begins at the midpoint of the groove and extends rostrally ("toward the top") and caudally ("toward the tail"). Both ends of the groove initially remain open. The rostral end begins to close at about the 24th day, followed by the caudal end 2 days later (for good introductions to brain development see Kandel, Schwartz, & Jessell, 1991; Nowakowski, 1987; Sidman & Rakic, 1982).

Before proceeding, it is important to note that some cells of the neural plate are not incorporated into the neural tube. These cells, which remain free between the ectoderm proper and the neural tube, form the *neural crest* (see Figure 6, panel C). It is from the neural crest that sensory and autonomic ganglia, cranial skeletal elements, and the autonomic nervous system develop.

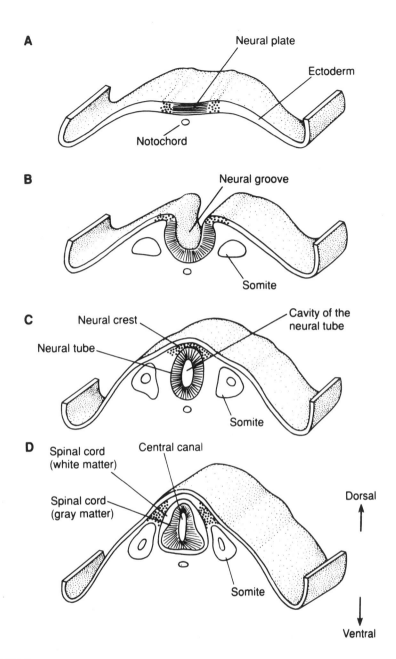

FIGURE 6. The process of neurulation, including formation of the neural plate (an outgrowth of the ectodermal layer of the embryo; panel A), neural groove (panel B), and neural tube (panel C). The conversion of neural plate to neural tube takes place between the 3rd and 4th prenatal weeks. Reprinted from *Principles of Neural Science* (3rd ed., p. 297) by E. R. Kandel, J. H. Schwartz, and T. M. Jessell, 1991, Norwalk, CT: Appleton & Lang. Copyright 1991 by Appleton & Lang. Adapted from ''The Development of the Brain'' by W. M. Cowan, 1979, *Scientific American, 241*(3). Copyright 1979 by Scientific American. Reprinted and adapted by permission.

Provided that the neural tube closes properly (the result of improper or insufficient closure is a neural tube defect, such as anencephaly or spina bifida), growth of the neural tube is greatest at the cranial end, where the cortex will eventually appear. Toward the end of the 4th week, three primary vesicles have begun to form. These are the *forebrain* (*prosencephalon*), *midbrain* (*mesencephalon*), and *hindbrain* (*rhombencephalon*; see Figure 7). The rest of the neural tube becomes the spinal cord.

By approximately the 5th week of development, the forebrain subdivides further into the *telencephalon* and *diencephalon*, whereas from the hindbrain emerges the *metencephalon* and *myelencephalon*. The midbrain changes very little. Central to this discussion is the development of the forebrain structures (see Figure 7, panel B).

It is from the telencephalon that the cerebral hemispheres will develop. The two hemispheres comprise about 75% of all central nervous cells, which first appear as two lateral diverticula (i.e., "sacs") of the prosencephalon. The cranial end of the hemispheres becomes the frontal pole, whereas the caudal end turns ventrally first, then cranially, to form the temporal pole. The occipital pole emerges as new outgrowth of the hemispheres.

The initial formation of the cortical plate (surface) begins at about the 6th week of development and occurs by the migration of cells to the deepest layer of the cortex, which is followed by subsequent migrations to more superficial layers, in what is called an "inside-out" pattern. In this manner, young (postmitotic) neurons leave their zone of origin (the so-called "ventricular" zone) and typically migrate past older cells to reach their final position. As a result, the earliest formed cells inhabit the deepest cortical layer (layer VI), whereas progressively later formed cells occupy positions at progressively more superficial layers. (It should be noted that the cerebellum, which lags in development in relation to the cortex, forms in an "outside-in" pattern.)

Cell proliferation and migration vary from area to area, but in general, these processes are complete by about 5–6 months after conception. The exceptions include cerebellar structures and glial cells,[2] all of which continue to develop and/or be produced postnatally.

---

[2]Glial cells come in many varieties and provide for a number of support services to the brain as a whole and to neurons in particular, such as the removal of debris (phagocytes), the formation of myelin

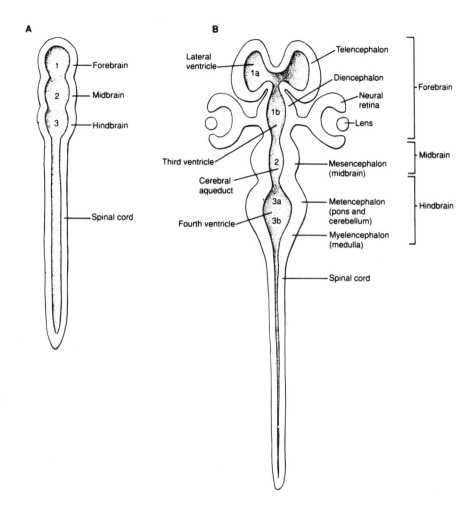

FIGURE 7. Differentiation of the three major subdivisions of the developing central nervous system. In the upper left-hand portion of the figure (panel A) is represented the early three vesicle stage of forebrain, midbrain, and hindbrain. Illustrated in the upper right-hand portion (panel B) is further subdivisions of these three vesicles. From *Principles of Neural Science* (p. 299) by E. R. Kandel, J. H. Schwartz, and T. M. Jessell, 1991, Norwalk, CT: Appleton & Lang. Copyright 1991 by Appleton & Lang. Reprinted by permission.

(Schwann cells), and so on. Most such cells are generated from the subventricular zone (in contrast to neurons, most of which come from the ventricular zone). Both the subventricular and ventricular zones are outgrowths of an early epithelial layer of cells that line the neural tube (for a discussion see Nowakowski, 1987).

As the hemispheres are formed, the otherwise smooth surface of the hemispheres becomes convoluted. Such convolutions appear by about the 5th–6th month and continue through the 1st postnatal year. It should be added, however, that it is at about the 5th prenatal month that the migration of cells into the cortex ends, and thus further growth of the cortical surface is the result of glial proliferation and neuron differentiation.

Once cells have reached their target destination, they begin the process of differentiation, which can range from the death of the cell to the development of axons and dendrites and ultimately synapses. This latter process, *synaptogenesis*, can be very protracted. For example, after an initial overproduction of synapses, adult levels of synapses in the occipital cortex are not reached until nearly 6 years of age; and in the frontal cortex, adult levels are not reached until adolescence (Huttenlocher, 1979, 1990, in press; Huttenlocher, De Courten, Garey, & Van Der Loos, 1982).

Development of Some Specific Brain Areas Relevant to Temperament

Having described the development of the central nervous system in very general terms, I would now like to examine some specific structures that are central to temperament. I focus my attention on the development of the three major areas that should play central roles in behavioral approach and withdrawal: the striatum, which involves the motor planning routines involved in approach or avoidance; the hippocampus, amygdala, and related temporal lobe structures, which are involved in the coding of emotion and the formation of memory; and the prefrontal regions, which are concerned with overseeing the operation of approach and withdrawal and with planning the subject's reaction to positive or rewarding versus novel or threatening stimuli and events.

Striatum

The striatum plays a central role in the regulation of voluntary movement. It appears that the structures that comprise the striatum (including the caudate, the putamen, and the globus pallidus; see Figure 3) are differentiated at birth; indeed, the striatum is the first of the telencephalic structures to begin myelinating.[3] Within the striatum, the inner segment of the globus pallidus is well myelinated by the 8th postnatal month, although the outer segment does not reach adult levels of myelination until beyond the 1st postnatal year. In terms of metabolic activity, Chugani (1993) and Chugani and Phelps (1986) reported that the basal ganglia (which subsume the striatal structures plus the amygdaloid complex and claustrum) display increases in glucose activity earlier than most regions of the cortex. Given that glucose is a major source of energy, from such increases one can infer the emergence of brain function.

These data suggest that the structures involved in regulating voluntary movement develop early in life. Needless to say, one need only observe the choreoformlike movements of the young infant to know that development of this region is far from complete, even within the first few years of life. Naturally, not all the blame should be attributed to the relative immaturity of these structures; after all, sophisticated, adultlike movements depend considerably on the development of the motor cortex (which lies in the frontal lobe) and not insignificantly on the muscles and limbs that are to be moved. When considered in this context, my main point is that the striatum does, in fact, achieve some level of functional maturity relatively early in life—clearly within the 1st year, possibly sooner.

Hippocampus

In general, a great deal more is known about the development of the hippocampus than is known about the development of the striatum. Early in the 4th prenatal month, the subiculum, the hippocampus, and the dentate gyrus acquire individual characteristics. At 13–14 weeks, the pyramidal cell fields are all distinguishable (Sidman & Rakic, 1982). By the 4th prenatal month, the presubiculum and the entorhinal cortex separate out (see Figure 5), with the presubiculum developing before the entorhinal cortex (13–14 weeks vs. 16–17 weeks; Sidman & Rakic, 1982). Finally, the

---

[3]Myelin is a lipid–protein substance produced by Schwann cells that coats certain axons and in so doing greatly increases the speed (and by default, efficiency) at which information can be transmitted (i.e., conduction velocity increases).

granule cell layer (in the dentate gyrus; see Figure 5) develops last. Given that axons in the entorhinal cortex go through the subiculum to reach the dentate gyrus and that efferents from the dentate gyrus feed back to other hippocampal structures, the development of the dentate would seem to play an important role in the general neural circuitry of the hippocampal formation.

Having described when these various structures differentiate, let me add some other observations. First, at least in the monkey, the distribution of muscarinic receptors (i.e., receptors for acetylcholine) in the limbic cortex are adultlike at birth, in contrast to those in the cortex, which mature later (Bachevalier, Ungerleider, O'Neill, & Friedman, 1986; O'Neill, Friedman, Bachevalier, & Ungerleider, 1986). Second, the volume of human limbic cortex and the size of relevant limbic structures (e.g., the hippocampus) rapidly become adultlike in the second half of the 1st year of life (Humphrey, 1966; Kretschmann, Kammradt, Krauthausen, Sauer, & Wingert, 1986; O'Neill et al., 1986; Paldino & Purpura, 1979). Third, the subiculum (which links the entorhinal cortex with the hippocampus) and the hippocampus proper mature relatively early in postnatal development (Nowakowski & Rakic, 1981). Fourth, dendritic development in the hippocampus precedes that of the visual cortex, a structure known to be quite functional by the second half of the 1st year of life (cf. Aslin, 1989). Fifth, metabolic activity in the temporal lobes increases substantially by the 3rd postnatal month, which precedes that of prefrontal cortex by several months (Chugani & Phelps, 1986). Finally, from a functional perspective, it appears that the hippocampus is "on-line" by 15–30 days of age, at least in the monkey. Specifically, Bachevalier (1991) and Brickson and Bachevalier (1984) reported that memory performance in the visual paired comparison procedure is impaired after 15 days of age following bilateral removal of the hippocampus and amygdala.

Collectively, then, the hippocampal region appears to mature relatively early in life. On the basis of the best available evidence, it seems reasonable to propose that at least some hippocampal function emerges in the first few months of life, with more adultlike function in place by about 1 year of age, possibly sooner (cf. Nelson, 1993b). Before summarizing the implications that this might have for reactivity to novelty and for memory, let me comment on the development of another temporal lobe structure.

Area TE

An important temporal lobe region implicated in memory that lies outside of the hippocampus is the inferior temporal region TE. There are two reasons for discussing the development of this structure in the context of temperament. First, this structure lies in close proximity to the temporal pole, an area known to play a role in emotion (see earlier discussion). However, because the temporal pole has not been examined developmentally in humans, I decided to examine the development of area TE as a tentative model for the development of the temporal pole. Second, area TE appears to be an area that receives projections from the limbic system and, therefore, plays a large role in the development of memory.

It has recently been reported that in the monkey, adult levels of glucose utilization are not obtained in area TE until approximately 4 months of age (corresponding to 12–16 months of age in humans; cf. Bachevalier, Hagger, & Mishkin, 1991).[4] As mentioned earlier, such evidence can be taken to reflect the emergence of brain function. Second, early (neonatal) lesions of this area appear to have no impact on performance on either the visual paired comparison or delayed nonmatching-to-sample tasks, although later lesions profoundly affect performance on the latter task. This suggests that (a) this structure develops late and (b) may be responsible for what in animals has been termed *explicit memory* (cf. Bachevalier, 1991, 1992; Nelson, 1993b).

What are the implications of the differential rates of development of area TE in relation to that of the hippocampus? First, early hippocampal development likely makes possible the range of memory phenomena that involve reactivity to novelty, for example, memory evaluated through the visual paired comparison procedure and the habituation procedure. However, as I have argued previously, novelty reactions at this age may be obligatory, and thus this "type" of memory may be more primitive than

---

[4]For many species of monkey, 1 month of life (depending on the species) corresponds to approximately 3–4 months of human life (V. M. Gunderson, personal communication, October 1992).

what develops toward the end of the 1st year (cf. Nelson, 1993a, 1993b; Nelson & Collins, 1991). This more mature form of memory, which in the adult literature is called explicit memory, likely develops closer to 1 year of age when cortical area TE starts to come on-line. As Bachevalier and colleagues have argued, the phenomenon of infantile amnesia may be due to the immaturity of this cortical area in the 1st year or 2 of life (cf. Bachevalier, 1992; Webster, Ungerleider, & Bachevalier, 1991a, 1991b). The reason is that the memories formed and consolidated by the hippocampus have no forwarding address, and thus long-term *episodic memory* may not be possible.

Amygdala

Unfortunately, much less is known about this structure (see Figure 4) than those just described, although it would appear that it, like the hippocampus, develops early. Indeed, many investigators have suggested that this should not be surprising, given that the hippocampus and the amygdala are deep structures, and thus cell migration for these structures would be completed earlier than for structures that lie in more superficial laminae. By the 3rd prenatal month, the cells of the human amygdala are differentiated. By the 4th month, they have distinct nuclei, and in the 6th month, all areas are well distinguished, although the cells are still differentiating. In the last (9th) month, final differentiation occurs. In general, the periamygdaloid cortex is distinguishable by the 6th prenatal month, which is earlier than for any other deep nuclei.

More is known about the development of the amygdala in the monkey than in the human. For example, Bachevalier (1990) and Brickson and Bachevalier (1984) demonstrated that neonatal damage to either the amygdala or the hippocampus appears to disrupt memory performance in the infant monkey, which suggests that the amygdala develops on a time frame similar to that of the hippocampus. Second, Bachevalier (1992) made a number of intriguing observations about monkeys that had incurred early amygdaloid lesions. When interacting with normal monkeys at 2 months of age, infants with amygdaloid–hippocampal lesions had more temper tantrums when first placed in a novel play cage, showed more passive behavior, and manipulated objects less than did unoperated controls. At 6 months of age, these monkeys displayed even more striking pathology in that they showed a complete lack of social contact, extreme submissiveness including active withdrawal, and gross motor stereotypies. Also at 6 months of age, the monkeys with amygdaloid–hippocampal lesions displayed blank and unexpressive faces, little eye contact, and poor body expression (for a discussion see Bachevalier, 1991).[5]

Collectively these data suggest that (a) the amygdala, like the hippocampus, likely develops within the 1st year of postnatal life, perhaps earlier; and (b) from a functional perspective, the amygdala is not only involved in memory but is also involved in modulating normal emotional reactions in social situations, and does so from an early age.

Prefrontal Cortex

I begin the discussion of this final area with an overview of the physiological and anatomical changes that transpire over the last part of gestation and the 1st year or 2 of postnatal life. I then discuss the functional development of this area.

Physiological and anatomical development
Rakic, Bourgeois, Zecevic, Eckenhoff, and Goldman-Rakic (1986) reported that synaptogenesis in monkeys occurs concurrently over diverse regions of the cortex (e.g., the prefrontal cortex, the hippocampus, the visual cortex), with the peak of overproduction occurring between the 2nd and 4th postnatal month, and a subsequent decline to adult levels over the next 8 or so months. It is not clear whether this model applies to the human, however. For example, Huttenlocher reported that the highest synaptic density occurs at 4 months of age in primary visual cortex and at 1 year of age in the medial gyrus of the prefrontal cortex. This peak is essentially retained until about 4 years of age in visual cortex and until about 7 years of age in prefrontal cortex. After about 4 years of age, these synapses undergo a process of elimination, such that adult levels of synaptic density are reached at 5–6 years of age in the visual cortex and at

---

[5]Although one must interpret comparative data cautiously, such findings are of great use in providing a model of development, one that will hopefully guide subsequent studies in humans.

16 years of age in the prefrontal cortex (Huttenlocher, 1979, 1990, in press; Huttenlocher et al., 1982). In addition, neuronal density was reported to be less in the middle frontal gyrus than in the primary visual cortex, and the decline (to adult numbers) in neuronal density occurs at a slower rate in the middle frontal gyrus. On the basis of the human data, it would appear that synaptogenesis and neuronal differentiation follow a more protracted course in the prefrontal cortex than in more posterior regions of the brain.

Turning now to a discussion of myelination, it appears that the prefrontal association cortex continues myelinating through the 3rd decade of life, well after other areas of the brain have completed myelination (e.g., Yakovlev & LeCours, 1967). However, there is some evidence to suggest that myelin develops in the orbital prefrontal regions before it does in the dorsolateral region (Orzhekhovskaya, 1975 [cited in Fuster, 1980]); the latter region, of course, is known to be involved in spatial working memory (cf. Goldman-Rakic, 1987).

In terms of metabolic function, Chugani and Phelps (1986), using PET to analyze human infants, reported that regional glucose metabolism in most of the frontal lobe is low during the 2–4-month postnatal period. Indeed, this is the last region of the brain to undergo a maturational rise in glucose metabolism. These investigators also reported that maturation of the lateral portion of the frontal lobe occurs between the 6th and 8th month, thereby preceding that of the phylogenetically newer dorsolateral prefrontal region, which occurs between the 8th and 12th month.

In summary, on the basis of the anatomical and physiological data, it seems reasonable to posit that development of the prefrontal cortex broadly construed lags well behind that of most other areas of the brain. As should be apparent shortly, however, in the case of the prefrontal cortex, function may not follow form.

Functional development
Unfortunately, little is known about the functional development of the OFC; more is known about the development of the dorsolateral prefrontal cortex (which, as indicated earlier, may develop more slowly than the OFC). For example, Goldman-Rakic (Goldman, 1971) investigated the role

of the dorsolateral prefrontal cortex in delayed response performance in infant monkeys. It was initially demonstrated that neonatal lesions of the dorsolateral prefrontal cortex had little effect on performance during the later infancy period (i.e., 8 months; see Goldman, 1971). More recently, however, Diamond (1990) and Diamond and Goldman-Rakic (1989) demonstrated that when lesions are done later in the infancy period (at approximately 4½ months of age) and testing soon thereafter (1 month later), performance on the delayed-response and Piagetian A-not-B tasks are deleteriously affected. Although this finding suggests that this region of the brain is functional early in life (i.e., 5th–6th postnatal month in the monkey; perhaps 15th–24th postnatal month in humans) and mediates performance on these tasks, it must be kept in mind that Goldman (1985) proposed that other, more developmentally mature structures in the general prefrontal circuitry might subserve performance on these tasks during infancy. Such structures include the OFC (Goldman, 1971) and the anterodorsal caudate nucleus (Goldman & Rosvold, 1972). Only later in life (after 12–16 months) does the dorsolateral prefrontal cortex take over.

Summary

In general, the prefrontal cortical areas develop later than do other areas of the brain in general and, specifically, later than do the limbic or striatal areas. Although the physiological and anatomical data suggest that the prefrontal cortex develops quite late in relation to other areas, the behavioral data are slightly more liberal in their estimates; for example, on the basis of such data, one might argue that some prefrontal function emerges by the 1st–2nd postnatal year, although considerably more development is in store over the ensuing years.

Brain–Temperament Relations in Infancy

After describing earlier in this chapter the association between behavioral approach and behavioral inhibition, as well as the structure and function of the striatal, limbic, and prefrontal cortices that are thought to be involved in these behaviors, I then described the development of these brain areas. I did so to lay the groundwork for speculating about the emergence of different temperament traits in the infancy period. It is with discussion of this last topic that I conclude this chapter. I begin with an exposition of behavioral approach and withdrawal and then briefly discuss novelty reactions. I remind the reader that the speculations described herein are tentative at best and are based on a less than thorough knowledge of temperament (for a more enlightened view of brain–temperament relations see Rothbart et al., chapter 4 in this book).

Approach/Withdrawal

Several observations are worth noting about the emergence and functional development of behavioral approach and withdrawal based on the developmental neuroscience data reviewed herein. First, although striatal structures may develop relatively early, they are not fully developed, nor are the motor areas to which they project. Such immaturity somewhat limits the gross motor expressions (e.g., walking, running) of approach and withdrawal. In their place are expressions of approach/withdrawal behaviors that are conveyed through nonlocomotor routines, such as the expression of positive and negative affect through the facial and vocal musculature (e.g., crying, laughing). Such speculation appears well warranted in light of reports that infants by 1–2 years of age display a range of facial expressions that approaches that of the adult (e.g., Hiatt, Campos, & Emde, 1979; Malatesta, 1985).

Second, given the relatively early development of the amygdala, even young infants should have little problem experiencing and encoding emotional events (for reviews of socioemotional development see Barrett & Campos, 1987; Campos, Barrett, Lamb, Goldsmith, & Stenberg, 1983). Similarly, the relatively early development of the limbic structures that are involved in memory (e.g., hippocampus) likely make possible (after 6–8 months) the infant's ability to encode for somewhat brief periods of time memory for emotional events. However, given the relatively "late" development of the cortical structures that are involved in memory (e.g., area TE), it is likely that long-term explicit memory for specific emotionally laden episodes will not be present until well after the 1st year of life, probably closer to the 2nd. Unfortunately, memory researchers have not yet begun to examine the former issue, although there is much speculation about the latter, particularly in the context of infantile amnesia (cf. Bach-evalier, 1992; Howe & Courage, 1993).

The missing neural link to the development of approach/withdrawal behavior and the associated expression of positive affect versus negative affect is the prefrontal cortex. Although the OFC may develop before the dorsolateral prefrontal cortex does (see Bachevalier & Hagger, 1991; Gold-man, 1975; Goldman, Crawford, Stokes, Galkin, & Rosvold, 1974), the OFC still develops later than do the limbic and striatal structures that have been mentioned. Thus, although the development of the amygdala and hippocampal formation may allow infants to experience and encode emo-tional events from early in life, the late development of the prefrontal cortex should make infants who are younger than 1–2 years experience difficulty in organizing consistent responses to stimuli that are perceived as aversive or pleasurable (thereby possibly accounting for the instability in temperament ratings across the first 1–2 years of life; see Bates, 1987). I do not argue that they cannot detect such events or retrieve such events from memory once they have been stored; rather, they have difficulty in mounting a response to such events, which is why, I suspect, they have difficulty in holding on-line whatever course of action they have settled on long enough to actually implement this action. Of course, immaturity in the motor cortex also likely limits the kind of response they can initiate and, perhaps, sustain.

Novelty Reactions

In the context of memory research, novelty reactions appear in devel-opment at or shortly after birth (e.g., Slater, in press) and have proven to be a robust phenomenon for well over 20 years (for reviews see Fagan, 1990; Olson & Sherman, 1983). Furthermore, individual differences in this domain have also been extensively studied (cf. Colombo & Mitchell, 1990). What likely makes novelty reactions possible is the relatively early de-velopment of the hippocampus (for a discussion see Diamond, 1990; Nel-son, 1993b). However, as shown by a variety of behavioral paradigms (e.g., delayed nonmatching-to-sample; cf. Overman, Bachevalier, Turner, & Peuster, 1992) as well as through the use of electrophysiological proce-dures (e.g., event-related potentials; e.g., Nelson & Collins, 1991, 1992), it appears that a qualitative shift in novelty reactions occurs sometime shortly before the 1st year of life. I attribute this shift to the functional development of cortical areas within the temporal lobe, notably area TE (for elaboration see Bachevalier & Hagger, 1991; Bachevalier, Hagger, & Mishkin, 1991; Nelson, 1993b). This shift likely reflects the emergence of a more mature form of explicit memory.

Responding differentially to a novel versus familiar stimulus as evidenced by looking time is quite different, of course, than the way novelty reactions are thought of in the context of temperament research. In the latter, a variety of behaviors are observed as infants are confronted with strange or unusual (i.e., novel) toys, situations, and people. In these cases infants must do much more than simply look longer at the novel event: They must evaluate the event, determine whether it has been experienced before, decide whether the event merits approach or avoidance behavior, and ultimately, initiate approach or avoidance behavior (be these behaviors locomotor, such as crawling away, or facial, such as displaying fear). Because of the relatively early development of limbic structures (subserving the comparator mechanism), the evaluation process may emerge within the first 6–12 months of life; however, due to delayed maturation of the OFC, mounting a consistent and sustained behavioral reaction to a novel situation may prove problematic. As discussed earlier, although infants may express positive or negative affect to novel situations early in the 1st year, whether they can implement an appropriate course of action (and do so for a sustained period of time) is likely not possible until well after the 1st year, possibly closer to the 2nd.

Future Research Directions

The just-presented speculations have by design been relatively unencumbered by developmental data. In this context I briefly mention the research of Davidson, Fox, and colleagues, who have used the electroencephalogram (EEG) to examine behavioral approach and withdrawal (e.g., Calkins & Fox, 1992; Davidson, Ekman, Saron, Senulis, & Friesen, 1990; Davidson & Fox, 1989; Fox, 1991; Fox, Bell, & Jones, 1992). In general, these investigators reported greater right frontal EEG activation in infants who were labeled as high in negative affect, whereas they detected a trend for greater left frontal activation in infants who expressed greater positive affect. At first glance, these data appear to be at odds with the PET data (reviewed earlier), which tend to indicate either (a) greater left orbito-frontal and amygdaloid activation under conditions of negative affect or (b) no lateral differences at all. Although one might initially question the validity of either the PET or EEG data, a few points are worth noting. First, the PET data were all collected from relatively small numbers of adults, and often these were adults with demonstrated psychopathology. In contrast, for the EEG data that were collected by both Davidson and Fox, the sample sizes were larger, the subjects ranged in age from a few months old to adults, and the subjects included both normal and pathological populations. Second, PET and EEG provide for different levels of analysis, and thus they may be indicating different things. For these reasons, it is not surprising that the PET and EEG data are in some disagreement. Given this context, it seems advisable to conduct EEG studies simultaneously with PET studies, as Davidson is currently doing (R. J. Davidson, personal communication, March 14, 1993). Second, PET studies should be conducted with infants, as de Schonen, Dervelle, Mancini, and Pascalis (1993) have done in France, as well as to include infants in studies using other neuroimaging procedures, such as event-related potentials and perhaps functional (i.e., "fast") magnetic resonance imaging.

A more challenging issue is to go from the basic neuroscience literature to the literature that I have briefly reviewed herein and ask why one would find lateral differences of any sort; simply put, there is nothing in the anatomical or physiological literature, and nothing in Gray's (1991) model for example, that would predict any of the lateral differences that have been observed, be they from PET or EEG. An answer to this question clearly awaits further study, and therefore, I do not elaborate further on this point.

Conclusion

My goal in writing this chapter was to outline the possible neural bases of infant temperament. Given the paucity of data on this subject, a great deal more conjecture and speculation was required than I would have liked. In the long run, I think the only hope investigators have for mapping behaviors as complex as temperament onto the brain is to mount a serious effort to do what has happened in cognitive neuroscience; temperament researchers must essentially link arms with those who are studying neuroscience. This will necessitate the use of a variety of brain imaging procedures with young infants, and appropriate animal models will also need to be developed. In addition, I think it would be useful for those who are studying neuroscience to begin to pay heed to those who are studying temperament. In so doing, speculation about the brain bases of temperament (such as those offered herein) can be examined in an a priori fashion by the brain scientist (e.g., rather than infer the developmental course of the amygdala from that of the hippocampus, one could formally examine the amygdala and determine whether it plays the role suggested in this chapter). It is by adopting both of these suggestions that a complete account of the neurobiological bases of infant temperament will become possible, including exposition of the ever-important issue of individual differences.

References

Aggleton, J. P., & Mishkin, M. (1986). The amygdala: Sensory gateway to the emotions. In E. Plutchik & H. Kellerman (Eds.), *Emotion: Theory, research, and experience: Vol. 3. Biological foundations of emotion* (pp. 281–299). San Diego, CA: Academic Press.

Aslin, R. (1989). Visual and auditory development in infancy. In J. D. Osofsky (Ed.), *Handbook of infant development* (2nd ed., pp. 5–97). New York: Wiley.

Bachevalier, J. (1990). Ontogenetic development of habit and memory formation in primates. In A. Diamond (Ed.), *Development and neural bases of higher cognitive functions* (pp. 457–484). New York: New York Academy of Sciences Press.

Bachevalier, J. (1991). An animal model for childhood autism. In C. A. Tamminga & S. C. Schulz (Eds.), *Advances in neuropsychiatry and psychopharmacology: Vol 1. Schizophrenia research* (pp. 129–140). New York: Raven Press.

Bachevalier, J. (1992). Cortical versus limbic immaturity: Relationship to infantile amnesia. In M. R. Gunnar & C. A. Nelson (Eds.), *Minnesota symposia on child psychology: Vol. 24. Developmental behavioral neuroscience* (pp. 129–153). Hillsdale, NJ: Erlbaum.

Bachevalier, J., & Hagger, C. (1991). Sex differences in the development of learning abilities in primates. *Psychoneuroendocrinology, 16,* 177–188.

Bachevalier, J., Hagger, C., & Mishkin, M. (1991). Functional maturation of the occipito-temporal pathway in infant rhesus monkeys. In N. A. Lassen, D. H. Ingvar, M. E. Raichle, & L. Friberg (Eds.), *Brain work and mental activity* (pp. 231–240). Copenhagen, Denmark: Munksgaard.

Bachevalier, J., Ungerleider, L. G., O'Neill, J. B., & Friedman, D. P. (1986). Regional distribution of [^{3}H]naloxone binding in the brain of a newborn rhesus monkey. *Developmental Brain Research, 25,* 302–308.

Barrett, K. C., & Campos, J. J. (1987). Perspectives on emotional development: II. A functionalist approach to emotions. In J. D. Osofsky (Ed.), *Handbook of infant development* (2nd ed., pp. 555–578). New York: Wiley.

Bates, J. (1987). Temperament in infancy. In J. D. Osofsky (Ed.), *Handbook of infant development* (2nd ed., pp. 1101–1149). New York: Wiley.

Brickson, M., & Bachevalier, J. (1984). Visual recognition in infant monkeys: Evidence for a primitive memory process. *Society for Neuroscience Abstracts, 10,* 137.

Buss, A. H., & Plomin, R. (1984). *Temperament: Early developing personality traits.* Hillsdale, NJ: Erlbaum.

Calkins, S. D., & Fox, N. A. (1992). The relations among infant temperament, security of attachment, and behavioral inhibition at 24 months. *Child Development, 63,* 1456–1472.

Campos, J., Barrett, K., Lamb, M., Goldsmith, H., & Stenberg, C. (1983). Socioemotional development. In M. M. Haith & J. J. Campos (Eds.), *Handbook of child psychology: Vol. 2. Infancy and developmental psychobiology* (pp. 783–915). New York: Wiley.

Chugani, H. T. (1993). Developmental aspects of regional brain glucose metabolism, behavior, and plasticity. In G. Dawson & K. Fischer (Eds.), *Human behavior and the developing brain.* New York: Guilford Press.

Chugani, H. T., & Phelps, M. E. (1986). Maturational changes in cerebral function in infants determined by [18]FDG positron emission tomography. *Science, 231,* 840–843.

Churchland, P. S. (1986). *Neurophilosophy: Toward a unified science of mind–brain.* Cambridge, MA: MIT Press.

Collins, P. F. (1991). *Dopamine, the behavioral facilitation system, and the emotional structure of personality: Theory and psychophysiological measurement.* Unpublished manuscript.

Collins, P. F., & Depue, R. A. (1992). A neurobehavioral systems approach to developmental psychopathology: Implications for disorders of affect. In D. Cicchetti (Ed.), *Rochester symposia on developmental psychopathology: Vol. 4. Developmental perspectives on depression* (pp. 29–101). Rochester, NY: University of Rochester Press.

Colombo, J., & Mitchell, D. W. (1990). Individual differences in early visual attention: Fixation time and information processing. In J. Colombo & J. Fagen (Eds.), *Individual differences in infancy* (pp. 193–227). Hillsdale, NJ: Erlbaum.

Cowan, W. M. (1979). The development of the brain. *Scientific American, 241*(3), 112–133.

Davidson, R. J., Ekman, P., Saron, C. D., Senulis, J., & Friesen, W. (1990). Approach/ withdrawal and cerebral asymmetry: Emotional expression and brain physiology I. *Journal of Personality and Social Psychology, 58,* 330–334.

Davidson, R. J., & Fox, N. A (1989). The relation between tonic EEG asymmetry and ten-month-old infant emotional responses to separation. *Journal of Abnormal Psychology, 98,* 127–131.

de Schonen, S., Dervelle, C., Mancini, J., & Pascalis, O. (1993). Hemispheric differences in face processing and brain maturation. In B. de Boysson-Bardies, S. de Schonen, P. Jusczyk, P. MacNeilage, & J. Morton (Eds.), *Developmental neurocognition: Speech and face processing in the first year of life* (pp. 149–163). Norwell, MA: Kluwer Academic.

Diamond, A. (1990). The development and neural bases of memory functions as indexed by the AB and delayed response task in human infants and infant monkeys. In A. Diamond (Ed.), *Development and neural bases of higher cognitive functions* (pp. 267–317). New York: New York Academy of Sciences Press.

Diamond, A., & Goldman-Rakic, P. S. (1989). Comparison of human infants and rhesus monkeys on Piaget's AB task: Evidence for dependence on dorsolateral prefrontal cortex. *Experimental Brain Research, 74,* 24–40.

Drevets, W. C., Videen, T. O., Price, J. L., Preskorn, S. H., Carmichael, S. T., & Raichle, M. E. (1992). A functional neuroanatomical study of unipolar depression. *Journal of Neuroscience, 12,* 3628–3641.

Fagan, J. F. III (1990). The paired-comparison paradigm and infant intelligence. In A. Diamond (Ed.), *Development and neural bases of higher cognitive functions* (pp. 337–364). New York: New York Academy of Sciences Press.

Fowles, D. C. (1980). The three arousal model: Implications of Gray's two-factor learning theory for heart rate, electrodermal activity, and psychopathy. *Psychophysiology, 17,* 87–104.

Fox, N. A. (1991). If it's not left, it's right: Electroencephalogram asymmetry and the development of emotion. *American Psychologist, 46,* 863–872.

Fox, N. A., Bell, M. A., & Jones, N. A. (1992). Individual differences in response to stress and cerebral asymmetry. *Developmental Neuropsychology, 8,* 161–184.

Fuster, J. M. (1990). *The prefrontal cortex.* New York: Raven Press.

Goldman, P. S. (1971). Functional development of the prefrontal cortex in early life and the problem of neuronal plasticity. *Experimental Neurology, 32,* 366–387.

Goldman, P. S. (1975). Age, sex, and experience related to the neural basis of cognitive development. In N. A. Buchwald & M. A. B. Brazier (Eds.), *Brain mechanisms in mental retardation* (pp. 379–392). San Diego, CA: Academic Press.

Goldman, P. S., Crawford, H. T., Stokes, L. P., Galkin, T. W., & Rosvold, H. E. (1974). Sex-dependent behavioral effects of cerebral cortical lesions in the developing rhesus monkeys. *Science, 186,* 540–542.

Goldman, P. S., & Rosvold, H. E. (1972). The effects of selective caudate lesions in infant and juvenile rhesus monkeys. *Brain Research, 43,* 53–66.

Goldman-Rakic, P. S. (1985). Toward a neurobiology of cognitive development. In J. Mahler (Ed.), *Neonate cognition* (pp. 285–306). Hillsdale, NJ: Erlbaum.

Goldman-Rakic, P. S. (1987). Circuitry of the prefrontal cortex and the regulation of behavior by representational memory. In F. Plum & V. B. Mountcastle (Eds.), *Handbook of physiology: Section I. The nervous system: Vol. 5. Higher functions of the brain, Part 1.* (pp. 373–417). Bethesda, MD: American Physiological Society.

Gray, J. A. (1982). *The neuropsychology of anxiety.* New York: Oxford University Press.

Gray, J. A. (1990). Brain systems that mediate both emotion and cognition. *Cognition and Emotion, 4,* 269–288.

Gray, J. A. (1991). The neuropsychology of temperament. In J. Strelau & A. Angleitner (Eds.), *Explorations in temperament: International perspectives on theory and measurement* (pp. 105–128). New York: Plenum.

Greenough, W. T., & Black, J. E. (1992). Induction of brain structure by experience: Substrates for cognitive development. In M. R. Gunnar & C. A. Nelson (Eds.), *Minnesota symposia on child psychology: Vol. 24. Developmental behavioral neuroscience* (pp. 155–200). Hillsdale, NJ: Erlbaum.

Hiatt, S., Campos, J. J., & Emde, R. N. (1979). Facial patterning and infant emotional expression: Happiness, surprise, and fear. *Child Development, 50,* 1020–1035.

Howe, M. L., & Courage, M. L. (1993). On resolving the enigma of infantile amnesia. *Psychological Bulletin, 113,* 305–326.

Humphrey, T. (1966). The development of the human hippocampal formation correlated with some aspects of its phylogenetic history. In S. Hassler (Ed.), *Evolution of the forebrain* (pp. 104–116). Stuttgart, Germany: Thieme.

Huttenlocher, P. R. (1979). Synaptic density in human frontal cortex—Developmental changes and effects of aging. *Brain Research, 163,* 195–205.

Huttenlocher, P. R. (1990). Morphometric study of human cerebral cortex development. *Neuropsychologia, 28,* 517–527.

Huttenlocher, P. R. (in press). Synaptogenesis, synapse elimination, and plasticity in human cerebral cortex. In C. A. Nelson (Ed.), *Minnesota symposia on child psychology: Threats to optimal development. Integrating biological, psychological, and social risk factors.* Hillsdale, NJ: Erlbaum.

Huttenlocher, P. R., De Courten, C., Garey, L. G., & Van Der Loos, H. (1982). Synaptogenesis in human visual cortex—evidence for synapse elimination during normal development. *Neuroscience Letters, 33,* 247–252.

Jones, B., & Mishkin, M. (1972). Limbic lesions and the problem of stimulus–reinforcement associations. *Experimental Neurology, 36,* 362–377.

Kaada, B. R. (1960). Cingulate, posterior orbital, anterior insular, and temporal pole cortex. In J. Field & H. W. Magoun (Eds.), *Handbook of physiology: Section 1. Neurophysiology* (pp. 1345–1372). Washington, DC: American Physiological Society.

Kandel, E. R., & Schwartz, J. H. (1985). *Principles of neural science* (2nd ed.). New York: Elsevier Science.

Kandel, E. R., Schwartz, J. H., & Jessell, T. M. (1991). *Principles of neural science* (3rd ed.). Norwalk, CT: Appleton & Lang.

Kling, A. S. (1986). The anatomy of aggression and affiliation. In E. Plutchik & H. Kellerman (Eds.), *Emotion: Theory, research, and experience. Vol. 3. Biological foundations of emotion* (pp. 237–263). San Diego, CA: Academic Press.

Kling, A. S., & Steklis, H. D. (1976). A neural basis for affiliative behavior in non-human primates. *Brain, Behavior, and Evolution, 13*, 216–238.

Kretschmann, J.-J., Kammradt, G., Krauthausen, I., Sauer, B., & Wingert, F. (1986). Growth of the hippocampal formation in man. *Bibliotheca Anatomica*, No. 28, 27–52.

LeDoux, J. E. (1986). The neurobiology of emotion. In J. E. LeDoux & W. Hirst (Eds.), *Mind and brain: Dialogues in cognitive neuroscience* (pp. 301–354). New York: Cambridge University Press.

Malatesta, C. Z. (1985). Developmental course of emotion expression in the human infant. In G. Zivin (Ed.), *The development of expressive behavior* (pp. 183–219). San Diego, CA: Academic Press.

Nauta, W. J. H., & Feirtag, M. (1986). *Fundamental neuroanatomy*. New York: Freeman.

Nelson, C. A. (1987). The recognition of facial expressions in the first two years of life: Mechanisms of development. *Child Development, 58*, 889–909.

Nelson, C. A. (1993a). The development of recognition memory in the first postnatal year of life. In G. Dawson & K. Fischer (Eds.), *Human behavior and the developing brain* (pp. 269–313). New York: Guilford Press.

Nelson, C. A. (1993b). *The ontogeny of human memory: Perspectives from developmental psychology and cognitive neuroscience*. Unpublished manuscript.

Nelson, C. A. (1993c). The recognition of facial expressions in infancy: Behavioral and electrophysiological correlates. In B. de Boysson-Bardies, S. de Schonen, P. Jusczyk, P. MacNeilage, & J. Morton (Eds.), *Developmental neurocognition: Speech and face processing in the first year of life* (pp. 187–198). Norwell, MA: Kluwer Academic.

Nelson, C. A., & Collins, P. F. (1991). Event-related potential and looking time analysis of infants' responses to familiar and novel events: Implications for visual recognition memory. *Developmental Psychology, 27*, 50–58.

Nelson, C. A., & Collins, P. F. (1992). Neural and behavioral correlates of recognition memory in 4- and 8-month-old infants. *Brain and Cognition, 19*, 105–121.

Nowakowski, R. S. (1987). Basic concepts of CNS development. *Child Development, 58*, 568–595.

Nowakowski, R. S., & Rakic, P. (1981). The site of origin and route and rate of migration of neurons to the hippocampal region of the rhesus monkey. *Journal of Comparative Neurology, 196*, 129–154.

Olson, G. M., & Sherman, T. (1983). Attention, learning and memory in infants. In M. M.

Haith & J. J. Campos (Eds.), *Handbook of child psychology: Vol. 2. Infancy and developmental psychobiology* (pp. 1001–1080). New York: Wiley.

O'Neill, J. B., Friedman, D. P., Bachevalier, J., & Ungerleider, L. G. (1986). Distribution of muscarinic receptors in the brain of a newborn rhesus monkey. *Society for Neuroscience Abstracts, 12*, 809.

Orzhekhovskaya, N. S. (1975). Comparative study of formation of the frontal cortex of the brain of monkeys and man in ontogenesis. *Arkhiv Anatomii, Gistologii i Embriologii, 68*, 43–49.

Overman, W., Bachevalier, J., Turner, M., & Peuster, A. (1992). Object recognition versus object discrimination: Comparison between human infants and infant monkeys. *Behavioral Neuroscience, 106*, 15–29.

Paldino, A. M., & Purpura, D. P. (1979). Branching patterns of hippocampal neurons of human fetus during dendritic differentiation. *Experimental Neurology, 64*, 620.

Pardo, J. V., Pardo, P. J., & Raichle, M. E. (1993). Neural correlates of human self-induced dysphoria. *American Journal of Psychiatry, 150*, 713–719.

Penfield, W., & Jasper, H. (1954). *Epilepsy and the functional anatomy of the human brain*. Boston: Little, Brown.

Rakic, P., Bourgeois, J.-P., Zecevic, N., Eckenhoff, M. F., & Goldman-Rakic, P. S. (1986). Isochronic overproduction of synapses in diverse regions of primate cerebral cortex. *Science, 232*, 232–235.

Reiman, E. M., Fusselman, M. J., Fox, P. T., & Raichle, M. E. (1989). Neuroanatomical correlates of anticipatory anxiety. *Science, 243*, 1071–1074.

Reiman, E. M., Raichle, M. E., Butler, F. K., Herscovitch, P., & Robins, E. (1984). A focal brain abnormality in panic disorder, a severe form of anxiety. *Nature, 310*, 683–685.

Rolls, E. T. (1990). A theory of emotion, and its application to understanding the neural basis of emotion. *Cognition and Emotion, 4*, 161–190.

Sherry, D. F., & Schacter, D. L. (1987). The evolution of multiple memory systems. *Psychological Review, 94*, 439–454.

Sidman, R. L., & Rakic, P. (1982). Development of the human central nervous system. In W. Haymaker & R. D. Adams (Eds.), *Histology and histopathology of the nervous system* (pp. 3–145). Springfield, IL: Charles C Thomas.

Slater, A. (in press). Visual perception and memory at birth. In C. Rovee-Collier & L. P. Lipsitt (Eds.), *Advances in infancy research*. Norwood, NJ: Ablex Press.

Stuss, D. T., & Benson, D. F. (1984). Neuropsychological studies of the frontal lobes. *Psychological Bulletin, 95*, 3–28.

Stuss, D. T., & Benson, D. F. (1986). *The frontal lobes*. New York: Raven Press.

Thompson, R. F., & Robinson, D. N. (1979). Physiological psychology. In E. Hearst (Ed.), *The first century of experimental psychology* (pp. 407–454). Hillsdale, NJ: Erlbaum.

Webster, M. J., Ungerleider, L. G., & Bachevalier, J. (1991a). Connections of inferior temporal areas TE and TEO with medial temporal-lobe structures in infant and adult monkeys. *Journal of Neuroscience, 11*, 1095–1116.

Webster, M. J., Ungerleider, L. G., & Bachevalier, J. (1991b). Lesions of inferior temporal area TE in infant monkeys after cortico-amygdalar projections. *Neuro Report, 2*, 769–772.

Yakovlev, P. I., & LeCours, A.-R. (1967). The myelogenetic cycles of regional maturation of the brain. In A. Minkowski (Ed.), *Regional development of the brain in early life* (pp. 3–70). Oxford, UK: Blackwell Scientific.

CHAPTER 4

A Psychobiological Approach to the Development of Temperament

Mary K. Rothbart, Douglas Derryberry, and Michael I. Posner

Temperament research investigates constitutionally based individual differences in emotion, motivation, and attention (Bates, 1989). As a domain of study, it occupies a particularly interesting location with respect to psychology and neuroscience. Although most of the temperament research completed to date has been behavioral, temperament differences can also be studied at the neural systems level (see reviews by Gunnar, 1990; Rothbart, 1989b). It is nevertheless important to remember that behavior is itself biological, a critical part of the adaptive functioning of the organism (Gunnar, 1990).

Our approach to temperament follows the distinction we have made between temperament reactivity and self-regulation. We define *reactivity* as the characteristics of the individual's reactions to stimulus change, which are reflected in the temporal and intensive parameters of the so-

The research described in this chapter was funded, in part, by National Institute of Mental Health grant 43361 to Mary K. Rothbart and Michael I. Posner.

matic, endocrine, and autonomic nervous systems (Rothbart & Derryberry, 1981). We define *self-regulation* as the processes functioning to modulate this reactivity, including behavioral patterns of approach and avoidance, attentional orientation, and selection (Rothbart & Posner, 1985). In this chapter, we first consider recently identified broad behavioral dimensions of temperament, reviewing briefly some of the findings on higher order factors of individuality in temperament and personality. We then attempt to develop links between these broad dimensions and models from affective and cognitive neuroscience. Finally, we describe a developmental model resulting from this effort.

Behavioral Dimensions of Temperament and Personality

Over the past 4 decades, investigators of personality have used factor analytic methods to develop a taxonomy of individual differences (Goldberg, 1990). In recent years, research in this area has increasingly identified a limited set of higher order factors for describing personality (Digman, 1990; John, 1989; McCrae & Costa, 1987). Although there remains considerable variability across studies in exactly how these superfactors are to be measured and defined, five higher order factors (the "Big Five") have frequently been derived, including broad dimensions of (a) Neuroticism/Negative Emotionality, (b) Extraversion/Positive Emotionality, (c) Conscientiousness/Constraint, (d) Agreeableness, and (e) Openness. When only three such superfactors are reported (the Big Three), they tend to correspond to the first three superfactors identified in the Big Five: Neuroticism/Negative Emotionality, Extraversion/Positive Emotionality, and Conscientiousness/Constraint (Tellegen, 1985).

These taxonomic results have been exciting in a number of ways. First, the general factors appear to emerge regardless of whether the measures involve self-report or the report of others, and they emerge for both trait-descriptive adjectives and more specific behavioral items. Second, the general factors have emerged from research on children as well as adults (Digman, 1990). Finally and most important for this chapter, the Big Three, as well as four of the Big Five factors, show quite remarkable similarity to the dimensions of temperament that have emerged from studies on infancy and early childhood (Ahadi & Rothbart, in press; Martin, Wisenbaker, & Hutunen, in press; Rothbart, 1989b).

In behavioral observations of newborn temperament using the Brazelton Neonatal Behavioral Assessment Scale, four factors have frequently been identified, two of which include aspects of negative emotionality (for more detail see a review by Rothbart, 1989c). These two factors include (a) irritability, tension, and activity; (b) emotional state lability, rapidity of buildup, and self-quieting; (c) alert orienting; and (d) response decrement during drowsiness and sleep (Strauss & Rourke, 1978). Kaye (1978) identified a single negative reactivity factor that appears to combine the first two of Strauss and Rourke's factors, including peak of excitement, rapidity of buildup, and irritability.

Laboratory studies have found levels of neonatal distress proneness to predict observed distress at 1, 3, and 4 months of age (Birns, Barten, & Bridger, 1969); distress at 9 months of age; and distress, lower attentiveness to objects and persons, and more changeable activity level at 24 months of age (Matheny, Riese, & Wilson, 1985; Riese, 1987, in the Louisville Twin Study). Reports of stability of negative affect from the neonatal period to 15 months of age have also been reported (Larson, DiPietro, & Porges, 1987), although the Louisville study did not find predictability of negative affect from the neonatal period to 12 or 18 months of age (Matheny et al., 1985).

Most research on dimensions of temperament variability in older infants has used parental report questionnaires rather than laboratory observations, and most of the research has been based on the New York Longitudinal Study's (NYLS) nine dimensions of temperament (Thomas & Chess, 1977; Thomas, Chess, Birch, Hertzig, & Korn, 1963). Nevertheless, the results of item-level factor analytic research on the NYLS scales (Bohlin, Hagekull, & Lindhagen, 1981; Sanson, Prior, Garino, Oberklaid, & Sewell, 1987) combined with dimensions that have emerged from other theoretical approaches (Buss & Plomin, 1975, 1984; Rothbart, 1981) have identified a shorter list of higher order factors in infancy (Rothbart & Mauro, 1990). Two of these factors involve distress proneness. The first factor includes the infants' distress and behavioral inhibition to novel and challenging stimuli; it is sometimes called Fear. The second factor includes other Irritability, including distress to limitations or frustration. The third factor includes Positive Affect and Approach. The fourth involves attentional Persistence; the fifth involves Activity Level; and the sixth, a relatively small factor, is called Rhythmicity.

For older children, Ahadi and Rothbart (in press) and Ahadi, Rothbart, and Ye (in press) factor analyzed parental report temperament scales for children in the United States who were 4–5 and 6–7 years old and for children in the People's Republic of China who were 6–7 years old. The factors that have emerged from this research are quite similar to the Big Three in adulthood (Ahadi & Rothbart, in press; Ahadi et al., in press). They include a Surgency (Approach/Positive Affect) factor including scales that assess approach, high-intensity pleasure, and activity level, with a negative loading for shyness. For the Chinese children and for the 4–5-year-old U.S. children, this factor also includes smiling and laughter. The second factor—Negative Affectivity—is defined by positive loadings for discomfort, fear, anger/frustration, sadness, and shyness and a negative loading for soothability. For all three of the just-mentioned groups, Approach also loads moderately negatively on this factor. The third factor—Effortful Control—is defined primarily by inhibitory control, attentional focusing, low-intensity pleasure, and perceptual sensitivity. For the U.S. 6–7-year-olds only, smiling and laughter loaded chiefly on this factor. These factors show considerable similarity to the adult Big Three factors of Extraversion, Neuroticism, and Constraint, with Approach/Positive Affect mapping on Extraversion, the Negative Affectivity factor mapping on Neuroticism, and the Effortful Control factor mapping on Constraint.

For a very small sample of infants who were observed in the laboratory, Rothbart, Derryberry, and Hershey (1993) found infant laboratory measures to predict childhood parental-report measures of fear, approach, and anger/frustration when the children were 7 years old. They also found that infants' behavioral caution in the laboratory predicted later attentional focusing, whereas infants' activity level and smiling and laughter predicted later approach. These results suggest that even early measures of temperament assess variability in children's behavior that will be important in later life.

What conclusions might be drawn about results of these developmental studies? First, note that three of the higher order factors found in infancy are associated with basic emotions: Positive Affect, Fear, and Irritability/Frustration; note too that these factors are associated with the motivational dispositions that are related to each emotion: approach for Positive Effect, behavioral inhibition and avoidance for Fear, and attack for Irritability/Frustration. Second, developmentally, a general distress proneness disposition is observable during the neonatal period, earlier than dispositions toward positive affectivity and attentional control. Third, Fear and Irritability/Frustration sometimes appear together in a more general Negative Affectivity factor, for example, in the newborn infant and during childhood. In later infancy, they are more differentiated. The later developing Effortful Control factor (seen in children 4–7 years old and in adults) is of particular interest because it does not refer to individual differences in emotional reactivity but to individual differences in self-regulation that are related to attention.

If one considers these higher order factors to represent individual differences in basic emotions and related motivations, along with attentional control, then models for their underlying neurophysiology from the affective and cognitive neurosciences will aid in understanding them. For example, in LeDoux's (1989) view, emotions represent information processing circuits that assess the evaluative meaning of situations and events to the individual. The neural circuits that are involved in this analysis are genetically prepared, found in other species, and organized around events that are likely to be significant to the welfare of the organism. Outcomes of this affective analysis are organized responses that can be studied at physiological, cognitive, and behavioral levels.

Affective and Cognitive Neuroscience Models

We now consider affective and cognitive neuroscience models for the general factors that were described earlier. These models have implications for a developmental model of temperament that is discussed at the end of this chapter. We begin by considering proposed circuits for systems underlying Positive Affect/Approach, Fear, and Anger/Irritability. Each of these systems consists of a distributed set of circuits connecting cortical regions to limbic (e.g., amygdala and hypothalamus) regions and to brain stem (e.g., locomotor and autonomic nuclei) regions. In general, limbic components of the circuits appear to be specialized to recognize certain types of significant information (e.g., reward-related or threat-related information) that is transmitted from the cortex or thalamus. On detecting such signals, the limbic circuits coordinate the brain stem nuclei controlling motor and autonomic functions, which thereby orchestrates behavior that is appropriate to the situation. In discussing these networks, we briefly consider the relevant neural structures, the types of information to which they may respond, and their relevance to the dimensions of temperament.

Approach/Positive Affect

Three forms of evidence indicate that the limbic system contains specialized circuits for processing reward-related information. Single-cell recording studies have located cells within the orbital frontal cortex, the basolateral amygdala, and the lateral hypothalamus that respond when an animal is presented with a reward-related visual stimulus (e.g., Rolls, 1987). Lesion studies have shown that damage to the basolateral amygdala can impair the formation of associations between a stimulus and a reward (Everitt, Morris, O'Brien, & Robbins, 1991). In addition, many studies have investigated limbic circuits that appear to generate positive affect during intracranial self-stimulation (Robertson, 1989). Although progress has been made in mapping these circuits, whether they constitute a general reward system or a set of more specific reward systems remains unclear.

When activated by a rewarding stimulus, the limbic circuits regulate endocrine, autonomic, and motor activity by means of their projections to the brain stem. Approach behavior is controlled by projections to the nucleus accumbens and the pedunculopontine nucleus, two of the primary centers controlling locomotion (Bechara & van der Kooy, 1989). The limbic outputs can also facilitate approach by interacting with the midbrain dopamine systems that project from the substantia nigra and the ventral tegmental area. The dopamine projections influence many brain regions but are particularly important in facilitating the locomotor functions of the nucleus accumbens and the pedunculopontine nucleus (Robbins, Cador, Taylor, & Everitt, 1989). Many additional systems, such as the central opiate and serotonergic systems and the gonadal hormones, appear to interact with dopamine and to contribute to approach behavior (Spoont, 1992; Zuckerman, 1991).

Several theorists have discussed the role these circuits may play in temperament and personality. Gray (1987) proposed that they function as a *behavioral activation system* (BAS) in response to conditioned signals predicting reward or nonpunishment. When activated by reward signals, the BAS circuits generate a central emotional state that is related to hope and recruit the dopamine systems to facilitate approach behavior. When activated in aversive contexts by nonpunishing signals, the BAS circuits generate a state of relief, and they also facilitate active avoidance behavior. Gray (1987) further proposed that the reactivity of the BAS varies across individuals and underlies a temperament dimension of "impulsivity." Individuals with less reactive systems (low impulsives or stable introverts) are relatively unresponsive to signals of reward and nonpunishment and are thus less likely to show facilitated approach and active avoidance. In contrast, individuals with a more reactive BAS (high impulsives or neurotic extraverts) are more sensitive to reward and nonpunishment and more likely to exhibit approach and active avoidance.

A similar model can be found in Depue and Iacono's (1989) discussion of the dopamine-focused *behavioral facilitation system* (BFS). Like Gray's (1987) BAS, the BFS is presumed to facilitate approach behavior when given rewarding cues and avoidance behavior when given relieving cues. However, Depue and Iacono further suggested that when reward is blocked or when avoidance is impossible, the BFS may facilitate irritative aggressive behavior that is aimed at removing the frustrating obstacle or threat. They also proposed that dopaminergic activity increases the probability of switching or changing response strategies. Thus, individuals with a reactive BFS may be quick to initiate approach but may also demonstrate many shifts in their targets of approach. They will tend to experience strong positive affect given potential reward but may also be subject to frustration when their goals are blocked.

Another approach-related system is the *expectancy–foraging system* that was described by Panksepp (1982, 1986a). Like the two just-described models, Panksepp's expectancy system serves an anticipatory function that is engaged by reward-related stimuli, and its core is based around the dopamine systems. However, its functions appear more complex than those described by Gray (1987) and Depue and Iacono (1989), involving the activation and inhibition of multiple motor and autonomic reactions that are related to locomotion, exploration, and appetitive behaviors. These functions also give rise to emotional states that are described in terms such as curiosity, desire, and anticipatory eagerness. Panksepp (1982, 1986a) suggested that this command system influences attention, thereby adjusting the sensitivities of sensory mechanisms relevant to the activated behavior sequences. This attentional function is consistent with contemporary models of incentive motivation, which suggest that stimuli predicting reward regulate attentional as well as behavioral systems (Wise, 1987).

In general, these models suggest that the neural systems that are related to positive affect are closely tied to facilitated behavior, particularly in the form of approach. For the young child, behavioral facilitation may give rise to a high activity level, impulsive approach responses, and a tendency to seek out stimulation. Although initially tied to positive affect, this facilitation can also set the child up for negative affect, however. Facilitated approach may lead to frustration because parents may often have to block the child's approaches. Even if the parents do not intervene, many objects of approach will remain unobtainable.

It is also possible that strong approach tendencies may leave the child vulnerable to stress or anxiety. Although a more anxious child may withdraw from or cautiously approach threatening situations, the more impulsive child may at times rush into them (Fowles, 1988). Gunnar (chapter 7 in this book) has indeed found that the children entering preschool who show the highest cortisol reactivity to the situation tend to be children with temperament characteristics of high approach. More fearful children do not show signs of cortisol reactivity until later in their preschool experience, presumably when they also have ventured out.

It is important to remember that the affective consequences of a strong approach system depend not only on the system itself, but also on other self-regulatory systems that serve to constrain approach. The notion that the approach system interacts with other neural systems is clearly expressed in Fowles' (1988) discussion of "appetitive" and "aversive" motivational systems. Following Gray's (1987) general model, Fowles draws on the reciprocal inhibitory connections between these opponent systems to account for various types of appetitive behavior. Given this inhibitory influence, increased activity within the aversive system would serve to inhibit the appetitive system, leading to less positive affect and approach. Such a mechanism may help explain why some aversive states (e.g., anxiety) are often accompanied by decreased appetitive states (e.g., depression). Conversely, decreased activity within the aversive system would disinhibit the appetitive system, leading to enhanced approach. This type of mechanism may help explain certain "disinhibitory" disorders (e.g., excessive impulsivity, psychopathy). Approach may also be modulated via attention in inhibitory control, which is discussed later in this chapter.

Fear

We now consider one of the two negative affect systems that has been found to be differentiated in infancy—the fear circuitry. Like the neural mechanisms underlying positive affect, those related to fear consist of specialized information processing systems located in the limbic regions, which promote defensive behaviors by means of projections to the brain stem. Limbic structures that are related to fear include the hippocampus and the amygdala.

Gray's (1982) model of anxiety is based on a set of circuits involving the hippocampus, the subiculum, the septum, and related structures. Although these circuits serve many functions, Gray (1982) suggested that as a whole they constitute a *behavioral inhibition system* (BIS). The BIS responds to conditioned signals predicting punishment and nonreward, and also to novel stimuli and innate fear-related inputs. It functions to immediately inhibit ongoing behavior and to increase cortical arousal. In addition, the BIS directs attention to the relevant signals, thereby promoting an enhanced analysis of the threatening situation. Gray (1982) proposed that individual differences in the reactivity of the BIS underlie a dimension of "anxiety." Individuals with an unreactive BIS (low-anxiety persons or stable extraverts) are relatively unresponsive to signals of punishment, nonreward, and novelty and tend to be poor at passive avoidance. In contrast, individuals with a reactive BIS (high-anxiety persons or neurotic introverts) respond to such signals with behavioral inhibition, increased arousal, and attentional vigilance.

Additional evidence indicates that the central nucleus of the amygdala plays a crucial role in fear (Davis, 1992). Although it is interconnected with the approach-related cell groups of the basolateral nucleus, the amygdala's central nucleus forms a key component in an extended set of circuits interconnecting the orbitofrontal cortex, the amygdala, the bed nucleus of the stria terminalis, the lateral hypothalamus, the central gray region of the midbrain, and the multiple brain stem nuclei controlling specific motor and autonomic reactions (Heimer, De Olmos, Alheid, & Zaborszky, 1991). Within this circuitry, the central amygdala is particularly well positioned for monitoring incoming information and detecting potential threats. It receives sensory information following early processing within the thalamus and also after more detailed processing within the association areas of the cortex.

LeDoux (1987) found that the central nucleus responds within 50 ms to a shock-related tone, apparently by means of a direct sensory input from the thalamus. This thalamic input to the amygdala is developmentally interesting because it may provide a pathway supporting conditioned fear responses prior to extensive cortical and cognitive development. It is also worth noting that the amygdala may become spontaneously active, generating an anxious state in the absence of an eliciting stimulus (Davis, 1992). Whether elicited or spontaneous, this anxious state is orchestrated by amygdaloid projections to the brain stem cell groups that are involved in somatic and autonomic activity.

Fear activation is accompanied by more specific inhibition of ongoing motor programs and also by a more specific preparation of the response systems controlling coping options such as fleeing, fighting, and hiding. These general and specific effects are consistent with the descending output projections to brain stem cell groups that send nonspecific serotonergic and noradrenergic projections throughout the spinal cord. These projections are thought to act as a gain-setting system, enhancing the overall responsiveness of the spinal motor neurons (Holstege & Kuypers, 1987). More specific effects may be orchestrated through projections to brain stem cell groups that implement the discrete autonomic and somatic components of fear, such as motor inhibition, potentiated startle reflex, facial expression, cardiovascular and respiratory adjustments, and so on (see Figure 1; Davis, Hitchcock, & Rosen, 1987). The possibility of individual variation in the functioning of any of these subsystems may help to account for behavioral variability in the specific expression of fear, and this observation would apply to other affective motivational systems involving multiple components as well.

In addition to its effects on autonomic and somatic activity, the amygdala appears capable of influencing information processing within the cortex. As illustrated in Figure 2, this influence is exerted through three general sets of projections. The first includes projections to brain stem regions including the locus coeruleus, the ventral tegmental area, the raphe nuclei, and the nucleus basalis, which constitute the cellular sources of the widespread monamine projections (noradrenergic, dopaminergic, serotonergic, and cholinergic, respectively) that ascend to the cortex (Wallace, Magnuson, & Gray, 1992). The second influence is exerted through amygdaloid projections to component nuclei within the thalamus (e.g., mediodorsal, medial pulvinar, and intralaminar nuclei), which in turn project on relatively specific cortical fields (Gaffan & Murray, 1990). The third and perhaps most specific influence involves direct projections from the amygdala to the cortex. For example, the basolateral nucleus projects to the frontal and cingulate regions that are involved in the anterior attention system and to the ventral occipital and temporal pathways that are involved in processing object information (Barbas & De Olmos, 1990). The anterior attention system is later described in more detail (Posner & Petersen, 1990).

The anatomical connections between the amygdala and the cortex, including the anterior cingulate (see later discussion), are consistent with recent findings that anxious individuals show enhanced attention to threatening sources of information (e.g., Mathews, 1990). Threat-related attentional biases may cause the person to notice more threats in the world, worry more about potential dangers, and experience more intense

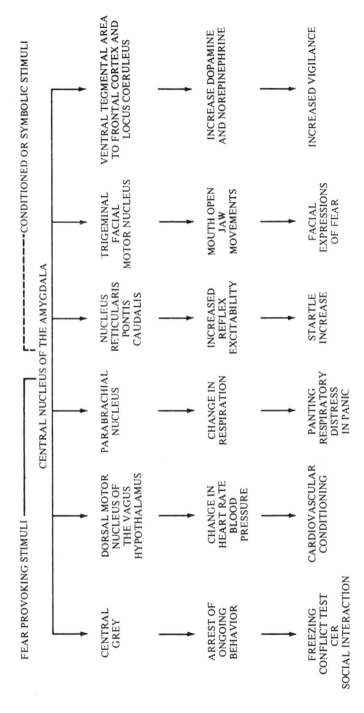

FIGURE 1. Connections of the central nucleus of the amygdala to a variety of target areas associated with fear. From *The Psychology of Learning and Motivation* (Vol. 21, p. 293) edited by G. Bower, 1987, San Diego, CA: Academic Press. Copyright 1987 by Academic Press.

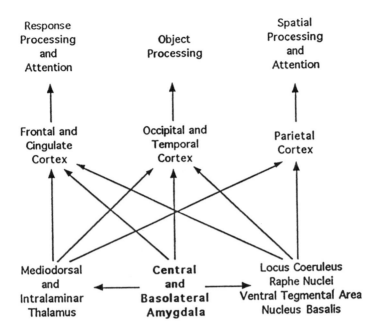

FIGURE 2. The effector system and the cortex.

anxiety. Such biases are particularly important from a developmental perspective because they may promote greater storage of information in memory. Relevant to this topic are findings that attention is required for certain types of learning (Cohen, Ivry, & Keele, 1990) and that some of the amygdala's targets (the cholinergic nucleus basalis and the noradrenergic locus coeruleus) are crucial in regulating synaptic plasticity within the cortex (Singer, 1987). By attending to threatening information across time, an anxious child may gradually build up representations emphasizing the threatening aspects of the world. These representations may then lead the child to develop within a threatening world, to some extent apart from the environment as experienced by others.

When viewed as an affective–motivational system, fear can also be seen to consist of both experiential and behavioral components. The behavioral aspects are most commonly emphasized and include the complex adjustments in motor activity and supporting autonomic and endocrine activity. As just discussed, research by LeDoux (1987, 1989), Davis (1992), and others has made great progress in studying this organization. The affective or experiential aspects of fear remain much more elusive, although amygdala–anterior cingulate connections may prove important in this regard (see later discussion). On one hand, the behavioral adjustments that accompany fear give rise to the interoceptive feelings, such as muscular tension and an accelerating heart rate, that are central to anxiety. At the same time, the environmental context activates related conceptual information stored in memory. Perhaps most important, attentional adjustments serve to select among available information, weaving together an experience based on these interoceptive, exteroceptive, and conceptual sources. Thus, fear is much more than a behavioral state, and investigators are only beginning to grasp its complexity.

Irritability/Anger

Neural pathways that are related to irritability and anger can be approached in terms of the circuitry underlying aggressive behavior. These pathways interconnect the basolateral and centromedial nuclei of the amygdala, the ventromedial nucleus of the hypothalamus, the central gray region of the midbrain, and the somatic and motor effector nuclei of the lower brain stem. In Gray's (1982) model, these circuits process information involving unconditioned punishment and nonreward, as opposed to the signals of conditioned punishment and nonreward that are processed by the hippocampal anxiety system. On detecting a painful or frustrating input, the amygdaloid, hypothalamic, and midbrain components function to coordinate the brain stem effectors in producing aggressive and defensive behavior. Individual differences in the reactivity of this "fight/flight" system are thought to underlie the aggressive aspects of Eysenck's psychoticism dimension.

Panksepp (1982) discussed similar circuitry in terms of a "rage" system. On the basis of evidence that lesions of the ventromedial hypothalamus dramatically increase aggression, Panksepp (1982) suggested that this brain region normally inhibits aggressive behaviors that are controlled by the midbrain's central gray area. By suppressing aggressive tendencies, the hypothalamic projections allow for friendly, trusting, and helpful behaviors between members of a species. Panksepp (1986b) further suggested that these prosocial behaviors depend on opiate projections from higher limbic regions (e.g., amygdala, cingulate cortex) to the ventromedial hypothalamus and pointed out that although brain opiates promote social comfort and bonding, opiate withdrawal promotes irritability and aggressiveness. Thus, Panksepp (1982, 1986b) suggested that the mechanisms underlying prosocial and aggressive behaviors are reciprocally related. This approach fits well with the two poles of the agreeableness–hostility dimension of Big Five models.

Other theorists have suggested that monoaminergic systems and gonadal hormones may also contribute to aggression and hostility. As mentioned earlier, the dopaminergic system of Depue and Iacono (1989) may facilitate irritable aggression aimed at removing a frustrating obstacle, which is consistent with findings that dopamine agonists (e.g., amphetamine) enhance aggressive behaviors. Spoont (1992) suggested that serotonergic projections from the midbrain's raphe nuclei help limit aggression by constraining information processing within the aggressive circuitry of the amygdala, the hypothalamus, and the brain stem. Many animal studies have also found a positive correlation between testosterone and intermale aggression, although their extension to humans is problematic (Zuckerman, 1991). Thus, the circuits that control aggressive behavior appear to be regulated by multiple neurochemical systems, and it may prove difficult to map a single "aggression" system onto a specific personality dimension.

Neurochemical Regulation

This brief review suggests that the neural systems related to various forms of positive and negative affect consist of separable systems that process significant information through a descending series of cortical, limbic, and brain stem circuits. To some extent, these pathways appear as parallel processing systems that may function independently. It is important to emphasize, however, that these descending systems are regulated by more general neurochemical systems such as the dopaminergic and serotonergic projections that arise from the midbrain and also by circulating substances such as the gonadal and corticosteroid hormones.

Although these general influences add to the complexity of emotional processing, they provide a valuable approach to understanding the coherence of emotional states within an individual and thus the more general factors of temperament. For example, the serotonergic projections from the midbrain raphe nuclei appear to constrain processing within the limbic circuits that are related to anxiety and aggression (Spoont, 1992). Low serotonergic activity may enhance an individual's vulnerability to both fear and frustration, thereby contributing to the general factor of negative emotionality. Similarly, the gonadal hormones appear related to positive affect (sociability) and aggressiveness (Zuckerman, 1991) and may promote coherence across positive and angry states. Although more research is necessary to clarify these relationships, the study of general as well as specific neural systems may provide a framework for understanding more general and differentiated temperament dimensions. In addition to their regulation by more general neurochemical systems, the emotional circuits of the limbic system are also influenced by the brain's attentional systems. We turn now to a discussion of attentional self-regulation.

Attention and Self-Regulation

The last 5 years have seen a tremendous increase in the understanding of the three networks that are involved in selective attention. Each network is involved in the selective aspects of attention in a somewhat different way (for a review see Posner & Peterson, 1990). We consider here the posterior, anterior, and vigilance attentional networks.

The Posterior Attention Network

The *posterior attention network* is involved in orienting to sensory stimuli. Most is known about visual orienting, but similar systems are available for the other modalities as well (Posner, 1990). The posterior attention network is involved in directing attention to relevant locations, as in visual search, in binding information to spatial locations in order to produce object perception, and in selecting a relevant scale for examining visual input. The metaphor of a zoom lens has been useful in guiding research in this area. The popularity of lens and spotlight metaphors despite their inadequacy in detail reflects the idea that selection is necessary because of the limited capacity of higher level systems. The reason for this limited capacity may be the importance of integrating features into objects and coordinating actions so that behavior can maintain coherence, rather than in any intrinsic limitation in the neural systems. At an empirical level, however, interference between signals can be used as an indicator of this capacity limitation.

When a person attends to a location in visual space, not only is information at that location increased in processing efficiency, but information at other locations is reduced over what it would be if attention had not been directed to the selected location (Posner & Presti, 1987). This basic selective property of attention has been demonstrated for the posterior attention network in cellular recording, electrical recording from the scalp, detection of near-threshold stimuli, and reaction time. There is evidence that injury to the posterior attention system is closely related to specific deficits in the ability to make selections from information contralateral to the lesion (Posner, 1990).

Anatomically, the posterior attention network involves at least portions of the parietal cortex, associated thalamic areas of the pulvinar and the reticular nucleus, and parts of the midbrain's superior colliculus. These areas cooperate in performing the operations needed to bring attention to a location in space. The posterior system also has close anatomical connections to anterior attention networks and to arousal or vigilance systems (Posner & Peterson, 1990). Indeed, the posterior system is heavily modulated by noradrenergic input from the locus coeruleus and can thus be influenced by the state of alertness of the organism.

The Anterior Attention Network

The second attention network—the *anterior attention network*—involves areas of the midprefrontal cortex, including the anterior cingulate gyrus and a closely related but more superior supplementary motor area, that together appear to be active in a wide variety of situations involving the detection of events and the effortful control of behavior (Posner & Peterson, 1990; Posner & Rothbart, 1991; Vogt, Finch, & Olsen, 1992). In adult humans, detection is most often indicated by a verbal response, which is taken to be one of a set of arbitrary detection responses indicating that the person is aware of the target. Some habitual responses to a target, such as orienting the eyes toward it, may occur without being consciously aware of the target. However, we regard arbitrary responses such as pressing a key or saying "I see it" as indicants that the person is aware the target has occurred.

Detection plays a special role in the production of interference. People can monitor many input channels at once with little or no interference, but if a target on any one channel is detected, the probability of detection on other channels is greatly restricted (Duncan, 1980). Interference may also occur in connection with effortful control, for which more than one response is potentiated, and the person must then effortfully choose one alternative. The anterior attention system is much more active during the effortful control that is involved in conflict blocks of the Stroop task (when the subject must name the color in which a color name is printed, e.g., "RED" printed in blue ink) than during nonconflict blocks (Pardo, Pardo, Janer, & Raichle, 1990). The anterior attention system is also active during tasks requiring subjects to detect target visual stimuli, regardless of whether the targets involve color, form, motion, or the semantics of words (Corbetta, Meizin, Dobmeyer, Shulman, & Petersen, 1990; Peterson, Fox, Snyder, & Raichle, 1990). The degree of activation of the brain's anterior attention system during detection tasks appears to be related to the number of targets presented (Posner, Petersen, Fox, & Raichle, 1988).

There is a great deal of cognitive evidence on the functional role of attention in relation to word association. Researchers have known for 15 years, for example, that words can have relatively automatic input to their semantic associations, at least under some conditions (Posner, 1978). However, attending to words can modify that effect. If one attends to one meaning of a word, activation of other meanings, at least within the left hemisphere, is suppressed (Burgess & Simpson, 1988). Attending to a word meaning also reduces the person's ability to detect unrelated words. That is, attending to a semantic category retards the speed at which words in other categories are detected. These effects are similar to the enhancements described previously for the posterior attention system when a visual location is attended. There is no direct evidence that these enhancements require activation of the anterior cingulate, but interpretation of extant data suggests that they are caused by anterior cingulate interaction with the lateral frontal areas.

The organization of the anterior cingulate both anatomically and behaviorally has been the subject of a great deal of recent research (Vogt et al., 1992). In their overview to a special issue of *Cerebral Cortex* that is devoted to the cingulate, Vogt et al. (1992) attempted to superimpose results from behavioral and neuroimaging studies of humans and animals on the known anatomical divisions of this area. They labeled its overall function as "executive" because it includes emotional, attentional, and motor aspects. There is strong evidence from positron emission tomography (PET) studies that tasks involving higher level control systems activate areas of the anterior cingulate. These include tasks involving the semantics of language (Pardo et al., 1990; Petersen, Fox, Posner, Mintun, & Raichle, 1989) as well as aspects of visual pattern recognition (Corbetta et al., 1990).

Evidence of the inhibitory nature of the attentional control of semantics in the Stroop task that was discussed earlier suggests that the anterior cingulate represents a part of the brain network involved in the temperament dimension of effortful control. The structure of the anterior cingulate in nonhuman primate species is consistent with its role in humans in the control of both semantic processing and orienting to visual stimuli. The results of cell-labeling research in the anterior cingulate indicate that alternate columns are connected to the lateral prefrontal cortex (which is involved in semantic processing in humans) and to the posterior parietal cortex (part of the posterior orienting network) (Goldman-Rakic, 1988).

The attentional areas of the anterior cingulate also lie in very close proximity to areas that are involved in human pain and in emotional vocalization in animals (Vogt et al., 1992). This is consonant with this area as an important outflow of the limbic system. It suggests that a physical system, which is known to be involved in inhibitory control, is in close proximity to both attentional and emotional processing. There is experimental evidence on the effects of lesions of the anterior cingulate on performance. Bilateral lesions of this area can cause akinetic mutism (Damasio & Van Hoesen, 1983), which tends to leave orienting intact but blocks the initiation of spontaneous activity. The presence of recovery of function from lesions in this area and the relatively benign effect of cingulotomy sometimes used in the case of psychiatric disorders, however, suggests that this area does not alone mediate attentional affects on emotion.

The operations of the brain's attentional system boost signals within various brain areas. For example, attention to a visual dimension increases blood flow and electrical activity in prestriatal areas, and attention to semantic associations boosts activity in lateralized frontal areas. What is the effect of this increase in signal strength? Objectively, it increases the probability of being able to detect the relevant signal. That objective fact is based on the increased probability of being aware or having the subjective experience of the signal. In this sense, attention selects the content for the individual's current awareness.

What requirements would be necessary for a mechanism that allows integration between different systems that act on a given input? First, any such mechanism would surely have to share input from many information sources. Second, it should also have close relationships to motor systems but be able to maintain its separation from them. Anatomically, the anterior cingulate has close relationships to the basal ganglia, which provide rich dopaminergic innervation from the ventral tegmental area. The anterior cingulate lies adjacent to and has close interconnections with the supplementary motor area. Third, the integration mechanism should have available a memory capacity to maintain a goal state while activating processes that are involved in integration. The anterior cingulate has rich connections to areas of the lateral cortical surface known to be important in holding information in temporary storage and to the hippocampus, which is involved in the formation of more permanent memories. The anterior cingulate is also an important cortical outflow of the limbic system, thereby allowing close integration with emotional systems (Buck, 1988; Vogt et al., 1992). The anterior attention network, therefore, appears to be well suited to provide integration of thought and behavior and to exert control on emotional experience and expression.

This control can be seen as being related to the dimensions of effortful control in childhood temperament and the dimensions of effortful control or constraint in adult personality. The child or adult with strong and flexible attentional control will have the ability to shift attention from negative affect and develop coping mechanisms for stressful situations that the child with lower attentional control will not share. Mischel, Shoda, and Peake (1990) found that young children's ability to delay gratification in a situation in which a reward is present, which often involves strategies of attentional control, is predictive of their later self-control and of lower levels of parent-reported negative emotionality. The results of laboratory studies also suggest that individuals who are particularly prone to anxiety may have difficulty shifting away from a negative focus, whereas those who are low in anxiety tend to shift away from negative information (Derryberry & Reed, 1993; MacLeod & Mathews, 1988). In studies in both China and the U.S., Ahadi et al. (in press) found that children who are high in effortful control also tend to be low in negative affectivity. Derryberry and Rothbart (1988) found similar negative relationships between adults' self-reports of attentional control and negative affect.

It is important to keep in mind the importance of brain stem dopaminergic systems in influencing the just-discussed operations of attention. The anterior cingulate is modulated by dopaminergic input from the ventral tegmental area of the basal ganglia. As noted earlier, dopaminergic systems are thought to influence temperament dimensions such as Approach and Irritability/Anger. Our primary model for the interaction of arousal systems with attention, however, has been the role of noradrenergic systems in maintaining vigilance. The next section reviews this interaction.

Vigilance

The third selective attention system is called the *vigilance system* (Posner & Petersen, 1990). We believe that this system involves locus coeruleus noradrenergic input to the cortex (for a review see Harley, 1987). When subjects are required to maintain the alert state in the foreperiod of a reaction time task or when they attend to a source of signal while waiting for an infrequent target to occur (vigilance), there is strong activity in this system (for a review of this evidence see Posner & Petersen, 1990). This activity is evident in PET scans in the right lateral frontal lobe. When lesioned, this area gives rise to deficits in the ability to develop and maintain the alert state. Animal studies have found cells of the locus coeruleus to be particularly responsive to threatening or aversive signals (Grant, Aston-Jones, & Redmond, 1988), which indicates an important role for this system in emotional states such as fear.

Cohen et al. (1988) found an area of the right lateral midfrontal cortex that appears to be the most active during an auditory vigilance task. This higher metabolic activation was accompanied by reduced activation of the anterior cingulate. If one views the anterior cingulate as related to target detection, this makes sense. For tasks in which one needs to suspend activity while waiting for low-probability signals, it is important not to interfere with detecting the external event. Subjectively, one feels empty-headed, avoiding any stray thoughts that might detract from detection of the signal. When one attends to a source of sensory input in order to detect an infrequent target, the subjective feeling is of emptying the head of thoughts or feelings. This subjective "clearing of consciousness" appears to be accompanied by an increase in activation of the right frontal lobe vigilance network and a reduction of neural activity in the anterior cingulate. The feeling of effort that is associated with target detection or inhibiting prepotent responses is accompanied by evidence of cingulate activation, whereas the clearing of thought is accompanied by evidence of cingulate inhibition. As in many other aspects of attention, the clearing of consciousness is frequently required in adaptive functioning. When parents or teachers ask children to switch from one activity to another or to follow instructions, attentional individual differences among children will make these activities easier for some children than for others.

In addition to its effect on the anterior attention system, vigilance also has a clear effect on the posterior attention system. It appears to tune the posterior attention system so that its interaction with accumulating information in object recognition systems is faster (Posner, 1978). Anatomically, it is known that the locus coeruleus has its primary noradrenergic input to the areas of the posterior attention system, including the parietal, pulvinar, and collicular systems (Morrison & Foote, 1986). Within these systems the receptive field sizes of cells can be altered by the simultaneous activity of locus coeruleus cells. Cognitively, this means that during vigilant states, the posterior attention network can interact more efficiently with the object recognition system of the ventral occipital lobe. In highly alert states, responses are faster, with more anticipatory reactions and higher error rates (Posner, 1978), similar to aspects of behavioral impulsivity noted earlier. Recent monkey studies have shown that blocking noradrenergic input abolishes the effect of warning signals, which suggests that norepinephrine plays a key role in maintaining the alert state.

Discussion

In this review of affective and cognitive neuroscience models, we have considered several findings that have general implications for the conceptualization of temperament. First, we found evidence for both general and more specific influences on emotional and attentional processing. These findings support the behavioral study of temperament in terms of the existence of both broad factors and more finely grained variables of temperament. Neuroscience models also remind investigators that variables of temperament are unlikely to be orthogonal in their relation to each other. Some neural systems facilitate others, for example, the facilitation of anger by approach systems. Some systems act in opposition to each other, as in the opposition of approach and fear. Attentional networks in particular not only select for action but also bring conscious choice into the domain of temperament (Posner & Rothbart, 1991). The existence of the anterior attention system means that self-regulation will not only be driven by the pleasure and pain associated with positive and negative reactivity but that it can take place at a cognitive level. This provides a neural framework for going beyond optimal levels of regulation in the understanding of self-regulatory aspects of temperament.

The study of neural models also emphasizes the important ways in which emotion and attention influence each other. Approach and fear systems affect alerting and selection; attentional selection modulates reactivity. Findings in adults and children that high attentional control is linked with low negative affectivity are congruent with the interpretation that attentional control allows humans to avoid or moderate negative reactions (Ahadi et al., in press; Derryberry & Rothbart, 1988). This correlation also fits with the close anatomical connections between emotional and attentional systems, for example, within the anterior cingulate.

Finally, our discussion suggests that there may be a neural substrate for a dimension of temperament or personality that has not previously been part of the model, although it was addressed briefly in a previous discussion of Cloninger's (1986, 1987) theory (Rothbart, 1989a). This is a dimension of *positive social orientation*, which is related to the Big Five agreeableness factor. This dimension includes positive social feelings that may act in opposition to cold or hostile feelings in promoting behavior toward others. This would be a late developing dimension, one that might be heavily based on early positive experiences with others, and it would provide an additional control mechanism to the controls of fear and attention on aggressive or antisocial behavior. Figure 3 adds a tentative social orientation dimension to the general model for the development of temperament that is discussed in the next section.

A Developmental Model

We now consider a tentative developmental model for conceptualizing the differentiation and integration of temperament systems (Figure 3). Amygdaloid structures are differentiated prenatally (see Nelson, chapter 3 in this book), and activity within the amygdaloid complex may be involved in the negative affect and related activities that are observed in the young infant (Kagan, Snidman, & Arcus, 1992). Earlier, we presented developmental data that are consistent with the predictability of both later irritability (Larson et al., 1987) and fear (Riese, 1987) from individual differences in newborn negative affect. In addition, Kagan and Snidman (1991) found that a combination of negative affect and motor activity to stimulation at 4 months of age predicts later measures of behavioral inhibition (i.e., fear). As discussed earlier, reduced serotonergic activity may also be related to general distress proneness.

Newborns demonstrate individual differences in general distress proneness. By 2 months of age, infants also demonstrate frustrative neg-

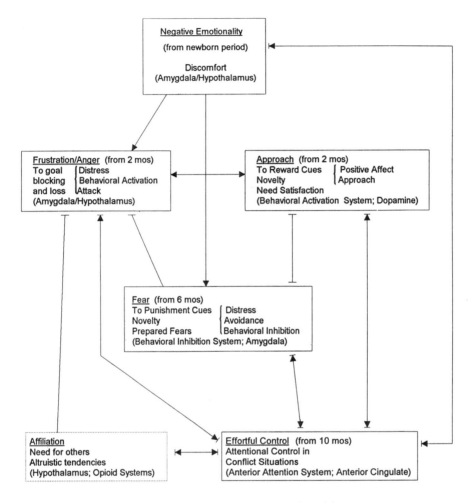

FIGURE 3. A developmental model.

ative affect when they can no longer produce an interesting effect by their own actions (Lewis, Alessandri, & Sullivan, 1990). We suggested earlier that anger/frustration may result when infants' motor activity or the goals of that activity are blocked, and goal blocking will occur more often when the infant is more approaching and sensitive to reward. Depue and Iacono's (1989) model also suggests that irritative aggression will be higher in connection with a stronger BFS. As determined by measures of anger/frustration by parental report or by laboratory study, frustration is consistently positively related to activity level (Rothbart, Derryberry, & Hershey, 1993). At no age in infancy is fear related to activity level.

A precise relationship between newborn distress proneness and the later development of fearfulness is not clear, but in addition to their sharing distress components, one might expect the distress prone individual to be more likely to experience punishment and thereby to develop more conditioned fear reactions. Throughout infancy, one would also expect both anger/frustration and fear to be related to general distress proneness. However, when inhibition is developmentally added to the behavioral output of the fear reaction (Rothbart, 1989a; Schaffer, 1974), anger and fear may become differentiated. Behavioral inhibition opposes approach reactions, as well as the behavioral expression of other emotions (Rothbart, 1989a). To the extent that fear in the latter half of the 1st year of life includes the inhibition of approach to expected punishment, one would expect fear to modulate approach generally, thereby making the occurrence of frustration less likely, even though both fear and frustration may continue to share a general component of negative emotionality seen very early in life. Thus, fear and anger reactions may come to oppose each other, either directly as fear inhibits the active expression of irritability, or indirectly via their relation to approach. In a laboratory study, Rothbart, Derryberry, and Hershey (1993) found fear and frustration measures to be positively correlated at 6 months of age; but by 10 and 13 months of age, the two measures were not related to each other. The novel and challenging environment of the laboratory might be especially likely to put these two responses into opposition (Rothbart, 1989c).

For middle childhood (ages 6–7 years), factor analysis (Ahadi & Rothbart, in press) revealed loadings of anger with the other negative affects, including discomfort, fear, and sadness. Nevertheless, anger continued to load positively (0.23) on the approach factor, and fear loaded negatively (-0.22) on the approach factor. Rothbart et al. (1993) found that high infant anger/frustration also predicts later higher approach, whereas infant fear predicts lower approach. Thus, although these two negative affects can be seen to be part of a negative emotionality factor in middle childhood, they continue to show differentiated relationships with other measures.

In adult measures, a general negative emotionality or neuroticism factor is often found, but in the Big Five factor structure, the separate factor of Agreeableness includes at its opposite pole a possible offshoot of anger/frustration that includes hostility, cruelty, and aggression. We have tentatively added to our model a social orientation dimension that would be related to this factor. Although expressions of positive social behavior versus aggression are probably strongly influenced by the individual's reinforcement history, temperament may make a contribution at the level of anger-proneness, as well as at the level of warmth and social orientation that may act as a control on aggression (see Panksepp's model for the opiate systems and the ventromedial hypothalamus described earlier). Fear would also serve as a control on the expression of aggression, via the aggressive act's potential for eliciting punishment from others; Rothbart, Ahadi, and Hershey (1993) found behavioral evidence that is consistent with this in mothers' reports on 6- and 7-year-olds' behavior. A third control system would be effortful control as discussed earlier in the functioning of the anterior attention network.

With the development of anterior attentional control during the 1st year of life and continuing to adolescence, the individual develops the capacity to selectively focus on a source of information and to increasingly integrate information from different channels of processing. Attentional inhibitory control is particularly important because it can be programmed via the socialization process, thereby assuming an important role in the development of conscience and the inhibition of aggression (Kochanska, 1991; Rothbart & Ahadi, in press; Rothbart et al., in press). The bidirectionality of emotional and attentional influences means that, as we previously suggested, a child might be particularly directed toward detecting threat, given distress and fear-proneness. That child's ability to shift and focus attention, however, can also serve to help modulate the negative emotion.

Block and Block (1980) identified two important ego control processes, which they have labeled *ego control* and *ego resiliency*. The first of these processes, ego control, may correspond chiefly to fear control; the second, ego resiliency, may correspond chiefly to attentional control, allowing the child to overcome reactions to stress and to act and think flexibly in situations that require it. Attentional capacities are particularly important in the study of temperament because of their role in self-regulation, thereby organizing the functioning of the reactive systems in new ways. Attentional capacities are also developmentally of special interest because they are among the latest developing temperament characteristics.

The model for the development of temperament that we briefly presented here combines information about higher order behavioral dimensions with information from affective and cognitive neuroscience models. As in the neural models described earlier, our model stresses the interactions between reactivity and self-regulation. We believe that in the future, both behavioral and neurophysiological components of individual differences will become more highly differentiated and that an approach to temperament characteristics that includes both levels of analysis will continue to contribute to the understanding of the development of temperament and personality.

References

Ahadi, S. A., & Rothbart, M. K. (in press). Temperament, development and the Big Five. In G. Kohnstamm & C. Halverson (Eds.), *The developing structure of temperament and personality from infancy to adulthood.* Hillsdale, NJ: Erlbaum.

Ahadi, S. A., Rothbart, M. K., & Ye, R. (in press). Child temperament in the U.S. and China: Similarities and differences. *European Journal of Personality.*

Barbas, H., & De Olmos, J. (1990). Projections from the amygdala to basoventral and mediodorsal prefrontal regions in the rhesus monkey. *Journal of Comparative Neurology, 300,* 549–571.

Bates, J. E. (1989). Concepts and measures of temperament. In G. A. Kohnstamm, J. E. Bates, & M. K. Rothbart (Eds.), *Temperament in childhood* (pp. 3–26). New York: Wiley.

Bechara, A., & van der Kooy, D. (1989). The tegmental pedunculopontine nucleus: A brainstem output of the limbic system critical for the conditioned place preferences produced by morphine and amphetamine. *Journal of Neuroscience, 9,* 3400–3409.

Birns, B., Barten, S., & Bridger, W. (1969). Individual differences in temperamental characteristics of infants. *Transactions of the New York Academy of Sciences, 31,* 1071–1082.

Block, J. H., & Block, J. (1980). The role of ego-control and ego-resiliency in the organization of behavior. In W. A. Collins (Ed.), *Minnesota symposium on child psychology* (Vol. 13, pp. 39–101). Hillsdale, NJ: Erlbaum.

Bohlin, G., Hagekull, B., & Lindhagen, K. (1981). Dimensions of infant behavior. *Infant Behavior and Development, 4*, 83–96.

Bower, G. (1987). *The psychology of learning and motivation* (Vol. 21). San Diego, CA: Academic Press.

Buck, R. (1988). *Human motivation and emotion.* New York: Wiley.

Burgess, C., & Simpson, G. B. (1988). Cerebral hemispheric mechanisms in the retrieval of ambiguous word meanings. *Brain and Language, 33*, 86–103.

Buss, A. H., & Plomin, R. (1975). *A temperament theory of personality development.* New York: Wiley.

Buss, A. H., & Plomin, R. (1984). *Temperament: Early developing personality traits.* Hillsdale, NJ: Erlbaum.

Cloninger, C. R. (1986). A unified biosocial theory of personality and its role in the development of anxiety states. *Psychiatric Developments, 3*, 167–226.

Cloninger, C. R. (1987). A systematic method for clinical description and classification of personality variants. *Archives of General Psychiatry, 44*, 573–588.

Cohen, A., Ivry, R. I., & Keele, S. W. (1990). Attention and structure in sequence learning. *Journal of Experimental Psychology: Learning, Memory, and Cognition, 16*, 17–30.

Cohen, R. M., Semple, W. E., Gross, M., Holcomb, H. J., Dowling, S. M., & Nordahl, T. E. (1988). Functional localization of sustained attention. *Neuropsychiatry, Neuropsychology and Behavioral Neurology, 1*, 3–20.

Corbetta, , M., Meizin, F. M., Dobmeyer, S., Shulman, G. L., & Petersen, S. E. (1990). Selective attention modulates neural processing of shape, color, and velocity in humans. *Science, 249*, 1556–1559.

Damasio, A. R., & Van Hoesen, G. W. (1983). Emotional disturbances associated with focal lesions of the limbic frontal lobe. In K. Heilman & P. Satz (Eds.), *Neuropsychology of human emotion* (pp. 85–99). New York: Guilford Press.

Davis, M. (1992). The role of the amygdala in fear and anxiety. *Annual Review of Neuroscience, 15*, 353–375.

Davis, M., Hitchcock, J. M., & Rosen, J. B. (1987). Anxiety and the amygdala: Pharmacological and anatomical analysis of the fear-potentiated startle paradigm. In G. Bower (Ed.), *The psychology of learning and motivation* (Vol. 21, pp. 263–305). San Diego, CA: Academic Press.

Depue, R. A., & Iacono, W. G. (1989). Neurobehavioral aspects of affective disorders. *Annual Review of Psychology, 40*, 457–492.

Derryberry, D., & Reed, M. A. (1993). *Attentional components of temperament: Orienting toward and away from positive and negative signals.* Manuscript submitted for publication.

Derryberry, D., & Rothbart, M. K. (1988). Arousal, affect and attention as components of temperament. *Journal of Personality and Social Psychology, 55*, 958–966.

Digman, J. M. (1990). Personality structure: Emergence of the five-factor model. *Annual Review of Psychology, 41,* 417–440.

Duncan, J. (1980). The locus of interference in the perception of simultaneous stimuli. *Psychological Review, 87,* 272–300.

Everitt, B. J., Morris, K. A., O'Brien, A., & Robbins, T. W. (1991). The basolateral amygdala–ventral striatal system and conditioned place preference: Further evidence of limbic–striatal interactions underlying reward-related processes. *Neuroscience, 42,* 1–18.

Fowles, D. C. (1988). Psychophysiology and psychopathology: A motivational approach. *Psychophysiology, 25,* 373–392.

Gaffan, D., & Murray, E. A. (1990). Amygdalar interaction with the mediodorsal nucleus of the thalamus and the ventromedial prefrontal cortex in stimulus–reward associative learning in the monkey. *Journal of Neuroscience, 10,* 3479–3493.

Goldberg, L. R. (1990). An alternative "Description of Personality": The Big-Five factor structure. *Journal of Personality and Social Psychology, 59,* 1216–1229.

Goldman-Rakic, P. S. (1988). Topography of cognition: Parallel distributed networks in primate association cortex. *Annual Review of Neuroscience, 11,* 137–156.

Grant, S. J., Aston-Jones, G., & Redmond, D. E. (1988). Responses of primate locus coeruleus neurons to simple and complex sensory stimuli. *Brain Research Bulletin, 21,* 401–410.

Gray, J. A. (1982). *The neuropsychology of anxiety.* London: Oxford University Press.

Gray, J. A. (1987). Perspectives on anxiety and impulsivity: A commentary. *Journal of Research in Personality, 21,* 493–509.

Gunnar, M. R. (1990). The psychobiology of infant temperament. In J. Colombo & J. Fagen (Eds.), *Individual differences in infancy: Reliability, stability, prediction* (pp. 387–410). Hillsdale, NJ: Erlbaum.

Harley, C. W. (1987). A role for norepinephrine in arousal, emotion and learning: Limbic modulation for norepinephrine and the key hypothesis. *Progress in Neuro-Pharmacology and Biological Psychiatry, 11,* 419–458.

Heimer, L., De Olmos, J., Alheid, G. F., & Zaborszky, L. (1991). "Perestroika" in the basal forebrain: Opening the border between neurology and psychiatry. In G. Holstege (Ed.), *Progress in brain research: Vol. 87. Role of the forebrain in sensation and behavior* (pp. 109–165). Amsterdam: Elsevier.

Holstege, G. J., & Kuypers, H. G. (1987). Brainstem projections to spinal-motor neurones: An update. *Neuroscience, 23,* 809–821.

John, O. P. (1989). Towards a taxonomy of personality descriptors. In D. M. Buss & N. Cantor (Eds.), *Personality psychology: Recent trends and emerging directions* (pp. 261–271). New York: Springer-Verlag.

Kagan, J., & Snidman, N. (1991). Infant predictors of inhibited and uninhibited profiles. *Psychological Science, 2,* 40–44.

Kagan, J., Snidman, N., & Arcus, D. M. (1992). Initial reactions to unfamiliarity. *Current Directions in Psychological Science, 1,* 171–173.

Kaye, K. (1978). Discriminating among normal infants by multivariate analysis of Brazelton scores: Lumping and smoothing. *Monographs of the Society for Research in Child Development, 43*(5–6, Serial No. 177), 60–80.

Kochanska, G. (1991). Socialization and temperament in the development of guilt and conscience. *Child Development, 62*, 1379–1392.

Larson, S. K., DiPietro, J. A., & Porges, S. M. (1987, April). *Neonatal and NBAS performance are related to development across at 15 months.* Paper presented at the meeting of the Society for Research in Child Development, Baltimore, MD.

LeDoux, J. E. (1987). Emotion. In F. Plum (Ed.), *Handbook of physiology: Sec. 1. The nervous system: Vol. 5. Higher functions of the brain, Part 1* (pp. 419–454). Bethesda, MD: American Physiological Society.

LeDoux, J. E. (1989). Cognitive–emotional interactions in the brain. *Cognition and Emotion, 3*, 267–289.

Lewis, M., Alessandri, S. M., & Sullivan, M. W. (1990). Violation of expectancy, loss of control, and anger expressions in young infants. *Developmental Psychology, 26*, 745–751.

MacLeod, C., & Mathews, A. (1988). Anxiety and the allocation of attention. *Quarterly Journal of Experimental Psychology, 40*, 653–670.

Martin, R. P., Wisenbaker, J., & Hutunen, M. (in press). The factor structure of instruments based on the Chess-Thomas model of temperament: Implications for the Big Five Model. In C. F. Halverson, G. A. Kohnstamm, & R. P. Martin (Eds.), *The developing structure of temperament and personality from infancy to adulthood.* Hillsdale, NJ: Erlbaum.

Matheny, A. P., Jr., Riese, M. L., & Wilson, R. S. (1985). Rudiments of infant temperament: Newborn to nine months. *Developmental Psychology, 21*, 486–494.

Mathews, A. (1990). Why worry? The cognitive function of anxiety. *Behavioral Research and Therapy, 28*, 455–468.

McCrae, R. R., & Costa, P. T., Jr. (1987). Validation of the five-factor model of personality across instruments and observers. *Journal of Personality and Social Psychology, 52*, 81–90.

Morrison, J. H., & Foote, S. L. (1986). Noradrenergic and serotonergic innervation of cortical, thalamic and tectal structures in old and new world monkeys. *Journal of Comparative Neurology, 143*, 117–118.

Panksepp, J. (1982). Toward a general psychobiological theory of emotions. *Behavioral and Brain Sciences, 5*, 407–467.

Panksepp, J. (1986a). The anatomy of emotions. In R. Plutchik & H. Kellerman (Eds.), *Emotion: Theory, research and experience: Vol. 3. Biological foundations of emotions* (pp. 91–124). San Diego, CA: Academic Press.

Panksepp, J. (1986b). The psychobiology of prosocial behaviors: Separation distress, play, and altruism. In C. Zahn-Waxler, E. M. Cummings, & R. Iannotti (Eds.), *Altruism and aggression: Biological and social origins* (pp. 19–57). Cambridge, UK: Cambridge University Press.

Pardo, J. V., Pardo, P. J., Janer, K. W., & Raichle, M. E. (1990). The anterior cingulate cortex mediates processing selection in the stroop attentional conflict paradigm. *Proceedings of the National Academy of Sciences USA, 87*, 256–259.

Petersen, S. E., Fox, P. T., Posner, M. I., Mintun, M., & Raichle, M. E. (1989). Positron emission tomographic studies of the processing of single words. *Journal of Cognitive Neuroscience, 1*, 153–170.

Petersen, S. E., Fox, P. T., Snyder, A. Z., & Raichle, M. E. (1990). Activation of extrastriate and frontal cortical areas by visual words and word-like stimuli. *Science, 249*, 1041–1044.

Posner, M. I. (1978). *Chronometric explorations of mind.* Hillsdale, NJ: Erlbaum.

Posner, M. I. (1990). Hierarchical distributed networks in the neuropsychology of selective attention. In A. Carramaza (Ed.), *Cognitive neuropsychology and neurolinguistics: Advances in models of cognitive function and impairment* (pp. 187–210). New York: Plenum.

Posner, M. I., & Petersen, S. E. (1990). The attention system of the human brain. *Annual Review of Neuroscience, 13*, 25–42.

Posner, M. I., Petersen, S. E., Fox, P. T., & Raichle, M. E. (1988). Localization of cognitive functions in the human brain. *Science, 240*, 1627–1631.

Posner, M. I., & Presti, D. (1987). Selective attention and cognitive control. *Trends in Neuroscience, 10*, 12–17.

Posner, M. I., & Rothbart, M. K. (1991). Attentional mechanisms and conscious experience. In M. Rugg & A. D. Milner (Eds.), *The neuropsychology of consciousness* (pp. 91–112). San Diego, CA: Academic Press.

Riese, M. L. (1987). Temperamental stability between the neonatal period and 24 months. *Developmental Psychology, 23*, 216–222.

Robbins, T. W., Cador, M., Taylor, J. R., & Everitt, B. J. (1989). Limbic–striatal interactions in reward-related processes. *Neuroscience and Biobehavioral Reviews, 13*, 155–162.

Robertson, A. (1989). Multiple reward systems and the prefrontal cortex. *Neuroscience and Biobehavioral Reviews, 13*, 163–170.

Rolls, E. T. (1987). Information representation, processing, and storage in the brain: Analysis at the single neuron level. In J. P. Changeaux & M. Konishi (Eds.), *The neural and molecular bases of learning* (pp. 503–540). New York: Wiley.

Rothbart, M. K. (1981). Measurement of temperament in infancy. *Child Development, 52*, 569–578.

Rothbart, M. K. (1989a). Behavioral approach and inhibition. S. Reznick (Ed.), *Perspectives on behavioral inhibition* (pp. 139–157). Chicago: University of Chicago Press.

Rothbart, M. K. (1989b). Biological processes of temperament. In G. Kohnstamm, J. Bates, & M. K. Rothbart, (Eds.), *Temperament in childhood* (pp. 77–110). New York: Wiley.

Rothbart, M. K. (1989c). Temperament and development. In G. Kohnstamm, J. Bates, & M. K. Rothbart (Eds.), *Temperament in childhood* (pp. 187–248). New York: Wiley.

Rothbart, M. K., & Ahadi, S. A. (in press). Temperament and the development of personality. *Journal of Abnormal Psychology*.

Rothbart, M. K., Ahadi, S. A., & Hershey, K. L. (1993). Temperament and social behavior in childhood. *Merrill-Palmer Quarterly, 40*, 21–39.

Rothbart, M. K., & Derryberry, D. (1981). Development of individual differences in temperament. In M. E. Lamb & A. L. Brown (Eds.), *Advances in developmental psychology* (Vol. 1, pp. 37–86). Hillsdale, NJ: Erlbaum.

Rothbart, M. K., Derryberry, D., & Hershey, K. (1993). *Stability of temperament in childhood: Laboratory infant assessment to parent report at seven years*. Unpublished manuscript.

Rothbart, M. K., & Mauro, J. A. (1990). Questionnaire measures of infant temperament. In J. W. Fagen & J. Colombo (Eds.), *Individual differences in infancy: Reliability, stability and prediction* (pp. 411–429). Hillsdale, NJ: Erlbaum.

Rothbart, M. K., & Posner, M. (1985). Temperament and the development of self-regulation. In L. C. Hartlage & C. F. Telzrow (Eds.), *The neuropsychology of individual differences: A developmental perspective* (pp. 93–123). New York: Plenum.

Sanson, A. V., Prior, M., Garino, E., Oberklaid, F., & Sewell, J. (1987). The structure of infant temperament: Factor analysis of the Revised Infant Temperament Questionnaire. *Infant Behavior and Development, 10*, 97–104.

Schaffer, H. R. (1974). Cognitive components of the infant's response to strangeness. In M. Lewis & L. A. Rosenblum (Eds.), *The origins of fear* (pp. 11–24). New York: Wiley.

Shoda, Y., Mischel, W., & Peake, P. K. (1990). Predicting adolescent cognitive and self-regulatory competencies from preschool delay of gratification: Identifying diagnostic conditions. *Developmental Psychology, 26*, 976–986.

Singer, W. (1987). Activity-dependent self-organization or synaptic connections as a substrate of learning. In J. P. Changeaux & M. Konishi (Eds.), *The neural and molecular basis of learning* (pp. 301–336). New York: Wiley.

Spoont, M. R. (1992). Modulatory role of serotonin in neural information processing: Implications for human psychopathology. *Psychological Bulletin, 112*, 330–350.

Strauss, M. E., & Rourke, D. L. (1978). A multivariate analysis of neonatal behavioral assessment scale in several examples. *Monographs of the Society for Research in Child Development, 43*(5–6, Serial No. 177), 81–91.

Tellegen, A. (1985). Structures of mood and personality and their relevance to assessing anxiety, with an emphasis on self-report. In A. H. Tuma & J. D. Maser (Eds.), *Anxiety and the anxiety disorders* (pp. 681–706). Hillsdale, NJ: Erlbaum.

Thomas, A., & Chess, S. (1977). *Temperament and development*. New York: Brunner/Mazel.

Thomas, A., Chess, S., Birch, H. G., Hertzig, M. E., & Korn, S. (1963). *Behavioral individuality in early childhood*. New York: New York University Press.

Vogt, B. A., Finch, D. M., & Olsen, C. R. (1992). Overview: Functional heterogeneity in cingulate cortex: The anterior executive and posterior evaluative regions. *Cerebral Cortex 2, 6,* 435–443.

Wallace, D. M., Magnuson, D. J., & Gray, T. S. (1992). Organization of amygdaloid projections to brainstem dopaminergic, noradrenergic, and adrenergic cell groups in the rat. *Brain Research Bulletin, 28,* 447–454.

Wise, R. A. (1987). Sensorimotor modulation and the variable action pattern (VAP): Toward a noncircular definition of drive and motivation. *Psychobiology, 15,* 7–20.

Zuckerman, M. (1991). *Psychobiology of personality.* Cambridge: Cambridge University Press.

CHAPTER 5

The Concepts of Arousal and Arousability as Used in Temperament Studies

Jan Strelau

W hen asking questions about the biological bases of temperament, independent of what might be comprised by the term *biology*, one is confronted with at least two basic difficulties. First, what is meant by temperament? Many discussions have arisen around this question (e.g., Goldsmith et al., 1987; Strelau, 1987a), which shows that the definition of temperament differs depending on the theory guiding the researcher, the population being studied (children, adults, animals), or the methods being used. To avoid misunderstanding, in this chapter, the concept of temperament refers to basic, relatively stable personality traits that apply mainly to the formal aspects of behavior. These traits are established early in life, and they occur in both humans and animals. Being primarily determined by inborn physiological mechanisms, temperament is subject to changes caused by maturation and by some environmental factors. In

The chapter was written during my fellowship (1992–1993) at The Netherlands Institute for Advanced Study in the Humanities and Social Sciences, Wassenaar, The Netherlands.

several of my previous publications, I discussed the differences between the concepts of temperament and personality by showing that the term *personality* is a broader one, which includes not only temperament but also other phenomena such as motivation, the self, values, interests, and so on (for a detailed discussion see Strelau, 1983, 1987a).

When studying the biology of temperament traits, one is also confronted with a second difficulty, namely, which and how many temperament traits should be studied. Researchers studying so-called basic personality dimensions (considered by some researchers as being equivalent to temperament) declare that there exist only three or five such dimensions. One set of three traits involves the Eysenckian Psychoticism, Extraversion, and Neuroticism (PEN; Eysenck, 1970, 1991). Other sets of three basic temperament traits, different from PEN, have also been postulated (e.g., Buss & Plomin, 1984; Gray, 1991; Strelau, 1983). Other researchers emphasize the five basic personality dimensions, known as the "Big Five." However, there is not full agreement concerning which dimensions belong to the Big Five or how to name them (Costa & McCrae, 1988; Digman, 1990; Zuckerman, Kuhlman, Thornquist, & Kiers, 1991).

Among child-oriented researchers, Thomas and Chess's (1977) 9 categories of temperament have gained high popularity. When discussing this issue, Kagan (1989) suggested that the number of possible temperament traits will be larger than 6 but probably less than 60. I recently identified 81 traits that could fall within the domain of temperament (Strelau, 1991).

These various traits differ in generalizability, which further complicates this issue. By using a factor analysis approach, one may say that some are first-order traits (e.g., motor impulsiveness), most of them are second-order traits (e.g., impulsivity), and some have a status of third-order traits (e.g., extraversion). According to Zuckerman (1992), narrower traits are probably closer to the biological phenomena than are broader traits. This might be considered as a kind of recommendation to center biological studies on the first- and second-order factors (traits). On the other hand, the richest evidence on the biology of temperament traits has been accumulated in reference to third-order factors, such as extraversion and neuroticism.

The ambiguity about the nature and number of dimensions being encompassed by the term *temperament*, as well as the diversity of meanings when referring to the same temperament label (see Strelau, 1991), does not allow for unequivocal conclusions regarding the biological bases of temperament. Furthermore, the postulate that temperament has a biological background is based on several assumptions and/or findings, some of which are not necessarily specific for this domain of research. Not pretending to list all of them, I now present six assumptions/findings.

1. Any psychological function depends on the activity of the brain. Therefore, if there exists a psychology of temperament (as well as of any other psychological function or trait), then there is ipso facto a neuropsychology of temperament (Gray, 1991, p. 105).

2. Behavioral genetics studies on temperament have shown the importance of genetic factors in determining individual differences in temperament traits (e.g., Braungart, Plomin, DeFries, & Fulker, 1992; Eaves, Eysenck, & Martin, 1989; Goldsmith, 1989; Loehlin, 1992; Matheny, 1990; Torgersen, 1987).

3. If genetic factors play an essential role in determining individual differences in temperament, then there must exist intervening variables of a biological nature (e.g., physiological, neurological, biochemical, hormonal) that are transferred genetically through generations (see Eysenck, 1991; Zuckerman, 1992).

4. The universality of temperament traits across cultures implies that there must be species-specific carriers of these traits that have a biological (genetic) background (Eysenck, 1991).

5. The presence of temperament traits and clear-cut individual differences in this domain since early childhood cannot be explained by environmental factors (e.g., Buss & Plomin, 1984).

6. The existence of temperament traits not only in humans but also in other mammalian species serves as the basis for two important assumptions. (a) In the process of biological evolution, temperament traits must have played an important adaptive function, as underlined already in the 1950s by Diamond (1957; see also Buss & Plomin, 1984; Strelau, 1987a; Zuckerman, 1991). (b) There must be some biological mechanisms in common for both humans and other mammals that mediate tempera-

ment traits (Eysenck, 1967, 1991; Pavlov, 1951/1952; Strelau, 1983; Zuckerman, 1991).

The strongest support in favor of the importance of the biological basis in individual differences in temperament stems from (a) behavioral genetics studies, (b) studies with neonatal infants, and (c) research aimed at identifying the physiological and biochemical variables that are supposed to mediate temperament characteristics in humans and other mammalian species. The two first approaches (a and b) allow only for general statements (*yes* or *no*) regarding the biological bases of temperament, whereas the third approach (c) has the potential to yield more specific information concerning the kinds of biological mechanisms underlying temperament.

In this chapter, I concentrate on the third approach by illustrating findings and conclusions centered around the constructs of arousal and arousability.

Forerunners of the Concept of Arousal

It was the 18th-century philosopher Immanuel Kant (1724–1804) who developed the idea that temperament may be characterized by means of life energy (*Lebenskraft*), which oscillates from excitability to drowsiness (Kant, 1912). This original idea was further developed by the German psychiatrist Gottfried Ewald (1888–1963). According to Ewald (1924), the life energy is limited by a so-called *biotonus* in which individuals differ. Biotonus refers to the quantitative aspects of behavior, expressed in intensity and tempo characteristics, which are regarded as the core of human temperament. Metabolic processes, the functioning of the endocrine system, and the sensitivity of the nerve cells were considered by Ewald as determinants of the biotonus. Ewald viewed mechanisms underlying the energetic characteristics of behavior (biotonus) as highly complex and in interaction with each other–a statement that corresponds with contemporary views on the determinants of the energetic characteristics of behavior.

Some of the first experiments on temperament that involved constructs referring to the *conceptual nervous system* (C.N.S.; Hebb, 1955) were undertaken by Pavlov (1951/1952) during the first 3 decades of this century. I refer specifically to Pavlov's concept of the excitatory processes, which relates to the "excitatory substance" of the cortex and subcortex. The excitatory substance can be viewed as a C.N.S. construct underlying the concept of arousal. According to Pavlov, the intensity of excitatory processes is, to a given extent, a function of the intensity of stimuli (the law of strength). After a critical point, excitation passes into protective (transmarginal) inhibition that is expressed in a decrease or disappearance of reactions (performance). The Pavlovian concept of protective inhibition is also used by contemporary researchers as a C.N.S. construct, which can be used to explain findings referring to such arousal-oriented traits as extraversion (Eysenck, 1970, 1991), augmenting–reducing (Buchsbaum, 1976), and sensation seeking (Zuckerman, 1979, 1991).

By manipulating hunger (now regarded as one of the drives that determines the level of arousal), Pavlov controlled the intensity of excitatory processes. Pavlov also manipulated different doses of caffeine (stimulant drug) and bromine (depressant drug) to pharmacologically change the level of excitatory processes.

On the basis of this research, Pavlov introduced the concept of *strength of excitation*, understood as a trait (similar to the construct of arousability), from which he was able to explain individual differences in the intensity of excitatory processes (for details see Gray, 1964b; Nebylitsyn, 1972; Strelau, 1983). Pavlov also established the "principle of nervism," by which he meant that all functions of the organism are regulated and integrated by the central nervous system, especially by the cortex.

Arousal and Activation Regarded as C.N.S. Constructs Referring to the Energetic Aspects of Behavior

The Concept of General Arousal

Ewald's (1924) concept of the biotonus is, in fact, very similar to the concept of *energy mobilization* that was developed in the 1930s by Elizabeth Duffy (1951, 1957). Duffy regarded this concept as being synonymous to such concepts as *arousal* and *activation*. According to Duffy

(1957), all kinds of behavior may be described as variations in either the direction of behavior or the intensity of behavior: "It is the intensity aspect of behavior which has been variously referred to as the degree of excitation, arousal, activation or energy mobilization" (p. 265). As Duffy (1957) noted, the historical roots of the concepts of arousal and activation go back to Cannon (1915), who discussed bodily changes under emotions. Like Ewald, Duffy hypothesized that the degree of energy mobilization (arousal, activity) is regulated through metabolic activity and may vary from deep sleep to extreme excitement (Duffy, 1951).

Duffy (1951, 1957) considered arousal (and its synonym, activation), as a general, undifferentiated phenomenon underlying temperament, which she identified with the intensity dimension of behavior. Arousal, which consists of the release of potential energy for use in activity or response, is determined by physiological factors such as endocrine secretion, food, drugs, and the degree of effort required by the situation (e.g., difficult task, stress). Energy release is reflected in a number of physiological processes, such as tension of the skeletal muscles, electrodermal activity (EDA), and electroencephalographic (EEG) activity. Duffy's (1957) statement that individuals differ in the level of arousal and responsiveness to stimulation was of special significance for studies on temperament. This idea was most extensively elaborated by Gray (1964b) when he introduced the concept of *arousability*.

Most representative of the research that lent support to Duffy's (1957) theory of arousal as a phenomenon based on the activity of the autonomic nervous system (ANS) were Wenger's studies (1938, 1943). Using children as subjects, these studies applied physiological indices as measures of the imbalance between the sympathetic and parasympathetic branches of the ANS. In a factor analysis of the physiological data, Wenger found a General Autonomic factor, which represents the functioning of the ANS. This factor comprised the following measures: salivary output (low), percentage of solids in saliva (high), heart rate (fast), sinus arrhythmia (little), palmar and nonpalmar sweating (much), basal metabolic rate (high), and pulse pressure (low). High scores for the General Autonomic factor indicated the predominance of the sympathetic branch of the ANS. It has to be added, however, that the results, in general, indicated that the correlations between the separate measures are rather low (see Wenger, 1943). Low correlations were among the reasons why many important physiological correlates, such as systolic and diastolic blood pressure, respiration rate, and dermographic scores, were not included by Wenger in his composite score of autonomic imbalance.

There are probably two reasons why neither Duffy nor Wenger gained the popularity among temperament researchers that they deserved. First, Moruzzi and Magoun's (1949) discovery of the significance of the reticular formation in mediating the level of arousal shifted interest from the behavioral to the neurophysiological component of arousal. Second, the results of studies that used ANS measures to assess arousal, as conceptualized by Duffy (1951, 1957) and other researchers from the 1930s through the 1950s (e.g., Freeman, 1948; Malmo, 1959; Wenger, 1938, 1943), do not support the concept of arousal as a general, homogeneous phenomenon (see Fahrenberg, Walschburger, Foerster, Myrtek, & Muller, 1983; Lacey, 1950, 1967; Venables, 1984).

Hebb (1955), after reviewing the many data on behavior under deprivation, arrived at three conclusions important for further studies relating concepts of arousal and/or activation to temperament characteristics. First, by analyzing sensory events, Hebb distinguished two main functions that stimulation plays in the organism. One function refers to the direction of behavior; the other function refers to the energetic background of any kind of behavior.

> In general terms, psychologically, we can now distinguish two quite different effects of a sensory event. One is the *cue function*, guiding behavior; the other, less obvious but no less important, is the *arousal* or *vigilance function*. Without a foundation of arousal, the cue function cannot exist. (Hebb, 1955, p. 249)

The dichotomy between the direction and energetic components of behavior had already been introduced by Duffy (1951, 1957), as noted earlier. The difference between the approaches of Duffy and Hebb consists mainly in the fact that Duffy primarily paid attention to the behavioral component of arousal, whereas Hebb centered on the stimulation determinants of arousal (see Gray, 1964b). Second, Hebb considered arousal as synonymous with *general drive state*: "The drive is an energizer, but not a guide; an engine but not a steering gear" (1955, p. 249). According to Hebb, this characteristic of a drive fully refers to the activity of the arousal system that he located, after Moruzzi and Magoun (1949), in the brain stem. By giving the concept of arousal the status of a general drive, Hebb intended to emphasize that a given level of arousal is indispensable for any behavior, regardless of whether in humans or animals. Third, Hebb believed that there exists an optimal level of arousal. The fact that a nonlinear (inverted-U-shaped curve) relation occurs between the intensity of stimuli (to which the concept of arousal refers) and the speed of learning was already known at the beginning of this century (Yerkes & Dodson, 1908). The level of arousal under which performance of any kind is most efficient is regarded as the optimal level of arousal (Schlosberg, 1954). Hebb developed this idea by showing that the level of arousal can be regarded as optimal not only from the point of view of efficiency of performance but also in respect to its rewarding functions. At low levels of arousal, an increase in drive intensity (high stimulation) may be rewarding; whereas at high levels of arousal, a decrease in drive intensity (low stimulation) has a rewarding value. An increase of arousal to the optimal level is accompanied by positive emotions, whereas a level of arousal that goes beyond the optimal level is a source of negative emotions.

The concept of optimal level of arousal has been broadly applied in several theories of temperament. In the theory of extraversion, this concept has been used by Eysenck (1967, 1970; Eysenck & Eysenck, 1985) to explain, among other things, the relation between level of performance and/or level of physiological responses, depending on the position an individual occupies on the extraversion–introversion dimension. In introverts, because of their chronically higher level of arousal, the optimal level of arousal occurs with lower levels of stimulation, compared with extraverts. In the regulative theory of temperament that I developed with my co-workers (Strelau, 1974, 1983, 1985), the optimal level of arousal is considered as a standard for stimulation regulation (Eliasz, 1981; Strelau, 1983). The concept of optimal level of arousal explains the role that temperament activity plays in regulating the stimulative value of behavior and the situation in which behavior occurs.

Arousal as a Neurophysiological Construct

The revolutionary discovery by Moruzzi and Magoun (1949) that the cat's brain stem reticular formation (BSRF) produces unspecific activation, and that the stimulation of the BSRF desynchronizes and increases EEG activity, had an essential influence on the concept of arousal. Since this discovery, arousal—besides its traditional role as a general construct—has also been treated as a neurophysiological construct. Lindsley (1952), Samuels (1959), and Berlyne (1960) showed that the activity of the ascending reticular activating system is responsible for the organism's levels of wakefulness (alertness), which is characterized by such states as coma and deep sleep on the one extreme and strong, excited emotions (fear, rage, anxiety) on the other extreme (Lindsley, 1952).

What must be emphasized is that most of the research that was centered on the neurophysiological constructs of arousal, including Lindsley's (1952) and Berlyne's (1960) essential contributions, was quite divergent from the field of temperament, as well as from the context of individual differences. Most of the studies were aimed at examining the role of neurophysiological states, as measured by EEG indices, in mediating emotional processes, orienting reactions, attention, conditioning, or perception. Research on arousal was mainly conducted with the aim of finding general laws and regularities, as is typical for general psychology.

However, the discovery that the BSRF constitutes the neurophysiological basis of arousal, which is understood to be nonspecific activation, has also influenced further investigations aimed at identifying the biological correlates of temperament traits. This is especially evident in the domains of extraversion, neo-Pavlovian central nervous system properties, sensation seeking, and impulsivity.

The fact that arousal has been related to behavior, as well as to two different categories of physiological processes (ANS activity and activity of the BSRF), led to the distinction of three different kinds of arousal—

behavioral arousal, autonomic arousal, and cortical arousal—a distinction to which temperament researchers often refer (e.g., Buss & Plomin, 1984). There are, however, other categories of arousal. For example, Routtenberg (1968) made a clear-cut distinction between two systems of arousal: *Arousal System I*, which refers to the BSRF, and *Arousal System II*, which is located in the limbic system. Arousal System II, as distinguished by Routtenberg, cannot be identified with ANS arousal. Rather, Arousal System II is regarded by Routtenberg as a reward system. Interestingly, Gray (1982a, 1982b) referred to the reward function of the limbic system when studying the biological basis of temperament.

Arousal and Activation

In some conceptualizations of temperament, there is a distinction between the constructs of arousal and activation. This distinction can be illustrated by referring to Eysenck's and Rothbart's theories of temperament.

After the discovery by Moruzzi and Magoun (1949), Eysenck (1967) revised his Pavlovian interpretation of extraversion in favor of the BSRF theory. According to Eysenck's view, individual differences in the level of activity in the corticoreticular loop determine the individual's position on the extraversion–introversion dimension. When he referred to activity of the corticoreticular loop, Eysenck used the construct "arousal"; the most direct physiological index of arousal is EEG activity (Eysenck, 1970, 1991; Eysenck & Eysenck, 1985). In contrast, the physiological basis underlying neuroticism (emotionality–stability) is located in the visceral brain, which controls ANS activity. In contrast to the activity of the BSRF, the activity of the visceral brain, "which produces autonomic arousal" (Eysenck, 1991, p. 248), has been labeled as "activation" (Eysenck, 1991; Eysenck & Eysenck, 1985). The fact that extraversion and neuroticism seem to be orthogonal to each other also influenced Eysenck's thinking about the relation between the two systems that determine the levels of arousal and activation. Unless high activation occurs, "these two systems are independent" (Eysenck, 1991, p. 248).

Thus, Eysenck's distinction between anatomical and physiological differentiation of arousal and activation is rather clear. However, the difference between the two concepts becomes less clear when their measurement indices are considered. When he measured the physiological correlates of extraversion, Eysenck used typical indices of cortical arousal such as EEG activity, evoked potentials, and contingent negative variations. But he, as well as others, also used visceral brain measures, which are considered as indices of the level of activation. For example, indices of EDA have been used in studies on extraversion (Stelmack, 1990; Stelmack & Geen, 1992). Similarily, Eysenck (1991) considered a finding by Wilson (1990), which showed predicted differences in daily tonic skin conductance changes for introverts and extraverts, as one of the strongest arguments for differences in chronic arousal between extraverts and introverts. The argument that Eysenck used to allow such measures as EDA, secretion of salivary glands, and pupillary dilation to be considered as indices of arousal is as follows: The activity underlying these measures is fully under the control of the central nervous system. The corticoreticular loop also controls ANS activity (Eysenck, 1991; Eysenck & Eysenck, 1985; see also Stelmack, 1990). Using this argument, one can conclude that all, or almost all, nervous and endocrine processes are under the control of the cortex or other higher nervous centers. By taking such a position, which is shared by many researchers (Gale & Edwards, 1983; Gunnar, 1990; Stelmack & Geen, 1992; Zuckerman, 1991), it is almost impossible to distinguish between physiological correlates that are typical for extraversion and those that are typical for neuroticism. This is also true for other traits of temperament. In fact, EDA is also considered as one of the most often used markers of neuroticism (Fahrenberg, 1992; Fahrenberg et al., 1983; Navateur & Baque, 1987).

The problem of distinguishing whether physiological markers refer to autonomic arousal (activation, according to Eysenck) or to cortical arousal (Eysenck's arousal) exists regardless of what terms are used to characterize the activity of the different neural structures. However, Eysenck's distinction between the terms *arousal* and *activation*, as concepts referring to the activity of two independent neural structures, has to be questioned given existing physiological data.

A different understanding of the C.N.S. constructs of arousal and activation is found in the biological model of temperament by Rothbart and Posner (Rothbart, 1989; Rothbart & Posner, 1985). These investigators defined these concepts within an information processing (cognitive)–oriented framework. Their position is comprehensible if one takes into account the two following facts. First, Rothbart included attention in the domain of temperament as one of the components of self-regulatory processes (see Rothbart, 1989; Posner & Rothbart, 1981). Attention is a psychological process that is rarely considered by existing theories of temperament. Second, Posner's main interests have centered for many years on the concepts of arousal and activation viewed within a cognitively oriented approach (e.g., Posner, 1982).

The concepts of arousal and activation, as used in Rothbart's (Rothbart, 1989; Posner & Rothbart, 1981) theory, derive from the research of Pribram. According to McGuinness and Pribram (1980),

> the involuntary modes have been redesignated as *arousal*, a phasic short-lived and reflex response to input, and *activation*, a tonic long-lasting and involuntary readiness to respond. (p. 99)

Arousal occurs when an input change produces a phasic change in physiological (e.g., EDA) or behavioral (e.g., head turning) reactions. Activation refers to a tonic readiness to respond and is reflected in an increase in cortical reactivity, for example, as measured by contingent negative variation and/or tonic heart rate deceleration.

Without going into the details and specific functions that arousal and activation play, according to McGuinness and Pribram (1980), arousal refers to phasic excitatory processes, whereas activation to tonic excitatory states. Such a distinction between arousal and activation has not previously been used in temperament research, with the exception of Rothbart (1989) and Rothbart and Posner (1981). Because of the specific meanings given by investigators to the concepts of activation and arousal, compared with their traditional use since the 1930s in temperament research, I hope that future studies will show how these C.N.S. constructs, taken from cognitively oriented researchers, are related to activation and arousal as applied in temperament studies. In this chapter, I use these concepts to underline the unspecific excitatory (i.e., energetic) components, whether related to the ANS, visceral brain, BSRF, or cortex.

Arousability as a Construct Underlying the Search for Links Between Different Dimensions of Temperament

The concepts of arousal and activation have different meanings to different individuals, which causes difficulties in communication between researchers when discussing the biological background of temperament. In an attempt to reinterpret the concept of strength of the nervous system in terms of level of arousal, Gray (1964b) distinguished three important aspects. These are *determinants, indices,* and *determinates* of arousal (see Figure 1), which must be taken into account when the level of arousal is considered. The meanings of *determinants* and *indices* of arousal are clear. Less obvious is the concept of determinates, as applied by Gray (1964b). According to him, *determinates* refer to the individual's states and processes as determined by the level of arousal. The distinction made by Gray (1964b) seems to be very important not only for understanding the links between the concepts of arousal and strength of the central nervous system but also for realizing how the just-reviewed concepts of arousal–activation relate to each other.

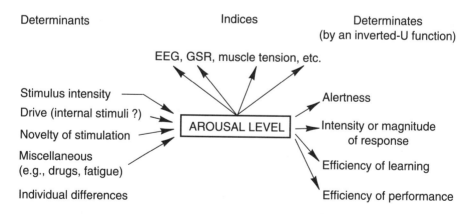

FIGURE 1.   Determinants, indices, and determinates of arousal level. EEG = electro-encephalogram; GSR = galvanic skin response. From *Pavlov's Typology* (p. 296) edited by J. A. Gray, 1964a, Elmsford, NY: Pergamon. Copyright 1964 by Pergamon. Reprinted by permission.

For studies aimed at identifying the physiological basis (at least correlates) of arousal-oriented temperament traits, the most important element in Figure 1 is labeled *determinants*. These are the individual differences in the physiological mechanisms (neurological or biochemical) that are considered as codeterminants of the level of arousal. Determinants have to be treated as this physiological component, which is directly related to individual differences in temperament traits.

If one assumes that temperament traits are characterized by some degree of stability, then one must also assume that the physiological mechanisms of arousal, to which many dimensions of temperament refer, must also show some degree of stability. The C.N.S. construct that fulfills this criterion is arousability. Gray (1964b) introduced this concept to underline the two following statements: (a) There are individual differences in the organismic determinants of arousal; and (b) because of these determinants, individuals have a chronic (more or less stable) level of arousal, which may be also called *arousal trait*. The relation between (cortical) arousal and arousability, according to Gray (1964b) is as follows:

> Individual differences in arousability are such that individuals low on this dimension respond to stimulation with relatively low degrees of nonspecific reticular bombardment of the cortex, whereas individuals high on this dimension respond to stimualtion with relatively high degree of such bombardment. (p. 307)

Gray (1964b) limited his considerations of arousability to the concept of cortical arousal, as related to strength of the central nervous system. My proposal is to use the term *arousability* as a broader construct. Whatever the mechanisms that regulate the level of arousal, individual differences in their functioning occur, and they reveal themselves in the fact that in some individuals stimulation of a given intensity (S_n) results in a higher level of arousal (A_{n+x}), whereas in others, the level of arousal to the same intensity of stimulation is lower (A_{n-x}). This might be expressed as follows:

$$S_n \longrightarrow A_{n+x} = \text{high arousability, whereas}$$

$$S_n \longrightarrow A_{-x} = \text{low arousability.}$$

In accordance with the concepts of arousal and activation as applied in temperament research, the indices of arousability may be of different kinds: behavioral characteristics (in correspondence with behavioral arousal), reactions referring to the activity of the ANS (autonomic arousal) or visceral brain (visceral arousal), as well as indices of EEG activity (cortical arousal).

Among the dimensions of temperament that are derived from different theoretical conceptualizations, a whole range of traits that refer to the construct of arousal may be mentioned. Researchers differ, however, in their views regarding the importance of the diversity of physiological, biochemical, and/or anatomical components taking part in determining the level of arousal. The following systems and/or components may be mentioned as the most important in regulating the level of arousal: the cortex, the reticular formation, the limbic system, the ANS, neurotransmitters as well as their enzymes, and hormones.

The following dimensions of temperament may be considered as possible candidates that can be interpreted in terms of the concept of arousability: extraversion–introversion, neuroticism, emotionality, sensation seeking, strength of excitation, reactivity, anxiety, impulsivity, augmenting–reducing, inhibited–uninhibited temperament, and approach–withdrawal. A very short summary of the hypothesized biological mechanisms underlying these dimensions follows.

Extraversion: As already mentioned, differences in the level of activity in the corticoreticular loop determine the individual's position on the extraversion–introversion dimension. Introverts are chronically more cortically aroused than are extraverts (Eysenck & Eysenck, 1985).

Neuroticism: The physiological bases of neuroticism as understood by Eysenck (1970, 1991) were described earlier in this chapter. Individual differences in neuroticism depend on the susceptibility of the visceral brain. "People who are high in neuroticism produce activity in the visceral brain (i.e., activation) more readily than those low in neuroticism" (Eysenck & Eysenck, 1985, p. 198).

Emotionality: Some investigators identify emotionality with the Eysenckian neuroticism dimension (see Eysenck, 1970; Eysenck & Eysenck, 1985; Fahrenberg, 1987). I refer to this concept as understood by Buss and Plomin (1984). According to these investigators, emotionality, which includes three basic emotional traits (distress, fear, and anger), is mediated by arousal of the ANS. Inherited individual differences in this system are thought to explain an essential part of the variance in emotionality. Individuals who are high in emotionality are chronically more highly aroused compared with individuals who are in a low position on this dimension.

Sensation seeking: Individual differences in sensation seeking, which were primarily interpreted by Zuckerman (1984) in terms of the corticoreticular loop, have recently been treated as being determined by the activity of the neurotransmitters (dopamine, norepinephrine, and serotonin) that are most prominently located in the limbic system. The biochemical factors determine the sensitivity of the neural system in such a way that sensation seekers are chronically less aroused than are sensation avoiders (Zuckerman, 1984).

Strength of the nervous system: Pavlov (1951/1952) did not give a physiological interpretation of this concept. This has been done, however, by Nebylitsyn (1972), who in his explanation referred to the ionic theory of the nerve cell. According to Gray (1964b), the individual's position on the strength dimension may be explained in different ways that are not necessarily contradictory to each other, that is, by individual differences: (a) in the brain stem's sensitivity to stimulation, (b) in sensitivity of the cortex to reticular activation, or (c) in the amount of epinephrine release in the reticular formation (see also Mecacci, 1987; Robinson, 1982).

Reactivity: The physiological mechanism of temperament reactivity, as understood in the regulative theory of temperament (Strelau, 1974, 1983), is a very complex one and includes all anatomical and physiological systems responsible for the release of stored energy. Which of those systems plays the dominant role in determining reactivity depends on the type of activity and situation. There exist not only inter- but also intraindividual differences in the physiological arousal mechanisms that are responsible for codetermining reactivity; thus, the concept of "neurobiochemical individuality" seems to be most relevant. In high-reactive individuals, this complex of physiological mechanisms enhances (augments) stimulation (whether external or internal). In low-reactive individuals, these mechanisms reduce (suppress) stimulation.

Anxiety: Gray (1982a, 1982b), who has conducted the most advanced studies devoted to the physiological mechanisms underlying anxiety, concluded that the functioning of the septohippocampal system regulates the level of anxiety. Functionally, this system constitutes the *behavioral inhibition system* (BIS), which is composed of the three following structures: the hippocampal formation, the septal area, and the Papez circuit (Gray, 1991). BIS has the status of a C.N.S. construct. Gray (1991) considered individual differences in operating parameters of the BIS (e.g., thresholds or ease of excitation) as the basis for individual differences in anxiety.

Impulsivity: Impulsivity, regarded by Gray (1983, 1991) as one of the most basic temperament dimensions, has its biological basis in the *behavioral approach system* (BAS; also a C.N.S. construct). Gray (1991) hypothesized that the key components of this system are the basal ganglia, the ascending dopaminergic fibers of the mesencephalon (which innervate the basal ganglia), thalamic nuclei, and neocortical areas. Analogous to the BIS, individual differences in operating parameters of the BAS have to be considered as the basis for individual differences in impulsivity. Schalling and Asberg (1985) argued that the physiological mechanism of impulsivity lies in the limbic-frontal connections, the sensitivity of which is modulated by the monoamine neurotransmitters.

Augmenting–reducing: Petrie (1967), who introduced the augmenting–reducing dimension, hypothesized that there exists a central stimulus intensity control mechanism, which is probably the general nonspecific arousal system. Buchsbaum (1976), who also used the concept of augmenting–reducing in studies on evoked potentials, interpreted this dimension in a way that was opposite Petrie's original view (for interpretations of these differences see Davis, Cowles, & Kohn, 1984; Kohn, Hunt, Cowles, & Davis, 1986). Buchsbaum (1976) argued that three types of neural pathways may be responsible for the individual differences in augmenting–reducing: "ascending inhibitory, nonspecific arousal, and cortical–cortical" (p. 110).

Inhibited–uninhibited temperament: The two temperaments distinguished by Kagan and co-workers (Kagan, 1989; Kagan, Reznick, & Snidman, 1988), *inhibited* and *uninhibited*, are considered by these investigators as qualitatively different. The inhibited temperament is characterized as consistently shy, quiet, and timid; whereas the uninhibited temperament is consistently sociable, talkative, and affectively spontaneous (Kagan et al., 1988). In spite of the supposed qualitative differences on the behavioral level, Kagan (1989) assumed that, in their physiological basis, the two temperaments differ quantitatively. The biological basis of inhibited temperament consists in "lower [as compared with uninhibited individuals] thresholds of reactivity in the limbic system, especially the amygdala and hypothalamus" (Kagan, 1989, pp. 671–672).

Approach/withdrawal: According to Thomas and Chess (1977), approach–withdrawal is defined by the nature of the initial response to new stimuli. Positive responses are regarded as approach, and negative responses are regarded as withdrawal. A good starting point for hypothesizing some biological mechanisms underlying this temperament dimension is the approach–withdrawal intensity hypothesis, as developed by McGuire and Turkewitz (1979), who considered approach–withdrawal in a much broader context, encompassing even infrahuman behavior. According to the intensity hypothesis, the threshold of approach behavior occurs when stimuli are at lower intensity levels, compared with the withdrawal threshold. This distinction is illustrated in Figure 2. If one assumes that (a) "intensity is defined in terms of the amount of neural

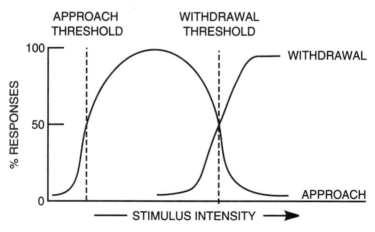

FIGURE 2. Relationship between approach and withdrawal responses over a wide range of stimulus intensities. From *Cognitive Growth and Development* (p. 65) edited by M. Bortner, 1979, New York: Brunner/Mazel. Copyright 1979 by Brunner/Mazel. Reprinted by permission.

activity" (McGuire & Turkewitz, 1979, p. 70) and (b) individuals differ in the tendency to approach or withdraw from new situations, then one may hypothesize that there exists a physiological mechanism that mediates the intensity of stimuli. Because withdrawal and approach responses are accompanied by changes in motor tension and by changes in the cardio-vascular system, as illustrated by McGuire and Turkewitz (1979), it is highly probable that components of the limbic system produce arousal and explain individual differences in approach–withdrawal behavior.

All of the just-mentioned dimensions or categories of temperament refer to neurophysiological and/or biochemical mechanisms of arousal. This means that, in spite of the differences in their psychological content as well as differences in their physiological interpretation, one may assume that they refer to a common phenomenon, that is, to arousability. A presumption is made (explicitly or implicitly), which is valid for all of these dimensions, that there exist more or less stable individual differences in physiological and/or biochemical mechanisms that explain the individual differences in temperament traits.

The specific physiological and/or biochemical mechanisms that are related to different traits do not explain individual differences in these traits. They refer to behaviors (to states) that are considered as expressions of given traits. The biological features underlying individual differences in behavior refer to more-or-less formal characteristics of these physiological and/or biochemical mechanisms. For example, one may hypothesize that such features as sensitivity of neurons' postsynaptic receptors or sensitivity in their synaptic transmission, the amount of neurotransmitters being released, and reactivity of neural structures (including receptors) to different kinds of stimuli, all take part in determining individual differences in the traits under discussion. These features are common for all neurobiochemical mechanisms associated with temperament characteristics. To give one example, it is not the BIS that determines individual differences in anxiety. The BIS construct is used by Gray (1983) to explain anxiety as a state (anxious behavior): The physiological bases for susceptibility to anxiety (as a trait) in which individuals differ "arise as a function of variation in the operating parameters (thresholds, ease of excitation, speed of operation, etc. ..." (p. 168).

Taking into account the two poles of the arousability dimension (low vs. high arousability), one may hypothesize that the 11 temperament traits just listed may be spread within this dichotomy in the way presented in Table 1.

Inserting the qualitatively different dimensions of temperament under one label does not mean, however, that they are similar or equivalent to each other. It means only that they are comparable with regard to the phenomenon of chronic arousal. One may characterize them from the point of view of whether they refer to chronically high or chronically low arousal. This does not deny that the mechanisms determining arousal may be different for each temperament trait under discussion. I (Strelau, 1987b) previously demonstrated some similarities between a selected number of temperament traits, taking into account behavioral components and physiological indices of arousal.

It is my as-yet-unproven conviction that, by using the C.N.S. construct of arousability, it is possible to integrate research on temperament traits stemming from different biologically oriented theories, or at least possible to throw some light on the links between those characteristics of temperament. The perspective drawn in this chapter seems to differ from other integrative approaches, such as the psychometric one, which is more commonly found in this domain of research.

TABLE 1

Arousability and Temperament Traits

High arousability	Low arousability
Introverts	Extraverts
Neurotics	Emotionally stable
High emotionality	Low emotionality
Sensation avoiders	Sensation seekers
Weak type of CNS	Strong type of CNS
High reactives	Low reactives
High-anxiety individuals	Low-anxiety individuals
Low impulsives	High impulsives
Augmenters (Petrie, 1967)	Reducers (Petrie, 1967)
Reducers (Buchsbaum, 1976)	Augmenters (Buchsbaum, 1976)
Inhibited temperament	Uninhibited temperament
Withdrawal tendency	Approach tendency

Note. CNS = central nervous system.

References

Berlyne, D. E. (1960). *Conflict, arousal, curiosity*. New York: McGraw-Hill.

Bortner, M. (Ed.). (1979). *Cognitive growth and development*. New York: Brunner/Mazel.

Braungart, J. M., Plomin, R., DeFries, J. C., & Fulker, D. W. (1992). Genetic influence on tester-rated infant temperament as assessed by Bayley's Infant Behavior Record: Nonadoptive and adoptive siblings and twins. *Developmental Psychology, 28*, 40–47.

Buchsbaum, M. S. (1976). Self-regulation of stimulus intensity: Augmenting/reducing and the average evoked response. In G. E. Schwartz & D. Shapiro (Eds.), *Consciousness and self-regulation* (Vol. 1, pp. 101–135). New York: Plenum.

Buss, A. H., & Plomin, R. (1984). *Temperament: Early developing personality traits*. Hillsdale, NJ: Erlbaum.

Cannon, W. B. (1915). *Bodily changes in pain, hunger, fear and rage*. New York: Appleton.

Costa, P. T., Jr., & McCrae, R. R. (1988). Personality in adulthood: A six-year longitudinal study of self-reports and spouse ratings on the NEO Personality Inventory. *Journal of Personality and Social Psychology, 54*, 853–863.

Davis, C., Cowles, M., & Kohn, P. (1984). Behavioural and physiological aspects of the augmenting–reducing dimension. *Personality and Individual Differences, 5*, 683–691.

Diamond, S. (1957). *Personality and temperament*. New York: Harper.

Digman, J. M. (1990). Personality structure: Emergence of the five-factor model. *Annual Review of Psychology, 41*, 417–440.

Duffy, E. (1951). The concept of energy mobilization. *Psychological Review, 58*, 30–40.

Duffy, E. (1957). The psychological significance of the concept of "arousal" or "activation." *Psychological Review, 64*, 265–275.

Eaves, L. J., Eysenck, H. J., & Martin, N. G. (1989). *Genes, culture and personality*. San Diego, CA: Academic Press.

Eliasz, A. (1981). *Temperament a system regulacji stymulacji* [Temperament and system of regulation of stimulation]. Warsaw, Poland: Panstwowe Wydawnictso Naukowe.

Ewald, G. (1924). *Temperature und Charakter* [Temperament and character]. Berlin: Springer.

Eysenck, H. J. (1967). *The biological basis of personality*. Springfield, IL: Charles C. Thomas.

Eysenck, H. J. (1970). *The structure of human personality*. London: Methuen.

Eysenck, H. J. (1991). Biological dimensions of personality. In L. A. Pervin (Ed.), *Handbook of personality* (pp. 244–276). New York: Guilford Press.

Eysenck, H. J., & Eysenck, M. W. (1985). *Personality and individual differences*. New York: Plenum.

Fahrenberg, J. (1987). Concepts of activation and arousal in the theory of emotionality (neuroticism): A multivariate conceptualization. In J. Strelau & H. J. Eysenck (Eds.), *Personality dimensions and arousal* (pp. 99–120). New York: Plenum.

Fahrenberg, J. (1992). Psychophysiology of neuroticism and anxiety. In A. Gale & M. W. Eysenck (Eds.), *Handbook of individual differences: Biological perspectives* (pp. 179–226). New York: Wiley.

Fahrenberg, J., Walschburger, P., Foerster, F., Myrtek, M., & Muller, W. (1983). An evaluation of trait, state, and reaction aspects of activation processes. *Psychophysiology, 20,* 188–195.

Freeman, G. L. (1948). *The energetics of human behavior.* Ithaca, NY: Cornell University Press.

Gale, A., & Edwards, J. A. (Eds.). (1983). *Physiological correlates of human behavior: Basic issues* (Vol. 1). San Diego, CA: Academic Press.

Goldsmith, H. H. (1989). Behavior–genetic approaches to temperament. In G. A. Kohnstamm, J. E. Bates, & M. K. Rothbart (Eds.), *Temperament in childhood* (pp. 111–132). New York: Wiley.

Goldsmith, H. H., Buss, A. H., Plomin, R., Rothbart, M. K., Thomas, A., Chess, S., Hinde, R. A., & McCall, R. B. (1987). Roundtable: What is temperament? Four approaches. *Child Development, 58,* 505–529.

Gray, J. A. (Ed.). (1964a). *Pavlov's typology.* Elmsford, NY: Pergamon.

Gray. J. A. (1964b). Strength of the nervous system and levels of arousal: A reinterpretation. In J. A. Gray (Ed.), *Pavlov's typology* (pp. 289–364). Elmsford, NY: Pergamon.

Gray, J. A. (1982a). The neuropsychology of anxiety: An inquiry into the functions of the septo-hippocampal system. London: Oxford University Press.

Gray, J. A. (1982b). Precis of the neuropsychology of anxiety: An inquiry into the functions of the septo-hippocampal system. *Behavioral and Brain Sciences, 5,* 469–534.

Gray, J. A. (1983). Where should we search for biologically based dimensions of personality? *Zeitschrift fur Differentielle und Diagnostische Psychologie, 4,* 165–176.

Gray, J. A. (1991). The neuropsychology of temperament. In J. Strelau & A. Angleitner (Eds.), *Explorations in temperament: International perspectives on theory and measurement* (pp. 105–128). New York: Plenum.

Gunnar, M. R. (1990). The psychobiology of infant temperament. In J. Colombo & J. Fagen (Eds.), *Individual differences in infancy: Reliability, stability, prediction* (pp. 387–409). Hillsdale, NJ: Erlbaum.

Hebb, D. O. (1955). Drives and the C.N.S. (conceptual nervous system). *Psychological Review, 62,* 243–254.

Kagan, J. (1989). Temperamental contributions to social behavior. *American Psychologist, 44,* 668–674.

Kagan, J., Reznick, J. S., & Snidman, N. (1988). Biological bases of childhood shyness. *Science, 240,* 167–171.

Kant, I. (1912). *Anthropologie in pragmatischer Hinsicht* [Anthropology from a pragmatic point of view] (5th ed.). Leipzig, Germany: Verlag von Felix Meiner.

Kohn, P., Hunt, R. W., Cowles, M. P., & Davis, C. (1986). Factor structure and construct validity of the Vando Reducer–Augmenter Scale. *Personality and Individual Differences, 7*, 57–64.

Lacey, J. I. (1950). Individual differences in somatic response patterns. *Journal of Comparative and Physiological Psychology, 43*, 338–350.

Lacey, J. I. (1967). Somatic response patterning and stress: Some revisions of activation theory. In M. H. Appley & R. Trumbull (Eds.), *Psychological stress: Issues in research* (pp. 14–37). New York: Appleton-Century-Crofts.

Lindsley, D. B. (1952). Psychological phenomena and the electroencephalogram. *Electroencephalography and Clinical Neurophysiology, 4*, 443–456.

Loehlin, J. C. (1992). *Genes and environment in personality development.* Newbury Park, CA: Sage.

Malmo, R. B. (1959). Activation: A neuropsychological dimension. *Psychological Review, 66*, 367–386.

Matheny, A. P., Jr. (1990). Developmental behavior genetics: Contributions from the Louisville Twin Study. In M. E. Hahn, J. K. Hewitt, N. D. Henderson, & R. H. Benno (Eds.), *Developmental behavior genetics: Neural, biometrical, and evolutionary approaches* (pp. 25–39). New York: Oxford University Press.

McGuinness, D., & Pribram, K. (1980). The neuropsychology of attention: Emotional and motivational controls. In M. C. Wittrock (Ed.), *The brain and psychology* (pp. 95–109). San Diego, CA: Academic Press.

McGuire, I., & Turkewitz, G. (1979). Approach–withdrawal theory and the study of infant development. In M. Bortner (Ed.), *Cognitive growth and development: Essays in memory of Herbert G. Birch* (pp. 57–84). New York: Brunner/Mazel.

Mecacci, L. (1987). Basic properties of the nervous system and arousal model in light of current neuropsychophysiology. In J. Strelau & H. J. Eysenck (Eds.), *Personality dimensions and arousal* (pp. 171–182). New York: Plenum.

Moruzzi, G., & Magoun, H. W. (1949). Brain stem reticular formation and activation of the EEG. *Electroencephalography and Clinical Neurophysiology, 1*, 455–473.

Naveteur, L. J., & Baque, E. F. (1987). Individual differences in the electrodermal activity as a function of subjects' anxiety. *Personality and Individual Differences, 8*, 615–626.

Nebylitsyn, V. D. (1972). *Fundamental properties of the human nervous system.* New York: Plenum.

Pavlov, I. P. (1951/1952). *Complete works* (2nd ed.). Moscow: SSSR Academy of Sciences. (in Russian)

Petrie, A. (1967). *Individuality in pain and suffering.* Chicago: University of Chicago Press.

Posner, M. I. (1982). Cumulative development of attentional mechanisms. *American Psychologist, 37*, 168–179.

Posner, M. I., & Rothbart, M. K. (1981). The development of attentional mechanisms. In J. Flowers (Ed.), *Nebraska symposium on motivation* (Vol. 28, pp. 1–52). Lincoln: University of Nebraska Press.

Robinson, D. L. (1982). Properties of the diffuse thalamocortical system and human personality: A direct test of Pavlovian/Eysenckian theory. *Personality and Individual Differences, 3,* 393–405.

Rothbart, M. K. (1989). Biological processes in temperament. In G. A. Kohnstamm, J. E. Bates, & M. K. Rothbart (Eds.), *Temperament in childhood* (pp. 77–110). New York: Wiley.

Rothbart, M. K., & Posner, M. I. (1985). Temperament and the development of self-regulation. In L. C. Hartlage & C. F. Telzrow (Eds.), *The neuropsychology of individual differences* (pp. 93–123). New York: Plenum.

Routtenberg, A. (1968). The two-arousal hypothesis: Reticular formation and limbic system. *Psychological Review, 75,* 51–80.

Samuels, I. (1959). Reticular mechanisms and behavior. *Psychological Bulletin, 56,* 1–25.

Schalling, D., & Asberg, M. (1985). Biological and psychological correlates of impulsiveness and monotony avoidance. In J. Strelau, F. H. Farley, & A. Gale (Eds.), *The biological bases of behavior: Theories, measurement techniques, and development* (Vol. 1, pp. 181–194). Washington, DC: Hemisphere.

Schlosberg, H. (1954). Three dimensions of emotion. *Psychological Review, 61,* 81–88.

Stelmack, R. M. (1990). Biological bases of extraversion: Psychophysiological evidence. *Journal of Personality, 58,* 293–311.

Stelmack, R. M., & Geen, R. G. (1992). The psychophysiology of extraversion. In A. Gale & M. W. Eysenck (Eds.), *Handbook of individual differences: Biological perspectives* (pp. 227–254). New York: Wiley.

Strelau, J. (1974). Temperament as an expression of energy level and temporal features of behavior. *Polish Psychological Bulletin, 5,* 119–127.

Strelau, J. (1983). *Temperament, personality, activity.* San Diego, CA: Academic Press.

Strelau, J. (Ed.). (1985). *Temperamental bases of behavior: Warsaw studies on individual differences.* Lisse, The Netherlands: Swets & Zeitlinger.

Strelau, J. (1987a). The concept of temperament in personality research. *European Journal of Personality, 1,* 107–117.

Strelau, J. (1987b). Personality dimensions based on arousal theories: Search for integration. In J. Strelau & H. J. Eysenck (Eds.), *Personality dimensions and arousal* (pp. 269–286). New York: Plenum.

Strelau, J. (1991). Renaissance in research on temperament: Where to? In J. Strelau & A. Angleitner (Eds.), *Explorations in temperament: International perspectives on theory and measurement* (pp. 337–358). New York: Plenum.

Thomas, A., & Chess, S. (1977). *Temperament and development.* New York: Brunner/Mazel.

Torgersen, A. M. (1987). Longitudinal research on temperament in twins. *Acta Geneticae Medicae et Gemellologieae, 36,* 145–154.

Venables, P. H. (1984). Arousal: An examination of its status as a concept. In M. G. H. Coles, J. R. Jennings, & J. P. Stern (Eds.), *Psychophysiological perspectives: Festschrift for Beatrice and John Lacey* (pp. 134–142). New York: Van Nostrand Reinhold.

Wenger, M. A. (1938). Some relationships between muscular processes and personality and their factorial analysis. *Child Development, 9,* 261–276.

Wenger, M. A. (1943). An attempt to appraise individual differences in level of muscular tension. *Journal of Experimental Psychology, 32,* 213–225.

Wilson, G. (1990). Personality, time of day and arousal. *Personality and Individual Differences, 11,* 153–168.

Yerkes, R. M., & Dodson, J. D. (1908). The relation of strength of stimulus to rapidity of habit formation. *Journal of Comparative Neurology and Psychology, 18,* 459–582.

Zuckerman, M. (1979). *Sensation seeking: Beyond the optimal level of arousal.* Hillsdale, NJ: Erlbaum.

Zuckerman, M. (1984). Sensation seeking: A comparative approach to a human trait. *Behavioral and Brain Sciences, 7,* 413–471.

Zuckerman, M. (1991). *Psychobiology of personality.* Cambridge, MA: Cambridge University Press.

Zuckerman, M. (1992). What is a basic factor and which factors are basic? Turtles all the way down. *Personality and Individual Differences, 13,* 675–681.

Zuckerman, M., Kuhlman, D. M., Thornquist, M., & Kiers, H. (1991). Five (or three) robust questionnaire scale factors of personality without culture. *Personality and Individual Differences, 12,* 929–941.

CHAPTER 6

Quantitative Genetics and Molecular Genetics

Robert Plomin and Kimberly J. Saudino

G enetics is a fundamental facet of the biological roots of temperament and a common denominator for other biological correlates of temperament such as neuroanatomy, neurophysiology, and endocrinology. Basic behavioral genetics approaches to individual differences in temperament have been previously reviewed (Goldsmith, 1989), as have

The preparation of this chapter and some of the quantitative genetics research that it describes were supported, in part, by National Institute of Aging grant AG-04563, National Institute of Child Health and Human Development (NICHD) grants HD-10333 and HD-18426, National Institute of Mental Health grants MH-43373 and MH-43899, National Science Foundation grant BNS-91-08744, and a grant from the John D. and Catherine T. MacArthur Foundation. Our current molecular genetics research is supported by National Institute on Alcohol Abuse and Alcoholism grant AA-08125, NICHD grant HD-27694, and National Institute on Drug Abuse grant DA-07171. The recombinant inbred mouse research is a collaborative project with D. Blizard, V. E. Erwin, B. C. Jones, and G. E. McClearn. The human quantitative trait loci–association research represents a collaboration with M. Chorney, D. K. Detterman, G. E. McClearn, P. McGuffin, M. Owen, and L. A. Thompson. In writing this chapter, Robert Plomin was supported by a James McKeen Cattell Sabbatical Award and a Fogarty Senior International Fellowship, and Kimberly J. Saudino was supported by a postdoctoral fellowship awarded by the Social Sciences and Humanities Research Council of Canada.

the evidence and unsolved puzzles concerning genetic influence on temperament (Plomin, Chipuer, & Loehlin, 1990). In the first part of this chapter, we briefly mention some new findings of this type. However, rather than reiterating these reviews, we provide a preview of the revolutionary advances in molecular genetics that will make it possible to identify some of the many genes that are responsible for the ubiquitous genetic contribution to temperament for both humans and nonhuman animals.

Genetic research on temperament and other behavioral dimensions and disorders will eventually be revolutionized by molecular genetics. However, at this early stage it is important to emphasize that behavior is fundamentally different from the single-gene diseases that have been the targets of molecular genetics research to date. For complex dimensions and disorders that are influenced by multiple genes and nongenetic factors, new strategies are required that can detect DNA markers that account for small amounts of behavioral variation. In short, molecular genetics techniques will need to be applied in a quantitative genetics framework that recognizes multiple-gene influences as well as nongenetic influences. The following section briefly describes quantitative genetics theory and methods before turning to molecular genetics techniques.

Although this chapter focuses on dimensions of personality that are typically regarded as temperament, the issues broached in the chapter also apply to behavioral dimensions and disorders outside the domain of temperament. For this reason, we do not discuss in detail the hoary issues concerning definitions of temperament. We merely assert that we agree with the general definition offered by Bates (1989) that temperament "consists of biologically rooted individual differences in behavior tendencies that are present early in life and are relatively stable across various kinds of situations and over the course of time" (p. 4). The biological roots that interest us are genetic, by which we mean DNA-based differences among individuals that are transmitted hereditarily.

To avoid the misunderstandings that abound concerning this definition, we should emphasize at the outset what we are not saying. Dictionaries define the word *definition* in two ways. The first definition involves "the setting of bounds" and the second is "a precise statement of the essential nature of a thing" (Onions, 1987, p. 507). We do not believe that the second type of definition is possible for temperament, but there is some merit in the first type of definition in order to distinguish temperament from the rest of personality and psychology.

In terms of heritability, we are not saying that heritability is a facet of the "essential nature of a thing" called temperament. Heritability is our attempt to limit what we mean by the term *biological roots*. Personality traits that show no genetic influence—such as neonatal behavior (Riese, 1990) and positive low-arousal emotions such as smiling (Plomin, 1987)—are of less interest to us in this context, although such dimensions of behavior may be of great interest to other constituencies. Similarly, the criteria of appearance early in life and relative stability are not absolute. Traits that emerge later in life such as achievement motivation, alienation, and artistic orientation—just to begin with the first letter of the alphabet—are simply of less interest to us in this context. Finally, stability does not mean immutability. Indeed we are quite interested in genetic sources of age-to-age change as well as continuity in temperament (Plomin & Nesselroade, 1990; Saudino & Eaton, 1993).

Our interest in heritable personality traits is not completely capricious, however. Because personality traits that we refer to as temperament are heritable, they permit us to think about the application of molecular genetics techniques to begin to identify some of the many genes responsible for heritable variation.

Quantitative Genetics

Quantitative genetics refers to the theory developed in the early part of this century that merged Mendel's single-gene theory of inheritance of qualitative single-gene traits with inheritance of quantitative dimensions (Fisher, 1918). The merger merely required the realization that multiple genes as well as environmental factors can affect traits, and if they do, then quantitative dimensions rather than qualitative dichotomies will be seen even though each gene operates according to Mendel's laws of discrete inheritance. Quantitative genetics methods have been developed to assess the "bottom line" of the genetic contribution to behavior of humans and nonhuman animals, regardless of the complexity of genetic modes of action or the number of genes involved (Plomin, DeFries, & McClearn, 1990).

Nonhuman Research

Quantitative genetics methods that are used to study animal temperament include comparisons of inbred strains and selection studies. Inbred strains are created by mating brother to sister for at least 20 generations. This severe inbreeding eliminates heterozygosity and creates animals that are virtually identical genetically. Temperament differences between different inbred strains that are reared under the same laboratory conditions are ascribed to genetic differences between the inbred strains. For example, two widely studied inbred strains of mice that happen to be very different genetically are called *C57BL/6*, a black mouse, and *BALB/c*, an albino. C57BL/6 mice are much more active than are BALB/c mice in a brightly lit open field—an aversive situation that is thought to assess emotional reactivity (DeFries, Gervais, & Thomas, 1978).

Over 1,000 behavioral investigations have been published involving inbred strains of mice (Sprott & Staats, 1981). Inbred strains permit many other interesting analyses. For example, crosses between C57BL/6 and BALB/c inbred strains are intermediate in open-field activity. In such hybrids, the strain of the rearing mother makes little difference (DeFries & Hegmann, 1970); ovary transplant experiments prove that there is no prenatal maternal effect (DeFries, Thomas, Hegmann, & Weir, 1967). Inbred strains that are reared in different environments represent a powerful experimental approach to genotype–environment interaction (Henderson, 1967).

Selection studies provide the most convincing demonstrations of a genetic contribution to temperament. The results of selection can be seen most dramatically in differences in temperament among dog breeds (Scott & Fuller, 1965), differences that testify to the great range of genetic variability within a single species and its effect on behavior. In the laboratory, several controlled selection experiments have been conducted that show successful selection for temperament. For example, in one of the longest mammalian selection studies of behavior, replicated high and low lines were selected for activity in the open field (DeFries et al., 1978). After 30 generations of selection, a 30–fold difference exists between the activity of the high and low lines—there is no overlap between them. Selection has been successful for dozens of other behaviors, again indicating a genetic contribution to temperament.

Human Research

For temperament in humans, family, twin, and adoption designs, and combinations of these, have been used to triangulate estimates of genetic effects. For both humans and nonhuman animals, a genetic contribution to temperament has seemed nearly ubiquitous, although rarely are genetic factors able to explain more than half of the variance. However, there are recent examples in which negligible genetic influence was found. These include a study of neonatal temperament (Riese, 1990) and an adoption study of parental ratings of temperament (Plomin, Coon, Carey, DeFries, & Fulker, 1991). The latter study conflicts sharply with the results for twin studies of parental ratings of temperament. These problems with parental ratings are offset by recent twin and adoption analyses using objective and observational data that show a genetic contribution to temperament (e.g., Braungart, Plomin, DeFries, & Fulker, 1992; Saudino & Eaton, 1991).

Rather than reviewing evidence for a genetic role in temperament, in the main section of this chapter we go beyond the basic question of nature and nurture to consider application of techniques of the "new genetics" of molecular biology to identify specific genes that affect temperament in humans and nonhuman animals. However, it should be noted that quantitative genetics research will not be replaced by molecular genetics. To the contrary, quantitative genetics research will become even more valuable as it guides the search to identify some of the many genes that are responsible for the genetic contribution to temperament. Evaluating the bottom line of the genetic contribution to behavior will continue to be important.

New Quantitative Genetics Methods

New developments in quantitative genetics can go well beyond the basic nature–nurture question in ways of particular importance to temperament research and to molecular genetics applications. Four examples follow:

multivariate genetic analysis, DF analysis of extremes, longitudinal genetic analysis, and analyses of the interface between nature and nurture.

Multivariate genetic analysis

Multivariate genetic analysis assesses the extent to which genetic effects on one dimension or disorder overlap with genetic effects on another (Eaves & Gale, 1974; Loehlin & Vandenberg, 1968; Martin & Eaves, 1977; Plomin & DeFries, 1979). Multivariate genetic analysis is generally recognized as crucial for addressing the key issues of heterogeneity and comorbidity in psychopathology (Hewitt, 1993; Plomin & Rende, 1991; Plomin, Rende, & Rutter, 1991). For researchers of temperament, an important but as yet unexplored multivariate genetic issue is the extent of genetic overlap between psychopathology and temperament.

DF analysis of extremes

A related issue involves a new method named *DF analysis* after its developers (DeFries & Fulker, 1985, 1988). DF analysis addresses the fundamental question of the etiological association between the normal and the abnormal. The DF method leads to an estimate of what is called *group heritability*, which refers to the genetic contribution to the average difference between a selected group such as children who meet diagnostic criteria for a disorder and the rest of the population. DF analysis assesses group heritability as the differential regression to the population mean of the cotwins of identical and fraternal twin probands for a quantitative measure. For example, temperament scores of cotwins of probands that are ascertained because of psychopathology are expected to regress toward the mean of the unselected population. However, to the extent that the psychopathology is due to genetic factors, the regression to the mean will be less for identical-twin cotwins than for fraternal-twin cotwins.

In terms of temperament, one issue is whether the genetic etiology of the extremes of a dimension of temperament differs from the etiology of the rest of the dimension. Another critical issue for temperament research that can be broached by DF analysis is the extent to which psychopathology represents the genetic extreme of continua of temperament (Plomin, 1991; Stevenson, Batten, & Cherner, 1992).

Genetic analysis of age-to-age change and continuity

Extension of multivariate genetic analysis to longitudinal data makes it possible to assess age-to-age change as well as continuity in genetic effects during development (Eaves, Long, & Heath, 1986; Hewitt, Eaves, Neale, & Meyer, 1988; Plomin & DeFries, 1981). It has been suggested that the best place to look for age-to-age change in genetic effects is temperament in infancy and early childhood (Plomin & Nesselroade, 1990), and recent research has provided evidence of such change (Braungart et al., 1991; Plomin et al., 1993; Saudino & Eaton, 1993).

Genetics and experience

Finally, recent research indicates that genetic factors contribute to widely used measures of the environment (Plomin & Bergeman, 1991). The key question is what processes mediate this genetic contribution. It has been suggested that temperament plays an important role at this interface between nature and nurture (Plomin, 1994; Plomin & Neiderhiser, 1992).

Molecular Genetics

Researchers are at the dawn of a new era in which molecular genetics techniques will revolutionize genetic research on behavior by identifying specific genes that contribute to genetic variance in behavioral dimensions and disorders (Aldhous, 1992; Plomin, 1990). We have begun to use these techniques in our research to identify specific genes that affect temperament in both mice and humans.

It was only 10 years ago that the now-standard techniques of the "new genetics" were first used to identify genes responsible for single-gene disorders. As described previously (e.g., Plomin et al., 1990), the discovery of restriction enzymes led to recombinant DNA, the ability to sequence DNA, and the discovery of thousands of new DNA markers. DNA markers are genetic differences among individuals that involve DNA itself rather than gene products such as the blood groups and other traditional genetic markers. These new DNA markers can be used to identify a chromosomal region and, eventually, to isolate a gene and a gene product for single-gene disorders.

Notable early successes in identifying genes in humans include cystic fibrosis and Duchenne muscular dystrophy. These are dichotomous traits, like Mendel's smooth versus wrinkled seeds, in which one gene is necessary and sufficient to explain the observed difference. Several thousand single-gene disorders, most very rare, have been reported, and many affect behavior (McKusick, 1990). However, this by no means implies that behavior is determined by a single gene. A "mutation" in any one of hundreds of parts of an automobile can impair its functioning, yet not one of those parts is by itself responsible for a fully functioning automobile. Behavior reflects the functioning of the whole organism. Moreover, behavior is dynamic, changing in response to the environment.

Genes that affect behavioral traits are transmitted hereditarily according to Mendel's laws in the same way as genes that affect any other phenotype. However, the genetics of behavior is special in three ways. First, unlike Mendel's smooth versus wrinkled seeds, most behavioral dimensions and disorders are not distributed in simple either–or dichotomies, although in psychopathology, one often pretends that a line exists that sharply separates the normal from the abnormal. Second, behavioral traits are substantially influenced by nongenetic factors: Heritabilities rarely exceed 50%. Third, behavioral dimensions and disorders are likely to be influenced by many genes, with each producing small effects.

Each of these points applies to dimensions of temperament as well as to the dichotomies of convenience that are called psychopathology. The challenge is to use DNA markers to find genes in these complex systems of behavior that involve multiple-gene effects as well as multiple nongenetic factors. Such multiple genes of varying effect size that contribute to quantitative traits are called quantitative trait loci (QTL; Gelderman, 1975).

The following sections describe approaches that are currently being used in the quest to find QTL for behavior in mice and humans.

The Quest for QTL in Mice: Recombinant Inbred Strains

A particularly powerful method for identifying genes that affect nonhuman behavior is the recombinant inbred (RI) strain method. The RI method refers to a series of inbred strains that are developed by systematic in-breeding of animals from an F_2 generation obtained from the F_1 cross derived from two progenitor inbred strains (Bailey, 1971; Taylor, 1989). For example, the most widely used RI series in mice, called *BXD RI*, is derived from the C57BL/6 and DBA/2J inbred strains. These two progenitor inbred strains are crossed-mated, which produces an F_1 (first filial generation, as Mendel called it), and the F_1 animals are then mated to produce F_2 individuals. F_2 individuals segregate for genetic differences between the progenitor lines according to the laws of inheritance that were worked out by Mendel. That is, Mendel's monohybrid genotypic segregation ratio for a locus (A) with two alleles (A_1 and A_2) means that F_2 individuals will segregate for that locus according to a 1:2:1 ratio in which 25% of the individuals have A_1A_1 genotypes, 50% have A_1A_2, and 25% have A_2A_2. Inbreeding of many inbred strains begins with brother–sister matings in this F_2 generation. Each incipient inbred strain continues to be mated brother to sister for 20 generations. As noted earlier, in-breeding decreases heterozygosity, which means that heterozygous A_1A_2 genotypes become increasingly distributed as homozygous A_1A_1 and A_2A_2 genotypes as inbreeding proceeds. In the case of the BXD RI series, 26 inbred strains have been successfully derived.

The word *recombinant* in *recombinant inbred series* refers not to recombinant DNA but to recombination, the process of crossing over during meiotic divisions. Crossing-over breaks up original linkage relationships. Re-inbreeding locks in new ones. For each chromosome, there-fore, each RI strain presents a unique linear patchwork of segments that are derived from one or the other progenitor strain.

RI strains were introduced for the purpose of mapping genes to chromosomes. The RI method is the primary reason why the genetic map of the mouse is at least as complete as the human map. For every locus for which the progenitor strains differ, half of the RI strains are expected to be inbred for one allele and half for the other allele. The pattern of the marker across the 26 BXD RI strains is called a *strain distribution pattern* (SDP). For example, for a particular marker, the SDP might be BDBDDDBDBDBDDDBDBDDDBBDBBD for the 26 RI strains in the BXD RI series, where B refers to a BB genotype and D refers to a DD genotype. (This is the actual SDP for dopamine D2 receptor found in our laboratory;

Smith et al., 1992.) Two markers will have the same SDP only if the markers are close together on the same chromosome, within about a million nucleotide base pairs. A single SDP difference indicates that the markers are distinct. Association of two markers can be detected reliably up to a distance of about 10 centimorgans (cM, which corresponds to about 10 million base pairs, roughly a 10th of the distance of an average chromosome). The more two markers' SDPs differ, the farther apart the loci are on a chromosome. If the SDP for two markers differs for half of the RI strains, the loci are assumed to be on different chromosomes.

Even 5 years ago, several hundred markers had been mapped for the BXD RI series across the 1,600 cM of the mouse genome, with distinct markers available every 6.5 cM on average (Taylor, 1989). The number of markers is increasing almost daily, and the mouse genome map is far better than the human map, with 1,518 new markers resulting in an average genome map density of 0.6 cM reported in October 1993 (Copeland et al., 1993). Given that associations can be detected for distances up to 10 cM, the chromosomal location of any new marker is thus likely to show an association with one of the existing BXD markers.

An additional benefit of the RI method is the test that it provides for the existence of a single-gene effect. If a trait is influenced by a single gene or a major gene (a gene that is primarily but not totally responsible for a genetic effect), then the RI strains should be distributed into two distinct groups of approximately equal size. That is, for any gene that differs for the progenitor strains, about half of the RI strains should lock on to one allele during inbreeding and half should lock on to the other allele. Thus, if a single or major gene that differed between the progenitor strains affected a trait, then the strains should be distributed bimodally. If such a dichotomous or at least bimodal SDP is obtained, then the SDP can be used to map the gene.

However, when the RI method was first applied to behavioral phenotypes in the late 1970s, bimodal distributions of RI means that are characteristic of major-gene effects were seldom found. These results provide the best available evidence that behavioral traits rarely show major-gene effects. For this reason, the RI method lay fallow for the analysis of behavior. That is, if a continuous SDP is found for a phenotype, then it is not possible to classify the RI strains as being like one progenitor parent or the other. Without such a dichotomous classification, there is no SDP to be compared with SDPs for genetic markers in order to map genetic effects.

In the late 1980s, researchers realized that the RI method could be applied to quantitative traits that yield a continuous strain distribution pattern. The method was called RI QTL analysis (McClearn, Plomin, Gora-Maslak, & Crabbe, 1991; Plomin, McClearn, Gora-Maslak, & Neiderhiser, 1991b). Using RI data, it is possible to identify a QTL that affects a quantitative trait if the QTL is relatively close to a marker and if its effect size is sufficient to be detected with the statistical power available. Most simply considered, the RI QTL approach compares the mean temperament scores of those RI strains that are genetically like one progenitor to those like the other for each marker, considered one at a time. A significant difference between the mean temperament scores of those RI strains possessing the allele of one progenitor strain and those RI strains possessing the allele of the other progenitor strain is evidence that there exists, somewhere in the vicinity of that locus, a QTL that influences the trait. A significant QTL association could be the result of a nearby QTL with small effect or a far-away QTL with large effect.

Use of the same RI series across studies capitalizes on the cumulative and integrative nature of the RI approach. Because RI strains are inbred, individuals are comparable across time and across studies. This benefit has a particularly important corollary: Once an RI series has been characterized for a particular quantitative trait, all strain distribution patterns for markers that have previously been typed for the RI series are immediately available for the search for QTL associations. In other words, a researcher who assesses temperament in an RI series can conduct a molecular genetics search for QTL without doing any molecular genetics research. The BXD RI series has been the choice of most researchers for three reasons. First, the BXD RI series is one of the largest. Second, the progenitor inbred strains (C57BL/6 and DBA/2J) are among the two most different inbred strains in terms of breeding history as well as documented genetic differences (Roderick, 1980). Third, many more markers are available for the BXD RI series than for any other RI series.

An Example of RI QTL Analysis for Activity Level

Previously published RI data relevant to temperament were re-analyzed to illustrate the potential utility of the RI QTL approach (Plomin, Mc-Clearn, Gora-Maslak, & Neiderhiser, 1991a). In this section, new data for activity level that were collected as part of our ongoing RI QTL study of alcohol-related processes are presented.

Subjects

A production colony of the BXD RI strains was established at Penn State University in 1990 in which all 26 BXD RI strains are represented. Testing begins at 60 days of age. The goal is to test 20 mice in each of the BXD RI strains. The present preliminary analyses are based on 15 BXD RI strains with an average of 10 mice per strain.

Activity measure

Activity was assessed in the Omnitech apparatus (Omnitech Electronics, 1992), which assesses diverse behavioral measures and continuously records responses directly into the computer. Each animal was assessed for 30 minutes. Factor analyses of 21 basic measures that were recorded by the Omnitech apparatus yielded a general activity factor that included such variables as total distance, movement time, and horizontal activity.

Reliability of RI strain means

The RI enterprise rests on the reliable and replicable determination of the rank order of the RI strain means (not the reliability of scores of individual animals). Without adequate reliability of strain means, RI QTL analyses are unlikely to yield more than a chance number of significant QTL associations, and these are not likely to replicate across studies. Reliability of strain means is a function of the number of animals tested per strain.

We assessed reliability by creating two randomly selected "split halves." The strain means for half of the sample were correlated with the strain means for the other half of the sample and corrected using the Spearman–Brown formula to estimate reliability for the entire sample. Reliability for our activity measure was .91.

Results

The SDP for activity for 15 BXD RI strains and the 2 progenitor inbred strains is shown in Figure 1. The frequency histogram is obviously continuous, the typical outcome for RI analyses of behavioral traits (Plomin et al., 1991b). In addition to the frequency histogram, the nonparametric Epanechnikov kernel density function (Wilkinson, 1988) is also shown in Figure 1. (As explained previously by Belknap et al., 1992, this continuous function portrays RI strain distributions more accurately than does the inherently discontinuous frequency histogram [Silverman, 1986].)

The activity SDP in Figure 1 raises an important point about RI QTL analyses. Although the progenitor strains (C57B and DBA in Figure 1) differ for many behaviors, they do not differ much on this activity measure.

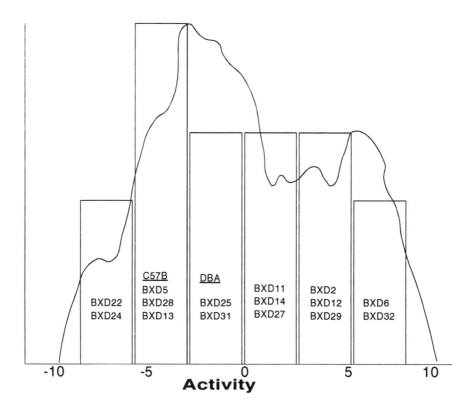

FIGURE 1. BXD RI strain distribution pattern for activity level. C57B and DBA refer to the progenitor inbred strains, C57BL/6 and DBA/2J.

However, some RI strains have lower activity scores than do the progenitor strains, whereas other RI strains have considerably higher activity scores. Although the single-gene RI approach requires that the progenitor strains differ, the RI QTL approach does not. For example, if there were 10 genes that affect activity level, then C57BL/6 and DBA/2J might each have five "positive" alleles and five "negative" alleles for activity level, but a different combination of these alleles. Despite similar average phenotypic scores for C57BL/6 and DBA/2J, when these alleles segregate in the RI strains, some RI strains are likely to have more than five positive alleles, and some will have fewer than five. Thus, the case represented in Figure 1 in which the RI strains have higher and lower scores than do the progenitors is to be expected from an RI QTL point of view.

Because the SDP is continuous for activity, classical RI analysis is not applicable because it is not possible to dichotomize the RI strains into those like one progenitor and those like the other. Table 1 presents preliminary RI QTL results. Because of the importance of replication, we conducted the analyses separately for the two half samples described earlier. QTL associations were assessed for each half sample using cor-

TABLE 1

BXD Markers That Show Significant ($p < .03$) Quantitative Trait Loci (QTL) Correlations With Activity in Both Half Samples

Marker	Chromosome	cM	QTL correlations Half A	Half B
PV40	5	6	.59*	.69**
D5MIT1	5	?	.58*	.73**
D5MIT2	5	?	−.63*	−.59*
XMMV27	6	30	−.65**	−.57
PMV18	7	7	.66**	.53*
CYP2B	7	?	.71**	.59*
D11NDS1	11	?	.54*	.57*
MS65	14	17	.77**	.73**
RB1	14	27	.60*	.62**
ES10	14	28	.56*	.59*
CTLA6	14	?	.60*	.56*
D14MCC1	14	?	.60*	.63*

Note. cM refers to centimorgan, an index of chromosomal position. A question mark indicates that the position is not known with certainty.
*$p < .03$. **$p < .01$.

relations between genotype (coded as 0 for the C57BL/6 allele and 1 for the DBA/2J allele) and the mean activity score rather than the equivalent t test comparing mean activity scores for the two genotypes.

Table 1 lists unique (i.e., with distinct SDP) BXD markers that yielded a significant ($p < .03$) QTL correlation for activity in both half samples. This significance level was chosen because a QTL association that is significant at $p < .03$ in both half samples will have a significance level on the order of $p < .001$. Because only 1 in 1,000 significant associations would be expected by chance, this criterion means that significant QTL are not expected by chance alone because the number of unique markers examined in this analysis is 398. Although there are currently 555 unique markers for the BXD RI series, many markers that have unique SDP for the 26 BXD RI strains have the same SDP for our subsample of 15 BXD RI strains. Although many QTL will be missed when such a stringent criterion for significance is used, we used this criterion to begin the search for QTL with the largest effects. We can of course return to these data and examine smaller QTL effects using a less severe criterion for significance.

As indicated in Table 1, markers on five chromosomes show QTL correlations that are significant ($p < .03$) in both half samples. One region that is indexed by marker Ms6–5 at 17 cM on Chromosome 14 is significant at $p < .01$ in both half samples. The other Chromosome 14 markers are close enough to the Ms6–5 marker (and thus have very similar marker SDP) that they would also show significant correlations. This finding does not imply that Ms6–5 is itself the QTL that codes for a product that affects activity level. Rather, the results suggest that a gene somewhere in this region of Chromosome 14 affects activity level. Other candidate chromosomal regions are suggested on Chromosomes 5, 6, 7, and 11. It should be noted that all of the significant QTL correlations (except for D5MIT2 and XMMV27) are in the expected positive direction in that C57BL/6 are somewhat less active than DBA/2J (see Figure 1) and the C57BL/6 allele is scored as 0 and the DBA/2J allele is scored as 1.

As mentioned earlier, one of the major benefits of the RI QTL approach is that genetic correlations with measures that are used in different studies and their QTL underpinnings can be explored. A search for genetic correlations between activity level in our study and dependent measures in the many other studies using BXD RI strains was conducted using the RI QTL Collaborative Data Bank (Plomin et al., 1991a). However, no more than a chance number of significant genetic correlations emerged. Thus, it is not possible to use activity level in relation to genetic correlations across studies and then identify QTL regions responsible for the genetic correlation (for a discussion of this issue see Plomin & McClearn, 1993).

Several strategies can be used to replicate and extend RI QTL analysis. The goal is to find markers closer and closer to the QTL itself and eventually identify the gene itself. The strategy of our laboratory is described in the next section, followed by a discussion of the ultimate extension of this research, which is to identify candidate genes for humans.

Replications and Extensions of RI QTL Analysis

In summary, RI QTL analysis of activity suggests several candidate chromosomal regions. However, because the unit of analysis for RI QTL analysis is the RI strain mean, the statistical power of the analysis depends on the number of RI strains. Although the BXD RI series is one of the largest RI series, it includes only 26 strains (and the present preliminary analysis includes only 15 strains). Another problem is the Type II error of false negatives. Type II problems are not so important at this stage of research because the QTL quest is not to find all of the genes that affect a trait but just some of them. A more serious problem is the Type I error of false positives. Because many markers are examined, some significant associations may be spurious. As explained earlier, the preliminary approach that we used was to replicate the results in two half samples.

Nonetheless, replication remains important, greater power is needed to detect QTL of smaller effect size, and strategies are needed to get closer to the QTL itself. We and our colleagues are using a three-stage strategy of successively finer screens to elect candidate QTL that have been nominated by RI QTL analysis (Plomin & McClearn, 1993).

RI F_1 QTL analysis
The first step is to use F_1 crosses between RI strains to increase the power to detect smaller QTL effects and replicate RI QTL results. With 26 BXD

RI strains, hundreds of F_1 could be generated. The most valuable feature of RI F_1 QTL analysis is that it does not require genotyping the animals because their genotypes are known from the genotypes of their RI parents. Because F_1 crosses are heterozygous for any alleles that differ between their inbred parents, the RI F_1 approach also extends QTL research to consideration of heterozygosity and dominance. Specifically, we are currently collecting activity data for 60 RI F_1 crosses to replicate the RI QTL results reported in Table 1. Of the 60 RI F_1 strains, for a particular marker, 30 strains would be expected to be BD heterozygotes, 15 would be BB homozygotes, and 15 would be DD homozygotes. QTL analysis of the BB and DD homozygotes for each candidate QTL marker provides a replication of RI QTL results as well as an extension of the results to a genetic background that includes heterozygosity at other loci. Analysis of the activity scores of the heterozygotes for the marker permits exploration of dominance effects.

F_2 QTL analysis
Other strategies to increase power and to replicate RI QTL results require genotyping. The next step in our screening strategy involves F_2 animals. F_2 individuals can provide potentially unlimited power to detect QTL in addition to replicating RI QTL results and extending them to the more natural genetic situation of genetically segregating individuals. Using the BXD progenitors to create an F_2 population appropriately limits the replication to the same polymorphic alleles that are involved in the RI QTL analysis. F_2 that are derived from crosses of other inbred strains could be used to test the generalization to other genetic backgrounds.

The F_2 strategy is the same as that for the QTL allelic association approach used in humans, which is discussed in the next section. It is relatively inexpensive to test large numbers of mice on measures such as activity level, but extraction of DNA and genotyping is expensive. For this reason, an efficient and powerful strategy for F_2 QTL association analysis is to test as large a sample of F_2 individuals as possible and select a small group of individuals at the extremes of the distribution. The frequency of the candidate QTL marker (or preferably, several markers in the candidate chromosomal region) can be compared for the high and low groups. This approach maximizes the likelihood of identifying even a small QTL association and minimizes the expense of genotyping. Specifically, we are testing a sample of 200 F_2 individuals from C57BL/6 and DBA/2J crosses, and we will then select the most and least active animals. We will compare the allelic frequencies for the high- and low-activity groups for candidate QTL markers that were nominated by RI QTL analysis and that survive replication in the RI F_1 analysis.

Heterogeneous-stock QTL analysis

QTL associations in F_2 animals are limited to the genetic differences between their C57BL/6 and DBA/2J progenitors. Moreover, F_2 animals are only subject to two generations of recombination. For these reasons, in our program of research the third stage from nomination to election of a QTL is to replicate candidate QTL markers that survive the RI F_1 and F_2 QTL analyses using heterogeneous-stock (HS) mice. HS mice are more representative of the mouse genome by virtue of their derivation from random intercrossing among eight inbred strains. Like humans, HS mice are outbred because scores of generations of recombination have broken up all but the tightest associations between markers and QTL. The procedure for HS QTL analysis is the same as that for F_2 QTL analysis: Test a large number of individuals, genotype the extremes for candidate QTL markers, and assess allelic frequency differences between the extreme groups.

QTL in Mice and Humans

A particularly exciting possibility is that RI QTL research may begin to bridge the gap between temperament in mice and humans at the fundamental level of DNA. Specifically, candidate genes such as the dopamine D2 receptor in mice that are shown to be temperament-related QTL can be used as candidate genes for human temperament research. Indeed, mouse DNA probes can be used as probes in human studies and vice versa because genes in the two species have enough DNA in common to use one species' DNA to fish out the other species' homologous gene.

Most polymorphisms (genetic markers that differ from person to person) are not in regions of genes called *exons*, which are the segments of DNA that are transcribed and then translated into amino acid sequences. In most cases, a DNA marker for a QTL association is not in an exon. Thus, the marker does not produce a functional difference in the nervous system. However, such markers may be close enough to a functional QTL that they are markers for the QTL. In this case, temperament-related QTL chromosomal regions in mice that are syntenic to human chromosomes can be used as candidate chromosomal regions for QTL association studies in humans. *Synteny* refers to a chromosomal segment that shows at least two homologous genes between the species (Nadeau, 1989). Currently, 157 syntenic regions are known between mice and humans, which accounts for about one sixth of the mouse genome. For example, the DNA marker for the dopamine D2 receptor in BXD RI maps to a region of Chromosome 9 that is syntenic to the q23 region of human Chromosome 11 (Smith et al., 1992). This region of human Chromosome 11 is already known to be the location of the human gene for the dopamine D2 receptor.

For this reason, temperament-related QTL in mice that are located in chromosomal regions syntenic with human chromosomes have special significance as possible candidate chromosomal regions for QTL association studies of human temperament. In Table 1, the significant activity-related QTL regions on Chromosomes 7 and 14 in mice are known to be syntenic with human chromosomes. Replication of these findings would suggest that these regions could be used as candidate chromosomal regions for exploration of activity-related QTL in the human species.

The Quest for QTL in the Humans

Because behavior in humans is at least as complex as that in mice, it is unlikely that major-gene effects will be found for human behavior if they cannot be found for mouse behavior. How can QTL for temperament be identified in humans? Given the breathtaking pace of technological advances in molecular genetics, the safest bet is that by the turn of the century researchers will be investigating multiple-gene influences for complex dimensions and disorders using completely different techniques from those in use today. However, one strategy that we are using in the meanwhile in our laboratory is very similar to the allelic association method discussed earlier for F_2 and HS mice. There is no approach for humans that would be as powerful as RI QTL analysis to nominate candidate chromosomal regions. Nonetheless, the quest for QTL can begin by using quasi-candidate genes relevant to the nervous system. The following section argues that linkage, the standard method for attempting to identify genes for single-gene disorders in humans, is not likely to be successful in identifying QTL.

Linkage

For a single-gene trait, linkage is a method guaranteed to find the chromosomal location of the gene, even when nothing is known about the gene product. In mice, powerful test crosses between inbred strains are available to pin down linkage of a single gene. The most important method, discussed earlier, is the RI strain method. In humans, the problem is much more difficult because humans are outbred, even more so than HS mice. This means that the process of recombination—crossing over of parts of chromosomes during meiosis—breaks up any associations ("linkage disequilibrium") between alleles (alternate forms of a gene) that happen to be inherited on the same chromosome. For this reason, human linkage analysis traces the cotransmission of a DNA marker and a single-gene disorder within a large family pedigree (Ott, 1985). Within a family, a marker allele and a disease allele that happen to be on the same chromosome will be inherited together if their loci (locations on chromosomes) are close together. If the loci are close (linked), then recombination is unlikely to separate the allele of the DNA marker and the allele of the single-gene disorder because recombination occurs only a few times per chromosome per generation within a family.

The problem is that linkage can only identify a major gene that is largely responsible for a disorder. Moreover, linkage techniques generally depend on the assessment of a qualitative dichotomy (which is expected if a single gene is at work) rather than a quantitative dimension. Temperament, however, involves multiple genes and dimensions rather than dichotomies.

The alternative view espoused here is that major genes will not be found for human behavior in either the population or the family. Rather, for each individual, many genes make small contributions to variability and vulnerability. In this view, the genetic quest is to find not *the* gene for a behavioral trait but the multiple genes that affect the trait in a probabilistic manner rather than a predetermined manner. Although some sledgehammer effects of major genes may be found, it seems more likely that many other alleles nudge development up as well as down for many individuals and do not show dramatic effects as in the classical single-gene disorders.

New strategies are needed to identify genes that affect behavioral traits, even when the genes account for only a small amount of variance, when nongenetic factors are important, and when the traits are quantitatively distributed. In short, researchers need to use molecular genetics techniques in a quantitative genetics framework. One possibility is to apply a strategy called QTL allelic association, which is similar to the method discussed earlier for mice.

Allelic Association

Linkage refers to loci rather than alleles. That is, linked traits such as hemophilia and color-blindness do not occur together in the population. In contrast, allelic association occurs when a DNA marker is so close to a trait-relevant gene (or is part of the gene) that its alleles are correlated with the trait in unrelated individuals in the population (Edwards, 1991). For example, allelic associations have been found between disease states and markers in the HLA histocompatibility complex (Tiwari & Terasaki, 1985). That is, particular HLA alleles increase risk for certain diseases. For normal variation, the best example of allelic association is serum cholesterol levels for which about a quarter of the variance can be explained by four apolipoprotein gene markers (Sing & Boerwinkle, 1987). In psychiatry, a marker in the dopamine D2 receptor has been reported in several studies to be associated with severe alcoholism (Noble, 1993). The frequency of an allele of this marker appears to be greater in severe alcoholics than in controls, although failures to replicate have also been reported (Gelernter, Goldman, & Risch, 1993). The most important recent success of the allelic association approach for a behavioral disorder involves a gene associated with the cognitive decline of late-onset Alzheimer's disease (Corder et al., 1993). The E4 allele of apolipoprotein E shows a frequency of 31% in control groups, 64% in sporadic Alzheimer's cases, and 80% in familial Alzheimer's cases. This finding has electrified the Alzheimer's scientific community because it is the first DNA marker shown to be related to this common form of dementia late in life.

The best situation is when the marker is the relevant gene itself. As mentioned earlier, the marker polymorphism can involve a coding region of a gene and thus code for actual polypeptide differences among individuals. Of the thousands of known markers, only a handful are known to involve polymorphisms in coding sequences (exons). Examples of markers that happen to be in coding sequences are markers for two of the five types of dopamine receptors, the D3 and D4 receptors. Dopamine is one of the catecholamine neurotransmitters and is centrally involved in diverse brain functions including drugs of abuse and antipsychotic drugs. In the case of the dopamine D4 receptor, it is known that receptor binding differs for people with different marker genotypes. However, most of the current markers are likely to be in noncoding regions because natural selection does not screen out such variation in noncoding DNA. Finding such functional markers is a high priority for research because of the power they provide for finding QTL (Sobell, Heston, & Sommer, 1992).

Allelic association makes it possible to use markers that are not functional themselves but are very close to functional genetic variation. A particular combination of a marker allele and a functional variation in DNA that happen to be on the same chromosome is rarely separated by recombination (meiotic crossing over of chromosomes) if the marker and the functional DNA polymorphism are very close together on the chromosome.

A major advantage of allelic association analysis is that it uses samples of unrelated individuals, whereas linkage requires pedigrees of related individuals. By increasing the sample size of relatively easy-to-obtain unrelated subjects, allelic association analysis can be made sufficiently powerful to detect small genetic effects. In addition, allelic association is just as applicable to quantitative traits as to disorders.

A problem is that there are so many DNA markers. Unlike the analogous HS approach in mice, for humans there is nothing like an RI QTL analysis to nominate candidate markers. The allelic association approach is like a myopic search for a few needles in a haystack. In contrast to linkage, which can detect a major gene far away from a marker, allelic associations can only be detected when a marker is very near a gene that affects the trait. For behavioral traits that are influenced by many genes as well as by nongenetic factors, a near-sighted strategy such as allelic association is needed to provide statistical power to detect QTL. Nonetheless, there are so many markers that randomly drawing straws from the haystack is unlikely to pay off. The odds can be loaded in one's favor by beginning the search using markers in or near genes of neurological relevance. The odds can also be improved by using large samples and well-measured extreme groups to increase the power to detect small effects. The goal is to identify some, certainly not all, genes that contribute to the ubiquitous genetic variance that is found for behavioral traits.

Candidate Gene Allelic Association: An Example of Activity Level in Children

The candidate gene allelic association approach has recently been used in an attempt to identify QTL associated with cognitive ability (Plomin & Thompson, 1993). In this section, we use DNA marker data from this study to provide a concrete example of the approach for temperament research. DNA markers are used that are in or near genes with possible neurological relevance, such as the many neuroreceptor genes and genes that are involved in the regulation of these genes. From a sample of more than 500 children, from 7 to 15 years of age, three groups of Caucasian children were selected: 24 children with the highest IQ scores, 21 with average IQ scores, and 18 with the lowest IQ scores. The average IQ scores of the three groups were 130, 104, and 80, respectively.

We obtained blood from these children and established permanent cell lines by transforming the lymphocytes with Epstein-Barr virus. Permanent cell lines provide unlimited amounts of DNA for marker analyses as well as a permanent resource for future DNA analyses of these samples.

This ongoing study compared allelic frequencies for these groups for neurologically relevant DNA markers, including the dopamine D1 and D3 receptors, monoamine oxidase B, neurofilament protein, and fragile X repeat length. The study also included an independent replication sample that included more than 20 children with even higher IQ scores and more than 20 children with even lower IQ scores.

To provide a concrete example of this QTL approach for temperament, we analyzed activity level for the 63 children with DNA marker data. Given that activity level and IQ are uncorrelated, we expected the 63 children to be roughly normally distributed in terms of activity level. This is, of course, a very preliminary analysis because the sample is small compared with the high and low IQ groups who were selected from a sample of more than 500 children. Nonetheless, these data will serve to illustrate the QTL allelic association approach.

Maternal activity ratings on the Colorado Childhood Temperament Inventory (Rowe & Plomin, 1977) were used to select the top and bottom quartiles of the reasonably normal distribution. When merged with the marker data, the sample consisted of 9 children in the high-activity group and 9 children in the low-activity group. We compared allelic frequencies for the children in the high- and low-activity groups. Although the children have been genotyped for more than 20 DNA markers, many of these markers are multiple-allele markers that lose power because the sample is spread out over the various alleles. We examined the 12 markers that have only two alleles. Of these 12 markers, 1 yielded a significant frequency difference between the high- and low-activity group. This marker is in a gene for the enzyme tyrosinase, which is involved in tyrosine metabolism. For the most common of the two alleles, the allelic frequency in the high-activity group was 72% (13/18), whereas in the low-activity group the allelic frequency was 39% (7/18). (The denominator is 18 because each child has two alleles.) The chi-square for this 2×2 contingency table is 4.05 with one degree of freedom, which yields $p < .05$.

Although this first preliminary attempt to harness the power of molecular genetics to study temperament suggests a potentially exciting result, until we have an opportunity to verify the finding in the replication sample, it is best interpreted only as indicative of the promise of this approach.

Conclusion

It seems clear that genetics plays an important role in the etiology of individual differences in temperament. Molecular genetics provides powerful tools that can be used by behavioral scientists to identify relevant DNA differences among individuals without relying on familial resemblance. In addition to providing indisputable evidence of the role of genetics, it will revolutionize behavioral genetics by providing measured genotypes for investigating the multivariate and longitudinal genetic issues, the links between the normal and abnormal, and the interactions and correlations between genotype and environment. In a broader perspective, it will contribute to the integration of genetic research on humans and nonhuman animals at the universal level of DNA. It will also help to integrate the increasingly fractionated biological and behavioral sciences. The much-used phrase *paradigm shift* seems no exaggeration for advances of this magnitude.

References

Aldhous, P. (1992). The promise and pitfalls of molecular genetics. *Science, 257*, 164–165.

Bailey, D. W. (1971). Recombinant inbred strains. *Transplanation, 11*, 325–327.

Bates, J. E. (1989). Concepts and measures of temperament. In G. A. Kohnstamm, J. E. Bates, & M. K. Rothbart (Eds.), *Temperament in childhood* (pp. 3–26). New York: Wiley.

Belknap, J. K., Sampson, K. E., Crabbe, J. C., Plomin, R., McClearn, G. E., O'Toole, L. A., & Gora-Maslak, G. (1992). Single locus control of saccharin intake in BXD/Ty recombinant inbred mice: Some methodological implications for RI strain analysis. *Behavior Genetics, 22*, 81–100.

Braungart, J. M., Plomin, R., DeFries, J. C., & Fulker, D. W. (1992). Genetic influence on tester-rated infant temperament as assessed by Bayley's Infant Behavior Record: Nonadoptive and adoptive siblings and twins. *Developmental Psychology, 28*, 40–47.

Copeland, N. G., Jenkins, N. A., Gilbert, D. J., Eppig, J. T., Maltais, L. J., Miller, J. C., Dietrich, W. F., Weaver, A., Lincoln, S. E., Steen, R. G., Stein, L. D., Nadeau, J. H., & Lander,

E. S. (1993). A genetic linkage map of the mouse: Current applications and future prospects. *Science, 262,* 57–66.

Corder, E. H., Saunders, A. M., Strittmatter, W. J., Schmechel, D. E., Gaskell, P. C., Small, G. W., Roses, A. D., Haines, J. L., & Pericak-Vance, M. A. (1993). Gene dose of apolipoprotein E type 4 allele and the risk of Alzheimer's disease in late onset families. *Science, 261,* 921–923.

DeFries, J. C., & Fulker, D. W. (1985). Multiple regression analysis of twin data. *Behavior Genetics, 15,* 467–473.

DeFries, J. C., & Fulker, D. W. (1988). Multiple regression analysis of twin data: Etiology of deviant scores versus individual differences. *Acta Geneticae Medicae et Gemellologiae, 37,* 205–216.

DeFries, J. C., Gervais, M. C., & Thomas, E. A. (1978). Response to 30 generations of selection for open-field activity in laboratory mice. *Behavior Genetics, 8,* 3–13.

DeFries, J. C., & Hegmann, J. P. (1970). Genetic analysis of open-field behavior. In G. Lindzey & D. C. Thiessen (Eds.), *Contributions of behavior–genetic analysis: The mouse as a prototype* (pp. 23–56). New York: Appleton-Century-Crofts.

DeFries, J. C., Thomas, E. A., Hegmann, J. P., & Weir, M. W. (1967). Open-field behavior in mice: Analysis of maternal effects by means of ovarian transplantation. *Psychonomic Science, 8,* 207–208.

Eaves, L. J., & Gale, J. S. (1974). A method for analyzing the genetic basis of covariation. *Behavior Genetics, 4,* 253–267.

Eaves, L. J., Long, J., & Heath, A. C. (1986). A theory of developmental change in quantitative phenotypes applied to cognitive development. *Behavior Genetics, 16,* 143–162.

Edwards, J. H. (1991). The formal problems of linkage. In P. McGuffin & R. Murray (Eds.), *The new genetics of mental illness* (pp. 58–70). London: Butterworth-Heinemann.

Fisher, R. A. (1918). The correlation between relatives on the supposition of Mendelian inheritance. *Transactions of the Royal Society of Edinburgh, 52,* 399–433.

Gelderman, H. (1975). Investigations on inheritance of quantitative characters in animals by gene markers: I. Methods. *Theoretical and Applied Genetics, 46,* 319–330.

Gelernter, J., Goldman, D. Risch, N. (1993). The A1 allele at the D_2 dopamine receptor gene and alcoholism. *Journal of the American Medical Association, 269,* 1673–1677.

Goldsmith, H. H. (1989). Behavior–genetic approaches to temperament. In G. A. Kohnstamm, J. E. Bates, & M. K. Rothbart (Eds.), *Temperament in childhood* (pp. 111–132). New York: Wiley.

Henderson, N. D. (1967). Prior treatment effects on open field behavior of mice—a genetic analysis. *Animal Behaviour, 15,* 365–376.

Hewitt, J. K. (1993). The new quantitative genetic epidemiology of behavior. In R. Plomin & G. E. McClearn (Eds.), *Nature, nurture, and psychology* (pp. 401–415). Washington, DC: American Psychological Association.

Hewitt, J. K., Eaves, L. J., Neale, M. C., & Meyer, J. (1988). Resolving cause of developmental continuity or "tracking." I. Longitudinal twin studies during growth. *Behavior Genetics, 22*, 293–317.

Loehlin, J. C., & Vandenberg, S. G. (1968). Genetic and environmental components in the covariation of cognitive abilities: An additive model. In S. G. Vandenberg (Ed.), *Progress in human behavior genetics* (pp. 261–285). Baltimore: Johns Hopkins University Press.

Martin, N. G., & Eaves, L. J. (1977). The genetical analysis of covariance structure. *Heredity, 38*, 79–95.

McClearn, G. E., Plomin, R., Gora-Maslak, G., & Crabbe, J. C. (1991). The gene chase in behavioral science. *Psychological Science, 2*, 222–229.

McKusick, V. A. (1990). *Mendelian inheritance in man* (9th ed.). Baltimore: Johns Hopkins University Press.

Nadeau, J. H. (1989). Maps of linkage and synteny homologies between mouse and man. *Trends in Genetics, 5*, 82–86.

Noble, E. P. (1993). The D2 dopamine receptor gene: A review of association studies in alcoholism. *Behavior Genetics, 23*, 119–129.

Omnitech Electronics. (1992). *User manual: Digiscan animal activity monitor, model RXYZCM(8)*. Columbus, OH: Author.

Onions, C. T. (1987). *The shorter Oxford English dictionary on historical principles*. Oxford, UK: Clarendon Press.

Ott, J. (1985). *Analysis of human genetic linkage*. Baltimore: Johns Hopkins University Press.

Plomin, R. (1987). Developmental behavioral genetics and infancy. In J. Osofsky (Ed.), *Handbook of infant development* (2nd ed., pp. 363–417). New York: Wiley-Interscience.

Plomin, R. (1990). The role of inheritance in behavior. *Science, 248*, 183–188.

Plomin, R. (1991). Genetic risk and psychosocial disorders: Links between the normal and abnormal. In M. Rutter & P. Casaer (Eds.), *Biological risk factors for psychosocial disorders* (pp. 101–138). Cambridge, UK: Cambridge University Press.

Plomin, R. (1994). *Genetics and experience: The developmental interface between nature and nurture*. Newbury Park, CA: Sage.

Plomin, R., & Bergeman, C. S. (1991). The nature of nurture: Genetic influence on "environmental" measures. *Behavior and Brain Sciences, 14*, 373–427.

Plomin, R., Chipuer, H. M., & Loehlin, J. C. (1990). Behavioral genetics and personality. In L. A. Pervin (Ed.), *Handbook of personality theory and research* (pp. 225–243). New York: Guilford Press.

Plomin, R., Coon, H., Carey, G., DeFries, J. C., & Fulker, D. W. (1991). Parent–offspring and sibling adoption analyses of parental ratings of temperament in infancy and early childhood. *Journal of Personality, 59*, 705–732.

Plomin, R., & DeFries, J. C. (1979). Multivariate behavioral genetic analysis of twin data on scholastic abilities. *Behavior Genetics, 9,* 505–517.

Plomin, R., & DeFries, J. C. (1981). Multivariate behavioral genetics and development: Twin studies. In L. Gedda, P. Parisi, & W. E. Nance (Eds.), *Progress in clinical and biological research: Twin research 3. Part B: Intelligence, personality, and development* (Vol. 69B, pp. 25–33). New York: Alan R. Liss.

Plomin, R., DeFries, J. C., & McClearn, G. E. (1990). *Behavioral genetics: A primer* (2nd ed.). New York: W. H. Freeman.

Plomin, R., Emde, R. N., Braungart, J. M., Campos, J., Corley, R., Fulker, D. W., Kagan, J., Reznick, J. S., Robinson, J., Zahn-Waxler, C., & DeFries, J. C. (1993). Genetic change and continuity from 14 to 20 months: The MacArthur Longitudinal Twin Study. *Child Development, 64,* 1354–1376.

Plomin, R., & McClearn, G. E. (1993). Quantitative trait loci (QTL) analyses and alcohol-related behaviors. *Behavior Genetics, 23,* 197–211.

Plomin, R., McClearn, G. E., Gora-Maslak, G., & Neiderhiser, J. M. (1991a). An RI QTL cooperative data bank for recombinant inbred quantitative trait loci analyses. *Behavior Genetics, 21,* 97–98.

Plomin, R., McClearn, G. E., Gora-Maslak, G., & Neiderhiser, J. M. (1991b). Use of recombinant inbred strains to detect quantitative trait loci associated with behavior. *Behavior Genetics, 21,* 99–116.

Plomin, R., & Neiderhiser, J. M. (1992). Genetics and experience. *Current Directions in Psychological Science, 1,* 160–163.

Plomin, R., & Nesselroade, J. R. (1990). Behavioral genetics and personality change. *Journal of Personality, 58,* 191–220.

Plomin, R., & Rende, R. (1991). Human behavioral genetics. *Annual Review of Psychology, 42,* 161–190.

Plomin, R., Rende, R., & Rutter, M. (1991). Quantitative genetics and developmental psychopathology. In D. Cicchetti & S. Toth (Eds.), *Rochester Symposium on Developmental Psychopathology: Vol. 2. Internalizing and externalizing expressions of dysfunction* (pp. 155–202). Hillsdale, NJ: Erlbaum.

Plomin, R., & Thompson, L. A. (1993). Genetics and high cognitive ability. In G. R. Bock & K. Ackrill (Eds.), *The origins and development of high ability* (pp. 67–84). New York: Wiley. (Ciba Foundation Symposium 178)

Riese, M. L. (1990). Neonatal temperament in monozygotic and dizygotic twin pairs. *Child Development, 61,* 1230–1237.

Roderick, T. H. (1980). Strain distributions of genetic polymorphisms in the mouse. In H. J. Heiniger & J. J. Dorey (Eds.), *Handbook on genetically standardized JAX mice* (pp. 19–34). Bar Harbor, ME: Jackson Laboratory.

Rowe, D. C., & Plomin, R. (1977). Temperament in early childhood. *Journal of Personality Assessment, 41,* 150–156.

Saudino, K. J., & Eaton, W. O. (1991). Infant temperament and genetics: An objective twin study of motor activity level. *Child Development, 62*, 1167–1174.

Saudino, K. J., & Eaton, W. O. (1993). *Genetic influences on activity level: An analysis of continuity and change from infancy to early childhood.* Manuscript submitted for publication.

Scott, J. P., & Fuller, J. L. (1965). *Genetics and the social behavior of the dog.* Chicago: University of Chicago Press.

Silverman, B. W. (1986). *Density estimation for statistics and data analysis.* London: Chapman & Hall.

Sing, C. F., & Boerwinkle, E. A. (1987). Genetic architecture of inter-individual variability in apolipoprotein, lipoprotein and lipid phenotypes. In G. Bock & G. M. Collins (Eds.), *Molecular approaches to human polygenic disease* (pp. 99–122). New York: Wiley.

Smith, D. L., Julian, A. J., Erwin, V. G., Jones, B. C., Chorney, M., McClearn, G. E., & Plomin, R. (1992). Dopamine D^2 RFLP in BXD RIs and assignment to chromosome 9. *Mouse Genome, 90*, 439–440.

Sobell, J. L., Heston, L. L., & Sommer, S. S. (1991). Delineation of genetic predisposition to multifactorial disease: A general approach on the threshold of feasibility. *Genomics, 12*, 1–6.

Sprott, R. L., & Staats, J. (1981). Behavioral studies using genetically defined mice—a bibliography (August 1979–July 1980). *Behavior Genetics, 11*, 73–84.

Stevenson, J., Batten, N., & Cherner, M. (1992). Fears and fearfulness in children and adolescents: A genetic analysis of twins data. *Journal of Child Psychology and Psychiatry, 33*, 977–985.

Taylor, B. (1989). Recombinant inbred strains. In M. F. Lyon & A. G. Searle (Eds.), *Genetic variance and strains of the laboratory mouse* (2nd ed., pp. 773–789). London: Oxford University Press.

Tiwari, J., & Terasaki, P. I. (1985). *HLA and disease associations.* New York: Springer.

Wilkinson, L. (1988). *Sygraph.* Evanston, IL: Systat.

PART TWO

Temperament, Biology, and Individual Adaptation

Psychoendocrine Studies of Temperament and Stress in Early Childhood: Expanding Current Models

Megan R. Gunnar

T he relationship between temperament and stress vulnerability has been the focus of considerable research in the last decade. Much of this research has been directed at understanding the psychobiology of behavioral inhibition (Clarke, Mason, & Moberg, 1988; Davidson, 1992; Kagan, Reznick, & Snidman, 1988; Matheny, 1989). Kagan, Snidman, and Arcus (1992) argued that about 15–20% of all Caucasian children are born with a physiology that biases them to become behaviorally inhibited in their 2nd year when confronted with unfamiliar people, places, or events.

The research reported in this chapter was supported by National Institute of Child Health and Human Development research grant HD-16494 and by National Institute of Mental Health Research Scientist Award MH-00946. I thank the many collaborators on the research cited herein, as well as Lynn Galle and the staff and students of the Shirley G. Moore Laboratory Nursery School in Minneapolis, Minnesota. I also thank Kaye O'Geay for her secretarial help. A portion of these data was presented at the 23rd Congress of the International Society of Psychoneuroendocrinology, Madison, Wisconsin, August 1992, and at the 60th meeting of the Society for Research in Child Development, New Orleans, Louisiana, March 1993.

Another 30–35%, they argued, are born with a physiology that biases them to approach the unfamiliar. Kagan et al. (1992) further argued that the physiologies that contribute to inhibition involve the amygdala and its projections to the motor system, the cingulate and frontal cortices, the hypothalamus, and the sympathetic nervous system. Inhibited children are described as having lower limbic thresholds for activation of the sympathetic–adrenomedullary system, whereas uninhibited children are described as having a higher threshold for the activation of this system.

The sympathetic–adrenomedullary system is one of the two major neuroendocrine stress-sensitive systems; the other major system is the hypothalamic–pituitary–adrenocortical (HPA) system (Palkovitz, 1987). Both systems affect metabolism, thereby increasing the energy available for action (Palkovitz, 1987). Both systems also influence emotions and cognitions (deWied & Croiset, 1991) as well as activity of the immune system (Borysenko, 1984). The sympathetic–adrenomedullary system produces its catecholamine end products—adrenaline and noradrenaline—very rapidly, and these catecholamines have a very short half-life. This system tends to be viewed as a quick response system. The HPA system, however, takes minutes to produce its end product, cortisol (although the releasing hormone, corticotropin releasing hormone, and the trophic hormone, ACTH, are produced quickly and also participate in behavioral aspects of the stress response). Some effects of cortisol may be observed as early as 10–20 min after stressor onset (de Kloet, 1991). However, many of the effects of cortisol occur over hours and even days. Thus, the HPA system is viewed as the long-acting response arm of the stress system.

Kagan's (Kagan et al., 1992) theory of behavioral inhibition emphasizes the sympathetic–adrenomedullary system. Nonetheless, all of the brain structures that Kagan et al. (1992) mention play a role in regulating both the sympathetic–adrenomedullary and HPA systems. Does behavioral inhibition also involve the HPA system? At one time it was expected that elevated cortisol levels would be characteristic of the behaviorally inhibited child. Indeed, Kagan, Reznick, and Snidman (1987) presented oft-cited evidence of higher cortisol levels in inhibited children compared with uninhibited children. However, elevated cortisol levels have not been consistently noted among behaviorally inhibited children (see Tennes &

Kreye, 1985), although evidence of increased sympathetic activity has been found more consistently (Kagan et al., 1992). As a result, researchers who are interested in behavioral inhibition have narrowed their attention to the sympathetic–adrenomedullary system, although some (e.g., Porges, 1992) have argued that the parasympathetic nervous system should also be considered.

Heart period and heart period variance have been used by Kagan (e.g., Kagan et al., 1987) and others to assess the sympathetic correlates of inhibition. Inhibited children are expected to have high and less variable cardiac activity. Both the parasympathetic and the sympathetic arms of the autonomic nervous system influence activity of the heart. Porges (1992) argued that cardiac activity in response to new situations and mild cognitive challenges, such as those used in research on inhibition, is largely parasympathetically mediated. Only when challenge has become intense and events are experienced as requiring "fight–flight" responses does the sympathetic–adrenomedullary system become highly involved. However, Kagan and colleagues (e.g., Kagan et al., 1987) measured urinary catecholamines, a more direct measure of sympathetic activity, and found higher concentrations for extremely inhibited children compared with uninhibited children. It seems likely that both sympathetic and parasympathetic arms of the autonomic nervous system support the greater and vigilant wariness noted among inhibited children.

Good evidence now exists that the psychological correlates of sympathetic–adrenomedullary and HPA activity differ dramatically. Lundberg and Frankenhaeuser (1980) showed that increased sympathetic activity is associated in adults with self-reports of attention, vigilance, and effort. In contrast, increased HPA activity is associated with reports of emotional distress. Ursin, Baade, and Levine (1978) noted similar results in a factor analytic study of cortisol and emotion among parachute trainees. Ursin et al. found that sympathetic activity accompanied effort, excitement, and vigilance, whereas HPA activity accompanied fear and other negative affects. Therefore, increased sympathetic activity may reflect increased effort and vigilance; however, whether this effort and vigilance is accompanied by distress and the activation of the HPA system may depend on other facets of the individual and the situation.

In this chapter, I argue that behavioral inhibition may actually function to reduce the likelihood of an HPA stress response in certain new situations. Behavioral inhibition may serve as a coping response that reduces the child's engagement with overly arousing and unpredictable events. This coping function of behavioral inhibition has been overlooked, perhaps because of the nearly exclusive focus on the sympathetic–adrenomedullary system—a system that tracks effort and not distress. Shifting focus to the HPA system, I present data showing that the coping context moderates the relationships between temperament and HPA activity. I also present data showing that in new situations, when social groups are first forming, shy children often have lower, not higher, cortisol levels compared with bold children. However, these relationships appear to reverse when social groups become more familiar. These patterns of relationships between behavioral inhibition and HPA activity require an expansion of current models of temperament and stress.

Coping Models

The model shown in Figure 1 is an expanded version of standard coping models of stress. It includes temperament and other factors that influence initial state. Aside from these variables, such models typically involve some form of appraisal, although the appraisal may be very rudimentary (cf. Lazarus & Folkman, 1984). When an event is encountered, if the child anticipates threat or is uncertain about whether bad things could happen, then attention and vigilance are heightened, and the child must attempt to cope somehow with the threat. To cope, the child must, on some level, appraise his or her resources. Resources include both the child's competencies (behavioral repertoire, abilities, etc.) and the affordances of the social and nonsocial environment. If resources are adequate, then the situation may be reappraised as benign. Alternatively, the situation may still be seen as threatening, but the child may expect that the people in the situation or his or her own actions will provide protection from threat. In either case, expectation of personal harm should be low and elevations in cortisol and yet greater increases in sympathetic–adrenomedullary activity should be avoided.

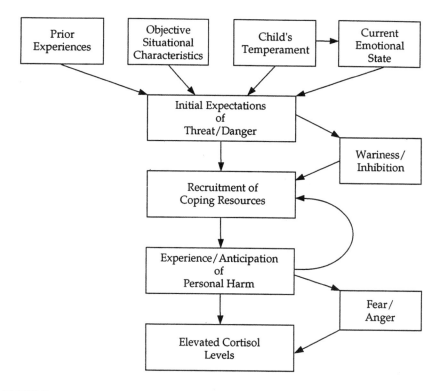

FIGURE 1. The "coping processes" component to an expanded model of the relationships of temperament with activation of the stress response of the adrenocortisol system (see Figure 6 for the full model).

Activity of the HPA system has been shown to be extremely sensitive to the moderating effects of coping resources and behaviors (Levine & Wiener, 1988). In the presence of adequate coping resources, the HPA stress response is often reduced or prevented even when the potential threat is quite salient. Temperament can be easily placed in the model by assuming that it is one of the factors that influences the child's initial response. Along with temperament, prior experiences, the objective characteristics of the event, and the child's emotional state at the time of the event are probably also important.

Inhibited children, as just discussed, are expected to have a lower threshold for anticipating threat in new, unfamiliar situations. They are, thus, expected to be in a state of vigilance more often or more intensely than are other children. The physiological differences noted for inhibited children may support these children's greater vigilance and wariness. Nonetheless, what actually happens among inhibited children after they have become vigilant in different contexts has not been explored. This information is essential if researchers are to make accurate predictions about the developmental sequelae of behavioral inhibition.

Coping Resources and Behavioral Inhibition in Early Childhood

Application of a coping model to the study of stress and behavioral inhibition requires attention to the coping resources of the young child. Because young children typically cannot cope with threat and uncertainty on their own, caregivers are the major coping resource (Campos, 1987). In research on nonhuman primates, Levine and Wiener (1988) showed that the presence of familiar conspecifics, especially the mother, reduces elevations in cortisol in response to threatening situations. My students and I have taken this one step further by examining whether the sensitivity and responsiveness of the caregiver also plays a role in modifying the HPA response.

Gunnar, Larson, Hertsgaard, Harris, and Brodersen (1992) experimentally manipulated the sensitivity and responsiveness of adult caregivers who were assigned to baby-sit 9-month-old infants during a 30-min period of maternal separation. In the low-responsiveness condition, labeled *caretaker*, female baby-sitters were instructed to interact very little with the baby as long as the baby did not fuss or cry. Once the baby became fussy, however, the caretaker baby-sitter responded sensitively and responsively. In the high-responsiveness condition, labeled *playmate*, the baby-sitter was instructed to be sensitive and responsive to the baby throughout the separation period. If the baby was content, then the baby-sitter sensitively supported the child's play; if the baby was fussy, then the baby-sitter sensitively comforted the child. At no time did the playmate baby-sitter withdraw her attention from the baby, as was the case in the caretaker condition.

To obtain baseline cortisol values, Gunnar et al. (1992) tested each child twice: once with the mother and once with the baby-sitter. The mothers were also asked to follow the baby-sitter protocol. Thus, some subjects experienced both their mother and the baby-sitter acting in the caretaker mode, whereas others experienced both the mother and baby-sitter acting in the playmate mode. The order of mother and baby-sitter sessions was, of course, counterbalanced, with about 1 week between each of these sessions. The results were striking (see Figure 2). There were no differences in salivary cortisol levels between the two conditions

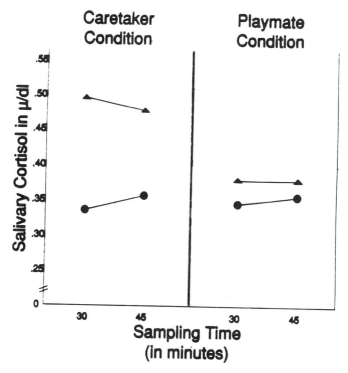

FIGURE 2. The relationships between caregiver behavior and cortisol responses to separation among 9-month-old infants who were randomly assigned to low-responsive (caretaker) versus high-responsive (playmate) condition. Lines with filled circles (no separation) depict salivary cortisol levels when the infants were with their mothers. Lines with filled triangles (separation) depict levels 30 and 45 min after the onset of a 30-min separation. From "The Stressfulness of Separation Among 9-Month-Old Infants: Effects of Social Context Variables and Infant Temperament" by M. Gunnar, M. Larson, L. Hertsgaard, M. Harris, and L. Brodersen, 1992, *Child Development, 63*, p. 295. Copyright 1992 by the Society for Research in Child Development. Reprinted by permission.

when the infants were with their mothers. However, when they were separated from their mothers, only the infants who were randomly assigned to the caretaker condition experienced a significant increase in cortisol. The more sensitive and responsive mode of caregiving completely prevented the HPA response to separation.

Gunnar et al. (1992) also found that the behavior of the caregiver moderated the relationships between temperament and the infant's cortisol response to separation. Loss of control is a potent stimulus of the adrenocortical stress response (Hanson, Larson, & Snowdon, 1976). Distress-to-limitations temperament can be viewed as a reflection of the infant's reactance to loss of control. Separation from mother involves a number of salient "losses" of control. Not only is the child blocked from access to the mother (loss of control over proximity), but the child also loses the mother's help in controlling the internal and external environment. Gunnar and Brodersen (1991) previously noted that distress-to-limitations temperament predicted cortisol responses to separation in several studies with 9-month-old infants. However, this relationship was also moderated by the behavior of the baby-sitter. Gunnar et al. (1992) found that the moderation of separation was significant in the caretaker condition ($r = .60, p < .01$) but not in the playmate condition ($r = -.16$, $ns; Z = 2.86, p < .01$; difference between the two correlations). Thus, the results of the Gunnar et al. (1992) caretaker–playmate study not only demonstrated the importance of the caregiver's behavior in mediating the effects of a stressor on the infant's HPA system, they also demonstrated that caregiver behavior moderates the relationships between temperament and HPA activity.

The analysis of the effects of quality of care has been extended to studies of the parent–child relationship. Nachmias and collegues (Colton et al., 1992; Nachmias, 1993) examined the responses of 18-month-old infants to three arousing events: a live female clown, a clown robot, and a puppet show. The events were chosen to examine toddler coping behaviors (Parritz, 1989), including their tendencies to approach versus avoid unfamiliar events. In many ways the events were similar to those used by Kagan (e.g., Kagan et al., 1987) and others to study behavioral inhibition. However, in this paradigm, the mother only remained silent for the first 3 min with each stimulus. For the last 3 min, the mother could do whatever she would normally do to help the child feel comfortable. The entire session took about 30 min, with breaks in between each stimulus event. Measures of salivary cortisol were taken at the beginning and at the end of the session. One week later, the toddlers and their mothers returned to the laboratory, and the Ainsworth Strange Situation (Ainsworth & Wittig, 1969) was conducted to examine the security of the attachment relationship. There is some evidence, although not uniform (e.g., Goldsmith & Alansky, 1987), that children in secure attachment relationships have a history of more sensitive and responsive parenting than do children in insecure attachment relationships.

To examine the role of attachment security in mediating HPA reactivity to the arousing event for inhibited toddlers, Nachmias and colleagues (Colton et al., 1992; Nachmias, 1993) first created groups of toddlers who were high and low on behavioral inhibition, which was determined by analyzing toddler inhibition during the first 3 min with each of the unfamiliar events. These scores were significantly correlated across the three stimulus events (range of rs = .25–.33, ps <.05), and the average of the three scores was also significantly correlated with parental reports of fearfulness that were completed before the child was brought in for testing (r = .36, p < .001). In all, the inhibition scores appeared to be reasonable indexes of temperament inhibition. The average inhibition score was then divided at the median to create two groups: high and low inhibition.

Before describing the results, I describe the predictions that were made based on the coping model outlined in Figure 1. First, elevations in cortisol should only be observed for the toddlers who were inhibited. The uninhibited toddlers should not be experiencing the situation as threatening and thus should not show elevations in cortisol. For the more inhibited toddlers, the coping model predicts elevations in cortisol only if the toddler is in an insecure attachment relationship. Toddlers who are in secure relationships should have sufficient coping resources (i.e., the sensitive and responsive parent) to reduce or prevent an HPA stress response even though they may remain behaviorally inhibited in response to the arousing, unfamiliar events.

The results of Colton et al. (1992) and Nachmias (1993) strongly bore out the predictions. Figures 3 and 4 depict the cortisol data from both the session with the three arousing, unfamiliar events and the strange-situation session. As predicted, the less inhibited children showed no evidence of an HPA response in either test session. However, both the inhibited A (avoidant-attached) infants and the inhibited C (resistant-attached) infants experienced significant elevations in cortisol, especially during the session with the three new events. In contrast, the inhibited secure infants did not experience any elevation in cortisol. The correlations between the maternal reports of toddler fearfulness and the children's cortisol responses were also examined. As found in Gunnar et al. (1992), the correlation was significant for the toddlers in insecure relationships who were theoretically receiving less sensitive care, $r = .39$, $p < .08$, but it was not significant for the toddlers in secure relationships who were theoretically receiving more sensitive care, $r = .16, ns$. Although

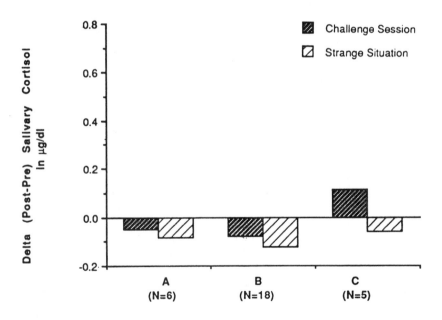

FIGURE 3.   Salivary cortisol change scores for low-inhibited toddlers as a function of attachment classification (A = avoidant, B = secure, C = resistant). Bars with shaded hatching (challenge session) reflect cortisol changes during testing with three novel events; hatched bars reflect data from the strange situation paradigm that was conducted 1 week later.

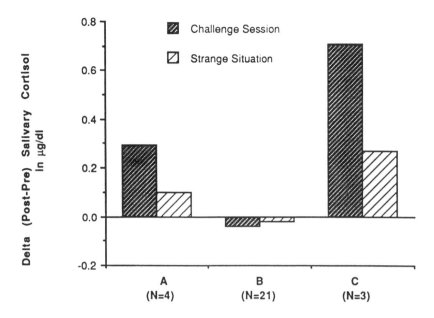

FIGURE 4. Salivary cortisol change scores for high-inhibited toddlers as a function of attachment classification (A = avoidant, B = secure, C = resistant). Bars with shaded hatching (challenge session) reflect cortisol changes during testing with three novel events; hatched bars reflect data from the strange situation paradigm that was conducted 1 week later.

these two correlations do not differ significantly from one another, quality of care again appeared to modify the relationships between temperament and HPA activity.

These data underscore the need to include "quality of care" in making predictions about the sequelae of behavioral inhibition (see also Suomi, 1987). Any prediction about the cumulative effects of exposure to threat on the developing nervous systems (cf. Gold, Goodwin, & Chrousos, 1988) would certainly have to be qualified by information on quality of care. Because Colton et al. (1992) did not select extreme groups of inhibited and uninhibited toddlers, there is no certainty that security of attachment would prevent a cortisol response among extremely inhibited toddlers. Nevertheless, it is possible. Of course, these data also suggest that an inhibited child in an insecure attachment relationship might frequently experience elevated cortisol levels even when encountering only mildly unfamiliar or threatening events.

Coping Behaviors and Inhibition

The repertoire of coping behaviors possessed by the child and the child's style of coping are part of the resources available to the child in unfamiliar or strange situations. Based on the research of Parritz (1989), Nachmias (1993) examined three major groups of coping behaviors that are observable in young children: (a) distraction–object orientation strategies (e.g., attending to familiar toys, putting objects between self and threatening event), (b) social strategies involving the seeking and sharing of information (e.g., affective sharing, social referencing), and (c) proximity and contact maintenance with caregivers (fuss at caregiver, approach caregiver, cling). As would be expected, more fearful or inhibited children use the first and third types of strategies more so than do less fearful or inhibited children. There are also developmental changes in the frequency with which these strategies are used. Parritz (1989) examined these changes between 12 and 18 months of age and found that social–informational strategies increased in frequency. This would be expected given the increase in language and cognitive skills between these ages (see also Kopp, 1989). However, despite the increase in social–informational strategies, these strategies were still used less often by toddlers than were distraction and proximity maintenance. Children also differ in which of these strategies they use most (Parritz, 1989). It seems reasonable to expect that strategy preference will influence the developmental trajectory of behavioral inhibition. Unfortunately, little is known about how temperament and coping styles interact or how they affect the child's subsequent behavior. This is an area that is much in need of research.

Researchers have not yet followed children to determine whether these differences in strategy styles persist and affect later inhibition. However, Nachmias and colleagues (Colton et al., 1992; Nachmias, 1993) did examine the relationships between these styles and attachment security. By covarying inhibition, these researchers found that distraction–object strategies were used more by avoidant-attached infants, social–informational strategies were used more by securely attached infants, and proximity maintenance was exhibited more by both the avoidant- and resistant-attached toddlers (see Figure 5). I suspect that fearful avoidant-attached infants do attempt to gain proximity with their attachment figure

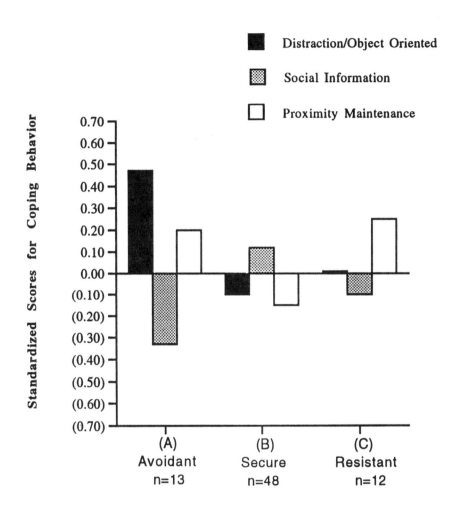

Attachment Classifications

FIGURE 5. Behaviors analyzed for toddlers exploring three novel, arousing events with inhibition covaried. Behaviors were grouped a priori into those organized around distraction–object manipulation, sharing and requesting information from mothers, and proximity and contact maintenance. The mother was free to help the child during the period when these data were scored. A = avoidant attachment, B = secure attachment, C = resistant attachment.

when not threatened by separation, as in the strange-situation paradigm. Use of this strategy would be consistent with the argument that avoidance is a defensive response for these children and not an indication of less intense attachment (Ainsworth, Blehar, Waters, & Wall, 1978). Interestingly, reliance on these strategies and differences among attachment groups increased once the mother was allowed to do whatever she would normally do to help the child, which suggests that whatever the mothers were doing increased the differences among these toddlers in their coping styles.

Stress Reactivity and the Assertive, Dominant Child

Coping models are perfectly adequate for predicting when behavioral inhibition might fail to result in elevated stress hormone levels. They are not adequate to explain why greater adrenocortical stress reactivity is sometimes associated with outgoing, assertive behavior. This pattern of relationships between cortisol and behavior has been noted in studies of nonhuman primates as well as in studies of humans (adults and children). Thus, in monkeys during the formation of social groups, the males who become dominant show greater activation of the HPA system than do the males who will assume more subordinate ranks (e.g., Manoque, Leshner, & Candland, 1975). Once the group has been together for a time, the dominant male has the lowest cortisol levels; however, when stressors are imposed on the group, the dominant animal once again mounts the greatest HPA stress response. Regarding human adults, Rose, Jenkins, Hurst, Livingston, and Hall (1982) reported similiar findings in their study of air traffic controllers. In this group, Rose et al. found that the men who exhibited the greatest increases in cortisol on high-traffic versus low-traffic days were the ones who were viewed as leaders by their peers and as the "best" at their jobs by their supervisors. Thus, during periods of increased demand and during periods of group formation, individuals who act as leaders appear to have higher, not lower, production of cortisol compared with less dominant, assertive individuals.

In three recent studies (deHaan, Buss, & Wegesin, 1993; Granger, Stansbury, Gunnar, Lopez, & Kauneckis, 1993; Gunnar, 1992), the investigators noted similar relationships in preschool children. All three studies were conducted with normally developing groups of middle-class to upper-middle-class children. The children were studied during their transition into either new nursery school classes (two studies) or play groups associated with mothers' groups (one study). Briefly, in a study of children who were entering the Shirley G. Moore Laboratory Nursery School classes for 2-year-olds at the University of Minnesota, deHaan et al. (1993) found that children who had higher cortisol levels on the first few days of school emerged as leaders later in the year according to teacher report, $r(18) = .45$, $p < .05$. The 2-year-olds who scored higher on teacher-reported leadership also engaged in more aggressive social interactions, $r(22) = .56$, $p < .01$, as might be expected among 2-year-olds. More aggressive social behaviors were also predicted by higher cortisol levels on the first days of class, $r(20) = .51$, $p < .05$. Finally, higher cortisol levels on the first days of class also tended to be correlated with parental reports of greater proneness to angry temperament using Goldsmith's Toddler Behavior Assessment Questionnaire, $r(15) = .46$, $p < .06$. None of the measures that might reflect greater behavioral inhibition (i.e., teacher reports of internalizing behavior, observations of more solitary play, or parental reports of social fearfulness) were associated with cortisol levels on these first days of class.

Similar results were obtained in a study of 2–5-year-old children who were studied during their first two sessions of a play group that was conducted as part of a mothers-of-preschoolers (MOPS) support group (Granger et al., 1993). Children who showed increases in cortisol from the beginning to the end of these 1.5-hr sessions were compared with children who showed stable or decreasing cortisol levels. The children who exhibited increased HPA activity (i.e., increased cortisol) during these initial sessions engaged in more appropriate social interactions, $F(1, 34) = 8.04$, $p < .01$, and were rated by observers to be less overcontrolled (i.e., less isolated, worried, fearful, concerned, anxious) than were the children who showed stable or decreasing cortisol levels, $F(1, 34) = 13.82$, $p < .01$. Using Rothbart's Child Behavior Questionnaire, parents also tended to describe their children who increased in cortisol as more prone to anger–frustration, $F(1, 22) = 3.24$, $p < .10$, and less shy, $F(1, 22) = 3.93$, $p < .10$, than children who exhibited stable or decreasing cortisol concentrations.

Finally, Gunnar (1992) examined the adrenocortical activity of 3–5-year-old children during the 1st few weeks of a new nursery school year. Most of the children in the study were familiar with the school; however, they were adjusting to new classmates and, in all but two cases, a new head teacher. Perhaps because many of the children were familiar with the school and one another, cortisol on the 1st day of class was not correlated with child temperament or later behavior. Because there were so many cortisol samples per child, the distribution of each child's cortisol values could be examined. Some children had approximately the same cortisol concentrations for each day of testing. Others, however, frequently showed evidence of slight elevations in cortisol. These children had a distinct positive skew in their cortisol distributions. This positive skew was captured by computing the difference between the 75th and 50th percentile of each child's distribution of cortisol values. Children with higher difference scores exhibited more positive skew. These values ranged from 0.01 µg/dl to 0.24 µg/dl during this period of transition into nursery school.

Median and positive skew measures for cortisol should reveal different aspects of HPA activity and regulation. The median value should reflect basal cortisol activity in the nursery school context because it is extremely difficult to produce chronic elevations of cortisol even under extremely stressful circumstances (for a review see Rose, 1980). Self-righting processes operating at every level of the HPA system tend to return cortisol to basal ranges of concentration with prolonged or repeated stress. The positive skew measure, in contrast, should reflect the extent to which HPA activity escaped from basal regulation intermittently in the nursery school context. I suspect that a greater positive skew reflects the child's experience of stress or challenge in the classroom. Thus, median (possibly basal activity) and positive skew (possibly reactivity) cortisol measures may be correlated with different aspects of temperament, and this is exactly what was found.

Children with greater positive skew in their distribution of cortisol values were described by parents (Rothbart's Child Behavior Questionnaire) as being more active, $r(18) = .64, p < .01$, more drawn to highly stimulating play, $r(18) = .49, p < .05$, more impulsive, $r(18) = .46, p < .05$, and less shy, $r(18) = -.41, p < .10$. Higher median cortisol values during this period of transition or group formation were correlated modestly with teacher reports (completed 6–8 months later) of less internalizing behaviors, $r(28) = -.32, p < .10$, greater popularity, $r(28) = .39$, $p < .05$, and more independent, competent classroom behavior, $r(28) = .40, p < .05$.

Several possible confounds of these results have been examined and ruled out. Moderate activity, such as exercise associated with playing tennis among adults, does not elevate cortisol (Nicolson, 1992). Among these nursery school children, cortisol levels following an exercise period in the gym did not differ from levels following an equal period of classroom activity, although running was encouraged in the gym and prohibited in the classroom. Thus, it is unlikely that physical activity differences caused the just-noted correlations with temperament. So far, these studies have failed to find significant sex differences, nor have they found that controlling for age affects the cortisol–temperament correlations.

Coping models can explain why inhibited children might fail to show increased cortisol levels during group formation in contexts that are rich with coping resources and options. However, coping models do not explain why the more assertive, outgoing children show increases in HPA activity. Why do they not show similarly low cortisol levels?

In Figure 6, an expanded coping model is depicted that might account for these findings. When coping resources are adequate, shy children can reduce feelings of personal threat by engaging in familiar, pleasant, solitary activities and by using their teachers as sources of security and comfort. These same resources are available to assertive, outgoing children; however, outgoing children approach new situations in a very different manner. Rather than avoiding new and exciting elements of the situation, they are drawn to them. In particular, they are drawn to interactions with other children. Interacting with other preschoolers, especially unfamiliar ones, contains elements of uncertainty and risk. In addition to the occasional hit, slap, or punch, there are frequent mild conflicts over toys and playmates. These mild conflicts provide pre-

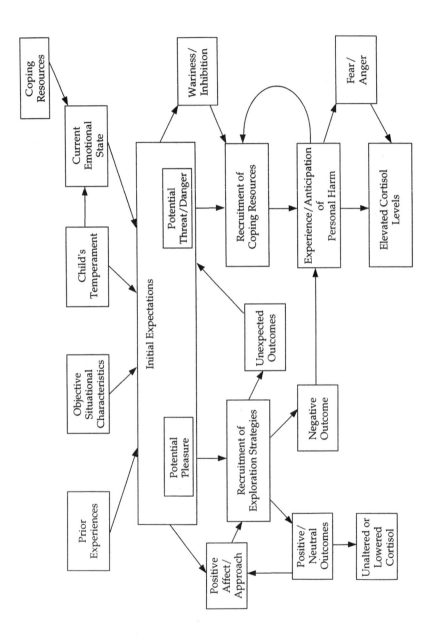

FIGURE 6. Expanded model of stress–temperament relationships including approach, as well as an inhibition–avoidance component.

schoolers with opportunities to develop more mature social skills. There-fore, although teachers keep an eye on such conflicts, they encourage children to manage them as independently as possible. It seems likely that the preschooler who chooses to play with other children risks more frequent conflicts. During group formation, the outcome of these conflicts may be less certain, thus enhancing their stressfulness.

Returning to the model in Figure 6, one may assume that assertive, outgoing children take more risks, especially social risks. When entering a new class or play group, this risk-taking may sometimes result in pleasant experiences but may also increase the chance that the child will have negative encounters with other children. When the encounters are negative, and especially if they involve physical aggression, the child may experience personal harm, which may produce elevated cortisol concen-trations. Even when physical aggression is not involved, the outgoing child may experience anger and frustration, which are emotions that may stimulate increased cortisol. For socially competent children in low-risk group-care settings, these frustrating outcomes should decrease in fre-quency as the child becomes more familiar with the other children and the rules of the class. Thus, one would expect that HPA reactivity would be associated with more active, outgoing, and assertive behavior, primarily when social relationships are unstable. In well-run classes with normally developing peers, once the group has been together for a period of time, outgoing children should be less likely to exhibit elevations in cortisol. In contrast, over time in safe contexts, shy children should begin to attempt more risky social interactions. Teachers will certainly begin to encourage this once the shy children have had a chance to adjust. There-fore, over time, HPA reactivity would be positively correlated more with shy, fearful temperament in safe group-care contexts.

Data that are consistent with this latter expectation were obtained from studies (Pierce, Tout, & deHaan, 1993; Tout, Hart, Pierce, & Wegesin, 1993) of the morning and afternoon classes ($N = 61$) at the Shirley G. Moore Laboratory Nursery School later during the school year (i.e., winter and spring quarters). Cortisol was again sampled over a number of class days, and median values and positive skew scores for each child were calculated. The winter–spring distribution of positive skew values was truncated at the high end, which suggests less HPA reactivity than during the fall quarter group-formation period. Furthermore, in contrast to the period of group formation, winter–spring positive skew was negatively correlated with teacher reports of leadership, $r = -.32$, $p < .05$, and positively correlated with teacher-reported internalizing behaviors, $r = .24$, $p < .06$, and parental reports of sensitivity to discomfort, $r = .31$, $p < .05$ (Pierce et al., 1993). Winter–spring observations of the children during class (Tout et al., 1993) revealed that children with a more positive skew to their cortisol distributions during the winter–spring period also played less with the other children, $r = -.37$, $p < .004$, and spent more time playing alone, $r = .41$, $p < .001$.

Thus, children who were more negatively reactive to stimulation and less outgoing exhibited more HPA reactivity than did more assertive, outgoing children when the social situation was stable and familiar. These results, taken together with those of the three group-formation studies (deHaan et al., 1993; Granger et al., 1993; Gunnar, 1992) that were described earlier, suggest that there is a reorganization of relationships between temperament and stress reactivity with the transition from group formation to stable, low-conflict group periods. My students and I are currently collecting data to replicate and extend the examination of this reorganization.

Summary and Conclusion

Current models of stress and temperament fail to predict many of the results that are described in this chapter. These models fail because they do not take coping processes into account, nor do they consider the role of temperament in children's selection of lower versus higher risk activities. Using measures of activity of the HPA system, I have shown that the availability of coping resources mediates the impact of potentially stressful events for children. I argued that, for young children, adults control most of the child's coping resources via the adults' sensitivity and responsiveness to the child 's signals. Furthermore, I showed that sensitive and responsive care and secure emotional relationships reduce or prevent the HPA response to potentially threatening situations. These buffering effects are most apparent for children whose temperaments predispose them to respond to the stressor.

I described the results of three studies (deHaan et al., 1993; Granger et al., 1993; Gunnar, 1992), all of which showed assertive, outgoing children to be more stress-reactive during periods of group formation. Because these are precisely the situations that one would expect to be highly threatening to more inhibited, shy children, these results point strongly to the need for more complex coping models of stress–temperament relationships. I argued that children's temperaments affect their choice of activities in new situations and that children modulate the impact of new events through these choices. Shy children reduce the likelihood of threatening encounters through playing more by themselves, whereas assertive, outgoing children increase the risk of such encounters by seeking out interactions with unfamiliar peers.

The expanded coping model of stress–temperament relationships provided in Figure 6 should help guide predictions in future studies. In particular, this model should be useful in the choice of situations and groups to study. What happens to stress–temperament relationships under conditions of less competent, secure adult caregiving? In more chaotic group-care situations with fewer toys, poorly trained caregivers, and/or more disruptive and aggressive peers, it is very possible that assertive, outgoing children would continue to be more HPA-reactive even after the groups have been together for long periods. This should place the assertive children at greater risk than inhibited children for the negative neuroendocrine consequences of stress (e.g., impaired immune functioning, altered cognitive processes). Alternatively, if quality of care and other factors affecting coping resources are too greatly reduced, or if the adult caregivers become major sources of threat (e.g., abuse and neglect), then differences in HPA activity that are related to child temperament may become altered, and all children may become highly HPA stress-reactive. To the extent that reactivity of neuroendocrine systems affect neurobiological development and help to determine normal and pathological developmental trajectories, it is crucial that researchers understand the coping processes that affect stress reactivity and the impact of different caregiving contexts in supporting or impeding children's coping competencies. Only after these processes and contexts have been integrated into models will researchers be in a position to make accurate predictions about the sequelae of individual differences in emotional temperament.

References

Ainsworth, M. D. S., Blehar, M. C., Waters, E., & Wall, S. (1978). *Patterns of attachment: A psychological study of the strange situation.* Hillsdale, NJ: Erlbaum.

Ainsworth, M. D. S., & Wittig, B. A. (1969). Attachment and the exploratory behavior of one-year-olds in a strange situation. In B. M. Foss (Ed.), *Determinants of infant behavior*, (Vol. 4, pp. 113– 136). London: Methuen.

Borysenko, J. (1984). Stress and coping and the immune system. In J. D. Matarazzo, S. M. Weiss, J. A. Herd, N. E. Miller, & S. M. Weiss (Eds.), *Behavioral health* (pp. 248–260). New York: Wiley.

Campos, B. E. (1987). Coping with stress during childhood and adolescence. *Psychological Bulletin, 101,* 393–403.

Clarke, A. S., Mason, W. A., & Moberg, G. P. (1988). Differential behavioral and adrenocortical response to stress among three macaque species. *American Journal of Primatalogy, 14,* 37–52.

Colton, M., Buss, K., Mangelsdorf, S., Brooks, C., Sorenson, D., Stansbury, K., Harris, M., & Gunnar, M. (1992, May). *Relations between toddler coping strategies, temperament, attachment and adrenocortical stress responses.* Poster presented at the 8th International Conference on Infant Studies, Miami, FL.

Davidson, R. J. (1992). Emotion and affective style: Hemispheric substrates. *Psychological Science, 1,* 39–43.

deHaan, M., Buss, K., & Wegesin, D. (1993, March). *Development of peer relations: Effects of prior experience, temperament, and stress reactivity on adjustment to preschool.* Poster presented at the 60th annual meeting of the Society for Research in Child Development, New Orleans, LA.

de Kloet, E. R. (1991). Brain corticosteroid receptor balance and homeostatic control. *Frontiers in Neuroendocrinology, 12,* 95–164.

deWied, D., & Croiset, G. (1991). Stress modulation of learning and memory processes. In G. Jasmin & L. Proschek (Eds.), *Stress revisited: 2. Systemic effects of stress: Vol. 15. Methodological achievements in experimental pathology* (pp. 167–199). Basel: Karger.

Gold, P. W., Goodwin, F. K., & Chrousos, G. P. (1988). Clinical and biochemical manifestations of depression: Relation to the neurobiology of stress, part 2. *New England Journal of Medicine, 319,* 413–449.

Goldsmith, H. H., & Alansky, J. A. (1987). Maternal and infant temperamental predictors of attachment: A meta-analytic review. *Journal of Consulting and Clinical Psychology, 55,* 805–816.

Granger, D. A., Stansbury, K., Gunnar, M., Lopez, S., & Kauneckis, D. (1993). *Relations between behavioral style and behavioral and neuroendocrine responses to social challenge in preschoolers.* Manuscript submitted for publication.

Gunnar, M. (1992, August). *Psychoendocrine studies of adaptation in normally functioning nursery school children.* Invited address for the XXIII Congress of International Society of Psychoneuroendocrinology, Madison, WI.

Gunnar, M., & Brodersen, L. (1991). Infant stress reactions to brief maternal separations in human and nonhuman primates. In T. Field, P. McCabe, & N. Schneiderman (Eds.), *Stress and coping in infancy and childhood* (pp. 1–18). Hillsdale, NJ: Erlbaum.

Gunnar, M., Larson, M., Hertsgaard, L., Harris, M., & Brodersen, L. (1992). The stressfulness of separation among 9-month-old infants: Effects of social context variables and infant temperament. *Child Development, 63,* 290–303.

Hanson, J. D., Larson, M. E., & Snowdon, C. T. (1976). The effects of control over high intensity noise on plasma cortisol levels in rhesus monkeys. *Behavioral Biology, 16,* 333–338.

Kagan, J., Reznick, J. S., & Snidman, N. (1987). The physiology and psychology of behavioral inhibition. *Child Development, 58,* 1459–1473.

Kagan, J., Reznick, J. S., & Snidman, N. (1988). Biological bases of childhood shyness. *Science, 240,* 167–173.

Kagan, J., Snidman, N., & Arcus, D. M. (1992). Initial reactions to unfamiliarity. *Current Directions in Psychological Science, 1,* 171–174.

Kopp, C. B. (1989). Regulation of distress and negative emotions: A developmental view. *Developmental Psychology, 25,* 343–354.

Lazarus, R. S., & Folkman, S. (1984). *Stress, appraisal and coping.* New York: Springer.

Levine, S., & Wiener, S. G. (1988). Psychoendocrine aspects of mother–infant relationships in nonhuman primates. *Psychoneuroendocrinology, 13,* 143–154.

Lundberg, U., & Frankenhaeuser, M. (1980). Pituitary–adrenal and sympathetic–adrenal correlations of distress and effort. *Journal of Psychosomatic Research, 24,* 125–130.

Manoque, K. R., Leshner, A. I., & Candland, D. K. (1975). Dominance status and adrenocortical reactivity to stress in squirrel monkeys (*Saimiri sciureus*). *Primates, 16,* 457–463.

Matheny, A. P. (1989). Children's behavioral inhibition over age and across situations. *Journal of Personality, 57,* 215–235.

Nachmias, M. (1993, March). *Maternal personality relations with toddler's attachment classification, use of coping strategies, and adrenocortical stress response.* Paper presented at the 60th annual meeting of the Society for Research in Child Development, New Orleans, LA.

Nicolson, N. A. (1992). Stress, coping and cortisol dynamics in daily life. In M. W. deVries (Ed.), *The experience of psychopathology: Investigating mental disorders in their natural settings* (pp. 219–232). New York: Cambridge University Press.

Palkovitz, M. (1987). Organization of the stress response at the anatomical level. *Progress in Brain Research, 72,* 47–55.

Parritz, R. H. (1989). *An examination of toddler coping in three challenging situations.* Unpublished doctoral thesis, University of Minnesota.

Pierce, S., Tout, K., & deHaan, M. (1993, March). *Individual differences in neuroendocrine activity in preschoolers: Relations to temperament characteristics.* Poster presented at the 60th annual meeting of the Society for Research in Child Development, New Orleans, LA.

Porges, S. W. (1992). Vagal tone: A physiologic marker of stress vulnerability. *Pediatrics, 90,* 498–504.

Rose, R. M. (1980). Endocrine responses to stressful psychological events. *Psychiatric Clinics of North America, 3,* 251–275.

Rose, R. M., Jenkins, C. D., Hurst, M., Livingston, L., & Hall, R. P. (1982). Endocrine activity of air traffic controllers at work: II. Biological, psychological and work correlates. *Psychoneuroendocrinology, 7,* 113–123.

Suomi, S. J. (1987). Genetic and maternal contributions to individual differences in rhesus monkey biobehavioral development. In N. A. Krasnegor, E. M. Blass, M. A. Hofer, & W. P. Smotherman (Eds.), *Prenatal development: A psychobiological perspective* (pp. 397–420). San Diego, CA: Academic Press.

Tennes, K., & Kreye, M. (1985). Children's adrenocortical responses to classroom activities and tests in elementary school. *Psychosomatic Medicine, 47,* 451–460.

Tout, K., Hart, J., Pierce, S., & Wegesin, D. (1993, March). *Day-by-day correspondences between preschoolers' social behavior and fluctuations in salivary cortisol levels.* Poster presented at the 60th annual meeting of the Society for Research in Child Development, New Orleans, LA.

Ursin, H., Baade, E., & Levine, S. (1978). *Psychobiology of stress.* San Diego, CA: Academic Press.

CHAPTER 8

Individual Differences in the Biological Aspects of Temperament

Susan D. Calkins and Nathan A. Fox

I n this chapter, we examine data from our own laboratory that provides evidence for a biology–temperament link. In presenting these data, we pose a number of specific questions regarding the relationships between biology and temperament, including the issue of identifying individual differences and establishing stability of such differences. We also address the question of environmental influences on temperament and examine the interplay between biology and environment in producing particular outcomes. In trying to answer questions regarding the biological component of temperament, we discuss in some detail the findings of two longitudinal samples of infants who were followed from birth to 4 years of age and birth to 14 months of age, respectively. The first study involved

The research presented in this chapter was funded, in part, by National Institutes of Health grant HD-17899 to Nathan A. Fox and by a grant from the John D. and Catherine T. MacArthur Foundation Transitions in Early Childhood Network. A summary of the data in this chapter was presented at the Ninth Occasional Temperament Conference, Bloomington, Indiana, October 1992.

an unselected sample of infants (Calkins & Fox, 1992; Fox, 1989; Stifter & Fox, 1990) and examined the role of the attachment relationship as a regulator of early infant reactivity. The second longitudinal study examined the links among biology, temperament, and social behaviors in a sample of infants selected for their profiles of extreme negative and positive reactivity (Calkins, Fox, & Marshall, in press). These studies allow us to address the issue of the underlying biological component of temperament and the role of the environment in modifying temperament. We conclude with suggestions for the manner in which studies of the origin and outcome of the biology–behavior link may be addressed in future research.

What Do We Mean When We Say That Temperament Is "Biologically Driven"?

The premise that is inherent in most theories of temperament is that the infant's expressed personality or behavioral disposition is a function of some early biological or genetic tendency (Goldsmith et al., 1987). The degree to which this early tendency exerts its influence, and the way in which it may be altered by environmental factors, differs according to theorists (Buss & Plomin, 1984; Goldsmith & Campos, 1982; Rothbart, 1981, 1989). For this reason, much of the research in the area of infant and child temperament has focused on two issues. First, a number of laboratories have undertaken the task of studying physiological or biological phenomena early in life in an effort to relate such phenomena to the display in infancy of particular behavioral traits (Fox, 1989; Fox, Bell, & Jones, 1992; Gunnar, Manglesdorf, Larson, & Hertsgaard, 1989; Kagan, Reznick, & Snidman, 1987; Porges, 1991; Stifter & Fox, 1990). The second focus of a considerable amount of temperament research has been the dual issues of the role of the environment in altering early behavioral tendencies and the consequent stability through infancy and early childhood of these tendencies (Calkins & Fox, 1992; Carey, 1981; Lerner & Lerner, 1983; Matheny, Wilson, & Nuss, 1984; Matheny, Wilson, & Thoben, 1987; Riese, 1987; Rothbart, 1986). It is important to note, however, that these two foci—biology and environment—within the temperament literature often overlap, with most researchers acknowledging the difficulty of isolating one from the other.

In our own research, we have examined the biology–temperament link in several studies using measures of regional brain electrical activity (the electroencephalogram; EEG) in infants and young children (Calkins et al., 1993; Davidson & Fox, 1989; Fox et al., 1992; Fox & Davidson, 1988, 1991). Researchers who are interested in the pattern of activation between the right and left hemispheres have computed ratio scores of the difference in power or energy between the two hemispheres. These ratio or difference scores reflect relative differences in power and indicate the degree to which one hemisphere or region in a hemisphere exhibits greater activation than does a homologous region in the other hemisphere. There is an extensive literature on asymmetrical EEG patterns during verbal versus spatial tasks (Davidson, Chapman, Chapman, & Henriques, 1990) and during the expression and perception of different emotions (Davidson, 1984; Fox & Davidson, 1986). Research on brain lateralization and emotion has provided insights into the understanding of the central nervous system components that are involved in both the expression and modulation of affect. Studies on the relationships between patterns of brain electrical activity and emotion in human infants (Davidson & Fox, 1982, 1989; Dawson, Hill, Panagiotides, Grofer, & Levy, 1989; Fox & Davidson, 1986, 1987, 1988) were, in fact, motivated by an attempt to explain variations in emotional reactivity and regulation that were the result of brain injury or surgical intervention (see Fox & Davidson, 1984). This research led to speculation that individual differences in threshold for either negative or positive affects are, in part, a function of the pattern of hemispheric activation, particularly in the frontal region.

In our research, we have examined the relationship between the pattern of brain electrical activity found in the frontal scalp leads and the dimension of temperament that has been described by different researchers as *approach–withdrawal* or *sociability–inhibition* (Buss & Plomin, 1984; Kagan, Reznick, Clarke, Snidman, & Garcia-Coll, 1984; Thomas, Chess, & Birch, 1970). Fox (1991) argued that one significant function of lateralization of approach–withdrawal tendencies is to allow the individual expression of emotions that are associated with either approach or withdrawal.

In observing infant behavior, differences in this personality dimension are quite apparent. Some infants are quick to approach, explore, and express positive affect under conditions of novelty, whereas others are more reticent in such circumstances and, in extreme cases, may display intense negative affect and withdrawal when confronted with novel situations. These differences appear quite early in infancy and have been tied by Kagan and colleagues to differences in the limbic system that are observable in heart rate and cortisol changes (Kagan et al., 1987; Kagan, Reznick, & Snidman, 1988; Kagan & Snidman, 1991).

We have studied infant approach and withdrawal responses to a host of different stimuli and have correlated these responses with asymmetrical activity in the left or right anterior scalp regions (Fox & Davidson, 1986, 1987). These data indicate that when approach behaviors are elicited there is greater relative left frontal activation, that is, greater power suppression in the EEG over the left frontal region. In contrast, when withdrawal behaviors are elicited, we have found greater relative right frontal activation, that is, greater power suppression in the EEG over the right frontal region. These differences have been observed in children from very early infancy through preschool age (Calkins & Fox, 1992; Fox, 1991; Fox et al., 1992; Fox & Davidson, 1986). In infancy, these EEG findings probably reflect subcortical asymmetries, quite possibly in the amygdala, the nuclei of which are involved in fear conditioning and emotional responses and which have direct connections to the anterior frontal regions of the cortex.

The asymmetry index that we compute reflects the relative degree of power in each of the two homologous regions. It assumes that suppression of power in a particular frequency band reflects activation in that band (Lindsley & Wicke, 1974). The score is derived by subtracting left power from right power. A positive score indicates left activation, whereas a negative score indicates right activation. The difference between the two hemispheres in any region is not, however, static and is constantly dynamically changing. Thus, there are at least two ways in which a left or right asymmetry score can be obtained. To obtain a left asymmetry score, right power could increase while left power remains unchanged. The difference would be positive and reflect greater relative left activation; or right power could remain static and left power could decrease, which again would produce a positive difference score and a left asymmetry index. Two similar paths could be produced for the negative asymmetry score that reflects right activation.

Fox (in press) argued that these different means to a positive or negative asymmetry index reflect different functional processes of approach or withdrawal. For example, a left (positive) asymmetry index may be the result of left activation (increased approach behavior) or right hypoactivation (decreased modulation of approach–loss of inhibition). Similarly, a right (negative) asymmetry index may be the result of right activation (increased withdrawal behavior) or left hypoactivation (decreased approach or decreased positive affect). Obviously, these represent only four distinct possibilities, and there are many others. We have, however, used this model to examine differences between infants and children in the manner in which left or right frontal asymmetry is expressed (Fox et al., 1994). We have attempted to determine whether the manner in which the two hemispheres are dynamically interrelated may be associated with the behavioral tendencies of the infant or child (Fox et al., 1994).

Recent research from our lab has confirmed these activation–behavior patterns (Fox et al., 1994). We observed a group of 4-year-old children in same-gender play quartets. The quartet session consisted of a 15-min free-play period, a clean-up session, a period during which each child had to stand and talk about his or her recent birthday party, a ticket sorting–cooperation task, and a second 15-min free-play period. The children's behaviors were coded using Rubin's Play Observation Scale (1989), and measures of inhibited behavior, social competence, and compliance were computed. In a separate session, each child returned to the lab, and EEG was recorded. We examined relationships between the pattern of EEG activity and the child's behavior in the quartet (Fox et al., 1994). To examine the effects of specific changes in left or right frontal EEG power, we devised a metric that allows us to compute site-specific power for each EEG scalp lead (Fox et al., 1994). We then examined relationships between left and right frontal power and sociability and inhibition at 4 years of age. The results suggest that both patterns of behavior are a function of activation or hypoactivation of the left frontal region. Children who exhibited high degrees of sociability displayed increased left frontal activation, whereas those who exhibited inhibition and reticence were likely to display increased left frontal hypoactivation (absence of approach behaviors).

In describing the EEG–behavioral findings from our studies, we have focused on the importance of the frontal region of the cortex and its role in emotion. It is well known that the frontal region has direct connections with certain areas of the limbic system and, in particular, those areas that are involved in the conditioning of certain emotions (Nauta, 1971; LeDoux, 1987). In addition, the frontal region plays an important role in the modulation of emotion and, by extension, in the regulation of certain temperament dispositions.

Our approach to the study of temperament is guided by the research of Goldsmith and Campos (1982) and Rothbart (1981). They view temperament as the pattern of expression of specific discrete emotions. An infant's tendency to express either positive or negative emotions, the intensity of that expression, and the modulation of that expression are the factors involved in defining temperament. Frontal activity and the development of both frontolimbic and frontoparietal connections are most probably involved in the ontogeny of modulation of emotional reactivity and hence the regulation of temperament behaviors (Fox, in press). Our research is actively involved in identifying the patterns of frontal activity that are associated with the expression of certain temperament-associated positive or negative emotions and the change in frontal activity that is associated with the modulation of this emotional expression.

How Early in Life Can These Biological Differences Be Detected?

In our recent longitudinal study (Calkins et al., 1993), we have examined behavioral tendency differences in infants at 4 months of age and have identified three discrete groups whose responses to novel stimulation are markedly different. We examined the pattern of brain electrical activity exhibited by these infants, as well as their responses to novelty, or tendency to display inhibited behavior, during early toddlerhood (Calkins et al., 1993). Kagan and Snidman (1991) argued that inhibited behavior has its roots in the child's threshold for arousal, which may be evident as early as 4 months of age. Children who displayed high amounts of negative affect and motor activity in response to novel stimuli, for example, tended to be fearful at 9 and 14 months of age (Kagan & Snidman, 1991). A recent finding of our laboratory complements the Kagan finding of early negative reactivity, which is reflected in high amounts of motor activity accompanied by irritability. We found a relationship between early irritability, insecure attachment, and behavioral inhibition in toddlerhood (Calkins & Fox, 1992). If high motor activity–high negative reactivity reflects a temperament pattern that predicts subsequent problems in social development, then it is possible that infants who display these behaviors in the 1st year of life also display right frontal activation. Asymmetrical frontal activation may be a physiological correlate of the predisposition to display behavioral inhibition in the face of novelty.

To address the possible relationships between early behavioral and physiological reactivity, we selected infants on the basis of their responses to a series of novel visual and auditory stimuli at 4 months of age. The first group that we selected exhibited high amounts of motor activity and negative affect in response to the procedures at 4 months of age. The second group displayed high amounts of motor activity accompanied by positive affect, whereas the third group was low on the three dimensions. When these infants were seen in the laboratory at 9 months of age, we found, as predicted, differences in frontal EEG asymmetry as a function of 4-month-old motor–affect group membership. Infants who were selected for high motor activity–high negative affect exhibited greater relative right frontal activation, whereas infants who were selected for high motor activity–high positive affect exhibited left frontal activation. The infants who had been classified as low motor activity–low affect could not be classified as showing a distinctly left or right pattern of activation. Thus, selection of infants on the basis of specific behavioral patterns was related to the pattern of brain electrical activity that was recorded when these same infants were 9 months of age. It is of obvious importance to examine whether this EEG pattern is present at the age that infants were identified in this study, and we are currently in the process of collecting EEG data on a new cohort of infants at 4 months of age.

A second finding from Calkins et al. (1993) suggests that the identification of early behavioral or temperament reactivity differences may help predict social behaviors during the 2nd year of life. The infants from our longitudinal study returned to the laboratory at 14 months and were observed in a series of brief episodes that were designed to elicit approach versus withdrawal in the face of novelty. The infants spent 5 min in a novel playroom with their mothers. The time spent near the mother, the negative affect they displayed during the episode, and their latency to speak spontaneously and play with the toys were summed and used as an index of inhibition. A stranger then entered the room, and similar measures of inhibition were obtained during a 3-min episode as the stranger tried to engage the child in play. Finally, the stranger presented the child with a novel toy (a battery-powered robot), and again, measures of inhibition were coded from the episode. The scores from the novel room, novel person, and novel toy episode were summed to create a single index of inhibited behavior. In examining the behavior of the three groups of infants, it was found that there were significant differences among them. Infants who displayed high motor activity–high negative reactivity at 4 months of age were the most withdrawn and inhibited infants in the laboratory at 14 months of age. Infants who displayed high motor activity–high positive reactivity were the most approach-oriented and uninhibited. Furthermore, although there was no direct association between 9-month EEG and inhibition, it was found that infants who were highly reactive and had negative affect at 4 months of age and who displayed a pattern of right frontal activation at 9 months of age were most inhibited at 14 months of age (Calkins et al., 1993). These findings, which link early behavioral and physiological reactivity to subsequent social behavior, suggest that researchers might be able to identify early in infancy the temperament precursors to social interaction and social adjustment. In the next section, we address the issue of the continuity of such early traits.

How Stable Are the Individual Differences in Biological–Behavioral Links?

In assessing the stability of biological–behavioral indices of temperament, consideration must be given to several issues beyond simply whether there is a correlation across age. First, with development, the structural characteristics of some behaviors often change in a nonlinear fashion. Although certain physical characteristics might change in a linear fashion with age, one will seldom observe linear behavioral change with age. Behaviors that reflect the approach–withdrawal dimension, for example, change as the child develops. Although it may be quite appropriate to measure the trait by assessing irritability or exploration to novelty at one age, such measures at an older age may be inappropriate to accurately assess this dimension. In part, the problem becomes one of assessing the degree to which the child has learned to regulate or manage the temperament tendency, and the researcher must devise ways of capturing such regulatory efforts (see also Gunnar, chapter 7 in this book).

A second issue that has particular relevance for the biological assessment of temperament concerns the change in the unit of measurement itself. This issue is particularly relevant for the study of EEG relationships in infancy and early childhood. As the child develops, there is an increase in power in higher frequencies (Bell & Fox, in press). For example, in infancy, the majority of power is in the lower frequency bands, in the range that would be termed delta or theta (1–3 Hz or 4–7 Hz). With age, power increases in the higher frequency bands and decreases in the lower bands (Bell & Fox, in press). This change in the pattern of EEG spectral power clearly makes the problem of studying the stability of EEG complex.

Using the longitudinal data from our infants studies, we have addressed this issue of EEG stability and have identified a number of interesting patterns (Fox et al., 1992). Unlike the data from adult studies, the correlations for EEG power that we have observed for a given frequency band are significant but quite low (.3 to .4, compared with correlations of .9 found in adult studies). Second, the correlations for EEG asymmetry are similarly low but are higher for selected samples (e.g., the high motor activity–high negative affect group) than they are for the general population. This observation complements quite nicely the findings regarding the behavior of selected groups of infants. For example, Reznick, Gibbons, Johnson, and McDonough (1989) observed only modest stability among unselected samples of infants and young children. However, these behavioral tendencies are more coherent and stable among the group of infants who fall at the extremes of the behavioral dimensions of irritability and arousal. For this reason, Kagan and colleagues have maintained that infants who exhibit these behaviors represent a distinct type of temperament (Kagan et al., 1988), which is observed in some 10–15% of the population (Kagan & Snidman, 1991).

The issues that are related to the assessment of behavioral and physiological aspects of temperament suggest that there is a degree of stability that may be measured across the infancy and early childhood period but that this stability may be found most often within a group of infants who display a distinct temperament profile. One important issue that is relevant to the question of stability concerns the extent to which both behavioral and biological aspects of temperament are subject to modification through the influence of environmental forces. We address this issue in the next section.

What Effect Does the Environment Have on Individual Differences in Temperament?

In describing our biological model of temperament, we acknowledge that the predisposition to display withdrawal–negative affect versus approach–positive affect must be regulated and adapted to the changing and varied environments with which the infant is confronted. Although we have focused much of our research on the biological component of temperament, it is clear that these behavioral patterns occur within a social context. Responsivity to the approach of a stranger and maternal separations, for example, are not independent of the child's history and experience in dyadic interactions. Indeed, our view is that the expression of certain temperament dispositions involves both an expressive component and a regulatory component.

The emotion that the infant displays, then, is a function of both the event and the process of socialization experienced by the infant. Although the individuality of temperament plays a role in infant behavioral and physiological responsivity, and this responsivity influences social interactions, there is also a clear process of parental feedback that allows the child to modulate emotional responses. That is, the child's interactions with a parent provide the context for learning skills and strategies for managing emotional reactivity (Calkins, in press).

Using data from our earlier longitudinal study of infant temperament, attachment, and the development of behavioral inhibition in an unselected sample (Calkins & Fox, 1992; Fox, 1989; Stifter & Fox, 1990), we proposed a model to describe the ways in which the child's environment, and specifically the parental caretaking to which the child is exposed, influences the display of particular early reactive tendencies (Calkins & Fox, 1992; Fox & Calkins, 1993). Specifically, the model hypothesizes that early emotional reactivity influences caretaking style, which in turn affects the child's ability to cope with emotion-eliciting events. This model was tested by examining data from a longitudinal study (Calkins & Fox, 1992) from birth to 2 years of age. Emotional reactivity at birth was examined using a pacifier withdrawal procedure. At 5 months of age, infant response to arm restraint and a novel visual display was observed, and negative affect to these events was thought to reflect frustration and fear, respectively. At 14 months of age, the infants and mothers were observed in the Ainsworth strange situation paradigm (Ainsworth & Wittig, 1969). At 24 months of age, the infants' reactions to novelty (a novel playroom, stranger, clown, robot, and tunnel) were observed. Relationships were found between attachment and inhibited behavior, which thereby suggests that some elements of the infant's attachment relationship may influence the infant's ability to cope with novelty. Specifically, infants whose attachment relationship with their mother was classified as insecure–resistant at 14 months of age were significantly more likely to display inhibited behavior in the laboratory at 24 months of age than were infants who were classified as insecure–avoidant. Furthermore, there was evidence that early negative reactivity interacted with attachment classification to produce inhibited behavior. Infants who were classified as insecure–resistant, and who had not cried in response to the arm restraint procedure, were the most inhibited 2-year-olds in the study. These infants had also been more likely than their insecure–avoidant counterparts to cry in response to the presentation of novel stimuli at 5 months of age.

The results of this longitudinal study led to a number of conclusions regarding the role of infant emotional reactivity in development. First, there seem to be multiple types of reactivity in early infancy. In that study, two types—reactivity to frustration and reactivity to novelty—were identified, and psychophysiological correlates of at least one type of reactivity were found (for a full account of these findings see Stifter & Fox, 1990). The child who is reactive to frustrating events may not be reactive to novel events. Second, infants with a characteristic pattern of reactivity may display their own styles of adaptive regulatory strategies that allow them to deal effectively with novelty. Children who, early on, have difficulty regulating their distress may be difficult to sooth and may use withdrawal as a means of coping with novelty. Children with a low tolerance for frustration may regulate their reactivity through approach and interest behaviors. In addition, parents may assist children in coping with their reactivity. Infants with a low tolerance for frustration may be allowed enough autonomy that they often approach novelty and avoid proximity to the parent. Infants with a low threshold for negative affect may not have as much autonomy and may therefore fail to approach novelty. These infants would also likely experience added stress in a novel situation when the parent is not present to provide support. Gunnar's chapter (chapter 7 in this book) provides additional data on this general point.

Although this model of parental and self-regulation explains the changes that one may see in infant reactivity as a function of modulation of affect, the degree to which the modification of behavioral tendencies affects the underlying physiological substrate is not clear. Indeed, the observation that the underlying biological predisposition predicts early behavioral tendencies, which are then subject to both internal and external sources of regulation, suggests that the biology–environment relationship is characterized by the dynamic interaction of the two, as opposed to one force subjugated to the other. In the next section, we examine this idea more fully.

Do Biology or Environment Work Singly or in Combination to Predict Behavioral Outcomes?

Data from both our selected (Calkins & Fox, 1992; Fox, 1989; Stifter & Fox, 1990) and unselected (Calkins et al., 1993) samples are clearly relevant to the discussion of the relative influence of biology and environment on the display of behavioral traits. First, recall that the 14–month behavior of the infants in the selected sample seemed to be a function of the types of reactivity that they displayed at 4 months of age. The early behavioral profiles of these infants, which reflected their reactivity to novel stimuli, were predictors of later behavior in response to novel people and events. In addition, the type of reactivity that was displayed at 4 months of age was related to the pattern of brain electrical activity that was observed at 9 months of age. The pattern of relationships confirms past affect–EEG findings and encourages us to hypothesize that the greater relative right frontal activation found in the sample of irritable and active infants is an important physiological correlate of early infant temperament.

However, an important issue from this selected sample concerns the lack of an observed relationship between brain electrical activity and inhibited behavior at 14 months of age. There are several possible explanations for this finding. First, it is possible that the behavior that was observed at 14 months of age reflects normative fear responses as well as individual difference–based fear responses. Some infants may display inhibited behavior in this situation due to normal developmental responses to strangers, whereas the inhibited behavior of other infants may reflect the lower threshold to novel stimuli that is integral to the profile of the inhibited child. The EEG–behavior relationships may be confounded by these different types of fear reactions that are observed at 14 months of age. A second hypothesis is that the pattern of brain electrical activity, although a correlate of some infant temperament reactivity, is not a direct predictor of behavior at 14 months of age due to some as-yet untested environmental influence. The responses of the infants to novel events and people at 14 months of age may reflect, to some degree, both their level of reactivity to these types of events as well as the regulation of that reactivity. This study has not yet assessed the role of external regulators of infant reactivity that may serve to modulate their affective response to particular events. So, for example, it is possible that some infants who display early manifestations of negative reactivity and right frontal activation are successful in managing distress due to the intervention of a competent caretaker. As we continue our research with this selected sample, we may be able to identify these sorts of external influences on infant and toddler behavior.

The data that we have collected to this point, from both unselected (Calkins & Fox, 1992) and selected longitudinal samples (Calkins et al., 1993), indicate that there are individual differences in reactivity during the first few months of life. Furthermore, these differences predict the child's responses to a variety of developmental challenges, particularly the ability to regulate affective response to novelty. Our research with a selected sample of 4-month-olds who were followed to age 14 months indicates that these differences may best be described in terms of (a) patterns of affective and motor reactivity and (b) brain electrical activity. The physiological and behavioral differences in arousal of either the approach or withdrawal system that were observed in the sample of selected infants may have important consequences for social–personality development. Importantly, although these predispositions by themselves are not necessarily sufficient to predict social outcome, it is most likely that at least two factors interact in this process. The first factor (discussed in the previous section) is parental response to infants with certain extreme patterns of temperament. Our demonstration of differences in inhibited behavior among infants with insecure–resistant and insecure–avoidant attachment relationships leaves open the possibility that caretakers' responses to particular displays of temperament may mold the child's repertoire of social behaviors. Caregivers may reinforce, ignore, or intervene in the case of a child who has a low threshold for novelty. Each pattern may produce a different pathway and end point in social development. Our research has yet to explore the many complex pathways that are possible. The second factor involved in the outcome of social behavior is the number of novel or stressful events to which the infant is exposed. Infant negative reactivity may be exacerbated in the case of a child who is exposed to a high degree of stress or novelty, and the child's responses to subsequent exposures may be marked by more extreme displays of fear and withdrawal.

Our data indicate, then, that differences in frontal asymmetry, by themselves, do not predict subsequent social development. Across a number of studies, we have identified clear early relationships between behavioral and physiological reactivity (Calkins et al., 1993; Fox, 1989; Stifter & Fox, 1990). Nevertheless, we assume that these relationships work in concert with both internal and external sources of regulation that serve to manage behavioral displays of reactivity. Biology and environment interact in a dynamic fashion to produce particular behavioral outcomes. Our position is that biology is the motivating force and that the extent of the environment's influence will depend on both how extreme an infant's disposition or temperament is as well as the strength of the environmental forces that may act on the endogenous disposition.

Conclusion

In this chapter, we have used data from our longitudinal studies of the physiological underpinnings of early infant temperament to support a model of temperament that we view to be biologically based. We described two longitudinal studies, which provide evidence that there are clear individual differences in both early infant reactivity to novel events as well as later individual differences reflecting differential abilities to manage affect and behavioral response tendencies in the face of novel social and nonsocial events. In the first study, we identified a relationship between attachment classification and later behavior toward novel events. In the second longitudinal study with a selected sample of infants, we identified a strong link between this early reactivity and brain electrical activity. Important evidence is lacking, however, on the best way to predict the relative power of biology versus environment in predicting outcome. That is, how may we predict whether there will be a direct influence of early biological predispositions that may be impervious to external influence, or whether early predispositions may be ameliorated by caretaker intervention? We believe that this question represents a significant challenge to the study of the biological component of temperament; the goal for future investigations will be to develop methodologies to examine this issue.

References

Ainsworth, M. D. S., & Wittig, B. A. (1969). Attachment and the exploratory behavior of one-year-olds in a strange situation. In B. M. Foss (Ed.), *Determinants of infant behavior* (Vol. 4, pp. 113–136). London: Metheun.

Bell, M. A., & Fox, N. A. (in press). Brain development over the first year of life: Relations between EEG frequency and coherence and cognitive and affective behavior. In G. Dawson & K. Fischer (Eds.), *Human behavior and the developing brain.* New York: Guilford Press.

Buss, A., & Plomin, R. (1984). *Temperament: Early developing personality traits.* Hillsdale, NJ: Erlbaum.

Calkins, S. D. (in press). Origins and outcomes of individual differences in emotion regulation. In N. A. Fox (Ed.), *Monographs of the Society for Research in Child Development: The biology and behavior of emotion regulation.* Chicago: Society for Research in Child Development.

Calkins, S. D., & Fox, N. A. (1992). The relations among infant temperament, attachment, and behavioral inhibition at 24 months. *Child Development, 63,* 1456–1472.

Calkins, S. D., Fox, N. A., & Marshall, T. R. (in press). Behavioral and physiological antecedents of inhibition in infancy. *Child Development.*

Carey, W. B. (1981). The importance of temperament–environment interactions for child health and development. In M. Lewis & L. Rosenblum (Eds.), *The uncommon child* (pp. 31–55). New York: Plenum.

Davidson, R. J. (1984). Affect, cognition and hemispheric specialization. In C. E. Izard, J. Kagan, & R. Zajonc (Eds.), *Emotion, cognition and behavior* (pp. 320–365). New York: Cambridge University Press.

Davidson, R. J., Chapman, J. P., Chapman, L. J., & Henriques, J. B. (1990). Asymmetrical brain electrical activity discriminates between psychometrically-matched verbal and spatial cognitive tasks. *Psychophysiology, 27,* 528–543.

Davidson, R. J., & Fox, N. A. (1982). Asymmetrical brain activity discriminates between positive and negative affective stimuli in human infants. *Science, 218,* 1235–1237.

Davidson, R. J., & Fox, N. A. (1989). The relation between tonic EEG asymmetry and ten-month-old infant emotional responses to separation. *Journal of Abnormal Psychology, 98*, 127–131.

Dawson, G., Hill, D., Panagiotides, H., Grofer, L., & Levy, A. (1989, April). *Frontal EEG activity of female and male toddlers during emotion-eliciting situations.* Paper presented at the annual meeting of the Society for Research in Child Development, Kansas City, MO.

Fox, N. A. (1989). Psychophysiological correlates of emotional reactivity during the first year of life. *Developmental Psychology, 25*, 364–72.

Fox, N. A. (1991). If it's not left, it's right: Electroencephalogram asymmetry and the development of emotion. *American Psychologist, 46*, 863–72.

Fox, N. A. (in press). Dynamic cerebral process underlying emotion regulation. In N. A. Fox (Ed.), *Monographs of the Society for Research in Child Development: The biology and behavior of emotion regulation.* Chicago: Society for Research in Child Development.

Fox, N. A., Bell, M. A., & Jones, N. A. (1992). Individual differences in response to stress and cerebral asymmetry. *Brain and Cognition, 8*, 161–184.

Fox, N. A., & Calkins, S. D. (1993). Pathways to aggression and social withdrawal: Interactions among temperament, attachment, and regulation. In K. Rubin & J. Asendorpf (Eds.), *Social withdrawal, inhibition and shyness in childhood* (pp. 81–100). Hillsdale, NJ: Erlbaum.

Fox, N. A., & Davidson, R. J. (1984). Hemispheric specialization and the development of affect. In N. A. Fox & R. J. Davidson (Eds.), *The psychobiology of affective development* (pp. 353–381). Hillsdale, NJ: Erlbaum.

Fox, N. A., & Davidson, R. J. (1986). Taste-elicited changes in facial signs of emotion and the asymmetry of brain electrical activity in human newborns. *Neuropsychologia, 24*, 417–22.

Fox, N. A., & Davidson, R. J. (1987). EEG asymmetry in ten-month-old infants in response to approach of a stranger and maternal separation. *Developmental Psychology, 23*, 233–240.

Fox, N. A., & Davidson, R. J. (1988). Patterns of brain electrical activity during the expression of discrete emotions in ten-month-old infants. *Developmental Psychology, 24*, 233–236.

Fox, N. A., & Davidson, R. J. (1991). Hemispheric specialization and attachment behaviors: Developmental processes and individual differences in separation protest. In J. L. Gewirtz & W. M. Kurtines (Eds.), *Intersection points in attachment research* (pp. 147–164). Hillsdale, NJ: Erlbaum.

Fox, N. A., Rubin, K. H., Calkins, S. D., Marshall, T. R., Coplan, R. J., Porges, S. W., & Long, J. M. (1994). *Frontal activation asymmetry and social competence at four years of age: Left frontal hyper- and hypoactivation as correlates of social behavior in preschool children.* Manuscript submitted for publication.

Goldsmith, H. H., Buss, A. H., Plomin, R., Rothbart, M. K., Thomas, A., Chess, S., Hinde, R., & McCall, R. B. (1987). Roundtable: What is temperament? Four approaches. *Child Development, 58,* 505–529.

Goldsmith, H. H., & Campos, J. J. (1982). Toward a theory of infant temperament. In R. N. Emde & R. J. Harmon (Eds.), *The development of attachment and affiliative systems* (pp. 231–283). New York: Plenum.

Gunnar, M. R., Manglesdorf, S., Larson, M., & Hertsgaard, L. (1989). Attachment, temperament and adrenocortical activity in infancy: A study of psychoendocrine regulation. *Developmental Psychology, 25,* 355–363.

Kagan, J., Reznick, J. S., Clarke, C., Snidman, N., & Garcia-Coll, C. (1984). Behavioral inhibition to the unfamiliar. *Child Development, 55,* 2212–2225.

Kagan, J., Reznick, J. S., & Snidman, N. (1987). The physiology and psychology of behavioral inhibition in children. *Child Development, 58,* 1459–1473.

Kagan, J., Reznick, J. S., & Snidman, N. (1988). Biological bases of childhood shyness. *Science, 240,* 167–171.

Kagan, J., & Snidman, N. (1991). Infant predictors of inhibited and uninhibited profiles. *Psychological Science, 2,* 40–44.

LeDoux, J. E. (1987). Emotion. In S. Plum (Ed.), *Handbook of physiology: The nervous system. Vol. 5: Higher functioning of the brain* (pp. 419–460). Bethesda MD: American Physiological Society.

Lerner, J. V., & Lerner, R. M. (1983). Temperament and adaptation across life: Theoretical and empirical issues. In P. B. Baltes & O. G. Brim (Eds.), *Life-span development and behavior* (pp. 197–231). San Diego, CA: Academic Press.

Lindsley, D. B., & Wicke, J. D. (1974). The electroencephalogram: Autonomous electrical activity in man and animals. I. R. Thompson & M. N. Patterson (Eds.), *Bioelectric recording techniques* (pp. 465–479). San Diego, CA: Academic Press.

Matheny, A. P., Jr., Wilson, R. S., & Nuss, S. M. (1984). Toddler temperament: Stability across settings and over ages. *Child Development, 55,* 1200–1211.

Matheny, A. P., Jr., Wilson, R. S., & Thoben, A. S. (1987). Home and mother: Relations with infant temperament. *Developmental Psychology, 23,* 323–331.

Nauta, T. W. H. (1971). The problem of the frontal lobes: A reinterpretation. *Journal of Psychiatric Research, 8,* 161–187.

Porges, S. W. (1991). Vagal tone: An autonomic mediator of affect. In J. Garber & K. A. Dodge (Eds.), *The development of emotion regulation and dysregulation* (pp. 69–88). New York: Cambridge University Press.

Reznick, J. S., Gibbons, J., Johnson, M., & McDonough, P. (1989). Behavioral inhibition in a normative sample. In J. S. Reznick (Eds.), *Perspectives on behavioral inhibition* (pp. 25–49). Chicago: University of Chicago Press.

Riese, M. L. (1987). Temperament stability between the neonatal period and 24 months. *Developmental Psychology, 23,* 216–222.

Rothbart, M. K. (1981). Development of individual differences in temperament. In M. E. Lamb & A. L. Brown (Eds.), *Advances in developmental psychology* (pp. 37–86). Hillsdale, NJ: Erlbaum.

Rothbart, M. K. (1986). Longitudinal observation of infant temperament. *Developmental Psychology, 22*, 356–365.

Rothbart, M. K. (1989). Biological processes in temperament. In G. A. Kohnstamm, J. E. Bates, & M. K. Rothbart (Eds.), *Temperament in childhood* (pp. 77–110). New York: Wiley.

Rubin, K. H. (1989). *The Play Observation Scale (POS)*. University of Waterloo, Waterloo, Ontario, Canada.

Stifter, C. A., & Fox, N. A. (1990). Infant reactivity: Physiological correlates of newborn and 5-month temperament. *Developmental Psychology, 26*, 582–588.

Thomas, A., Chess, S., Birch, H. G. (1970). The origin of personality. *Scientific American, 223*(2), 102–109.

CHAPTER 9

Impulsive Unsocialized Sensation Seeking: The Biological Foundations of a Basic Dimension of Personality

Marvin Zuckerman

An ancient Hindu belief asserts that the world rests on a giant turtle. A student asked his guru what that turtle rests on. The master replied: "Another larger turtle." The student pressed on: "And what does that turtle rest on?" The guru answered as before. The student persisted with the same question and the guru, growing more testy with each query, responded with the same answer. When they reached the seventh turtle, the guru stopped the regress by proclaiming: "And there it ends because seven is a magic number."

The seven psychobiological turtles of personality are shown in Figure 1. At the top are broad personality traits (Turtle 1), which are based on specific forms of consistent social behavior patterns and covert, but habitual, cognitive reactions to certain classes of situations (Turtle 2). Social behavior and cognitive constructions depend on learning (Turtle 3). But individual differences in what is learned from the broad range of

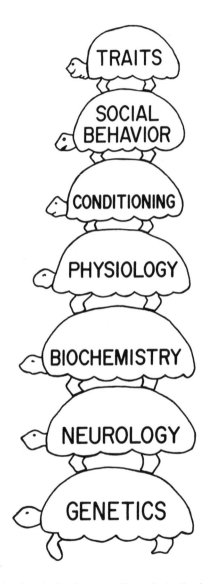

FIGURE 1. Levels of analysis of personality traits in the form of seven turtles.

social models depend on differences in biological makeup as well as specific learning experiences. Two individuals who are exposed to the same range of environmental influences may not learn the same things. This was axiomatic to Pavlov and his students, who developed a biologically based theory of temperament to account for individual differences in conditionability (Pavlov, 1927/1960). Pavlov proposed that differences in cortical physiology (Turtle 4) were the basis of differences in conditioning and social behavior, and this approach developed into arousal theories for personality (H. J. Eysenck, 1967; Strelau & Eysenck, 1987). Differences in physiology, in turn, depend on differences in the biochemistry of the nervous system, including neurotransmitters, regulatory enzymes, and hormones (Turtle 5). Specific neurotransmitters define neurological pathways and neural nuclei that vary in structural characteristics among individuals (Turtle 6). Up to this point, there is an arguable "turtle or egg" problem: Which level is more basic in the causal sense? Does a turtle move because of the movements of turtles below it, or does the movement of the turtle above disturb the turtle below and cause it to move? However, Turtle 7 (genetics) is quite basic because it is the fertilized turtle egg (zygote) from which all other turtles emerge and is largely responsible for the differences in neurological structure and biochemical trait characteristics of the organism.

This "levels" approach is not reductionistic. Each turtle is a separate animal worthy of study in itself. But a complete understanding of a particular turtle's movements requires observation of the turtles below because when one of them moves, the turtles above must also move. The converse is definitely possible but not inevitable. After all, turtles have rather thick shells.

This is a psychobiological model. An equivalent set of social turtles could be constructed from the individual to the family, to the class, to the society, and to the culture. These would be influences on Turtle 2 in the psychobiological hierarchy, but this would strain the limits of the metaphor and the reader may already be thinking that this is a "shell game."

There are two approaches to the definition of the levels underlying a personality trait. The "top-down" approach starts by defining the basic personality traits in humans and then studying their characteristic manifestations in behavior and correlated physiological phenomena. When one gets to pharmacological and neurological levels, it usually becomes necessary to use animal models because the biological activities and structures in the brain are not directly accessible to direct observation or experimentation in humans. At the genetic level, studies of the traits or behavior in human twins and adoptees may be used to disentangle and weigh the relative influences of heredity and environment, but experiments in selective breeding and correlational studies of pure strains must be confined to other species.

A "bottom-up" approach begins with significant biological substrates of behavior that can be studied by direct brain stimulation or selective lesioning of brain structures or neurochemical pathways. Animal models for human traits are used. Concepts of the behavioral functions of the biological systems that are developed from these experiments are then extended upward to human behavior and traits through correlational studies using indirect measures of activity in the relevant brain systems, such as the metabolites of brain neurotransmitters found in blood, urine, or cerebrospinal fluid. The positron emission tomography scan offers some possibility for direct observation of brain activity below the levels accessible to the electroencephalograph, but it is generally too expensive to use in experiments and too limited in definition of structures to be of much use in personality research, although some research using positron emission tomography has been performed (e.g., Haier, Sokolski, Katz, & Buchsbaum, 1987).

The research of Eysenck (H. J. Eysenck, 1967; H. J. Eysenck & Eysenck, 1985) and Zuckerman (1991) are examples of the top-down approach, whereas the research by Gray (1982) represents the bottom-up approach. Theoretically, the two approaches could yield the same solutions, and in some areas they do. But in other areas, the answers may be different because the human and animal models of behavior are not really equivalent, and the functions of biological systems may differ across species. To equate the activity of jogging in a human with the activity of a rat in a running wheel may be overlooking some important functional differences in determining activity in the two species.

An Alternative Five-Factor Model for Personality Traits

The trait that is the central focus of this chapter is part of a five-factor model that differs from what has been called the "Big Five." The alternative five-factor model (Zuckerman, in press) emerged from factor analyses (Zuckerman, Kuhlman, & Camac, 1988; Zuckerman, Kuhlman, Thornquist, & Kiers, 1991) of scales regarded by psychobiological theorists as measures of basic personality or temperament and extensively used in psychobiological research (e.g., impulsivity, sensation seeking, activity, emotionality, sociability, aggression, socialization). Highly replicable three- and five-factor models were found. The five-factor model included Sociability, Neuroticism–Anxiety, Impulsive Unsocialized Sensation Seeking (ImpUSS), Aggression–Hostility, and Activity. The ImpUSS factor consisted of Sensation-Seeking, Impulsivity, and Autonomy scales at the positive pole and Socialization, Need for Cognitive Structure (planning), Inhibition of Aggression, and Responsibility scales at the negative pole. Eysenck's (S. B. G. Eysenck, Eysenck, & Barrett, 1985) Psychoticism (P) scale was the best marker for the ImpUSS factor.

Questionnaire scales were developed for the alternative five-factor model (Zuckerman, Kuhlman, Joireman, Teta, & Kraft, 1993). A factor analysis of these scales and the primary scales from the revised Eysenck Personality Questionnaire (S. B. G. Eysenck et al., 1985) and Costa and McCrae's (1992) NEO Personality Inventory revealed substantial convergence between the Eysenck Big Three, the Big Five, and the alternative five-factor models. Impulsive sensation seeking was part of a factor that was also defined by Eysenck's P scale and Costa and McCrae's Conscientiousness scale. Impulsive sensation seeking also correlated highly with other impulsivity and sensation-seeking scales, as well as Block and Block's (1980) Ego Control scale.

Social and Risky Behavior Associated With P-ImpUSS

Most of the relationships between the P-ImpUSS dimension and social behavior have thus far been demonstrated with only one or two of the components of the P-ImpUSS supertrait, particularly sensation seeking (Zuckerman, 1979, 1983a, 1984) and the P scale (H. J. Eysenck & Eysenck, 1976). Sensation seeking and P are strongly associated with social deviance as expressed in criminal or rule-violation behaviors (H. J. Eysenck & Eysenck, 1976; Horvath & Zuckerman, 1993; Newcomb & McGee, 1991), excessive use of alcohol and illegal drugs (H. J. Eysenck & Eysenck, 1976; Newcomb & McGee, 1991; Zuckerman, 1983b, 1987), and reckless and drunken driving or speeding (Arnett, 1991; Donovan, Queisser, Salzberg, & Umlauf, 1985; Furnham & Saipe, 1993; Zuckerman & Neeb, 1980).

P-ImpUSS types also tend to engage in more varied types of sexual behavior with many partners (H. J. Eysenck & Eysenck, 1985; Zuckerman, Tushup, & Finner, 1976). Sensation seeking in college men is correlated with sexual activities that put them at higher risk for AIDS despite the recognition of the riskiness of their behavior (Horvath & Zuckerman, 1993). Appraised risk also does not prevent high-sensation seekers from smoking (Zuckerman, Ball, & Black, 1990) or using illegal drugs (Zuckerman, 1983b). P and impulsivity are also associated with multiple substance abuse (O'Boyle & Barratt, 1993). P-scale scores for gay or bisexual men who are infected with the HIV virus correlate with the continuation of unsafe sexual behavior despite the risks for others (McCown, 1993).

The social behavior of high-sensation seekers who are observed in the laboratory shows that they express high levels of verbal and nonverbal positive social affect through eye-gaze, smiling, laughing, vocalizing, and self-disclosure (Capella & Green, 1984; Franken, Gibson, & Mohan, 1990). Sensation-seeking women interacting with their male partners engage in more eye-gaze and verbalization than do low-sensation seekers (Thornquist, Zuckerman, & Exline, 1991). Love relationships of high-sensation seekers tend to be casual and hedonistic with a lack of strong commitment and a history of many relationships. But despite this pattern in relationships, there tends to be a high level of assortative mating for the trait: High-sensation seekers tend to marry "highs," and low-sensation seekers tend to marry other "lows" (Farley & Davis, 1977; Farley & Mueller, 1978; Lesnik-Oberstein & Cohen, 1984).

Demographic Characteristics

Age and gender are the major demographic variables influencing P-ImpUSS. Scores for both the P and Sensation-Seeking scales decline steadily with age from the teens through the 60s (see Figures 2 and 3), and men's scores are higher than those for women, particularly in the younger age groups (H. J. Eysenck & Eysenck, 1976; Zuckerman, 1979; Zuckerman & Neeb, 1980). Antisocial personality disorder in the general population is 4 to 7 times more prevalent in men than in women and declines with age after a peak in the 20s (Robins et al., 1984). Why are men more antisocial than women, and why does the trait and diagnosis decline with age after the early adult years? Socialization may account for some of the gender differences, and acquired wisdom may account for the decline with age, but it is also possible that age changes in certain neurotransmitters, enzymes, and gonadal hormones may influence the age and gender differences in P-ImpUSS and antisocial behavior.

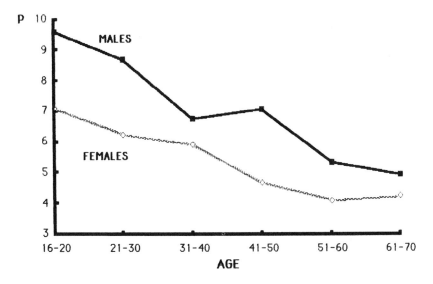

FIGURE 2. Relationship between age and male and female scores on the Psychoticism (P) scale from the revised Eysenck Personality Questionnaire. The data are from "A Revised Version of the Psychoticism Scale" by S. B. G. Eysenck, H. J. Eysenck, and P. Barrett, 1985, *Personality and Individual Differences, 6*, pp. 21–30. Copyright 1985 by Pergamon Press.

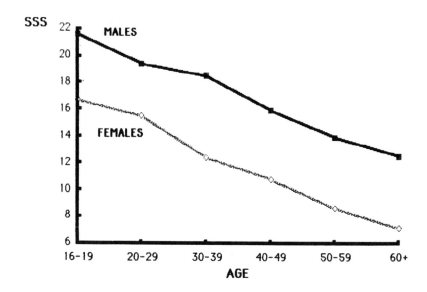

FIGURE 3.   Relationship between age and male and female scores on the Sensation-Seeking scale (SSS; total score), form V. From "Sensation Seeking in England and America: Cross-Cultural, Age, and Sex Comparisons" by M. Zuckerman, S. B. G. Eysenck, and H. J. Eysenck, 1978, *Journal of Consulting and Clinical Psychology, 46*, p. 143. Copyright 1978 by the American Psychological Association.

Psychopathology

H. J. Eysenck and Eysenck (1976) interpreted the P dimension as a broad latent tendency toward psychoticism. *Psychoticism* is used in the sense of a spectrum that includes schizophrenia, major mood disorders, antisocial personality and criminality in general, and even creative but deviant thinking in the nonpsychotic population. I have questioned this broad concept and suggested that *psychopathy* (antisocial tendencies) may be a better term if a clinical label must be used at all for the ImpUSS dimension (Zuckerman, 1989). Delinquents and adult prisoners do score high on P, but schizophrenics score only slightly higher than does the general population, and endogenous depressives score at normal levels.

Criminals with antisocial personalities score higher than do nonpsychopathic criminals on sensation seeking (Blackburn, 1969; Emmons

& Webb, 1974). Ratings of psychopathy in prisoners correlate significantly with the P and Sensation-Seeking scales (Harpur, Hare, & Hakstian, 1989). These correlations would probably be higher if a noncriminal population were included because psychopathy in a criminal population represents a restricted range at the high end for the general population.

Bipolar mood disorder in its manic phase represents a caricature of sensation seeking and impulsivity. It is therefore not surprising that individuals with bipolar mood disorders have high scores on these traits. But "bipolars" score high on the trait measure of sensation seeking even when they are in a normal phase (Zuckerman & Neeb, 1979) or even in a depressed phase (Cronin & Zuckerman, 1992) of the disorder, which shows that the relationship is not state dependent. Offspring of individuals with bipolar mood disorders also score higher on sensation seeking, particularly disinhibition (Nurnberger et al., 1988), which suggests that the personality trait may be part of the genetically transmitted disposition for the disorder.

In contrast, individuals with unipolar depression score low on sensation seeking even immediately after recovery from an episode (Carton, Jouvent, Bungener, & Widlücher, 1992). Schizophrenics, particularly withdrawn and inactive ones, also tend to be low-sensation seekers (Kish, 1970). These findings are a challenge to Eysenck's view that all kinds of psychosis define the high end of the P dimension (Zuckerman et al., 1988, 1991).

Learning–Conditioning

As discussed in the previous section, psychopaths do seem to represent a clinical extreme on the P and Sensation-Seeking scales. Consequently, studies of learning processes in psychopaths probably have some relevance for the broader P-ImpUSS trait. Although psychopaths are generally not less intelligent than other criminals, they do seem to have problems in learning not to repeat behaviors that have led to punishment in the past. Psychopaths spend more time in prison for repeated offenses than do other types of prisoners. Their recidivism could be accounted for by their need for excitement (sensation seeking) or their impulsivity in response to prospects of reward. Another possibility lies in an insensitivity to stimuli associated with punishment.

Newman and Kosson (1986) found that when both reward and punishment are possible, psychopaths seem to focus on the reward possibilities and ignore the prospects of punishment. As a consequence, they show more errors of commission (i.e., responding when they should not do so), which shows a deficiency in passive avoidance learning. Thornquist (1993) found that rated psychopathy correlated with errors of commission, but only among White prisoners. The Zuckerman–Kuhlman Personality Questionnaire impulsive sensation-seeking score correlated with these types of errors in the total group. Thus, both impulsive sensation seeking as a personality trait and psychopathy as a diagnostic trait are related to a deficit in passive avoidance learning.

Psychophysiology

Arousability in Response to Stimuli Associated With Reward and Punishment

Gray (1982) suggested that psychopathic types are underresponsive to signals of punishment. A lack of autonomic arousal could explain the deficit in passive avoidance learning in psychopaths who score high on the ImpUSS dimension because arousal may inhibit response in more anxious persons. Psychopaths tend to be underaroused when arousal is measured by skin conductance level (Hare, 1978) or heart rate (Venables, 1987; Wadsworth, 1976). Psychopaths display less arousability as measured by skin conductance response (SCR; Hare, 1978), but they actually show high heart rate response (HRR) to stimuli that have been conditioned to punishment (Hare & Craigen, 1974). SCR has been interpreted as an activation of a *behavioral inhibition system*, whereas HRR has been described by Fowles (1980) as indicating activation of a *behavioral approach system*. Both reactions are also indications of the activation of a nonspecific arousal system. It is not clear how one differentiates the arousal component from the inhibition or approach aspects of the responses if only SCR or HRR is measured. Furthermore, an accelerative HRR may be indicative of a defensive reflex (Graham, 1979), which is more likely to be related to withdrawal than to approach.

Psychopaths tend to exhibit weak SCRs in response to stimuli that are associated with punishment, but this could be more a function of low anxiety levels in primary psychopaths than a function of the ImpUSS traits in psychopathy itself. Punishment itself, as conveyed by feedback, appears to elicit less arousal (HRR or SCR) in psychopaths than in nonpsychopaths, which possibly indicates less processing of the feedback stimuli in psychopaths (Arnett, Howland, Smith, & Newman, 1993). This failure to process feedback stimuli could account for their failure to learn from punishment.

Response to Neutral Novel Stimuli: Attention and Orienting Responses

Another reason that psychopaths might not be aroused by the signals of punishment in a reward–punishment conflict is that either they do not attend to these signals or they attend too strongly to the reward cues compared with the punishment cues. Harpur (1993) postulated that the psychopath's oversensitivity to reward leads to a dominant response set that overrides their capacity to modulate their behavior in response to competing punishment stimuli. However, Ball and Zuckerman (1992) found that high-sensation seekers showed better focused attention to all stimuli in a dichotic listening task regardless of whether the stimuli were neutral words or words of particular interest to high-sensation seekers.

Novel stimuli may be intrinsically rewarding (Zuckerman, 1984) or fear-provoking (Gray, 1982). The effect that appears may depend on the individual's level of sensation seeking (Zuckerman, 1990). Neary and Zuckerman (1976) found that high-sensation seekers showed stronger SCR orienting responses to novel visual and auditory stimuli than did low-sensation seekers, but they found no difference in response to repeated stimulation. Although further studies using SCR orienting responses could not replicate these results, a study by Smith, Perlstein, Davidson, and Michael (1986) demonstrated that high-sensation seekers showed strong SCR orienting responses in response to loaded stimuli that were of interest to them but that they did not differ from low-sensation seekers in response to neutral stimuli. In another study, Smith, Davidson, Smith, Goldstein, and Perlstein (1989) found that high-sensation seekers showed greater SCR orienting responses to high-intensity words with strong sexual or violent connotations, which is consistent with their interest in these kinds of stimuli in the media (Zuckerman & Litle, 1986).

In contrast to the SCR, the HRR is biphasic: It can show either acceleration or deceleration in response to a stimulus. Deceleration is regarded as an orienting response that reflects interest in or openness to the stimulus, whereas acceleration may be either a defensive reflex or a startle reflex, depending on stimulus and response characteristics (Graham, 1979). Orlebeke and Feij (1979) and Ridgeway and Hare (1981) found that high-sensation seekers, particularly those who were high in disinhibition, tended to show HRR deceleration, whereas low-sensation seekers responded with HRR acceleration to tones of moderate intensity (see Figure 4). The results of these studies reveal that sensation seekers attend more strongly to novel stimuli even if the stimuli have no reward or punishment significance. The defensive reflex of low-sensation seekers

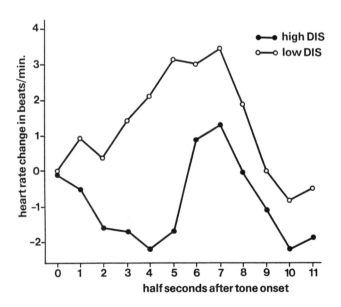

FIGURE 4. Heart rate responses to a moderate-intensity tone (1000 Hz, 80 dB) by individuals who are high in disinhibition (high DIS) and those who are low in disinhibition (low DIS). From *The Orienting Reflex in Humans* (p. 579) edited by H. D. Kimmel, E. H. van Olst, and J. F. Orlebeke, 1979, Hillsdale, NJ: Erlbaum. Copyright 1979 by Erlbaum. Reprinted by permission.

seems to represent an inhibition of attention to novel stimuli or perhaps a cognitive withdrawal rather than approach (information seeking) to such stimuli. The Disinhibition scale is an excellent marker for the general P-ImpUSS dimension and is the sensation-seeking subscale most highly related to psychopathy and impulsivity (Zuckerman, 1979).

Processing of Stimulus Intensity: Augmenting Versus Reducing of the Cortical Evoked Potential

The cortical reaction to a brief stimulus, such as a light flash or tone burst, may be assessed by repeating the stimulus many times, recording the cortical reaction using the electroencephalograph, and averaging the response in a computer. This operation yields a point-by-point response curve for an individual subject. Figure 5 shows typical visual evoked potential (EP) curves for humans, cats, and rats. The complex wave forms of humans to a particular stimulus are highly heritable; the curves for many identical twins can be nearly superimposed (see Figure 6) and look like the repeated measures for a single individual (Buchsbaum, 1974).

Buchsbaum and Silverman (1968) developed a technique for comparing the early cortical EP component (P1–N1) shown in Figure 6. This EP component represents an early cortical reaction that occurs 100–140 ms after the stimulus. Individuals who show a markedly increasing EP amplitude as a function of increasing stimulus intensity (positive slope) are called *augmenters*, whereas those who show little increase or a decrease in EP amplitude at the highest intensities (negative slope) are called *reducers*. Although this terminology suggests a dichotomy, the distribution of EP–stimulus intensity slopes is continuous and normal.

Reducing may represent a cortical protective function. Augmenting may be construed as a failure of cortical inhibition or a marker for a strong nervous system in the Pavlovian sense of resistance to transmarginal inhibition from the effects of intense stimulation.

As with the heart rate orienting response–defensive reflex response, the augmenting or reducing of the EP is most clearly related to scores on the Disinhibition (Dis) subscale of the Sensation-Seeking scale. Dis measures the seeking of novelty and excitement through other people, as in uninhibited parties and varied sexual experience. Figure 7 shows

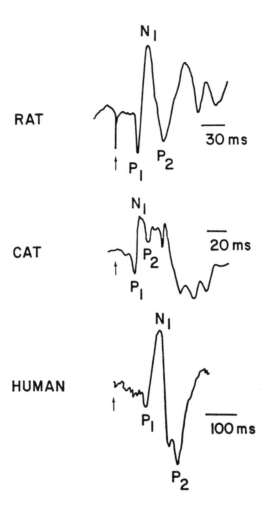

FIGURE 5. Typical visual evoked potential curves for humans, cats, and rats. From *Slow Potential Changes in the Brain* (p. 154) edited by W. Haschke, E. J. Speckman, and A. I. Roitbak, 1993, Cambridge, MA: Birkhauser Boston. Copyright 1993 by Birkhauser Boston. Reprinted by permission.

the contrast of visually evoked EPs between subjects who scored high or low on Dis (Zuckerman, Murtaugh, & Siegel, 1974). High disinhibitors are augmenters, whereas low disinhibitors tend to be reducers. These findings have been replicated many times for visual and auditory stimuli (Zuckerman, 1990). Impulsivity has also been related to EP augmenting (Barratt, Pritchard, Faulk, & Brandt, 1987).

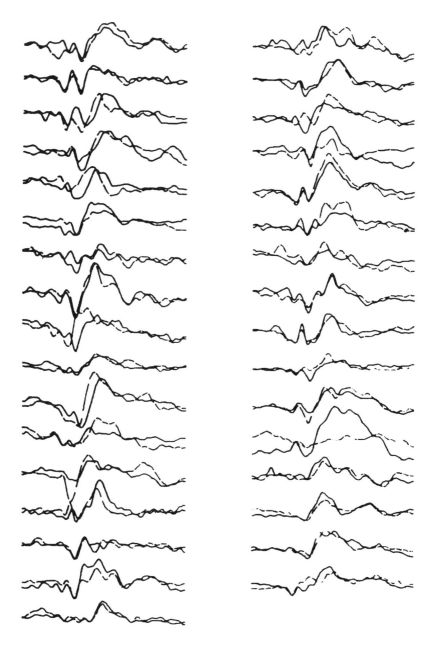

FIGURE 6. Averaged visual evoked potentials of pairs of identical twins, with one twin shown as a solid line and the other twin as a broken line. From "Average Evoked Response and Stimulus Intensity in Identical and Fraternal Twins" by M. S. Buchsbaum, 1974, *Physiological Psychology, 2,* p. 367. Copyright 1974 by the American Psychological Association. Reprinted by permission.

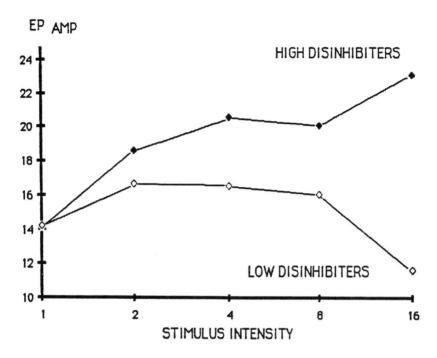

FIGURE 7.   Mean visual evoked potential amplitudes (P1–N1) at five levels of light intensity for low and high scorers on the Disinhibition subscale of the Sensation-Seeking scale. From "Sensation Seeking and Cortical Augmenting–Reducing" by M. Zuckerman, T. T. Murtaugh, and J. Siegel, 1974, *Psychophysiology, 11, p. 539. Copyright 1974 by the Society for Psychophysiological Research. Reprinted by permission.*

EP augmenting is characteristic of individuals with bipolar mood disorders (even when not in a manic state), alcoholics, and male delinquents (Zuckerman, Buchsbaum, & Murphy, 1980). Reducing is characteristic in acute schizophrenics, but augmenting is more typical in chronic schizophrenics or acutes with a poor prognosis. Gender differences are inconsistent, but augmenting tends to change to reducing as a function of age.

Animal Models for Augmenting–Reducing

The P1–N1 component can be seen in the EPs of cats and rats, as well as those of humans, (Figure 5) which provides the possibility for comparative studies of these species. "Augmenter " cats tend to be more exploratory, active, and show fight or approach reactions to a novel stimulus, whereas "reducer" cats tend to be emotional and tense and withdraw in reaction to a novel stimulus (Hall, Rappaport, Hopkins, Griffin, & Silverman, 1970; Lukas & Siegel, 1977, Saxton, Siegel, & Lukas, 1987). Using conditioning paradigms, Saxton et al. found that augmenter cats were more reactive on a fixed interval schedule, for which reward is simply a function of bar-pressing activity, but reducer cats performed better on a schedule that required them to maintain a low rate of response to get reward. The latter kind of schedule punishes impulsive responding and requires a capacity to inhibit response to avoid punishment (loss of reward). Augmenter cats, therefore, resemble impulsive sensation seekers and psychopaths in their deficit in passive avoidance learning.

Siegel, Sisson, and Driscoll (1993) extended the augmenting–reducing paradigm to rats, using strains of Roman high-avoidance (RHA) and Roman low-avoidance (RLA) rats. These two strains were bred from the original Wistar stock for performance in acquisition of a two-way active avoidance task. The RHA rats rapidly learned to avoid shock, whereas the RLA rats tended to freeze rather than run and therefore took much longer to learn the avoidance.

Nearly all RLA and Wistar rats were either reducers or weak augmenters, whereas nearly all of the RHA rats were moderate-to-strong augmenters. There was little overlap in EP augmenting–reducing between RLA and RHA groups.

Because all members of a strain are almost like identical twins, sharing nearly all of their genes, generalizations can be made from strain differences found in other studies. The differences found between RLA and RHA strains are shown in Table 1. Apart from the difference in active avoidance, for which they were bred, the RLA strains (EP reducers) are less active and more fearful in the open-field test, are less aggressive when shocked, show little tolerance for barbiturates and little taste for alcohol, are more maternal to their pups, and show more hypothalamic and pituitary response to stress through release of serotonin (5-HT), corticotrophin-releasing factor, and ACTH. In response to stimulation of lateral hypothalamic areas that mediate intrinsic reward ("pleasure") in the brain, the RLA rat is more sensitive to low intensities but tends to show

TABLE 1
Characteristics of RLA and RHA Rats

Measure	RLA (reducers)	RHA (augmenters)
Active-avoidance	Less (freezing)	More
Open-field		
Activity	Less	More
Defecation	More	Less
Shock-induced aggression	Less aggressive	More aggressive
Alcohol drinking	Less	More
Barbiturates	Little tolerance	High tolerance
Maternal behavior	More time in nest	Less time in nest with young
Hypothalamic self-stimulation	More sensitive	Less sensitive to low intensities
	More escapes	Fewer escapes high intensities
Stress effects		
Prefrontal cortex	No change DA	Increased DA (DOPAC)
Hypothalamus	Increased 5-HT	Less change 5-HT
	Increased CRF	Less change CRF
Pituitary	Increased ACTH	Less change ACTH

Note. RLA = Roman low-avoidance; RHA = Roman high-avoidance; DA = dopamine; DOPAC = dihydroxyphenylacetic acid; CRF = corticotropin releasing factor; 5-HT = serotonin.

more escape when stimulated with high intensities of stimulation. The RHA rat, in contrast, is a suitable model for the impulsive, sensation seeking normal and psychopath: active, exploratory in new environments, aggressive, more susceptible to substance abuse, less nurturing toward young, a need for intense stimulation as reward and insensitivity to weaker rewards, and less hypothalamic–pituitary–adrenocortical arousal in response to stress. However, the RHA rat shows an increase in dopamine release in the prefrontal cortex in response to stress. Stimulant and opiate drugs that are used by human impulsive sensation seekers increase dopaminergic activity. This comparative connection thus points the way down to the next level: psychopharmacology.

Psychopharmacology

Monoamine Oxidase

The enzyme monoamine oxidase (MAO) is contained in the mitochondria of monoamine neurons and regulates the levels of neurotransmitters that are stored in the cells by catabolic degradation of the neurotransmitters after reuptake. MAO in living humans is usually assessed from blood platelets. Platelet MAO is type B, which is primarily associated with the regulation of dopaminergic neurons in the human brain.

Low levels of platelet MAO have been associated with high levels of sensation-seeking trait, whereas high levels of platelet MAO have been associated with low sensation seeking (summaries in Zuckerman, 1983a, 1984, 1991; Zuckerman et al., 1980). Low levels of MAO have also been related to high levels of social activity, criminality, and tobacco, alcohol, and illegal drug use in a normal population. Alcoholics and individuals with bipolar mood disorder and borderline personality disorder tend to have low MAO levels.

High-MAO babies are less active and coordinated than are low-MAO babies in the first 3 days after birth, which suggests a genetic influence in the relationship between MAO and behavioral traits in adults. In fact, MAO level seems to be nearly entirely genetically determined by one major gene with several alleles (Cloninger, von Knorring, & Oreland, 1985; Rice, McGuffin, & Shaskan, 1982; Zuckerman, 1991).

Individual differences in platelet MAO are fairly reliable and resistant to temporarily changing states. Cortical EP augmenters tend to have low MAO levels, whereas reducers tend to have high MAO levels, which provides another link between the two levels of phenomena. The demographics of MAO are consistent with those found for P-scale scores, sensation seeking, and psychopathy: Men are lower in MAO than are women, and MAO increases with age in both the brain and blood platelets.

Comparative MAO findings using monkeys living in a natural colony also provide support for the relationship between ImpUSS in humans (and sociability, as well) and platelet MAO. Low-MAO monkeys were observed to be more active, socially dominant, playful, sexual, and aggressive. High-MAO monkeys tended to be inactive, socially isolated, and low in the dominance hierarchy and tended to show little sexual or aggressive activity.

Dopamine β-Hydroxylase

In the dopaminergic neuron, the biochemical conversion of tyrosine to L-dopa to dopamine stops with the production of dopamine. But in the noradrenergic neuron, the enzyme dopamine β-hydroxylase (DBH) converts dopamine into norepinephrine (NE). Concentrations of DBH in cerebrospinal fluid (CSF) and plasma correlate highly (Ballenger et al., 1983), which suggests either that CSF and platelet DBH have a common source such as brain DBH or, more likely, that peripheral and brain noradrenergic systems are coordinated. Early studies (Ballenger et al., 1983; Kulcsár, Kutor, & Arató, 1984) found significant negative correlations between sensation seeking and plasma DBH, although recent studies (Calhoon, 1988, 1991) have not supported these findings. Low DBH levels would lead to the prediction of low NE levels, and Ballenger et al. also found a substantial negative correlation between CSF NE and sensation seeking.

Despite the uncertain relationship between DBH and sensation seeking, low DBH levels have been found in individuals with certain disinhibitory disorders, for example, alcoholics (Major et al., 1980) and children with undersocialized conduct and borderline personality disorders (Rogeness et al., 1984).

Monoamine System Functions in Other Species

A given neurotransmitter system usually serves several functions, not all of which are relevant to personality differences. Those functions that involve general motivation, activity, and emotional arousal are likely to be related to the mechanisms underlying personality traits. Some of these mechanisms may be involved in more than one trait. For example, nonspecific arousability may be involved in emotionality or the neuroticism trait, but it may also influence inhibition. Strelau (chapter 5 in this book) makes a similar point.

In the broadest sense, dopamine is essential in approach motivation that centers around basic biological drives as exemplified in the "four Fs": foraging, feeding, fighting, and (euphemistically) "frolicking." But dopamine is involved in a more generalized approach tendency as expressed in activity, exploration, and approach to novel stimuli, even in the absence of a specific drive state. In humans, this kind of behavior is found in sensation seekers who explore and seek novel experiences in all aspects of life (Zuckerman, 1979). Dopamine is essential for the intrinsic reward mechanism that is stimulated in brain areas such as the lateral hypothalamus, the nucleus accumbens, and the medial forebrain bundle. Many drugs that are abused by high-sensation seekers effect dopamine release.

The dorsal ascending noradrenergic system that originates in the locus coeruleus ascends to innervate all areas of the neocortex, where it serves general arousal and heightened attentional functions. High activity of this system has been related to expressions of anxiety in rats (Gray, 1982) and primates (Redmond, 1987), which suggests that it may also be related to the trait of anxiety in humans. Ballenger et al. (1983) found a negative correlation between NE in the CSF and the sensation-seeking trait in both men and women. ImpUSS, therefore, could be associated with a deficit in NE arousal or arousability.

5-HT seems to serve a behavioral and emotional inhibitory function in animals and humans (Soubrié, 1986). Behavioral inhibition is associated with states of high anxiety, but it also serves an important function in the restraint or modulation of approach behavior. In animals, 5-HT inhibits sexual and aggressive behaviors, which are stimulated by dopamine. Levels of the 5-HT metabolite 5-hydroxyindoleacetic acid in humans is negatively correlated with aggressiveness, hostility, and high P-scale scores. Low levels of 5-HT have been found in impulsive murderers and those who attempted or committed suicide in violent ways.

Low levels of activity or reactivity in 5-HT-mediated inhibition could underlie psychopathy, P-ImpUSS, and the impulsivity and failures of inhibition of approach behavior that underlie the disorder and trait. EP augmenters tend to be low in 5-hydroxyindoleacetic acid (the 5-HT metabolite) compared with EP reducers (von Knorring & Perris, 1981), and the 5-HT agonist zimeldine reduces the augmentation tendency (von Knorring & Johansson, 1980). These findings suggest a causal link between 5-HT and the psychophysiological marker for inhibition–disinhibition. These correlational and experimental studies suggest direct experimental tests of animals in which 5-HT or other putative neurochemical sources of the EP augmenting–reducing tendency could be tested by direct brain infusion or lesioning.

Experimental Studies in Humans

The evidence already cited on the functions of monoamine systems is largely based on experimental research in animals and correlational studies in humans. However, experiments with drugs that temporarily block (antagonists) or stimulate (agonists) activity in neurotransmitter systems are possible in humans.

Netter and Rammsayer (1991) gave the drugs halperidol, a dopamine antagonist, and L-dopa, a dopamine agonist, to normal subjects and measured performance on reaction time tasks and self-reported arousal. Low-sensation seekers had a marked decrease in performance and felt less relaxed after taking halperidol than after taking L-dopa. High-sensation seekers felt more relaxed after taking halperidol, and neither drug affected their performance much. These findings suggest that low-sensation seekers suffer more when dopamine effect is blocked and perform better when dopamine activity is enhanced. Perhaps they suffer from an underactive dopamine system. On the other hand, high-sensation seekers may have overactive dopaminergic systems and therefore may feel more relaxed when dopaminergic action is blocked. Halperidol is given in higher doses to calm overexcited manic and schizophrenic psychotics. But feeling relaxed may not represent an optimal affective state for high-sensation seekers or manics. This may be why they tend to use dopamine-releasing drugs like amphetamine and cocaine.

Hormones

Gonadal hormones, both testosterone and estrogen, are directly related to sensation seeking in males, particularly those who are of the disinhibition type (Daitzman & Zuckerman, 1980). These hormones are also negatively related to socialization and self-control—two other markers for the ImpUSS dimension—and to variety of heterosexual experience and numbers of heterosexual partners. Furthermore, estradiol in men is related to high scores on Minnesota Multiphasic Personality Inventory scales for schizophrenia, hypomania, and psychopathy. Testosterone in prisoners is related both to social dominance and extreme violence (Dabbs, Ruback, Frady, Hopper, & Sgoritas, 1988; Ehrenkranz, Bliss, & Sheard, 1974).

CSF cortisol and NE are inversely related to traits constituting the P-ImpUSS dimension (Zuckerman 1984). Cortisol is produced by activation of the hypothalamic–pituitary–adrenocortical stress pathway, whereas NE in the CSF may be partly a function of activity in the locus coeruleus and its descending pathways into the spinal cord. When faced with a natural stress, as while awaiting outcome of a criminal trial, nonpsychopathic prisoners show arousal in peripheral measures of NE and epinephrine, but psychopathic types show little change in adrenergic arousal (Lidberg, Levander, Schalling, & Lidberg, 1978).

A Psychopharmacological Model for P-ImpUSS

Any model for psychobiology must involve some oversimplification because there is generally extensive overlap of specific systems in regard to functional mechanisms and traits. A simple organism like the paramecium has one simple behavioral function: approach or withdrawal in response to a stimulus. One might even imagine unidimensional "personality" differences among paramecia in terms of the strength or sensitivity of this conditionable reaction. At a somewhat higher level of evolution, inhibitory mechanisms provide a second choice: doing nothing (i.e., "freezing") combined with high arousal and attention to the significant stimulus. Inhibition introduces more flexibility into behavior and allows for further information processing in organisms that are capable of such activity. In an organism facing a potential aggressor (e.g., predator vs. prey), approach may elicit aggressive confrontation and flight may provoke pursuit. But freezing may temporarily confuse the predator and give the prey a chance to choose the best alternative of possible actions. This kind of inhibition is associated with anxiety. Behavioral inhibition is also necessary in the predator because an overeager stalking approach may prematurely precipitate running in the prey before the predator is in capture range. This kind of inhibition is related to the human trait of impulsivity versus restraint. Another mechanism, arousal, mediates direction of attentional resources and mobilization of the internal environment for maximal support of muscular and brain action ("fight or flight"). This mechanism may serve any of the other mechanisms, that is, approach, withdrawal, or inhibition.

P-ImpUSS trait and psychopathy are hypothesized to be a combination of strong approach with weak inhibition and arousal mechanisms (Figure 8). The mesolimbic dopaminergic system, which runs from the ventral tegmental area to the nucleus accumbens through the medial forebrain bundle and the lateral hypothalamus and ascends to the frontal cortex, is central to the approach mechanism. The nigrostriatal dopaminergic pathways to the basal ganglia may be involved in the impetus for motor activity. The serotonergic system originating in the raphe nucleus may mediate behavioral and emotional inhibition. Deficits in activity or reactivity of this system may be related to the P-ImpUSS dimension, which accounts for the inability to inhibit approach behavior. Descending pathways from the orbitofrontal lobe of the cortex mediate inhibition of lower centers from cortical influences.

The noradrenergic dorsal tegmental bundle influences cortical arousal and peripheral autonomic arousal as well as arousal of the hypothalamic–pituitary–adrenocortical system. Activity in the system is involved in trait anxiety, but a deficit in the system could lead to underarousal and a deficiency in anticipation of punishment mediated by anxiety.

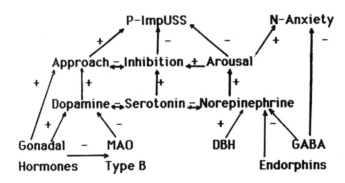

FIGURE 8. A psychopharmacological model for impulsive unsocialized sensation seeking (P-ImpUSS) and neuroticism–anxiety (N-Anxiety) with underlying behavioral mechanisms (approach, inhibition, and arousal) and neurotransmitters, enzymes, and hormones involved. Interactions between behavioral and biochemical factors are indicated by a plus sign for agonistic actions and by a minus sign for antagonistic actions. MAO = monoamine oxidase; DBH = dopamine β-hydroxylase; GABA = γ-aminobutyric acid.

The three behavioral mechanisms—approach, withdrawal, and inhibition—are also influenced by neuroregulators and hormones. The approach mechanism is potentiated by gonadal hormones, particularly testosterone. Testosterone probably interacts with dopaminergic systems in approach motivations like sex, social dominance, and aggression. MAO type B regulates dopamine disposal, and low levels of MAO are associated with a lack of inhibition of dopamine-influenced approach systems. A deficit in DBH may lower arousability because of a reduction in the production of NE from dopamine. Neurotransmitters other than 5-HT are involved in inhibition and suppression of arousal. For example, γ-aminobutyric acid and endorphins dampen arousal through inhibitory actions on the locus coeruleus and the dorsal noradrenergic system.

The interactions between neurotransmitters, enzymes, and hormones are complex. Strength in an approach agonistic system may have the same effect as a weakness in an inhibitory system. Differences in the strength of a neurotransmitter system may depend on an enzyme that regulates production or breakdown, receptors that effect transmission, receptors that regulate production through feedback, or receptors for other neurotransmitters that regulate activity in that transmitter. However, it is not necessary that the molecular mechanisms be fully understood before generalizations can be made about the relationships of molar pharmacology to behavior. If researchers had to wait for the results of a bottom-up approach, then the science of psychopharmacology would still be science fiction. The behavioral effects of drugs are usually known before the mechanisms for their actions are fully understood.

Genetics

The individual differences in biochemical and neurological systems underlying basic mechanisms have their origins in genetic variation. Animal strain differences in explorativeness, fearfulness, aggression, activity, and inhibition suggest genetic control of these traits. The results of selective breeding studies have confirmed the genetic influence, and cross-fostering experiments have provided controls for the possible effects of shared environment.

Biometric genetic studies of humans use twins and adoptees to estimate heritability. The Minnesota study of separated twins (Lykken, 1982) provided data of both types. The main personality test used in this study was the Tellegen (1985) Multidimensional Personality Questionnaire, which is scored for three factors resembling those in Eysenck's model. The third major factor is called *constraint*. This factor consists of three subscales: Control, Harm Avoidance, and Traditionalism, which are roughly the converse of Impulsivity, Sensation Seeking, and Unsocialized tendencies in the alternative five-factor model (Zuckerman et al., 1991). Table 2 shows correlations between identical (monozygotic) twins who were reared together and those who were reared apart on scores for the Constraint and Sensation-Seeking scales. Correlations for fraternal (dizygotic) twins raised together are also shown.

The correlations between identical twins who were reared apart are a direct estimate of heritability because these adopted twins were separated shortly after birth and reared in different family environments. The heritability for the Constraint (or Conscientiousness) factor, which is based only on separated twin correlations, is 61% (Bouchard, 1993). Data on the sensation-seeking component of ImpUSS was provided for separated twins by D. T. Lykken (personal communication, July 30, 1992) and are compared with data from identical and fraternal twins who were reared together from the study by Fulker, Eysenck, and Zuckerman (1980) in Table 2. The heritability from the separated identical twins alone is 54%.

TABLE 2

Correlations Between Twins: Minnesota Twin Study[a] and Sensation-Seeking Scale Data[c]

Measure	MZ apart	MZ together	DZ together
N	52[a]	553[a]	459[a]
Constraint	.61[a]	.59[a]	.38[a]
Sensation Seeking	.54[b]	.60[c]	.21[c]

Note. MZ = monozygotic; DZ = dizygotic.
[a]Bouchard (1993). [b]Lykken (personal communication, July 30, 1992). [c]Fulker et al. (1980).

The estimates of heritability for the Constraint factor and the sensation-seeking component are near the upper end of heritabilities assessed from twin studies (Zuckerman, 1991). There is little difference between the correlations for identical twins who were reared apart and those who were reared together, which indicates that shared environment is of little importance for these traits. This conclusion goes against the prevailing opinion that the family environment is largely responsible for socialization of children and that the greater similarity of identical twins who were reared together is because the identicals are treated more alike than are fraternal twins. The specific environment seems to play a more important role in these traits. This kind of influence is provided by different peers or other influences that affect one member of a family but not another.

In a study by Horvath and Zuckerman (1993), peer effects were found to be the strongest factors in criminality and rule violation. However, correlational studies such as this one cannot distinguish between genotype–environment correlational, interactional, and direct causal effects (Plomin, 1986). Peer behavior may correlate with self-behavior because people learn from their peers or because they select peers who are like themselves. Remarkable coincidences in the associations of separated identical twins suggest that the genotype can influence associations and interests through the phenotype. Genetic similarity in sensation seeking could account for some of this outcome, but the specificity of the expression found for the trait must be due to some kind of active genotype–environment correlation, which the researchers call *emergenesis* (Lykken, McGue, Tellegen, & Bouchard, 1992).

Chronic criminality is often an expression of an antisocial personality disorder and thus may represent the extreme manifestation of the ImpUSS trait. The results of studies of adopted children in Scandinavia show that there is a significant genetic influence from the biological parents but that there is less shared environmental influence from the adopting parents who rear the children (Cloninger & Gottesman, 1987; Mednick, Moffitt, Gabrielli, & Hutchings, 1986). However, specific environmental influences, such as peers, and socioeconomic status of the adopting parents (Mednick, Gabrielli, & Hutchings, 1987) may also play a role in criminal behavior as well as in the normal ImpUSS trait.

Summary: ImpUSS Turtles

Figure 9 summarizes the biological bases of the P-ImpUSS trait in terms of the seven turtles (levels) of analysis. The ImpUSS trait includes a variety of behaviors that can be summarized by the term *disinhibition*: criminality, sexual variety seeking, substance use and abuse, as well as risk-taking in financial and sports activities. Individuals with antisocial personalities and manic–depressives in the manic state illustrate disinhibition in its most vivid behavioral forms. These disorders represent the abnormal extremes of a normal dimension of personality. At the next level, we find a specific kind of conditioning deficit. ImpUSS types, particularly at the psychopathic extremes, have problems in passive–avoidance learning. For situations in which reward and punishment are both possible outcomes, they seem to ignore the signals of punishment and focus on the signals of reward. They have a strong capacity to focus attention on salient stimuli and ignore distracting stimuli, such as those for punishment. At the psychophysiological level, disinhibitors show this focused attention by exhibiting strong orienting reflexes to novel stimuli that may elicit defensive reflexes in low-sensation seekers. Disinhibitors also show augmentation of cortical reaction to intense stimuli that elicit cortical inhibition in low disinhibitors. This capacity to respond to intense and novel stimuli is summarized by the term *cortical accessibility*.

Below the physiological level are the biochemical systems that influence the broad behavioral mechanisms and psychophysiological reactions: dopaminergic (approach), serotonergic (inhibition), and noradrenergic (arousal and focused attention). The enzymes such as MAO and DBH that regulate these neurotransmitters, and hormones such as testosterone and cortisol, are also involved in this trait. A person who is high on P-ImpUSS probably has strong approach–disinhibitory tendencies and weak inhibitory and arousal tendencies. The implication is that they have an active or reactive dopaminergic system and inactive or unreactive serotonergic and noradrenergic systems. The converse would be true for those who are low on this trait: weak approach and strong inhibition or restraint with strong arousal or arousability by signals of punishment.

Neurological loci for personality traits suggest a new kind of phrenology. But this modern phrenology is based on relationships between

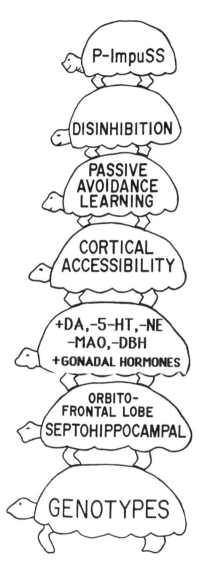

FIGURE 9. Levels of analysis (turtles) for impulsive unsocialized sensation seeking (P-ImpUSS) trait. Disinhibition is a summary term for the social behavior associated with the P-ImpUSS. Cortical accessibility refers to the physiological reactivity to novel and intense stimuli in high-sensation seekers and impulsives compared with the cortical inhibition or defensive reflexes that are characteristic of low-sensation seekers. DA = dopamine; 5-HT = serotonin; NE = norepinephrine; MAO = monoamine oxidase (type B); DBH = dopamine β-hydroxylase.

behavior and neurotransmitter-defined pathways and nuclei in the brain and not on the shape of the skull. Restraint or inhibition of behavior may originate in the orbitofrontal cortex, where damage seems to result in behavioral disinhibition. Excitatory influences from cortical sources descend to the septohippocampal comparator system (described by Gray, 1982, with reference to the trait of anxiety), where inhibition may be further potentiated. The central nucleus of the amygdala is also a source of behavioral inhibition and autonomic arousal. Each of these describes levels of inhibition from the relatively more deliberate (cortical) to the more reflexive and less conscious (amygdala).

An approach mechanism originates in the ascending mesolimbic dopaminergic system, beginning in the ventral tegmental area and traversing the medial forebrain bundle to the lateral hypothalamus and the nucleus accumbens and finally to the lateral and medial prefrontal cortices. Another system, which is mediated by the neurotransmitter NE and affects arousal, originates in the locus coeruleus and ascends to limbic structures including the amygdala, septum, and hippocampus and finally to all parts of the neocortex. A serotonergic inhibitory system originates in the raphe nucleus and ascends to the amygdala, hippocampus, hypothalamus, septum, striatum, and all areas of the neocortex.

Ultimately, individual differences in the structure and physiology of these systems depend on genotypes. ImpUSS has strong heritability, which is at the upper range of what is typical for personality traits. Unlike most other broad personality traits, however, sensation seeking shows substantial assortative mating, which suggests some evolutionary advantage in the trait. A high level of sensation seeking in men may have been involved in the motivations for hunting, exploration of new territory, seeking of mates, and sexual activity with a variety of partners, thereby enhancing acquisition of resources that are essential for survival and reproductive success. But too high levels of risk-taking would have been maladaptive so that selection would have been for an optimal midlevel range of the trait.

Evolutionary origins are highly speculative. Current functional significance of a trait and its biological correlates are more demonstrable. By this standard, ImpUSS is significant as one of the major supertraits, and further study of its biological bases from the genetic to the physiological is vital. We should resist the temptation to hide within the shell of our most familiar turtle.

References

Arnett, J. (1991). Still crazy after all these years: Reckless behavior among young adults aged 23–27. *Personality and Individual Differences, 12*, 1305–1313.

Arnett, P. A., Howland, E. W., Smith, S. S., & Newman, J. P. (1993). Autonomic responsivity during passive avoidance in incarcerated psychopaths. *Personality and Individual Differences, 14*, 173–184.

Ball, S. A., & Zuckerman, M. (1992). Sensation seeking and selective attention: Focused and divided attention on a dichotic listening task. *Journal of Personality and Social Psychology, 63*, 825–831.

Ballenger, J. C., Post, R. M., Jimerson, D. C., Lake, C. R., Murphy, D. L., Zuckerman, M., & Cronin, C. (1983). Biochemical correlates of personality traits in normals: An exploratory study. *Personality and Individual Differences, 4*, 615–625.

Barratt, E. S., Pritchard, W. S., Faulk, D. M., & Brandt, M. E. (1987). The relationship between impulsiveness subtraits, trait anxiety, and visual N100–augmenting–reducing: A topographic analysis. *Personality and Individual Differences, 8*, 43–51.

Blackburn, R. (1969). Sensation seeking, impulsivity, and psychopathic personality. *Journal of Consulting and Clinical Psychology, 33*, 571–574.

Block, J. H., & Block, J. (1980). The role of ego-control and ego-resiliency in the organization of behavior. In W. A. Collins (Ed.), *The Minnesota symposia on child psychology: Vol 13. Development of cognition, affect, and social relations* (pp. 39–101). Hillsdale, NJ: Erlbaum.

Bouchard, T. J., Jr. (1993). Genetic and environmental influences on adult personality: Evaluating the evidence. In J. Hettema & I. J. Deary (Eds.), *Foundations of personality* (pp. 15–44). Norwell, MA: Kluwer Academic.

Buchsbaum, M. S. (1974). Average evoked response and stimulus intensity in identical and fraternal twins. *Physiological Psychology, 2*, 365–370.

Buchsbaum, M. S., & Silverman, J. (1968). Stimulus intensity control and the cortical evoked response. *Psychosomatic Medicine, 30*, 12–22.

Calhoon, L. (1988). Explorations in the biochemistry of sensation seeking. *Personality Individual Differences, 9*, 941–949.

Calhoon, L. (1991). Sensation seeking, exercise, and dopamine beta hydroxylase. *Journal of Personality and Individual Differences, 9*, 903–907.

Cappella, J. N., & Green, J. O. (1984). The effects of distance and individual differences in arousability on nonverbal involvement: A test of discrepancy arousal theory. *Journal of Nonverbal Behavior, 8*, 259–286.

Carton, S., Jouvent, R., Bungener, C., & Widlücher, D. (1992). Sensation seeking and depressive mood. *Personality and Individual Differences, 7*, 843–849.

Cloninger, C. R., & Gottesman, I. I. (1987). Genetic and environmental factors in antisocial behavior. In S. A. Mednick, T. E. Moffitt, & S. A. Stack (Eds.), *The causes of crime: New biological approaches* (pp. 92–109). Cambridge, UK: Cambridge University Press.

Cloninger, C. R., von Knorring, L., & Oreland, L. (1985). Parametric distribution of platelet monoamine oxidase activity. *Psychiatry Research, 15*, 133–134.

Costa, P. T., Jr., & McCrae, R. R. (1992). *NEO-PI-R: Revised Personality Inventory.* Odessa, FL: Psychological Assessment Resources.

Cronin, C., & Zuckerman, M. (1992). Sensation seeking and bipolar affective disorder. *Journal of Personality and Individual Differences, 13*, 385–387.

Dabbs, J. M., Jr., Ruback, R. B., Frady, R. L., Hopper, C. H., & Sgoritas, D. S. (1988). Saliva testosterone and criminal violence among women. *Personality and Individual Differences, 9*, 269–275.

Daitzman, R., & Zuckerman, M. (1980). Disinhibitory sensation seeking, personality and gonadal hormones. *Personality and Individual Differences, 1*, 103–110.

Donovan, D. M., Queisser, H. R., Salzberg, P. M., & Umlauf, R. L. (1985). Intoxicated and bad drivers: Subgroups within the same population of high-risk men drivers. *Journal of Studies on Alcohol, 46*, 375–382.

Ehrenkranz, J., Bliss, E., & Sheard, M. H. (1974). Plasma testosterone: Correlation with aggressive behavior and social dominance in man. *Psychosomatic Medicine, 36*, 469–475.

Emmons, T. D., & Webb, W. W. (1974). Subjective correlates of emotional responsivity and stimulation seeking in psychopaths, normals, and acting-out neurotics. *Journal of Consulting and Clinical Psychology, 42*, 620–625.

Eysenck, H. J. (1967). *The biological basis of personality.* Springfield, IL: Charles C Thomas.

Eysenck, H. J., & Eysenck, M. W. (1985). *Personality and individual differences: A natural science approach.* New York: Plenum.

Eysenck, H. J., & Eysenck, S. B. G. (1976). *Psychoticism as a dimension of personality.* London: Hodder & Stoughton.

Eysenck, S. B. G., Eysenck, H. J., & Barrett, P. (1985). A revised version of the psychoticism scale. *Personality and Individual Differences, 6*, 21–29.

Farley, F. H., & Davis, S. A. (1977). Arousal, personality and assortative mating in marriage. *Journal of Sex and Marital Therapy, 3*, 122–127.

Farley, F. H., & Mueller, C. B. (1978). Arousal, personality, and assortative mating in marriage: Generalizability and cross-cultural factors. *Journal of Sex and Marital Therapy, 4*, 50–53.

Fowles, D. C. (1980). The three-arousal model: Implications of Gray's two-factor learning theory for heart rate, electrodermal activity and psychopathy. *Psychophophysiology, 17*, 87–104.

Franken, R. E., Gibson, F. J., & Mohan, P. (1990). Sensation seeking and disclosure to close and casual friends. *Personality and Individual Differences, 11*, 829–832.

Fulker, D. W., Eysenck, S. B. G., & Zuckerman, M. (1980). A genetic and environmental analysis of sensation seeking. *Journal of Research in Personality, 14*, 261–281.

Furnham, A., & Saipe, J. (1993). Personality correlates of convicted drivers. *Personality and Individual Differences, 14*, 329–336.

Graham, F. K. (1979). Distinguishing among orienting, defensive, and startle reflexes. In H. D. Kimmel, E. H. van Olst, & J. F. Orlebeke (Eds.), *The orienting reflex in humans* (pp. 137–167). Hillsdale, NJ: Erlbaum.

Gray, J. A. (1982). *The neuropsychology of anxiety: An enquiry into the functions of the septo-hippocampal system.* New York: Oxford University Press.

Haier, R. J., Sokolski, K., Katz, M., & Buchsbaum, M. S. (1987). The study of personality with positron emission tomography. In J. Strelau & H. J. Eysenck (Eds.), *Personality dimensions and arousal* (pp. 251–267). New York: Plenum.

Hall, R. A., Rappaport, M., Hopkins, H. K., Griffin, R. B., & Silverman, J. (1970). Evoked response and behavior in cats. *Science, 170*, 998–1000.

Hare, R. D. (1978). Electrodermal and cardiovascular correlates of psychopathy. In R. D. Hare & D. Schalling (Eds.), *Psychopathic behaviour: Approaches to research* (pp. 107–143). New York: Wiley.

Hare, R. D., & Craigen, D. (1974). Psychopathy and physiological activity in a mixed-motive game situation. *Psychophysiology, 11*, 197–206.

Harpur, T. J. (1993, June). *Mechanisms of attention that may mediate poor learning in psychopaths.* Paper presented at the symposium "Why Can't the Psychopath Learn From Experience?" at the annual meeting of the American Psychological Society, Chicago, IL.

Harpur, T. J. , Hare, R. D., & Hakstian, R. (1989). Two factor conceptualization of psychopathy: Construct validity and assessment implications. *Psychological Assessment: A Journal of Consulting and Clinical Psychology, 1*, 6–17.

Haschke, W., Speckman, E. J., & Roitbak, A. I. (Eds.). (1993). *Slow potential changes in the brain.* Cambridge, MA: Birkhauser Boston.

Horvath, P., & Zuckerman, M. (1993). Sensation seeking, risk appraisal, and risky behavior. *Personality and Individual Differences, 14*, 41–52.

Kimmel, H. D., van Olst, E. H., & Orlebeke, J. F. (Eds.). (1979). *The orienting reflex in humans.* Hillsdale, NJ: Erlbaum.

Kish, G. B. (1970). Reduced cognitive innovation and stimulus-seeking in chronic schizophrenics. *Journal of Clinical Psychology, 26*, 170–174.

Kulcsár, Z., Kutor, L., & Arató, M. (1984). Sensation seeking, its biological correlates and its relation to vestibulo-ocular functions. In H. Bonarius, G. van Heck, & N. Smid (Eds.), *Personality psychology in Europe: Theoretical and empirical developments* (pp. 327–346). Lisse, The Netherlands: Swets & Zeitlinger.

Lesnik-Oberstein, M., & Cohen, L. (1984). Cognitive style, sensation seeking, and assortative mating. *Journal of Personality and Social Psychology, 46*, 112–117.

Lidberg, L., Levander, S. E., Schalling, D., & Lidberg, Y. (1978). Urinary catecholamines, stress, and psychopathy: A study of arrested men awaiting trial. *Psychosomatic Medicine, 40*, 116–125.

Lukas, J. H., & Siegel, J. (1977). Cortical mechanisms that augment or reduce evoked potentials in cats. *Science, 196*, 73–75.

Lykken, D. T. (1982). Research with twins: The concept of emergenesis. *Psychophysiology, 19*, 361–373.

Lykken, D. T., McGue, M., Tellegen, A., & Bouchard, T. J., Jr. (1992). Emergenesis: Genetic traits that may not run in families. *American Psychologist, 47*, 1565–1577.

Major, L. F., Lerner, P., Goodwin, F. K., Ballenger, J. C., Brown, G. L., & Lorenberg, W. (1980). Dopamine-β-hydroxylase in CSF. *Archives of General Psychiatry, 37*, 308–310.

Mednick, S. A., Gabrielli, W. F., & Hutchings, B. (1987). Genetic factors in the etiology of criminal behavior. In S. A. Mednick, T. E. Moffitt, & S. A. Stack (Eds.), *The causes of crime: New biological approaches* (pp. 74–91). Cambridge, UK: Cambridge University Press.

Mednick, S. A., Moffitt, T., Gabrielli, W. F., & Hutchings, B. (1986). Genetic factors in criminal behavior: A review. In D. Olweus, J. Block, & M. Radke-Yarrow (Eds.), *Development of antisocial and prosocial behavior research theories and issues* (pp. 33–50). San Diego, CA: Academic Press.

McCown, W. (1993). Personality factors predicting failure to practice safer sex by HIV positive males. *Personality and Individual Differences, 14*, 613–616.

Neary, R. S., & Zuckerman, M. (1976). Sensation seeking, trait and state anxiety, and the electrodermal orienting reflex. *Psychophysiology, 13*, 205–211.

Netter, P., & Rammsayer, T. (1991). Reactivity to dopaminergic drugs and aggression related personality traits. *Personality and Individual Differences, 12*, 1009–1017.

Newcomb, M. D., & McGee, L. (1991). The influence of sensation seeking on general and specific problem behaviors from adolescence to young adulthood. *Journal of Personality and Social Psychology, 61*, 614–628.

Newman, J. P., & Kosson, D. S. (1986). Passive avoidance learning in psychopathic and non-psychopathic offenders. *Journal of Abnormal Psychology, 95*, 252–256.

Nurnberger, J. I., Jr., Hamovit, J., Hibbs, E. D., Pellegrini, D., Guroff, J. J., Maxwell, M. E., Smith, A., & Gershon, E. S. (1988). A high-risk study of primary affective disorder: Selection of subjects, initial assessment, and 1- to 2-year follow-up. In D. L. Dunner, E. S. Gershon, & J. E. Barrett (Eds.), *Relatives at risk for mental disorder* (pp. 161–177). New York: Raven Press.

O'Boyle, M., & Barratt, E. S. (1993). Impulsivity and DSM-III-R personality disorders. *Personality and Individual Differences, 14*, 609–611.

Orlebeke, J. F., & Feij, J. A. (1979). The orienting reflex as a personality correlate. In H. D. Kimmel, E. H. van Olst, & J. F. Orlebeke (Eds.), *The orienting reflex in humans* (pp. 567–585). Hillsdale, NJ: Erlbaum.

Pavlov, I. P. (1927/1960). *Conditioned reflexes: An investigation of the physiological activity of the cerebral cortex* (G. V. Anrep, Trans.). New York: Dover.

Plomin, R. (1986). *Development, genetics and psychology.* Hillsdale, NJ: Erlbaum.

Redmond, D. E., Jr. (1987). Neurochemical bases for anxiety and anxiety disorders: Studies of locus coeruleus in monkeys and hypotheses for neuropsychopharmacology. In H. Y. Meltzer (Ed.), *Psychopharmacology: The third generation of progress* (pp. 967–975). New York: Raven Press.

Rice, J., McGuffin, P., & Shaskan, E. G. (1982). A commingling analysis of platelet mono-amine oxidase activity. *Psychiatry Research, 7,* 325–335.

Ridgeway, D., & Hare, R. D. (1981). Sensation seeking and psychophysiological responses to auditory stimulation. *Psychophysiology, 18,* 613–618.

Robins, L. N., Helzer, J. E., Weissman, M. M., Orvarechel, H., Gruenberg, E., Burke, J. D., & Reiger, D. A. (1984). Lifetime prevalence of specific psychiatric disorders in three sites. *Archives of General Psychiatry, 41,* 949–967.

Rogeness, G. A., Hernandez, J. M., Macedo, C. A., Mitchell, E. L., Amrung, S. A., & Harris, W. R. (1984). Clinical characteristics of emotionally disturbed boys with very low activities of dopamine-β-hydroxylase. *Journal of the American Academy of Child Psychiatry, 23,* 203–208.

Saxton, P. M., Siegel, J., & Lukas, J. H. (1987). Visual evoked potential augmenting/reducing slopes in cats: Correlations with behavior. *Personality and Individual Differences, 8,* 511–519.

Siegel, J., Sisson, D. F., & Driscoll, P. (1993). Augmenting and reducing of visual evoked potentials in Roman high- and low-avoidance rats. *Physiology and Behavior, 54,* 707–711.

Smith, B. D., Davidson, R. A., Smith, D. L., Goldstein, H., & Perlstein, W. M. (1989). Sensation seeking and arousal: Effects of strong stimulation on electrodermal activation and memory test performance. *Personality and Individual Differences, 10,* 671–679.

Smith, B. D., Perlstein, W. M., Davidson, R. A., & Michael, K. (1986). Sensation seeking: Differential effects of relevant, novel stimulation on electrodermal activity. *Personality and Individual Differences, 7,* 445–452.

Soubrié, P. (1986). Reconciling the role of central serotonin neurons in human and animal behavior. *Behavioral and Brain Sciences, 9,* 319–364.

Strelau, J. (1983). *Temperament, personality, and arousal.* San Diego, CA: Academic Press.

Strelau, J., & Eysenck, H. J. (1987). *Personality dimensions and arousal.* New York: Plenum.

Tellegen, A. (1985). Structures of mood and personality and their relevance to assessing anxiety, with an emphasis on self-report. In A. H. Tuma & J. D. Maser (Eds.), *Anxiety and the anxiety disorders* (pp. 681–706). Hillsdale, NJ: Erlbaum.

Thornquist, M. H. (1993). *Psychopathy, passive–avoidance learning and basic dimensions of personality.* Unpublished doctoral dissertation, University of Delaware.

Thornquist, M. H., Zuckerman, M., & Exline, R. V. (1991). Loving, liking, looking and sensation seeking in unmarried college couples. *Personality and Individual Differences, 12,* 1283–1292.

Venables, P. H. (1987). Autonomic nervous system factors in criminal behavior. In S. A. Mednick, T. E. Moffitt, & S. A. Stack (Eds.), *The causes of crime: New biological approaches* (pp. 110–136). Cambridge, UK: Cambridge University Press.

von Knorring, L., & Johansson, F. (1980). Changes in the augmenter–reducer tendency and in pain measures as a result of treatment with a serotonin reuptake inhibiter: Zimeldine. *Neuropsychobiology, 6,* 313–318.

von Knorring, L., & Perris, C. (1981). Biochemistry of the augmenting–reducing response in visual evoked potentials. *Neuropsychobiology, 7,* 1–8.

Wadsworth, M. E. J. (1976). Delinquency, pulse rates, and early emotional deprivation. *British Journal of Criminology, 16,* 245–256.

Zuckerman, M. (1979). *Sensation seeking: Beyond the optimal level of arousal.* Hillsdale, NJ: Erlbaum.

Zuckerman, M. (1983a). A biological theory of sensation seeking. In M. Zuckerman (Ed.), *Biological bases of sensation seeking, impulsivity and anxiety* (pp. 37–76). Hillsdale, NJ: Erlbaum.

Zuckerman, M. (1983b). Sensation seeking: The initial motive for drug abuse. In E. H. Gottheil, K. A. Druley, T. E. Skoloda, & H. M. Waxman (Eds.), *Etiological aspects of alcohol and drug abuse* (pp. 202–220). Springfield, IL: Charles C Thomas.

Zuckerman, M. (1984). Sensation seeking: A comparative approach to a human trait. *Behavioral and Brain Sciences, 7,* 413–471.

Zuckerman, M. (1987). Is sensation seeking a predisposing trait for alcoholism? In E. Gottheil, K. A. Druley, S. Pashkey, & S. P. Weinstein (Eds.), *Stress and addiction* (pp. 283–301). New York: Brunner/Mazel.

Zuckerman, M. (1989). Personality in the third dimension: A psychobiological approach. *Personality and Individual Differences, 10,* 391–418.

Zuckerman, M. (1990). The psychophysiology of sensation seeking. *Journal of Personality, 58,* 313–345.

Zuckerman, M. (1991). *Psychobiology of personality.* Cambridge, UK: Cambridge University Press.

Zuckerman, M. (in press). An alternative five factor model for personality. In C. F. Halverson, G. A. Kohnstamm, & R. P. Martin (Eds.), *The developing structure of temperament and personality from infancy to adulthood.* Hillsdale, NJ: Erlbaum.

Zuckerman, M., Ball, S., & Black, J. (1990). Influences of sensation seeking, gender, risk appraisal, and situational motivation on smoking. *Addictive Behaviors, 15,* 209–220.

Zuckerman, M., Buchsbaum, M. S., & Murphy, D. L. (1980). Sensation seeking and its biological correlates. *Psychological Bulletin, 88,* 187–214.

Zuckerman, M., Eysenck, S. B. G., & Eysenck, H. J. (1978). Sensation seeking in England and America: Cross-cultural, age, and sex comparisons. *Journal of Consulting and Clinical Psychology, 46,* 139–149.

Zuckerman, M., Kuhlman, D. M., & Camac, C. (1988). What lies beyond E and N? Factor analyses of scales believed to measure basic dimensions of personality. *Journal of Personality and Social Psychology, 54,* 96–107.

Zuckerman, M., Kuhlman, D. M., Joireman, J., Teta, P., & Kraft, M. (1993). A comparison of three structural models for personality: The big three, the big five, and the alternative five. *Journal of Personality and Social Psychology, 65,* 757–768.

Zuckerman, M., Kuhlman, D. M., Thornquist, M., & Kiers, H. (1991). Five (or three) robust questionnaire scale factors of personality without culture. *Personality and Individual Differences, 12,* 929–941.

Zuckerman, M., & Litle, P. (1986). Personality and curiosity about morbid and sexual events. *Personality and Individual Differences, 7,* 49–56.

Zuckerman, M., Murtaugh, T. T., & Siegel, J. (1974). Sensation seeking and cortical augmenting–reducing. *Psychophysiology, 11,* 535–542.

Zuckerman, M., & Neeb, M. (1979). Sensation seeking and psychopathology. *Psychiatry Research, 1,* 255–264.

Zuckerman, M., & Neeb, M. (1980). Demographic influences in sensation seeking and expressions of sensation seeking in religion, smoking, and driving habits. *Personality and Individual Differences, 1,* 197–206.

Zuckerman, M., Tushup, R., & Finner, S. (1976). Sexual attitudes and experience: Attitude and personality correlations and changes produced by a course in sexuality. *Journal of Consulting and Clinical Psychology, 44,* 7–19.

PART THREE

Implications of Biological Models of Temperament

Methodological Implications of the Impending Engagement of Temperament and Biology

Warren O. Eaton

B ecoming a parent of a second child often signals the appearance of an interest in temperament and an appreciation of the individuality of infants and children. That second child seems so different than the first, yet the parent is hard-pressed to readily identify a situational explanation for the differences and begins to think about the possibility of inborn characteristics. My own interest in temperament emerged for some of the preceding reasons as well as my dissatisfaction with the hegemony of a situationism that formerly characterized theories of child development. It is understandable, then, to find an affinity between the interests of temperament researchers and the promise of biological models for understanding individual differences. As other contributions to this book well illustrate, however, there is a substantial gulf between individual differences at the behavioral level and the biological processes that presumably contribute to them. Can that gulf be bridged? Although I do not have an answer to that question, the possible marriage between temperamental and biological models has some interesting implications, and what follows are some thoughts of a biologically challenged behavioral researcher.

Are Temperament and Biology Compatible?

With the certainty that I am oversimplifying, I begin with the observation that, in their general approaches, temperament and biological models are identifiably different in their emphases. Consider the characteristics of each.

Temperament's emphasis on individual differences is a descendent of the psychometric tradition, which traces its lineage back to Francis Galton and Alfred Binet. This approach focuses on dimensions of individual difference and their relationships. The search is for between-person differences that show stability over time and situations. Indeed, without such stability, knowledge of a person's characteristics in one situation or at one age would be of little use in predicting their characteristics in another situation or at a later time. Stability in this context is the stability of an individual's rank within a group. Even though everyone within the group may have changed with regard to the characteristic in question, stability of the ranking within the group could still remain stable. Moreover, regularities in dimensions of difference are often seen to have structural properties of considerable generality and breadth (e.g., Goldberg, 1993).

As a behavioral researcher, I find it more difficult to characterize biological models, but in contrast to temperament models, they seem more numerous, more detailed, and more dynamic. Most fit within the superstructure of evolutionary theory and range in their coverage from nuclear DNA, to neural structures, to hormonal systems, and to behavioral adaptations. These models range in complexity, have multiple levels, and are hierarchical (Baldwin, 1980; Gottlieb, 1991). Two features, in particular, contrast with temperament models. First, unlike temperament models, biological ones generally do not focus a great deal on individual differences. Rather, they are more like those of experimental psychology in that they seek processes and structures that have general applicability across individual conspecifics. Second, biological models strike me as more change oriented and more elaborate than the trait taxonomies of the temperament models. Consider, for example, Steinmetz' (chapter 2 of this book, Figure 2) simplified version of the septohippocampal system, which is a loop-based system with interactions between neighboring structures.

Given the preceding differences in outlook between the two approaches, an integration of temperament and biological models appears to be a formidable task. How, then, can specific temperament constructs be linked to specific biological models?

Matchmaking

The identification of a simple relationship between individual differences on some temperament construct and on some biological structure or process is often the initial goal of research programs. However, the number of potential combinations of temperamental and biological variables is large. As an upper limit of the number of different temperament concepts that could be considered, Strelau (chapter 5 in this book) has identified 81 different scales that purport to measure temperament. If these 81 dimensions were combined one at a time with the 11 labeled parts of the limbic system in Steinmetz's Figure 2 (chapter 2), 891 biology–temperament combinations would result—assuming that there was only one established index of the function of each limbic area and of each dimension of temperament, and assuming that there were no dependencies or interactions among the limbic structures or among the dimensions of temperament. Such an empirical what–if correlational approach to linking temperament and biology would, of course, not be practical, although it could generate a lot of master's degree theses. My point is that the potential number of linkages between biology and behavior is extremely large, and the winnowing of the productive from the unproductive possibilities is a daunting task indeed.

There are several methods for such winnowing. One is to start with behavior that has clinical and applied relevance. Research on the concept of difficult temperament (Bates, Olson, Pettit, & Bayles, 1982) or a child's ability to cope with stressors (Gunnar, 1990) can be strongly motivated by such concerns. Theory provides excellent criteria by which to select a behavior–biology link to pursue (e.g., see Rothbart et al.'s [chapter 4 in this book] discussion of Gray's behavioral activation system). In addition to theoretical and clinical grounds, I would add a third, less scientifically correct, but important strategy—that of capitalizing on measurement advances.

This strategy is illustrated by the old joke about the drunk who is discovered crawling around under a streetlight and is asked what he is doing. He answers that he is looking for his wallet; when asked if that is where he lost it, he says no, but explains that that is where the light is. Ideally, we would look for answers where one's theory says they are lost. However, many scientific advances occur, not so much because of theoretical foresight, important although that is, but because technologies of measurement cast new light on an issue or problem.

Consider the case of fetal movement. There has been a long-standing medical interest (Richards, Newbery, & Fallgatter, 1938) in the validity of mothers' reports of fetal movement. If such reports were valid, then they could be used to measure fetal activity and its possible relationship to other obstetric variables. Earlier in this century, researchers compared mothers' reports of fetal activity with recordings made with mechanical devices (e.g., Kellogg, 1941, connected curved metal plates, which were placed over a pregnant woman's abdomen, to a strip chart recorder with a series of pulleys and threads). Although Kellogg concluded from his technique (and sample of 1!) that mothers' reports were valid, such cumbersome procedures were not very successful, and research on fetal movements waned until the advent of computer-aided ultrasound imaging in the 1970s. This now well-known technology, which allows visualization of the fetus, made validity studies of mothers' reports quite feasible. As a result, there is now substantial evidence that mothers' perceptions of fetal movement are reasonably accurate (Eaton & Saudino, 1992). The advent of ultrasound imaging was fortuitous with respect to Eaton and Saudino's (1992) research interests, but the availability of this measurement advance led to some new understandings in a topic domain quite removed from the medical concerns that originally prompted the development of the technique.

Given that the present question is one of where we can best see possible links between biology and temperament, measurement advances on the biological side will have much to say about an answer (e.g., see Plomin & Saudino, chapter 6 in this book). However, there are some hard-earned methodological lessons from the behavioral side that may prove important.

On Not Getting Our Hopes High

I believe that one should begin with the assumption that the likely magnitude for a hypothesized correlation between a dimension of temperament and a putative biological companion process will be between .20 and .30. Why such an apparently pessimistic and unromantic prediction?

First, there is the problem of "distance" between temperament and biological variables. Longitudinal researchers know that if you measure some variable over time, the resulting correlation matrix typically has a simplex pattern, that is, measurements that are taken close together in time tend to be more strongly correlated than those taken farther apart. Distance can also refer to the degree of dissimilarity between two variables. Two closely related variables, such as IQ and school achievement, will tend to be more strongly related than two less similar variables, such as IQ and neuroticism. By this reasoning, biological and temperament variables, measured as they are with quite different methodologies, will be distant, if only because they share almost no method variance. Consequently, it is highly unlikely that the correlation between them will be dramatic or large by conventional standards.

I argue, moreover, that researchers have unrealistic beliefs about the magnitude of a "large" effect. Quantitative reviews of the past 15 years in the behavioral sciences suggest that researchers have had overly romantic expectations about what constitutes a strong association or effect. Readers who are familiar with meta-analytic review procedures, which attempt to summarize research literature in terms of effect sizes, know that an effect of 0.5 standard deviations (equivalent to a correlation of .24) is a substantial effect, although one that has been found in various literature (Hunter & Schmidt, 1990). However, effects larger than this are uncommon, and an effect size of 0.5 standard deviations, which was once considered a medium effect by Cohen (1969), is now more fairly considered a large one. An example of an effect of this size is the well-known association between maternal smoking and lower infant birth weight, which has been replicated in dozens of studies (see Eaton, 1989). Thus, the assumption of a correlation in the .2–.3 range is one of optimism, not pessimism. The preceding brand of optimism has some interesting implications for the engagement of biology and temperament; these implications are elaborated in the next section.

Strategies for a Successful Engagement

Behavior at a given moment is subject to many influences, environmental as well as biological. Because of the many vectors of influence, a given sample of behavior is much like a single item on a test. As such, a single sample of behavior has a high degree of unreliability (Epstein, 1983), which attenuates the possible association between the behavior and other variables. As is now well known, an effective solution to this problem is to average over a large number of related behaviors. Such aggregation increases reliability and helps the true score signal to emerge from all of the background noise.

I learned the preceding lesson in my research on motor activity level, in which actometers, or small motion recorders, were used to measure individual differences in the activity levels of infants and young children. In an early study (Eaton, 1983), a group of preschoolers wore actometers for a series of 1–hr sessions during nursery school free play. It was subsequently calculated that the reliability of the actometers for assessing individual differences was .13 for a single session, but the reliability rose to .75 when averaged across sessions.

Most behavioral researchers are well aware of the aggregation advantage, but I suspect that more biologically oriented researchers are less cognizant of its importance. The same measurement principle applies to biological variables. A good example of an application of the aggregation principle can be found in the research of Gunnar (chapter 7 in this book), who averaged across daily salivary cortisol samples. She found that aggregated samples were far more reliable for the identification of individual differences than were single ones.

Aggregation as a strategy for a successful engagement is closely related to a second issue: statistical power. Virtually every researcher knows that a large sample size is, for statistical purposes, preferable to a small one, but the melding of the temperament and biological research models poses special sample-size problems. The cost of research on biological questions is very high in relation to the cost of paper-and-pencil temperament research. An informal survey of a journal such as *Developmental Psychobiology* will reveal many studies with *n*s of 10–30 subjects. Even with infrahuman subjects such as mice and rats, cell sizes rarely exceed 10. Such sample sizes may be quite satisfactory for designs that allow for randomization and the procedural control of unwanted variability, but they are wholly inadequate for most studies that are designed to assess uncontrolled individual difference variance.

This power problem has emerged in other research when individual differences questions are coupled with experimental designs. A good illustration of this can be found in four information-processing studies reported by Kyllonen, Tirre, and Christal (1991), who were investigating whether individual differences in breadth of verbal knowledge were related to rate of learning paired associates (it was). They emphasized that their success in linking individual differences to rate of learning was critically dependent on large sample sizes. And what were their sample sizes? They were 396, 708, 593, and 215! It should be noted that their research designs were complex mixed-model ones with many between-subjects factors and within-subjects trend analyses. A given temperament–biology question may not require such elaborate designs, but it will almost certainly require more subjects than biologically minded researchers are accustomed to using.

What about a simple design that compares two groups and for which the known effect is large (e.g., 0.5 standard deviations)? The implications for effect sizes of this magnitude are startling, as Schmidt (1992) illustrated. If one tested the previously mentioned hypothesis in multiple studies with sample sizes of 30 (15 per group), then 63% of those studies would return a nonsignificant result at the .05 alpha level because of sampling error alone. In other words, with a moderate-to-large effect and modest, but not uncommon, sample sizes, the power to detect that effect would be .37! If, as I have argued, a reasonably true correlation between a biological and a behavioral aspect of temperament is in the .2–.3 range, then sample sizes of 60 or more will be needed to have a 50–50 chance of detecting it.

Schmidt (1992) also highlighted a more subtle feature of this situation, namely that the body of published findings can overestimate the true relationship in some typical situations. For the previous example of a true effect of 0.5 standard deviations and a set of studies with ns of 30, the critical value for significance would be an effect size of 0.62. Presumably, only those studies with a significant outcome, and which displayed an effect that was greater than the true one, would be publishable. If one were to calculate the mean effect size for only these significant studies, one would find it to be 0.89 (Schmidt, 1992), which would clearly be greater than the true value of 0.50. Thus, estimates of the size of a relationship that are drawn from the literature may well be inflated, especially when small sample sizes characterize those studies.

One can find some cold comfort in the observation that the possible overestimation of some effects may well account for disappointing replications of initially exciting findings. A seminal, published study may, because of the requirement of significance, be an overestimate of a true effect, but subsequent studies will tend to return smaller, more accurate estimates of the true effect. They would also be more apt to be nonsignificant, unless they used larger sample sizes.

Even if a given replication study does return a significant finding, it is likely that in a series of studies some would be significant and some would not. As Schmidt (1992) noted, such a pattern of results can lead to a misguided search for some moderating variable that is inferred to be responsible for the differential results. Sampling error may well be the cause of the seemingly inconsistent findings, but its invocation as an explanation does not have the scientific lustre of a moderator variable.

In short, statistical power problems are apt to pose real difficulties for studies that are attempting to link biology and temperament. The sample-size constraints on the biological side of the equation could well mean that a significant outcome is very unlikely, even though a true effect is present. What can be done about such Type II errors? One strategy is to look for studies in which there are very strong theoretical predictions for a definite outcome under narrowly circumscribed conditions. A second strategy is to use biological (and temperament) measures that can be applied to relatively large samples, as in Gunnar's (chapter 7) use of salivary cortisol samples. Schmidt (1992) would probably add that a focus on statistical significance in individual studies should be replaced by attention to effect-size estimates that are drawn from meta-analytic syntheses of multiple studies. In any event, the investigator who does not have multiple studies to synthesize would be wise to assume that a simple relationship between temperamental and biological constructs will be a modest one.

Developing Common Interests

To study temperament is to also assume, tacitly or explicitly, that a meaningful part of the behavioral variability that is seen among individual *Homo sapiens* originates from within them and is not solely the product of differences in their current environments and life histories. In pursuing such an assumption, temperament researchers have sought to find temporal and cross-situational stabilities in behavior, because if the individual is the constant across varying occasions and situations, then the presence of behavioral stability is more readily attributable to the invariantly present person than to shifting circumstances. Thus, temperament research has taken as its default position the expectation of phenotypic stability in the characteristics of interest. A good deal of effort has been expended in searching for that stability.

The preceding emphasis on stable traits is a legacy of the study of adult personality. It has been common in psychology for a topic to have started with adults and then to be extended to children (e.g., see Stevenson, 1983, on theories of learning). Although the assumption of longitudinal stability is a defensible one for adult personality (McGue, Bacon, & Lykken, 1993), it is more troublesome for temperament in children because the behaviors and capacities of children change markedly with age. Intelligence testers circumvented this problem by conceptualizing IQ as a relationship between mental and chronological ages. They could then express intelligence with a score that was independent of developmental status. Although temperament researchers have not generated age-independent scores akin to the IQ score, they have accomplished the same end by generally attending to correlations while avoiding means. If change is studied at all, then it is from a correlational perspective, typically involving issues of changing factor structure, not ontogenetic change.

If one wishes to predict future temperament from current temperament, then it is very tempting to ignore individual differences in developmental trajectories. This is because, if such trajectories are largely uniform across individual children, the rank orderings of children on the variable of interest are not scrambled by vagaries in developmental timing. Thus, even if children become uniformly less fearful with increasing age, individual differences in relative fearfulness remain meaningful and predictive. The assumption of uniform developmental change on dimensions of temperament has been largely unstudied, probably because its examination would raise a variety of measurement complexities. Difficulties notwithstanding, I was interested in whether my favorite dimension of temperament, activity level, had an identifiable developmental trajectory—an issue that has largely been neglected in the literature. To remedy that neglect, I undertook a review that combined the results of many studies in a crude developmental meta-analysis (for details see Eaton, in press).

When I first considered this question, I had taken notes on the relationship between age and activity for a number of studies, each of which had included a measure of activity level. In most of the studies, only the general direction of the relationship could be determined. Faced with a choice between a precise index from a small number of studies or a crude index from a large set of studies, I chose the latter and classified studies only as to the direction of the age–activity relationship (i.e., positive or negative). My notes were on file cards (I was in my precomputer stage) and sorted by author name. In the hope that I would see a pattern in the set of studies, I arrayed the cards on the table and saw the jumble of inconsistent findings that are shown in panel A of Figure 1. Apparently, there was no relationship between age and activity level.

Sometime later, I was inspired to do a reanalysis after learning about a set of rules for bad data presentation (Wainer, 1984). One of Wainer's rules is to organize information along an irrelevant dimension. I realized that few dimensions were more irrelevant to understanding development

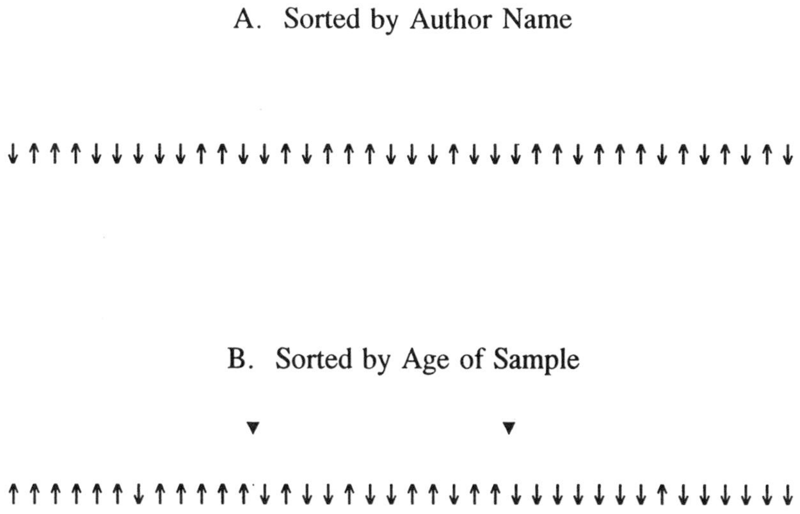

A. Sorted by Author Name

↓ ↑ ↑ ↑ ↓ ↓ ↓ ↓ ↑ ↑ ↑ ↓ ↓ ↑ ↓ ↑ ↑ ↑ ↓ ↓ ↓ ↑ ↓ ↓ ↓ ↑ ↑ ↑ ↓ ↑ ↑ ↑ ↓ ↑ ↓ ↑ ↓ ↑ ↓ ↑

B. Sorted by Age of Sample

▼   ▼

↑ ↑ ↑ ↑ ↑ ↑ ↓ ↑ ↑ ↑ ↑ ↑ ↓ ↑ ↓ ↓ ↑ ↓ ↑ ↑ ↑ ↓ ↑ ↑ ↓ ↓ ↓ ↓ ↓ ↓ ↓ ↑ ↓ ↓ ↓ ↓ ↓

FIGURE 1.   Two arrays of study outcomes for the relation between activity level and age. A: Sorted by author name. B: Sorted by age of sample. "Up" arrows indicate a positive relationship; "down" arrows indicate a negative relationship; inverted triangle symbols indicate ages of approximately 2 and 5 years, respectively. From *The Developing Structure of Temperament and Personality From Infancy to Adulthood* edited by C. F. Halverson, G. A. Kohnstamm, and R. P. Martin, 1993, Hillsdale, NJ: Erlbaum. Copyright 1993 by Erlbaum. Adapted by permission.

than an alphabetical ordering of results by author name. I consequently reshuffled my note cards in order of the mean age of each sample and was confronted by the pattern that is shown in panel B of Figure 1. Two break points in this array are suggested, and they are marked with the inverted triangle symbols. The first falls at approximately 2 years of age, with the second falling at approximately 5 years of age. The pattern of outcomes implies the presence of a curvilinear trajectory in the customary motor activity level of humans, a path that is characterized by increasing activity from the early days of postnatal life to sometime between 2 and 5 years of age and by decreasing motor activity levels thereafter.

I subsequently found corroboration for my inference: Curvilinear age patterns in activity have been reported in longitudinal studies of short-lived animal species (Campbell & Mabry, 1972; Owens, 1975; Reed, 1947); there is also at least one human study that covers the necessary age range and describes a curvilinear trajectory (MacFarlane, Allen, & Honzik, 1954). Curvilinearity does not in itself cause great difficulty with the reliance on rank order stability—unless there is variability in the timing of individuals' traversing of that path. Consider Figure 2, which depicts such a situation for a variable X. The profiles for each child are similar, with the major exception that one is traversing the same curvilinear developmental trajectory at an earlier age. How would we interpret such a pattern within a temperament framework? In a cross-sectional study, say at either Age A or Age C, one would be inclined to attribute the variability to temperament differences. However, if one conducted a longitudinal study and correlated Age A and Age B scores, then one would find no relationship; if one correlated Age A and Age C scores, then one would find a negative relationship! Without some evidence of longitudinal stability, as in these A–B and A–C correlations, the temperament model has little to offer.

The neglect of a developmental perspective was highlighted for me by the results of a recent longitudinal twin study (Saudino & Eaton, 1993). In this study, activity level was measured for 48 hr with mechanical motion recorders at two ages, 7 and 36 months. At each age, monozygotic (MZ)

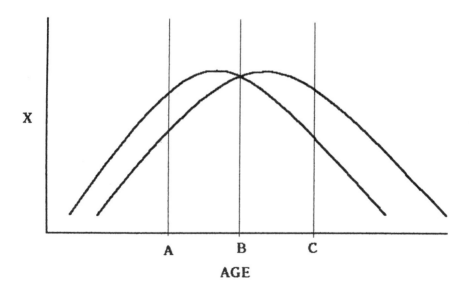

FIGURE 2.   Hypothetical longitudinal profiles for two individuals who vary in the timing of their development.

twins were more concordant on activity level than were their dizygotic (DZ) counterparts, a pattern that implies the presence of genetic contributions to individual differences at both ages. These were exciting findings because they corroborated with objective measures the results of twin studies that used parental reports. The case for activity level as a key dimension of temperament with a constitutional basis was also supported.

Because of its longitudinal design, the study also addressed some developmental questions. Specifically, the results of the study indicated that activity increased dramatically from 7 to 36 months of age. Moreover, MZ twins were more concordant on developmental change in that the amount of increase in activity for MZ cotwins was more similar than was the amount of increase for DZ cotwins. Thus, the evidence pointed to the presence of genetic contributions to developmental change. Given the preceding pattern of findings, one would assume that the traditional longitudinal stability (or phenotypic) correlation would be significant. It was not even close.

How is one to understand this situation in which there is evidence of genetic contributions at each age and for individual patterns of change, yet no age-to-age stability? My hypothesis is that genetically influenced, but different, activity-relevant processes are operating at the two ages. For example, activity differences at 7 months of age may be related to negative emotionality (e.g., crying and fussing); but at 3 years of age, other processes may be more salient. The 7-month-old is quite different from the 3-year-old, and it is naive to ignore these developmental realities.

The engagement of temperament and biology will, I believe, force temperament researchers to become more aware of the changing organism, in short, to become more developmentally oriented. Nelson (chapter 3 in this book) illustrates how the appearance of individual differences may be associated with underlying structural changes. A melding of biological models and temperament constructs will almost certainly require attention to such complexities of development.

Conclusion

The impending engagement of temperament and biology will undoubtedly take researchers' understanding in some surprising and unexpected directions. In addition to these surprises, there are several predictable implications for the engagement, and I have tried to make the case for two.

First, given the distance between the generalizations about individual differences in behavioral and biological processes and structure, the size of bona fide relationships between these two levels of analysis will, in correlational terms, probably not exceed the .20–.30 range. If this is true, then successful research programs will have to give careful attention to maximizing statistical power. A corollary of this need for power is the prediction that advances will be made where measurement technology will allow for the relatively inexpensive assessment of biologically relevant structures and processes.

Second, to be integrated with the complex, hierarchical, and dynamic biological models, static trait taxonomies and conceptualizations will have to become more elaborate and more developmentally sensitive. Although that will be a difficult task, it has the promise of invigorating future research on temperament.

References

Baldwin, A. L. (1980). *Theories of child development* (2nd ed.). New York: Wiley.

Bates, J. E., Olson, S. L., Pettit, G. S., & Bayles, K. (1982). Dimensions of individuality in the mother–infant relationship at six months of age. *Child Development, 53,* 446–461.

Campbell, B. A., & Mabry, P. D. (1972). Ontogeny of behavioral arousal: A comparative study. *Journal of Comparative and Physiological Psychology, 81,* 371–379.

Cohen, J. (1969). *Statistical power analysis for the behavioral sciences.* San Diego, CA: Academic Press.

Eaton, W. O. (1983). Measuring activity level with actometers: Reliability, validity, and arm length. *Child Development, 54,* 720–726.

Eaton, W. O. (1989). Childhood sex differences in motor performance and activity level: Findings and implications. In B. Kirkcaldy (Ed.), *Medicine and sport science: Vol. 29. Normalities and abnormalities in movement* (pp. 58–77). Basel, Switzerland: Karger.

Eaton, W. O. (in press). Temperament, development, and the five factor model: Lessons from activity level. In C. F. Halverson, G. A. Kohnstamm, & R. P. Martin (Eds.), *The developing structure of temperament and personality from infancy to adulthood.* Hillsdale, NJ: Erlbaum.

Eaton, W. O., & Saudino, K. J. (1992). Prenatal activity level as a temperament dimension?

Individual differences and developmental functions in fetal movement. *Infant Behavior and Development, 15,* 57–70.

Epstein, S. (1983). Aggregation and beyond: Some basic issues on the prediction of behavior. *Journal of Personality, 51,* 360–392.

Goldberg, L. (1993). The structure of phenotypic personality traits. *American Psychologist, 48,* 26–34.

Gottlieb, G. (1991). Experiential canalization of behavioral development: Theory. *Developmental Psychology, 27,* 4–13.

Gunnar, M. R. (1990). The psychobiology of infant temperament. In J. Colombo & J. Fagen (Eds.), *Individual differences in infancy: Reliability, stability, prediction* (pp. 387–409). Hillsdale, NJ: Erlbaum.

Halverson, C. F., Kohnstamm, G. A., & Martin, R. (1993). *The developing structure of temperament and personality from infancy to adulthood.* Hillsdale, NJ: Erlbaum.

Hunter, J. E., & Schmidt, F. L. (1990). *Methods of meta-analysis: Correcting error and bias in research findings.* Newbury Park, CA: Sage.

Kellogg, W. N. (1941). A method for recording the activity of the human fetus in utero, with specimen results. *Journal of Genetic Psychology, 58,* 307–326.

Kyllonen, P. C., Tirre, W. C., & Christal, R. E. (1991). Knowledge and processing speed as determinants of associative learning. *Journal of Experimental Psychology: General, 120,* 57–79.

MacFarlane, J. W., Allen, L., & Honzik, M. P. (1954). *A developmental study of the behavior problems of normal children between 21 months and 14 years.* Berkeley: University of California Press.

McGue, M., Bacon, S., & Lykken, D. T. (1993). Personality stability and change in early adulthood: A behavioral genetic analysis. *Developmental Psychology, 29,* 96–109.

Owens, N. W. (1975). Social play behaviour in free-living baboons, *Papio anubis. Animal Behavior, 23,* 387–408.

Reed, J. D. (1947). Spontaneous activity in animals. *Psychological Bulletin, 44,* 393–412.

Richards, T. W., Newbery, H., & Fallgatter, R. (1938). Studies in fetal behavior: II. Activity of the human fetus *in utero* and its relation to other prenatal conditions, particularly the mother's metabolic rate. *Child Development, 9,* 69–78.

Saudino, K. J., & Eaton, W. O. (1993). *Genetic influences on activity level: II. An analysis of continuity and change from infancy to early childhood.* Manuscript submitted for publication.

Schmidt, F. L. (1992). What do data really mean? *American Psychologist, 47,* 1173–1181.

Stevenson, H. (1983). How children learn—the quest for a theory. In W. Kessen (Ed.), *Handbook of child psychology: Vol. I. History, theory, and methods* (4th ed., pp. 213–236). New York: Wiley.

Wainer, H. (1984). How to display data badly. *American Statistician, 38,* 137–147.

CHAPTER 11

Toward Practical Uses for Biological Concepts of Temperament

John E. Bates, Theodore D. Wachs, and Robert N. Emde

The search for practical knowledge is a clear subtext throughout the literature on children's temperament, even in this book, which is focused on basic knowledge about biological factors in temperament. This chapter attempts to bring that practical subtext into the foreground. We are highly interested in applications that may be suggested by concepts of temperament. It can be argued that something is not really understood until it can be used. However, whether through research training, through clinical training, or by temperament, we are also cautious about overselling temperament as a clinical construct. This chapter is written for inquiring, research clinicians more than for ones who are looking for a set of well-defined, empirically validated techniques. Recommendations for use of concepts of temperament remain quite general and have seldom been empirically validated. Nevertheless, we do believe that well-considered practice with imperfect concepts can contribute to clients' welfare as well as to theoretical advances. In this chapter, we list current practices and suggest future approaches that might prove useful.

When concepts of temperament reemerged in models of child development, they were explanations of clinically relevant outcomes (Thomas, Chess, & Birch, 1968). The main emphasis at that phase and subsequently in the field has been on individual behavior patterns that are plausibly related to constitutional factors, excluding behavior that is mostly attributed to experience and cognitive factors, such as insecurity feelings and moral values (Thomas & Chess, 1989). Initially, specifics about the biological bases were generally lacking. More recently, there has been an explosion of interest in the biological bases of behavior, and concepts of temperament are becoming rooted in concepts of complex biological processes. There is movement toward consensus on some fairly broad biobehavioral systems that are relevant to personality development, as presented in three recent volumes by Kohnstamm, Bates, and Rothbart (1989), Strelau and Angleitner (1991), and Zuckerman (1991). Although the level of detail has increased exponentially, models of interactions between the various neuronal structures, biochemical processes, and behavior still remain tentative. Biopsychological detail seems clearest and most convergent across investigators in the basic descriptions of systems that are involved in discrete emotional and behavioral acts. It seems much less clear in the descriptions of the systems that operate over time to produce individual differences in patterns of behavior, as noted also by Eaton (chapter 10 in this book).

Two difficult issues that are embedded in concepts of temperament are important when one considers clinical applications. The first concerns the fact that temperament is an individual-differences construct. Temperament is usually thought of as characterizing individuality, but perhaps paradoxically, individual-differences approaches do not deal with individuality in the sense of the common notion of uniqueness. Instead, such approaches describe individuality according to differences and similarities among the members of a group. Knowledge that is based on differences and similarities is highly dependent on the group that is sampled, as well as on the variables chosen for study. Studies contributing to that knowledge are necessarily variable-centered rather than person-centered. Clinicians need to remember that one cannot make strong inferences from group-based studies of individual differences to particular individuals. Individual-differences studies of temperament that have been done in varying contexts and with different groups have accumulated knowledge about consistent patterns of behavior across development. The clinician faces the challenge of applying such general knowledge to the individual and to local circumstances. This chapter offers some guidelines for thinking about this challenge.

The second issue in considering clinical applications concerns the sense in which one considers temperament to be biological. Temperament is typically thought of as having an inborn, genetically influenced, biological basis (Bates, 1989b; Goldsmith, 1989). In addition, biological sources are often thought of as distinct from the environment and as acting on behavior in quasi-mechanistic, unidirectional ways. However, current biopsychological models incorporate multiple levels between gene, cell, and person. The levels of the system are hierarchically arranged, but they are interactive, with both environmental and genetic influences at all levels (Gottlieb, 1992; Hinde, 1992). Current knowledge suggests that the traits of temperament are regulated by multiple rather than single genes (Plomin & Saudino, chapter 6 in this book; Zuckerman, 1991). Complicating the picture even further, the genes turn on and off across development, responding to and regulating developmental processes. Genetic factors influence both continuity and change in temperament across development (Plomin et al., 1993). Clinical research indicates that individuals' patterns of temperament change across development in transaction with the social environment (Chess & Thomas, 1984, 1989). However, specification of the process and parameters in temperament–environment transaction has barely begun. Therefore, although there have been exciting developments in studies of genetics and other levels of the biological roots of temperament, one should not expect the search for biological bases for temperament to yield many simple correspondences between behavior and physical biology. Nevertheless, clinicians may profit from an awareness of the dynamic complexity of modern constructs of temperament, as well as from a glance at future constructs.

This chapter focuses on those concepts of temperament with the closest ties to current knowledge about biological systems and with the clearest relevance to concerns of psychologically oriented clinicians and educators. Current techniques that are based on concepts of temperament are considered first. At present, the practical implications of temperament that can be offered depend little on the specifics of biological structures and processes. As recent neuroscience and psychophysiology findings become known, however, and as biological measures of individuals advance, new applications will be increasingly based on biological information. Thus, this chapter concludes by envisioning possible benefits of more biologically specific concepts in future practice.

Current Applications of Temperament

Present applications of concepts of temperament are quite tentative, which is consistent with the state of knowledge on temperament. This is a conclusion not only offered by cautious academicians but also by scientifically oriented practicing clinicians, as seen in discussions at an international conference on temperament that was devoted entirely to clinical applications (Carey & McDevitt, 1989). Nevertheless, practicing clinicians have found some methods for using concepts of temperament. At this time, there is generally a lack of empirical evidence for the efficacy of these methods. Our summary of current practice relies not only on Carey and McDevitt's volume (1989) but also on the relevant sections of Strelau and Angleitner (1991), Kohnstamm et al. (1989), Chess and Thomas (1986), and other sources.

A fundamental appeal of temperament for the clinician is that its assumed component of biological predisposition allows transcendence over unidirectional and exclusively environmental-cause models, which many perceive as outmoded in an age of systems theory (e.g., Bates, 1989a; Chess & Thomas, 1989; Wachs, 1992). With a Temperament × Environment model, the child's behavior patterns are considered within complex social and developmental contexts (Carey, 1989a; Chess & Thomas, 1984, 1986). The child is seen as an active, selective responder, as well as an agent affecting others. If clinical assessment supports the plausibility of a temperament explanation, then the child's parents or teacher are given a psychobiological explanation that reduces blame, yet still allows novel action to resolve conflict between the child and the social environment

(Bates, 1989a). Novel action is considered crucial because of the tendency of problem–solution cycles to repeat themselves in inflexible and maladaptive ways (Fisch, Weakland, & Segal, 1982).

Assessment and Diagnosis: Current Practices

Clinical diagnosis has two aspects: (a) *classification* of disorder and (b) *assessment* of a particular individual in a particular context. Classification consists of the localization of the individual's symptoms and the clinician's observations of the individual within a widely accepted classification scheme for disorders, which thereby allows for linkages to knowledge about prognosis and intervention. Assessment consists of the many observations and measures that can be made of the individual's functioning, which can add to a clinician's ability to be helpful in a particular circumstance. We do not feel that knowledge of temperament is as yet applicable to classification of disorder. This section therefore deals with concepts of temperament in relation to assessment. Clinical discussions about assessment have revolved around two questions: (a) Which concepts of temperament are useful in guiding interventions? and (b) Which measures of those concepts are useful?

Which concepts of temperament should be assessed?
For clinical applications, it is important to identify particular concepts of temperament that imply specific interventions. A set of nine dimensions that were developed in the New York Longitudinal Study (NYLS) by Thomas, Chess, and colleagues (e.g., Thomas et al., 1968) has become a very widely used taxonomy for clinically oriented temperament researchers. The dimensions are activity, adaptability, approach, attention span–persistence, distractibility, intensity, mood, rhythmicity, and sensory threshold. Some clinicians (e.g., Turecki, 1989) use all nine NYLS concepts as temperament risk factors. Other clinicians emphasize a diagnosis of difficultness or easiness based on a configuration of temperament scales, such as the difficult, easy, and slow-to-warm-up categories (e.g., Carey, 1989a). Still others organize according to dimensions that are derived from factor analysis of the standard nine dimensions, for example, attention control and unadaptability (e.g., Martin, 1989a). There is a final group

of clinical researchers who have used factor-based taxonomies based on items that are based on NYLS concepts but who find factors that diverge from the nine NYLS dimensions (Bates, 1989b; Hagekull, 1989; Prior, Sanson, & Oberklaid, 1989).

Most recently, studies have begun to focus on several target concepts, which are based on the factorial summarization research showing three to seven dimensions in personality across developmental stages and cultures (Halverson, Kohnstamm, & Martin, in press; Kohnstamm, Halverson, Havill, & Mervielde, in press; Zuckerman, 1991). This chapter is organized around the three-variable systems—specifically Tellegen's (Tellegen & Waller, in press) and Zuckerman's (1991)—that we think not only will map well onto the leading models of temperament but also will reflect emerging knowledge on biological bases of temperament. What we present is a composite of these two systems—but not a perfect representation of either. The general dimensions are (a) *negative emotionality*, such as irritability and fearfulness; (b) *positive emotionality*, which would include reward seeking activity and sociability; and (c) *constraint*, which would include responsiveness to social controls and self-restraint versus impulsivity. These fixed axes can also be rotated to capture a whole circumplex of personality descriptors, which allows in principle for comparability of many different measures. These personality dimensions are being found in personality with many different measures, at different ages, and in different cultures (e.g., Goldberg, 1993; Halverson et al., in press; Rothbart, Derryberry, & Posner, chapter 4 in this book; Zuckerman, 1991). These dimensions also appear to have plausibly specific parallels in biological processes and structures.

Not all scales of temperament can be reduced to this three-dimensional system. Many argue that a five-variable (Goldberg, 1993) or even a seven-variable (Tellegen, 1993) array of dimensions is necessary to adequately characterize personality. Nor can researchers currently identify empirically established links between early childhood temperament and the basic personality dimensions (Halverson et al., in press; Wachs, in press). The three-dimensional system, however, has wide applicability (Zuckerman, 1991) and provides a conceptual focus. At least one major investigator (Zuckerman) has used "basic personality" as essentially equivalent to "temperament." It appears that several basic, second-order dimensions of personality have semantic overlap with a number of scales of temperament.

Which dimensions of temperament a clinician would choose to assess would depend on particular clinical decisions. A representative concern for many clinicians and educators is a misbehaving, unhappy child. To assess such a problem, the clinician desires concepts of temperament that provide insight into etiology and environmental sequences that should be changed. We can cite a little evidence on etiology: Several concepts of temperament have been found to covary with child adjustment, both concurrently and predictively. There are various operationalizations for each of the concepts, and not all correlations with adjustment have been observed with all measures of temperament in all situations; nor does a given measure always lead to identical patterns of findings in different samples. However, the general patterns of data have been reasonably consistent across samples and instruments.

The variables of temperament that have been found to be predictive of later adjustment (Bates, 1989a; Caspi, Henry, McGee, Moffitt, & Silva, 1992; Maziade, 1989), as conceptually mapped onto the three-dimensional personality system, include the following. (a) *Difficultness*: This construct has predicted both externalizing and internalizing symptoms. In infancy, difficultness seems to have elements of both frequent, intense negative affect expression and attention demandingness. This suggests that difficultness may be formed by intersecting dimensions of negative emotionality and impulsive sensation seeking or lack of constraint. According to theory, negative attention-demandingness could sometimes be related to unrestrained sensation seeking or impulsivity because suboptimal stimulation may be unpleasant and because impulsive individuals may tend to become irritable when their efforts are thwarted (Rothbart et al., chapter 4 in this book). (b) *Unadaptability and behavioral inhibition*: This construct has been found to be associated more clearly with internalizing symptoms than with externalizing ones. It appears to reflect primarily negative emotionality, with perhaps high constraint or low sociability tendencies. In addition, it may also reflect, at least at older ages, the presumably nontemperamental domain of slowness of verbal–intellectual development (Bates, 1989b; Martin, 1989b). Scales that describe (c) *task orientation* (Martin, 1989a), *tractability* (Matheny, Wilson, & Thoben, 1987), and conversely, *resistance to control* (Bates, 1989a) would probably fit best as reflections of the more general impulsivity-versus-constraint dimension. These scales have tended to be more clearly associated with externalizing, disruptive problems than internalizing, relatively self-contained ones. In addition to the constraint dimension, they may also contain a contribution from the positive affectivity dimension, in that an interested, reward-seeking child might be more likely to come in conflict with social limits.

The just-mentioned conceptual mapping of temperament in the misbehaving, unhappy child is plausible with current knowledge but is in need of empirical testing and refinement. At this time, there is no agreed-upon standard measure for any of the relevant concepts of temperament, but mapping individuals in a multidimensional space—even if only a two-dimensional one—may be useful in clinical decisions (e.g., Chess & Thomas, 1986; Turecki, 1989). For example, a clinician might suggest different parental behaviors for a child who is irritable due more to frustration of sensation seeking than for one who is irritable because of sensitivity to minor aversive stimuli and social novelty. Controlled demonstrations that such customizations of therapy actually improve child outcomes are lacking at the present time. This is one of many empirical issues in the field of temperament.

An important methodological discussion has concerned whether obtained correlations between measures of temperament and behavioral problems actually reflect etiological links between concepts of temperament and psychopathology, or are instead a reflection of item content contamination between the two kinds of measures (Bates, 1990; Rutter, 1989b; Sanson, Prior, & Kyrios, 1990). The contents of temperament scales do partially resemble the contents of adjustment checklists. Both temperament and behavior-symptom checklists refer to behavior and emotion in social relationships. It seems plausible that caregivers who report on the behavior of their children would give similar observations for content-similar scales dealing with temperament or with behavioral problems. Correlations between temperament and psychopathology, with both indexed at the same age, would be especially difficult to interpret as stemming from conceptually separate sources of variability. In fact, besides concurrent correlations there are also correlations between early individual differences on scales of temperament and later adjustment scores on behavioral checklists (Bates, 1989a; Bates et al., 1991; Earls & Jung, 1987; Graham, Rutter, & George, 1973; Maziade, 1989). This suggests a developmental continuity, even if there may also be some shared method variance. Maziade concluded that the equivalence of adverse temperament and psychopathology is unlikely because of the modest degree of linkage between the two kinds of variables in research so far. Further research needs to assess both temperament and psychopathology longitudinally, and evaluate the separate versus overlapping linkages between these antecedents and psychopathological (and temperament) outcomes. Further research also needs more precise definitions and measures of temperament characteristics, with improvements in both parent-report and observational assessments (Goldsmith & Rothbart, 1991). It will be important from the perspective of epidemiology to pursue Rutter's (1989a) question of

> whether temperament variation and psychiatric disorder have different determinants (such as genetic contributions or psychosocial adversity) and to test whether having differentiated temperament from disorder, temperament still predicts the later development of psychiatric problems. (p. 635)

A related methodological discussion concerns whether the continuities that are found in child temperament and behavioral adjustment are merely artifacts of stable source biases. It is reasonable to suppose that perceptual biases, such as social desirability response set, could account for some portion of any observer's report. This does appear to be so for situations in which parents are informants (see reviews by Bates, 1980, 1989a, in press) and could, in principle, be found for research staff observers. This is not to equate the two methods: Parental reports integrate observations over long time spans and can take account of rare yet salient events, whereas research observations are more limited in time but can be done with greater control over conditions of observation and perceptual biases. Nevertheless, the potential markers of parent-report biases have not been found to be correlated with scores of temperament any more strongly than markers based on unbiased, objective reporting (Bates & Bayles, 1984; Matheny et al., 1987). These findings call into question assumptions that parental reports are riddled with subjectivity and that research-observer reports are automatically more valid.

Furthermore, even if correlations between early temperament and later adjustment are attributed to source bias, one would still have to postulate a complex, rather than a simple, one-dimensional informant bias because qualitatively different dimensions of temperament predict comparable distinctions in types of behavioral problems in later childhood (Bates, 1990; Cameron, Hansen, & Rosen, 1989; Caspi et al., 1992; Maziade, 1989; Sanson et al., 1990), as just summarized. Instead of, or in addition to, the assumption that parental reports reflect multidimensional source bias, one could also make the perhaps more interesting assumption that some components of parental reports meaningfully reflect cross-situational, core temperament. Moreover, another interesting assumption still tenable is that the reports partly reflect the developing child–caregiver relationship. Research to date does not allow a clear choice of assumptions.

Which measures should be used?
Many measures have been developed for assessing child temperament. Questionnaire measures for parents' or teachers' reports are the most numerous (Slabach, Morrow, & Wachs, 1991) and most frequently used. Despite this, caregiver reports are often deprecated (Bates, in press), as seen for example in journal reviews and editorial decisions. There are also a few multidimensional laboratory tests of temperament (e.g., Goldsmith & Rothbart, 1991; Matheny et al., 1987) and naturalistic observation rating scales (e.g., Bates & Bayles, 1984). For basic research purposes, it is vital to have the laboratory and observational measures in addition to caregiver questionnaire measures. However, we are unaware of any constructs that have been demonstrated to have greater construct validity or to be of more practical value when assessed by one of the more objective, but much more costly, methods than when assessed by caregiver reports. There could be such an operational construct in principle, but for now,

we suggest that parental and teacher reports are of use to clinicians, as long as the potential inaccuracies are kept in mind (Bates, in press). Future assessment methods are considered in a later section.

Which of the questionnaire measures, then, provides the clinician with the most useful information? Slabach et al. (1991), after a comprehensive review of the literature, concluded that although there are many differences between temperament questionnaires, with each having its own shortcomings, various questionnaires might be adequate for research uses, depending on the specific purposes of one's research. Slabach et al.'s conclusion can be extended to clinical uses as well. The particular kind of problem would (or should) influence the specific variables of interest, and the specific variables would determine the choice of measures. One clinical scientist might be interested in the foundations of attention problems in school and would therefore be most interested in scales having to do with task orientation and attentional concepts such as impulsivity and distractibility (e.g., Keogh, 1989; Martin, 1989a). Another clinical scientist might be concerned with parent–child conflict and would pay particular attention to negative emotionality and associated attention-demandingness and resistance to control (Bates, 1989a).

Current Interventions

Many temperament-based interventions have been reported. Almost invariably, these reports have been accompanied by cautions about the formulations and assessments underlying the treatments, and about the efficacy of the treatments themselves. Nevertheless, concepts of temperament are being used, even if cautiously. For example, Rutter (1989b) pointed out the major conceptual and measurement problems that cast doubt on temperament's usefulness but concluded that there is empirical support for clinically relevant concepts of temperament, as long as researchers recognize that it is currently impossible to definitively separate the components of constitution and environment. We now summarize some of the more prominent perspectives, focusing completely on child problems.

Child psychiatry–clinical psychology

Chess and Thomas (e.g., 1986) have provided prototypical formulations for using temperament in clinical practice. In their 1986 book and in other sources, they have frequently discussed common behavioral adjustment problems found in their longitudinal research sample and in their clinical practice. They have assessed individual children, with strong attention to the developmental process, via a detailed interview of the parents. Their focus has been on the meshing of temperament, especially difficult versus easy versus slow-to-warm, with the environment, especially environmental demands for confronting novelty and challenges. Their assessment approach also has often included a playroom session with the child, as well as parent-report questionnaires when necessary. On the basis of an assessment that showed temperament–environment fit problems, Chess and Thomas (e.g., 1986) have provided guidance to the parents (or when the children were older, to the children themselves) on how to more productively cope with temperament–environment conflicts. Their basic objective has been to help people "see the positive side of traits they possess and to assist them to use these traits in adaptive ways," as Rutter (1989b, p. 474) put it. When temperament is a smaller part of the problem, and when psychopathology of child or parents is more severe, then direct psychotherapy has been recommended (Chess & Thomas, 1986).

Turecki (e.g., 1989) has dealt with similar issues in a private clinic for young children (as described by Turecki, 1989) and in a hospital-based clinic (as described by Chess & Thomas, 1986). Turecki's formulations resemble those of Chess and Thomas (1986); he considers all of the nine Thomas–Chess dimensions to be clinically relevant. After assessment, Turecki guides parents toward a more "educated and benign" parental leadership (Turecki, 1989), training them to apply a cognitive problem-solving algorithm for choosing in any given situation between gentle management versus effective, dominating punishment.

Cameron and colleagues (Cameron et al., 1989; Cameron, Hansen, & Rosen, 1991) have been concerned with management problems in very young children in a large health maintenance organization. They assess as many of the infants as possible in their health maintenance organization, using a shortened version of the widely used Carey and McDevitt

(1989) parent-report scales, which use the nine Thomas–Chess constructs. They then use these scores as the basis for customized, anticipatory guidance, for example, guidance about how a difficult child might respond to the challenges of parental limits at the time independent locomotion is achieved. Their goal is primary prevention of psychopathology. The research of Cameron et al. (1989, 1991) is distinctive in that it included controlled analysis of the efficacy of their treatments. Their results provide some support for the efficacy of the preventive intervention, especially when guidance is given face-to-face; however, the results also show that simple written guidance may not only be ineffective but may actually sensitize parents to possible problems.

Bates (e.g., 1989a) has applied concepts of temperament in various ways to common preschool- and middle-childhood problems in both low- and middle-income families, using parental and teacher reports on the dimensions of resistance to control, stimulation seeking, attention demandingness, irritability, and fearful versus approaching response to novelty. Interventions that are based on a formulation of temperament often, if not always, involve a benign reframing of the child's behavior pattern and guidance to the parents as to how to predict and constructively deal with challenging behavior by the child. Such an application is compatible with systems-oriented family therapy. Systemic therapy techniques have also been applied more directly to the child. One example involved changing the typical problem sequence by first formulating a 6-year-old boy's tantrums as having a temperament basis in need for control and action. This formulation, given in the presence of the child, took blame from the child and suggested that such emotional events would "need" to occur. However, at the same time, the therapist directed the child in the coming week to have some tantrums in particular situations, while the mother took careful notes on the details of how his tantrum varied across situations. In the ensuing week, the mother joined the spirit of the intervention by asking the child, on occasions when he was on the verge of a tantrum, whether this was one of his official tantrums and whether she needed to get her notebook. There were other aspects to the intervention (Bates, 1989a), but in this case, the child almost immediately and almost completely ceased his tantrums. Along with this important step to maturity, he continued to be an active, outgoing boy.

Pediatrics and pediatric psychology

Brazelton (e.g., 1969) has provided an influential example in pediatrics of organizing advice to parents of infants around temperament differences such as activity and by showing parents how to appreciate the developmental implications of such differences. The pioneering and programmatic research of Carey (e.g., 1989a, 1989b, 1993) has focused on behavioral problems in a pediatric practice, including poor adjustment to stressful events, as well as mild but more chronic behavioral problems and school problems. Carey has used parental questionnaires and consulting-room interviews and observations to assess temperament risk factors that include difficult, slow-to-warm-up, and low task-orientation traits, in transaction with environmental demands and stressors. Carey has emphasized the advantages of the pediatrician's longitudinal perspective on the child and family. He recommends the use of an assessment–intervention decision tree chart, which culminates in six different treatment choices, not all of which depend on the presence of temperament risk factors (Carey, 1989a, 1989b). The factors include (a) intervention on behalf of the child, (b) monitoring the problem or possible problem, (c) medical therapy, (d) referral to a psychotherapist, (e) pediatric counseling about temperament, and (f) pediatric counseling about nontemperament causes of the misbehavior (e.g., misperception of the child or other environmental and biological causes).

Weissbluth (e.g., 1989a, 1989b) has provided a pediatric focus on infants' and children's sleeping problems. Weissbluth's model of sleep problems involves environment–child transactions that produce alertness–sleepiness cycles and adrenal hormone cycles that are at odds with functional sleep patterns. Such patterns are dealt with in an easy infant by helping parents establish better timing and more soothing routines. In a difficult infant, intervention may need to consist of extinction of crying after the infant is put to bed.

Other pediatrics-related problems have been attacked with concepts of temperament in a less elaborated way than that of Carey (1989a, 1989b,

1993) and Weissbluth (1989a, 1989b) but deserve mention; they include maternal adaptation to a new baby (Hagekull & Bohlin, 1989), accident prevention (Matheny, 1989), diabetes (Garrison, 1989), and developmental handicaps (Goldberg & Marcovitch, 1989).

Educational psychology

Probably the most well known of the educational psychologists who are using concepts of temperament are Keogh (e.g., 1989) and Martin (e.g., 1989a, 1989b). Both began with the NYLS nine-dimensional system and discovered that teacher ratings can be decomposed into a much smaller number of consistently valid dimensions. For both psychologists, dimensions of task orientation and personal–social adaptability are of particular salience at school. Keogh has advised that teachers be aware of child temperament characteristics as one way to be able to predict and thus be able to prevent trouble. For example, with a highly active, distractible, or impersistent child, the teacher could be prepared to see the child as needing extra guidance at times of transition, instead of making negative attributions about the child's motivations. In a related vein, Pullis (1989) recommends helping teachers to manage their own negative feelings, to stop asking children to do things they are not suited for, and to provide extra help for a child when necessary.

Martin (1989a, 1989b) has emphasized the search for better formulations of academic underachievement. Martin believes that underachievement problems are the result of prenatal factors that affect temperament (especially the dimensions of attention control, activity, and adaptability), specific learning disabilities, and physiological–neurological problems such as those related to minor physical anomalies. Martin also believes that underachievement is the result of birth and childhood factors, including poor schooling and a lack of support in the home for education. The point being made by Martin (1989a), Rutter (1989b), and others is that the practitioner is presented with a whole child in a whole system. Therefore, it is not possible to identify traits of temperament separately from the developmental products of nontemperamental, biological characteristics and environmental shaping. This complex formulation for school problems is probably applicable to many others, not just those in school. It raises questions about how interventions that are based on formulations of temperament actually work.

How is temperament useful in intervention?
Temperament-based interventions, to the extent they are helpful, must succeed by hitting a largely unspecified target. The intervention must address interactions between the child and the child's social environment in a way that allows change, despite a vague model of how temperament is involved (Rutter, 1989b) and no assurance that the clinician actually has measured temperament rather than nontemperamental aspects of personality and social process. When a temperament-based intervention succeeds, it may do so by means of a relatively modest adjustment in the typical patterns of social interaction, rather than from better temperament–environment fit.

However, it is also possible that an intervention may succeed through an improved adaptation to the child's temperament by the social system. Strategic family therapists (e.g., Fisch et al., 1981; Haley, 1988) suggest that the key action of an effective clinician is to perturb the system in a way that allows a new level of flexible control, in place of the previous, stereotyped, ineffective transactions that were organized around "the child's problem." The intervention itself may have temporary effects, but ideally, it allows development to resume. If the parents are induced to be both more gentle and more persistent with a distractible child, as Chess and Thomas (1984, 1986) recommended, then this may lower the arousal level of the child, which may then allow the child to focus better. Such parental behavior may also increase the child's interest in a more rewarding adult, thereby eliciting more attention and cooperation. Environmental change could thus induce compensation for a temperament risk factor, thus reducing the frequency of problematic behavior.

It is also possible that the child's own pattern of attentional–affective reactions to stimuli could change over the course of development. When temperament is defined as the surface pattern of behavior, clearly temperament itself could change with maturation, changing circumstances, and systemic transactions at higher levels of individual and social complexity. More interesting, however, is the possibility that over time an intervention might produce change in the neurological organization that underlies temperament, for example, as when chronic levels of arousal are reduced at a neurohormonal level or when attentional, emotional, self-control, and reasoning structures in the child are developed more completely than they otherwise would have been. Steinmetz (chapter 2 in this book) suggests that transactions with the conditioning environment can affect functioning of temperament-relevant neural systems. The relevant studies to demonstrate such processes are just beginning to be done (see Wachs & King, chapter 12 in this book, for further discussion of this point).

To conclude this section, we argue that the current practical uses of temperament stem in a very general way from biological concepts, but they do not rely on specific biological models. For current applications, it is enough that a salient individual characteristic be identified and that it have some plausibility as a trait that is inborn and relatively stable. Most temperament-based interventions do not require a biological model of the child. Clinicians could often frame the same recommendations with environmental causation formulations. We believe that the more complete model of development that temperament-oriented clinicians hold provides greater efficiency in problem-solving, but there is not actually any evidence yet that this is so.

Future Practice

The preceding section on current practice was informed by biological research in terms of the dimensions of temperament that were emphasized. However, most of the section could easily have been written without the insights of research such as that described in this book. We doubt that this will be possible in 10 years. Looking deep into our crystal ball, we now attempt predictions as to how knowledge of biological factors in temperament will influence future practice.

Implications for Assessment

Partly due to advancing technologies for assessing brain functioning, we foresee an accelerating trend toward empirical identification of fairly basic biological structures and processes that more tightly specify what the variables of temperament are and how they operate in relationship to environment. Concepts of temperament have been of interest, not just because they account for early appearing traits, but especially because they also offer the hope of an objectification of the biological bases of adaptation. With advances in neuroscience, there have been corresponding advances in specifying biological processes underlying temperament (Kohnstamm et al., 1989; Strelau & Angleitner, 1991; Zuckerman, 1991a; also see the chapters in this book). One implication of this trend is the assessment of more basic biological states and events, as opposed to the assessment of patterns of social behavior. However, although psychophysiological or neurochemical data might avoid the interpretive problems of subjective biases, by themselves they are not sufficient.

As Fahrenberg (1991), Strelau (chapter 5 in this book), and others have cautioned, there are great challenges in finding meaningful individual differences in the physiological variables. According to research, two physiological variables that covary in one individual might well not covary in another individual. As a result, there are a great many possible patterns to consider. A second trend in research addresses this problem. Studies of basic biological patterns are increasingly being guided by multitrait–multimethod studies of behavior in context. Fahrenberg (1991) and Zuckerman (1991) have made especially eloquent calls for "top-down" approaches to guide biopsychological research. It appears likely that the superfactor, three- or five-dimensional approaches to the study of personality mentioned earlier in this chapter may be a matrix that facilitates linkages between the behavioral "top" and the biological "bottom." Behavioral research can work hand in hand with biological research; however, ultimately, researchers will probably learn to think of biological processes as not necessarily primary and, indeed, not necessarily separate from the psychosocial processes of behavior (see Wachs & King, chapter 12 in this book).

The most promising integrations of the two ends of the construct of temperament involve brain models of circuits affecting activation and inhibition of behavior (Fowles, 1988; Gray, 1991; Zuckerman, 1991), as discussed previously in this chapter and in much more detail in a number of the other chapters in this book. Temperament traits of positive and negative emotionality, activity, impulsivity, and distractibility, all of which have practical relevance, can be conceptually linked with neural systems. These neural systems have considerable empirical support as descriptors of basic emotional and attentional phenomena. However, these phenomena are not isomorphic with the construct of temperament, which refers to a pattern of behavior across situations and time. Furthermore, there is actually little specification of individual differences at the neural level.

Brain imaging techniques may someday advance to the point that metabolic and electrical activities of relatively small areas of the brain can be assessed without risk to the developing child. Similar advances toward less obtrusive assessments of neurochemical and peripheral events will probably also be achieved. Such developments may, in turn, provide the clinical scientist with opportunities to highlight subtle distinctions in behavioral patterns that might otherwise be ignored. At present, neuroscientists seem focused on describing the "circuitry" in basic events. Hence, they do not speculate much on larger patterns over time or on individual variations. In time, however, useful variables and measures will be discovered. These could include the numbers of nerve cells in a particular nucleus of the brain; the extensivity of synaptic linkages between different, interacting brain structures; temporal patterns of activity of a defined system of brain areas; or distinctive profiles of amounts of neurotransmitter substances.

One foretaste of such research is that of Calkins and Fox (chapter 8 in this book). Through electroencephalographic measures in 9-month-old infants, Calkins and Fox found that high levels of right frontal cortex activation (which may also reflect activity in corresponding areas such as the hippocampus and the amygdala) was observed in infants who at 4 months of age showed a pattern of high negative reactivity and high motor activity. Young infants who showed high negative reactivity and high motor activity also tended to be high in behavioral inhibition to novelty at 14 months of age. Also interesting were findings of the reverse pattern, in which greater relative left frontal activation at 9 months of age was associated with high positive affect plus high motor activity at 4 months of age. Kagan and colleagues (Kagan & Snidman, 1991a; Kagan,

Snidman, & Arcus, 1992) also found the high reactivity pattern at 4 months of age to predict novelty fears at 9 and 14 months of age; they also reported different, but conceptually related, psychophysiological markers of behavioral inhibition, such as heart rate acceleration and other indicators of sympathetic nervous system arousal.

Another way of describing the biological processes that are relevant to temperament is in the research of Lewis, Ramsay, and Kawakami (1993), who used cortisol, a by-product of stress reactions (see Gunnar, chapter 7 in this book). Lewis et al. studied 4-month-olds' stress reactivity, as indexed both by cortisol and by overt emotional expressions, while the infants were inoculated at the pediatrician's office. Although many infants were classified as being congruent on external expression and internal cortisol response, there were also a number of infants who showed an inverse relationship between the two indexes. Lewis et al. noted some cultural differences in these latter cases: Japanese infants were more likely than American infants to be internally distressed but overtly quiet; American infants were more likely to be low in cortisol but high in overt protest. Lewis et al. speculated that this may reflect culturally based differences in rearing patterns, especially the greater average proximity of Japanese parents to their infants, which is thought to imply corresponding differences in the signal value of crying. In addition, Lewis et al. suggested that inhibition of an overt expression might increase the internal cortisol response, whereas reinforcement of crying might decrease the cortisol response.

The findings of Lewis et al. (1993) suggest a number of questions for empirical research on adaptations within different environments: Will an infant with both cortisol and behavioral distress be different from one with high cortisol and low overt distress in later anxiety, depression, and somatic problems? Similarly, will an infant with low cortisol but high distress be different from a low cortisol–low distress child in later aggressiveness? In addition, will environmental differences correspond to concordant versus discordant biological–behavioral profiles? Answers to these questions would help distinguish between adaptations that may have some surface similarities (e.g., in amount of overt distress) but that may also have potentially crucial differences for tailoring effective treatments (e.g., amount of internal distress and family–cultural constraints on expression of negative emotions).

Studies of behavioral inhibition and stress response have been successful. It is plausible to predict that future research on the relationships between behavior and biology will advance beyond inhibition–approach and will consider longer developmental courses of individual differences. These advances will greatly enrich biological models of temperament. Nevertheless, as Calkins and Fox (chapter 8) emphasize, the fact that there is a biological system involved in behavioral variation does not imply that this system is directly responsible for the pattern; there are other facets of the developing child (e.g., qualities of child–caregiver relationships) that would play a role in outcomes separately and in interaction with the child's predispositions (also see Gunnar, chapter 7; Wachs & King, chapter 12).

Implications for Treatment

Given that the integration of biological and behavioral systems in individual development is underway, some intriguing possibilities for models of treatment are implied. One is that there may be more informed uses of goodness-of-fit models, which could amount to a more systematic tailoring of general treatments to particular cases, as called for by Dance and Neufeld (1988).

The coming specificity of knowledge about neural systems and quantitative genetics may be able to resolve an interesting issue—whether the adaptational implications of temperament are a function of continuous or discontinuous trait variation (Rutter, 1989a; Plomin & Saudino, chapter 6 in this book). Recently developed techniques in quantitative genetics (DeFries & Fulker, 1988) allow for the testing of whether the genetic–environmental influences for particular areas of a sample distribution are different in kind from the influences operating over the rest of the sample distribution. Thus, one can test in a large twin sample whether children at the extremes of behavioral inhibition show a unique pattern of genetic–environmental influences across time, as compared with all others who are not as extreme (Robinson, Kagan, Reznick, & Corley, 1992; Plomin et al., 1993). Such analyses will be important for identifying specific patterns of temperament that might be thought of as "syndromes" or phenotypes that reflect genotypic influences in some individuals. Using the example of behavioral inhibition, if such a pattern of behavior is a syndrome representing risk for anxiety disorder in only a minority of individuals, as some believe (e.g., Biederman et al., 1990, 1992; Kagan et al., 1990; Warren, 1993), and if this pattern can be elicited reliably in specifiable contexts (Kagan et al., 1992), then family tree studies may well reveal genetic markers when the human genome is mapped (see Plomin & Saudino, chapter 6). On the other hand, if behavioral inhibition is not a qualitatively distinct syndrome in some individuals, but instead is a dimensional trait characterizing all individuals, then such studies will not be fruitful. The clinical implications are vastly different.

Another paradigm for considering whether the adaptational significance of temperament depends on a critical level or pattern of temperament is seen in the research of Fox and colleagues. Calkins and Fox (chapter 8) report greater stability of electroencephalographic asymmetry for an extremely high negative behavior group than for an unselected sample. Similar questions could be raised for other variables of temperament, for example, early childhood sensation seeking: Do only the most highly sensation-seeking children have problems that could be diagnosed as attentional–hyperactivity disorder, or do more moderately sensation-seeking children also have an increased chance of this disorder? Perhaps this kind of question could be answered in terms of qualitative-versus-quantitative differences in brain structure or conditioning processes.

One particular treatment implication of the question of qualitative-versus-quantitative linkage between temperament and pathology is the choice between proportional and binary models of treatment. At the moment, especially in clinical child psychology and psychiatry, intervention systems are largely based on qualitative models of disorder. However, for situations in which adaptation and its underpinnings of temperament are continuously distributed, this might provide a basis for analog models of treatment. For example, a child who is moderately high on the dimension of impulsive sensation seeking would probably not be diagnosed as pathological, yet this child still might be helped to develop internal controls on behavior by moderate levels of assistance, which might serve to prevent later problems. Proportional intervention approaches might not only save professional time in treating already-developed disorders, through the use of proportional intensities of intervention, but might also allow efficient prevention of disorders.

On the other hand, if research shows that the core temperament components of psychopathology are only involved in the extremes of adaptation, then this too could be useful. Categorical diagnoses are convenient and lend themselves to treatment decisions that are based on answers to binary questions in a diagnostic flow chart. For example, if only extreme impulsive sensation seeking were found to be associated with genetic variations, then this might have prognostic and treatment implications. Perhaps at the extremes, where the loadings of temperament are highly salient, traditional interventions would need to be supplemented by some form of biological intervention to achieve initial change in behavior or to prevent relapse. Conversely, it might be found that the risk that is associated with less extreme impulsive sensation seeking might be relatively easily managed through environmental interventions.

Assuming that biologically rooted underpinnings of temperament for individual differences in behavioral activation and inhibition processes are likely, it seems plausible to expect that markers of such processes might also be discovered. That is, there may be certain factors in the ways in which an individual responds to a particular situation that indicate a particular biological condition, rather than more general learning history or nontemperamental biological characteristics. This might then provide grounds for more precisely targeted interventions than are currently used.

For example, some common forms of depression appear to have at least two components—relatively high levels of negative emotionality and relatively low levels of positive emotionality (Tellegen, 1985). A particular, phenotypic case of depression might be arrived at through a number of different paths. It might be useful in treatment to know the relative balances of the components, both concurrently and historically. With this knowledge, the combinations of pharmacological and behavioral interventions might be more precisely tailored to the individual's temperament predispositions. There need not be only one idealized state that is the target of all interventions. One depressed individual might need to reduce the level of negative affect but not increase the level of positive affect or extraversion, whereas another might need the reverse. Although skilled clinicians may know this intuitively, direct information on temperamental–biological underpinnings of adaptational history might aid in making diagnostic decisions that imply particular goals and methods for treatment.

Another route toward sharper treatment decisions of a biologically informed classification scheme, as suggested by the research of Lewis et al. (1993) and Gunnar (chapter 7), involves the assessment of both inner and outer expressions of distress in young children, for example, by both cortisol assays and behavioral indexes. It may be worthwhile to study the differential effectiveness of antianxiety treatments (e.g., graduated exposure) and behavior-suppression treatments (e.g., extinction) for children whose distress expressions are and are not congruent with certain physiological responses (e.g., activation of the hypothalamic–pituitary–adrenocortical system). Our intriguing, but cloudy, crystal ball hints that the findings of such research might help sharpen the comprehension of internalizing and externalizing behavioral problems, perhaps even suggesting useful strategies for caregivers in shaping adaptive behaviors at early ages.

Another example, then, would concern aggressive behavior disorders. Although typically one would think of an aggressive child as being low in the temperament traits of inhibition or fearfulness, there may be some children who are high on both aggressiveness and fearfulness, whereas others are high in aggression but low in anxiety. It seems likely that some parts of anxiety have a basis in temperament (Bates, 1989a; Kagan & Snidman, 1991a, 1991b). The distinction between high- and low-anxiety aggressive children has been drawn, with apparent implications for future adjustment, such as a lower degree of continuity of aggressiveness in high-anxiety children (Bates, Pettit, & Dodge, in press; Tremblay, 1992). If such distinctions can be sharpened through both behavioral and biological assessments of temperament, then it is possible that early interventions could be more efficiently targeted to prevent the terrible social costs of full-blown cases of conduct disorders, which are notoriously difficult to treat. Speculatively, young children who show the early behavioral pattern that is associated with later conduct disorder might be assessed for their profiles of temperament characteristics, as well as for other relevant characteristics, such as social information processing tendencies, with potentially important implications for screening and treatment.

The characteristics of temperament need not be assessed only in terms of naturally occurring behavioral patterns; they can also be assessed via responses to standardized, conditioning paradigms, such as psychophysiological and behavioral responses in an avoidance learning procedure. As in the speculative example concerning depression, more precise knowledge of the relative levels of inhibitory and activational processes might allow more precisely targeted behavioral and pharmacological interventions. For example, an individual whose aggressiveness is associated more with high levels of activation or extraverted exploration than with an absence of inhibitory responsiveness to aversive stimulation might be treated by changing the environment to provide more consistent, salient warnings and punishments. The reverse case, in which there is a relatively small basic response to aversive stimuli, might need intervention in which the escalating but ineffectual punishments are reduced and in which emphasis is placed on direct shaping of prosocial interests, skills, and cognitions. Again, skilled clinicians are probably intuitively aware of the relevant differences in reactive children who need gentle guidance versus unreactive children who need more intensive skills training and milder but still effective forms of punishment. However, diagnoses of these qualities are unsystematic and imprecise, which may contribute to the inefficiency of treatment and certainly to the inefficiency of evaluation of treatment effects. Again, assuming advances in biobehavioral diagnosis, it is also conceivable that environmental interventions for cases with an extreme deficit in ability to learn from aversive stimuli might someday be supplemented by drugs that compensate in a fairly precise way for the brain abnormalities that are associated with the conditioning deficit.

Conclusion

This chapter responds from a clinical perspective to the exciting developments in basic research on the neurobiological bases of temperamentlike behavior. The chapters of this book provide glimpses of a future in which individual differences in early appearing, relatively stable behavioral patterns will be related in specific ways to biological functioning, such as differences within the neural circuits supporting the individual's responses to signals of potential danger in the environment. The research on individual differences in such biological bases is not nearly as well developed as the research on normative characteristics of the systems. However, even without knowledge of specific biological bases, concepts of temperament are currently being applied to the solution of problems of individual children and their caregivers. The current solutions fundamentally rest on a benign reframing of pathology: Caregivers are taught to see the child's problems as representing a conflict between the developing child's constitutional temperament and the dynamic demands of a variable environment. When the reframing or professional guidance for the caregiver works, it is thought that changes are made that provide a better fit between temperament and environment. This formulation has not as yet received sufficient empirical evaluation. Assuming fulfillment of the current promise of research on biological bases of individual differences in temperament, future practice with concepts of temperament will involve assessments that draw distinctions between particular neural circuitry and interventions that directly address those distinctions.

We do envision a more biologically specific knowledge base for practice in the future. The trends are clearly already present. However, this does not mean that we believe the problems of individuals and social systems will be reduced to abnormalities in neural systems operating in a mechanistic, causal way. Developmental psychobiology suggests that a predetermined sequence of development is not coded in an individual's genes. Epigenesis is an emergent system in which all levels of biology and the environment are coacting and in continuous interplay (Gottlieb, 1992; Hinde, 1992; Plomin & Saudino, chapter 6). Even if biological inheritance and early events predispose one to certain kinds of responses in a particular environment, there will still be unpredictable courses of development and many possible paths to help people improve their adaptations.

References

Bates, J. E. (1980). The concept of difficult temperament. *Merrill-Palmer Quarterly, 26,* 299–319.

Bates, J. E. (1989a). Applications of temperament concepts. In G. A. Kohnstamm, J. E. Bates, & M. K. Rothbart (Eds.), *Temperament in childhood* (pp. 321–355). New York: Wiley.

Bates, J. E. (1989b). Concepts and measures of temperament. In G. A. Kohnstamm, J. E. Bates, & M. K. Rothbart (Eds.), *Temperament in childhood* (pp. 1–26). New York: Wiley.

Bates, J. E. (1990). Conceptual and empirical linkages between temperament and behavior problems: A commentary on the Sanson, Prior, and Kyrios study. *Merrill-Palmer Quarterly, 36,* 193–199.

Bates, J. E. (in press). Parents as scientific observers of their children's development. In S. L. Friedman & H. C. Haywood (Eds.), *Developmental follow-up: Concepts, genres, domains, and methods.* San Diego, CA: Academic Press.

Bates, J. E., & Bayles, K. (1984). Objective and subjective components in mothers' perceptions of their children from age 6 months to 3 years. *Merrill-Palmer Quarterly, 30,* 111–130.

Bates, J. E., Bayles, K., Bennett, D. S., Ridge, B., & Brown, M. M. (1991). Origins of externalizing behavior problems at eight years of age. In D. Pepler & K. Rubin (Eds.), *Development and treatment of childhood aggression* (pp. 93–120). Hillsdale, NJ: Erlbaum.

Bates, J. E., Pettit, G. S., & Dodge, K. A. (in press). Family and child factors in stability and change in children's aggressiveness in elementary school. In J. McCord (Ed.), *Coercion and punishment in long-term perspective.* Cambridge, UK: Cambridge University Press.

Biederman, J., Rosenbaum, J. F., Bolduc, E. A., Farone, S. V., Hirshfield, D. R., & Kagan, J. (1992, October). *A three year follow-up of children with and without behavioral inhibition (BI): Further evidence of an association between BI and childhood onset anxiety disorders.* Poster presented at the annual meeting of the American Academy for Child and Adolescent Psychiatry, San Francisco, CA.

Biederman, J., Rosenbaum, J. F., Hirschfeld, D. R., Faraone, S. V., Bolduc, E. A., Gersten, M., Meminger, S. R., Kagan, J., Snidman, N., & Reznick, J. S. (1990). Psychiatric correlates of behavioral inhibition in young children of parents with and without psychiatric disorders. *Archives of General Psychiatry, 47,* 21–26.

Brazelton, T. B. (1969). *Infants and mothers: Differences in development.* New York: Delacorte Press.

Cameron, J. R., Hansen, R., & Rosen, D. (1989). Preventing behavioral problems in infancy through temperamental assessment and parental support programs. In W. B. Carey

& S. C. McDevitt (Eds.), *Clinical and educational applications of temperament research* (pp. 155–165). Berwyn, PA: Swets North America.

Cameron, J. R., Hansen, R., & Rosen, D. (1991). Preventing behavioral problems in infancy through temperament assessment and parental support programs within health maintenance organizations. In J. H. Johnson & S. B. Johnson (Eds.), *Advances in child health psychology* (pp. 127–139). Gainesville: University of Florida Press.

Carey, W. B. (1989a). Practical applications in pediatrics. In G. A. Kohnstamm, J. E. Bates, & M. K. Rothbart (Eds.), *Temperament in childhood* (pp. 405–419). New York: Wiley.

Carey, W. B. (1989b). Temperament risk factors in general pediatric practice. In W. B. Carey & S. C. McDevitt (Eds.), *Clinical and educational applications of temperament research* (pp. 53–63). Berwyn, PA: Swets North America.

Carey, W. B. (1993). Specific uses of temperament data in pediatric behavioral interventions. In W. B. Carey & S. C. McDevitt (Eds.), *Prevention and early intervention: Individual differences as risk factors for the mental health of children—A festschrift for Stella Chess and Alexander Thomas*. New York: Brunner/Mazel.

Carey, W. B., & McDevitt, S. C. (1989). *Clinical and educational applications of temperament research*. Berwyn, PA: Swets North America.

Caspi, A., Henry, B., McGee, R. O., Moffitt, T. E., & Silva, P. A. (1992). *Temperamental origins of child and adolescent behavior problems: From age 3 to age 15*. Unpublished manuscript, University of Wisconsin, Madison.

Chess, S., & Thomas, A. (1984). *Origins and evolution of behavior disorders: From infancy to adult life*. New York: Brunner/Mazel.

Chess, S., & Thomas, A. (1986). *Temperament in clinical practice*. New York: Guilford Press.

Chess, S., & Thomas, A. (1989). The practical application of temperament to psychiatry. In W. B. Carey & S. C. McDevitt (Eds.), *Clinical and educational applications of temperament research* (pp. 23–35). Berwyn, PA: Swets North America.

Dance, K., & Neufeld, R. (1988). Aptitude–treatment interaction research in the clinical setting. *Psychological Bulletin, 104*, 192–213.

DeFries, J. C., & Fulker, D. W. (1988). Multiple regression analysis of twin data: Etiology of deviant scores versus individual differences. *Acta Geneticae Medicae et Gemellologiae, 37*, 205–216.

Earls, F., & Jung, K. G. (1987). Temperament and home environment characteristics as causal factors in the early development of childhood psychopathology. *Journal of the American Academy of Child and Adolescent Psychiatry, 26*, 491–498.

Fahrenberg, J. (1991). Differential psychophysiology and the diagnosis of temperament. In J. Strelau & A. Angleitner (Eds.), *Explorations in temperament: International perspectives on theory and measurement* (pp. 317–333). New York: Plenum.

Fisch, R., Weakland, J. H., & Segal, L. (1985). *The tactics of change: Doing therapy briefly.* San Francisco: Jossey-Bass.

Fowles, D. C. (1988). Psychophysiology and psychopathology: A motivational approach. *Psychophysiology, 25,* 373–392.

Garrison, W. T. (1989). Temperament methodology and physical chronic illness: An example from juvenile diabetes. In W. B. Carey & S. C. McDevitt (Eds.), *Clinical and educational applications of temperament research* (pp. 107–111). Berwyn, PA: Swets North America.

Goldberg, L. R. (1993). The structure of phenotypic personality traits. *American Psychologist, 48,* 26–34.

Goldberg, S., & Marcovitch, S. (1989). Temperament in developmentally disabled children. In G. A. Kohnstamm, J. E. Bates, & M. K. Rothbart (Eds.), *Temperament in childhood* (pp. 387–403). New York: Wiley.

Goldsmith, H. H. (1989). Behavior–genetic approaches to temperament. In G. A. Kohnstamm, J. E. Bates, & M. K. Rothbart (Eds.), *Temperament in childhood* (pp. 111–132). New York: Wiley.

Goldsmith, H. H., & Rothbart, M. K. (1991). Contemporary instruments for assessing early temperament by questionnaire and in the laboratory. In J. Strelau & A. Angleitner (Eds.), *Explorations in temperament: International perspectives on theory and measurement* (pp. 249–272). New York: Plenum.

Gottlieb, G. (1992). *Individual development and evolution: The genesis of novel behavior.* New York: Oxford University Press.

Graham, P., Rutter, M., & George, S. (1973). Temperament characteristics as predictors of behavior disorders in children. *American Journal of Orthopsychiatry, 43,* 328–339.

Gray, J. (1991). The neuropsychology of temperament. In J. Strelau & A. Angleitner (Eds.), *Explorations in temperament: International perspectives on theory and measurement* (pp. 105–128). New York: Plenum.

Hagekull, B. (1989). Longitudinal stability of temperament within a behavioral style framework. In G. A. Kohnstamm, J. E. Bates, & M. K. Rothbart (Eds.), *Temperament in childhood* (pp. 283–297). New York: Wiley.

Hagekull, B., & Bohlin, G. (1989). Greater impact of infant temperament in multiparous mothers' adaptation. In W. B. Carey & S. C. McDevitt (Eds.), *Clinical and educational applications of temperament research* (pp. 97–101). Berwyn, PA: Swets North America.

Haley, J. (1988). *Problem-solving therapy* (2nd ed.). San Francisco: Jossey-Bass.

Halverson, C. F., Kohnstamm, G. A., & Martin, R. P. (in press). *The developing structure of temperament and personality from infancy to adulthood.* Hillsdale, NJ: Erlbaum.

Hinde, R. A. (1992). Developmental psychology in the context of other behavioral sciences. *Developmental Psychology, 28,* 1018–1029.

Kagan, J., Reznick, J. S., Snidman, N., Johnson, M. O., Gibbons, J., Gersten, M., Biederman, J., & Rosenbaum, J. F. (1990). Origins of panic disorder. In J. C. Ballenger (Ed.), *Neurobiology of panic disorder* (pp. 71–87). New York: Wiley.

Kagan, J., & Snidman, N. (1991a). Infant predictors of inhibited and uninhibited profiles. *Psychological Science, 2,* 40–44.

Kagan, J., & Snidman, N. (1991b). Temperamental factors in human development. *American Psychologist, 46,* 856–862.

Kagan, J., Snidman, N., & Arcus, D. M. (1992). Initial reactions to unfamiliarity. *Current Directions in Psychological Science, 1,* 171–174.

Keogh, B. K. (1989). Applying temperament research to school. In G. A. Kohnstamm, J. E. Bates, & M. K. Rothbart (Eds.), *Temperament in childhood* (pp. 437–450). New York: Wiley.

Kohnstamm, G. A., Bates, J. E., & Rothbart, M. K. (1989). *Temperament in childhood.* New York: Wiley.

Kohnstamm, G. A., Halverson, C. F., Havill, V. L., & Mervielde, I. (in press). Parents' free descriptions of child characters: A cross-cultural search for the roots of the Big Five. In S. Harkness & C. Super (Eds.), *Parents' cultural belief systems: Cultural origins and developmental consequences.* New York: Guilford.

Lewis, M., Ramsay, D. S., & Kawakami, K. (1993). Differences between Japanese infants and Caucasian-American infants in behavioral and cortisol responses to inoculation. *Child Development, 64,* 1722–1731.

Martin, R. P. (1989a). Activity level, distractibility, and persistence: Critical characteristics in early schooling. In G. A. Kohnstamm, J. E. Bates, & M. K. Rothbart (Eds.), *Temperament in childhood* (pp. 451–461). New York: Wiley.

Martin, R. P. (1989b). Temperament and education: Implications for underachievement and learning disabilities. In W. B. Carey & S. C. McDevitt (Eds.), *Clinical and educational applications of temperament research* (pp. 37–51). Berwyn, PA: Swets North America.

Matheny, A. P., Jr. (1989). Injury prevention and temperament. In W. B. Carey & S. C. McDevitt (Eds.), *Clinical and educational applications of temperament research* (pp. 103–106). Berwyn, PA: Swets North America.

Matheny, A. P., Jr., Wilson, R. S., & Thoben, A. S. (1987). Home and mother: Relations with infant temperament. *Developmental Psychology, 23,* 486–494.

Maziade, M. (1989). Should adverse temperament matter to the clinician? An empirically based answer. In G. A. Kohnstamm, J. E. Bates, & M. K. Rothbart (Eds.), *Temperament in childhood* (pp. 421–435). New York: Wiley.

Plomin, R., Emde, R. N., Braungart, J. M., Campos, J., Corley, R., Fulker, D. W., Kagan, J., Reznick, J. S., Robinson, J., Zahn-Waxler, C., & DeFries, J. C. (1993). Genetic change and continuity from 14 to 20 months: The MacArthur Longitudinal Twin Study. *Child Development, 64,* 1354–1376.

Prior, M. R., Sanson, A. V., & Oberklaid, F. (1989). The Australian temperament project. In G. A. Kohnstamm, J. E. Bates, & M. K. Rothbart (Eds.), *Temperament in childhood* (pp. 537–554). New York: Wiley.

Pullis, M. (1989). Goodness of fit in classroom relationships. In W. B. Carey & S. C. McDevitt (Eds.), *Clinical and educational applications of temperament research* (pp. 117–120). Berwyn, PA: Swets North America.

Robinson, J. L., Kagan, J., Reznick, J. S., & Corley, R. (1992). The heritability of inhibited and uninhibited behavior: A twin study. *Developmental Psychology, 28,* 1030–1037.

Rutter, M. (1989a). Isle of Wight revisited: Twenty-five years of child psychiatric epidemiology. *Journal of Child and Adolescent Psychiatry, 28,* 633–653.

Rutter, M. (1989b). Temperament: Conceptual issues and clinical implications. In G. A. Kohnstamm, J. E. Bates, & M. K. Rothbart (Eds.), *Temperament in childhood* (pp. 463–479). New York: Wiley.

Sanson, A., Prior, M., & Kyrios, M. (1990). Contamination of measures in temperament research. *Merrill-Palmer Quarterly, 36,* 179–192.

Slabach, E. H., Morrow, J., & Wachs, T. D. (1991). Questionnaire measurement of infant and child temperament: Current status and future directions. In J. Strelau & A. Angleitner (Eds.), *Explorations in temperament: International perspectives on theory and measurement* (pp. 205–234). New York: Plenum.

Strelau, J., & Angleitner, A. (1991). *Explorations in temperament: International perspectives on theory and measurement.* New York: Plenum.

Tellegen, A. (1985). Structures of mood and personality and their relevance to assessing anxiety, with an emphasis on self-report. In A. H. Tuma & J. D. Maser (Eds.), *Anxiety and anxiety disorders* (pp. 681–706). Hillsdale, NJ: Erlbaum.

Tellegen, A. (1993). Folk concept and psychological concepts of personality and personality disorder. *Psychological Inquiry, 4,* 122–130.

Tellegen, A., & Waller, N. G. (in press). Exploring personality through test construction: Development of the Multidimensional Personality Questionnaire. In S. R. Briggs & J. M. Cheeks (Eds.), *Personality measures: Development and evaluation* (Vol. 1). Greenwich, CT: JAI Press.

Thomas, A., & Chess, S. (1989). Temperament and personality. In G. A. Kohnstamm, J. E. Bates, & M. K. Rothbart (Eds.), *Temperament in childhood* (pp. 249–261). New York: Wiley.

Thomas, A., Chess, S., & Birch, H. G. (1968). *Temperament and behavior disorders in children.* New York: New York University Press.

Tremblay, R. (1992). The prediction of delinquent behavior from childhood behavior: Personality theory revisited. In J. McCord (Ed.), *Facts, frameworks and forecasts: Vol. 3. Advances in criminological theory* (pp. 193–230). New Brunswick, NJ: Transactions.

Turecki, S. (1989). The Difficult Child Center. In W. B. Carey & S. C. McDevitt (Eds.),

Clinical and educational applications of temperament research (pp. 141–153). Berwyn, PA: Swets North America.

Wachs, T. D. (1992). *The nature of nurture.* Newbury Park, CA: Sage.

Wachs, T. D. (in press). Fit, context and the transition between temperament and personality. In C. Halverson, G. Kohnstamm, & R. Martin (Eds.), *The developing structure of temperament and personality from infancy to adulthood.* Hillsdale, NJ: Erlbaum.

Warren, S. L. (1993). *Childhood anxiety disorders: A developmental perspective on risk and course of disorder.* Unpublished manuscript, Department of Psychiatry, University of Colorado Medical School, Denver.

Weissbluth, M. (1989a). Sleep-loss stress and temperament difficultness: Psychobiological processes and practical considerations. In G. A. Kohnstamm, J. E. Bates, & M. K. Rothbart (Eds.), *Temperament in childhood* (pp. 357–375). New York: Wiley.

Weissbluth, M. (1989b). Sleep–temperament interactions. In W. B. Carey & S. C. McDevitt (Eds.), *Clinical and educational applications of temperament research* (pp. 113–116). Berwyn, PA: Swets North America.

Zuckerman, M. (1991). *Psychobiology of personality.* Cambridge, UK: Cambridge University Press.

CHAPTER 12

Behavioral Research in the Brave New World of Neuroscience and Temperament: A Guide to the Biologically Perplexed

Theodore D. Wachs and Beverly King

This summary chapter is presented expressly for the behaviorally oriented temperament researcher who, after repeated forays into the chapters contained in this book, may have wrongly concluded that he or she has little role to play in future temperament research. What we hope to show is that, paradoxically, increased understanding of the biological roots of temperament is not an impediment to future behavioral research in this area. Rather, we argue that increasing knowledge about the biological basis of temperament offers a unique set of research challenges that can only be answered via continued input from behaviorally oriented temperament researchers. Before dealing with this issue, we first summarize the main points that are raised in this book, by way of framing the issues to be discussed in an appropriate context (a good behavioral strategy).

We thank John E. Bates and Charles A. Nelson for their incisive comments on a preliminary draft of this chapter.

Biological Roots of Temperament: Common Themes

The chapters in this book have not only guided the reader toward the physiological, biochemical, and anatomical systems that are likely to be the most fruitful focus as researchers search for the biological roots of temperament, but they have hopefully also alerted the reader to voids to be filled and problems to be addressed in future biotemperament research endeavors.[1] This section addresses these two aspects.

Where Do We Find the Biological Roots of Temperament?

Strelau (chapter 5 in this book) presents a brief list of assumptive statements on which we base our consideration that temperament indeed may have a biological basis. One of these is the observation that any psychological function depends on the activity of the brain. Quoting Gray (1991, p. 105), Strelau states, "if there exists a psychology of temperament . . . . then there is ipso facto a neuropsychology of temperament."

Although this sentiment is echoed by many psychobiological researchers, acknowledging that the brain is ultimately the source of all behavior does not mean that one can localize all behavior within the brain, given the nervous system's complex set of circuits and interconnections (see Nelson, chapter 3 in this book). It is also true that the more "amorphous" the construct the more difficulty one can expect to encounter in locating its basis in the nervous system. Given that there are a host of often tenuously defined traits of temperament that one could potentially attempt to locate neurally (81 according to Strelau, chapter 5), out of necessity biotemperament researchers usually restrict their focus to a few options that either follow naturally from their current line of research or about which the database is broad enough to allow speculative theorizing. Table 1 presents a brief summary of the major systems that are emphasized by the contributors to this book. It should be immediately obvious that Steinmetz (chapter 2 in this book), Nelson (chapter 3), and Rothbart, Derryberry, and Posner (chapter 4 in this book) all

---

[1]We have derived the phrase "biotemperament research" as a substitute for the more cumbersome phrase "research on the biological roots of temperament."

present a similar outline concerning the brain systems that are involved in temperament. This is not surprising considering that they all draw heavily from Gray's (1991) detailed model of the neural substrates of emotion and personality.

Many of the structures that have been implicated as playing an important role in temperament behavior are those that have long been identified as being involved in emotional behavior. For example, the cingulate was identified by Papez (1937) as being involved in emotion via the hypothalamus. These, in turn, are part of the larger collection of structures known as the limbic system, which has been called the "emotional brain" (Goodwin, 1989). Indeed Nelson (chapter 3) describes the amygdala (a portion of the limbic system) as the organ that permits humans to have an emotional experience. One less cited area is the thalamus, which links portions of the hypothalamus and other parts of the limbic system that are involved in emotional behavior. The structure is worthy of more attention by developmental psychobiologists because the thalamus may mediate the development of conditioned fear responses prior to the maturation of cortical areas that are involved in cognitive functioning (Rothbart et al., chapter 4).

It is also apparent from Table 1 that different levels of analysis are represented. Any trait or behavioral dimension depends on several factors for its expression. In Zuckerman's (chapter 9 in this book) psychobiological model of personality, these factors include social behavior, conditioning, physiology, biochemistry, neurology, and genetics. Although Zuckerman cautions against hiding "within the shell of our most familiar turtle," it is usually a feasible choice for researchers to select one or two of these levels to include in their research repertoire.

Although a feasible strategy, the operation of multiple levels ultimately implies the necessity to go beyond the temperament researcher's preferred level of focus. For example, many of the chapters in this book provide the reader with a good overview of the anatomical structures that are likely to be involved in temperament. However, more information needs to be provided on cross-level detail concerning mechanisms of action, which in the brain involve neurotransmitters. Some authors mention the importance of the neurotransmitters that are involved in tem-

TABLE 1
Summary of Biological Roots of Temperament

Temperament dimension/trait	System(s) cited	Relevant structures/ neurochemicals	Researcher
Positive/negative affect Approach/behavioral inhibition	Hemispheric activation	Frontal cortex (with amygdala perhaps underlying EEG asymmetries in infancy)	Calkins & Fox
Stress Vulnerability	Hypothalamic–pituitary–adreno-cortical	System influenced by various structures including the amygdala and its projections to the motor system, cingulate and motor cortex and hypothalamus	Gunnar
Approach/positive affect Reactivity to novelty	Behavioral activation	Amygdala; temporal pole, orbitoprefrontal cortex; ventral striatum; ventral pallidum; motor cortices	Nelson
Withdrawal/negative affect Reactivity to novelty	Behavioral inhibition	Hippocampal formation and its surrounding structures (especially septal area, entorhinal area, dentate gyrus, hippocampus, subiculum, presubiculum); prefrontal cortex (including the orbitoprefrontal cortex); portions of the motor system	
Activity level	Genetic influence	Preliminary findings of marker for activity level in a gene for the enzyme tyrosinase which is involved in tyrosine metabolism	Plomin & Saudino

Approach/positive affect	Behavioral activation Behavioral facilitation	Limbic system projections to the brain stem and their interaction with various dopaminergic systems	Rothbart, Derryberry, & Posner
Behavioral/inhibition, avoidance/fear, response to novel stimuli	Behavioral inhibition	Hippocampus and related structures, as well as neurochemical processes	
Irritability/anger	Fight–flight	Basolateral and centromedial nuclei of the amygdala, ventromedial nucleus of the hypothalamus, central gray region of the midbrain, somatic and motor effector nuclei of the lower brain stem	
Emotionality	Interaction of limbic system with:	Includes septophippocampal system, limbic cortex, hypothalamus, amygdala	Steinmetz
	ANS and effector systems, and with:	Example = basal ganglia	
	Brain stem areas involved in arousal or vigilance	Examples = raphe nuclei and locus coerulus	
Arousability (which may subsume several temperament/personality traits)	Brain stem reticular formation	Cortex, reticular formation, limbic system, ANS, neurotransmitters, enzymes, hormones	Strelau
Impulsive unsocialized sensation seeking	Neurochemical and hormonal	Dopamine (approach), serotonin (inhibition), norephinephrine (arousal; attention focusing)	Zuckerman

Note. EEG = electroencephalographic; ANS = autonomic nervous system.

perament (e.g., Strelau, chapter 5), but more information is needed concerning their exact mechanism of influence in the physiology of individual differences. There are a multitude of possibilities including, but not limited to, differences among individuals in the manufacture or degradation of neurotransmitters, the relative deficit or overproduction of neurotransmitters, receptor sites and binding characteristics (such as sensitivity of neuronal postsynaptic receptors), and other elements of synaptic transmission.

The Need for a Developmental Framework

A number of authors emphasize the importance of viewing neural contributions to temperament in a developmental framework. It is known that prefrontal cortical areas mature later than do other areas of the brain such as the limbic or striatal areas (Nelson, chapter 3). Calkins and Fox (chapter 8 in this book) also hint at a developmental progression in brain system organization with their supposition that, in infancy, electroencephalographic (EEG) asymmetries may reflect subcortical asymmetries, possibly in the amygdala. It may be beneficial to present-day psychobiological research efforts to refocus attention on the concept that not all biological systems involved with a specific trait come on-line at the same time, as was pointed out by Anokhin (1964) in his theory of *systemogenesis*. One implication of the systemogenesis concept is that the nature of the relation among interacting biological systems may change as new systems come on-line. A second implication is that the way information is processed may vary across time, due to the differential maturation of the systems involved.

Differential development of neural systems may account for the instability of temperament ratings across the first 2 years of life. In general, available evidence indicates relatively limited long-term stability of specific dimensions of temperament (Slabach, Morrow, & Wachs, 1991). For the most part, behavioral researchers have construed these findings in terms of measurement problems with existing scales of temperament. However, the evidence presented in this book suggests that the cause may be biological rather than psychometric. As noted by both Nelson (chapter 3) and Rothbart et al. (chapter 4), not only are there different systems involved in different dimensions of temperament, but the components that define these neural systems come on-line at different ages. In terms of the implications for understanding stability, Rothbart et al. have shown that as different neural systems reach functional maturity, the nature of the child's behavioral patterns will change. If different neural subsystems are involved in specific temperament-related behaviors (see Table 1), and if these subsystems reach functional maturity at different points in time, then it is not surprising that stability would be relatively limited. Instability of measures of temperament will be a natural consequence if the behaviors that characterize a given dimension of temperament are rooted in a neural system that is still developing.

A similar conclusion can be drawn in regard to the question of interparent agreement. Available evidence indicates only modest ($r = .3–.4$) agreement among parents about the nature of their child's temperament (Slabach et al., 1991). Again, the processes underlying this finding may reflect biological rather than psychometric influences. In chapter 3, Nelson nicely illustrates how young infants may have a capacity for short-term reactivity to existing stimulation, but that this capacity may be situation-specific. Because the neural areas that are involved in long-term emotional memory develop more slowly, and because emotional memories that are encoded early in life have no particular neural home, one should not expect emotional consistency across situations. If the young child's existing neural structure does not allow consistency of response across situations, then it is therefore not surprising that mothers and fathers may see different aspects of the young child's temperament. Mothers and fathers may be providing different situations for the infant, either by treating the child differently (MacDonald & Parke, 1984), or by the two parents together providing a different context than does one parent (Clarke-Stewart, 1978). This type of information serves to illustrate why low stability or low interparent agreement may not be a flaw in our methodology but rather may reflect naturally occurring variability in children's temperament as a consequence of the nature of central nervous system (CNS) development.

Besides maturational development of the nervous system, change over time may be due to other influences. The subsequent impact of this change on temperament, behavior, and physiology is a common topic in this book. For example, Plomin and Saudino (chapter 6) are interested in strategies that will detect genetic sources of age-to-age change as well as continuity in temperament. One candidate identified by these authors is the extension of multivariate genetic analysis to longitudinal data. Similarly, Rothbart et al. outline a developmental model of temperament systems, highlighting behavioral measures that correlate at one age but not at another (e.g., fear and frustration). Although normal maturational factors may play a role in these correlational shifts, there also may be comparatively sudden reorganizations in the nervous system, comparable to Emde's (1989) concept of biobehavioral shifts. Resolving this issue will necessitate the longitudinal assessment of children, both physiologically and behaviorally, at enough ages to determine whether the changes are more gradual than precipitous or vice versa.

Zuckerman's theory may also be relevant to the issue of physiological change over time, although his theory is not strictly developmental in nature. Zuckerman (chapter 9) states that sensation-seeking scores decline steadily with age from the teens through the 60s, and that these age changes may be mediated by certain neurotransmitters, enzymes, and gonadal hormones. Extending the study of this construct downward from the teens could provide valuable information in terms of when and how this genetically related trait first appears in development, and whether the physiological, biochemical, and hormonal correlates of the trait in adulthood hold for the preteen years as well. For example, although the comparison is a stretch, Zuckerman (chapter 9) reports that low levels of platelet monamine oxidase are found in both high-activity babies and adults with high levels of social activity. This suggests that researchers might be able to trace the developmental course of physiological correlates of sensation seeking such as platelet monoamine oxidase levels.

Finally, in understanding change across time in the biological processes underlying temperament, of critical importance is the accumulation of normative data as it relates to physiological or psychophysiological measures that are likely to be used in biotemperament studies. For example, for EEG studies, Lindsley's now classic research (e.g., Lindsley, 1939) documented the longitudinal sequence of EEG changes during development in human infants. In more recent research, Calkins and Fox (chapter 8) have discovered age-related changes in the pattern of EEG spectral power. Specifically, there appears to be a power shift from lower to higher frequency bands as infants get older. This type of change confounds the study of EEG stability and necessitates comparison to normative age data. Developmental psychobiologists have a responsibility to accumulate information on the nature and extent of change in the physiological–psychophysiological measures that supposedly underlie the behavioral expressions of temperament across time. Assumptions about the reliability and predictive validity of particular measures will not be possible until developmental psychobiologists retest the same population on different occasions across a wider age range than has been used up to now.

How Does One Assess the Biological Roots of Temperament?

Another common theme running through this book involves methodological approaches to assessing the biological roots of temperament. Summarizing the multitude of strategies and techniques available to aid in the search for the biological roots of temperament is important for behavioral scientists. A familiarity with the experimental strategies and techniques of neuroscience and other disciplines will result not only in less fragmented communication between the disciplines but will also provide an understanding of where the resulting data fits in regard to mapping neural functions onto structure.

A number of chapters in this book use extreme groups, presumably to increase stability ratings for the behavioral dimensions under investigation. There is some danger when doing this in psychophysiological studies of individual differences. According to Gale and Edwards (1986):

> Extreme group designs sample only some of the distribution, waste available information, and cannot warrant assertions about general relationships between variables (e.g., whether they are linear, monotonic, or curvilinear). (p. 498)

Do the possible benefits outweigh the possible risks of extreme groups? Extreme-group analysis can be beneficial in the study of genetics, as in the search for allelic association (Plomin & Saudino, chapter 6). Plomin and Saudino also describe a new genetic method named *DF analysis of extremes*. One issue this method can address is whether the genetic etiology of the extremes of a dimension of temperament differs from the etiology of the rest of the dimension. Plomin and Saudino also suggest that a related issue can be dealt with by using DF analysis of extremes. That is, to what extent does psychopathology represent the genetic extremes of a temperamental continuum? A detailed discussion of this question is found in the previous chapter on clinical implications.

A second methodological theme involves the use of animal models. Although some psychophysiologists (e.g., Gale & Edwards, 1986) assert that animal research may reveal little about human experience and behavior, nonhuman research has been invaluable at the level of genetic analysis (Plomin & Saudino, chapter 6). Animal models also have great flexibility in terms of behavioral manipulation, as illustrated by Steinmetz's animal model for evaluating the effects of learning and memory on temperament-relevant behaviors. Animal studies also can provide researchers with information that would be impossible to obtain otherwise (e.g., pharmacological and lesioning experiments). It appears as if most researchers are cognizant of the fact that animal analogues of temperament are models and may not always transfer directly to the human experience. The extent of transfer may depend on the species used. For example, research has been done on the response to stress using inbred rat strains (Zuckerman, chapter 9), but nonhuman primate studies may be more applicable, such as the research of Levine and colleagues (e.g., Levine & Wiener, 1988) on cortisol production in threatening situations.

Going beyond infrahuman research, a number of chapters suggest techniques that may be applicable to human populations. At the human level, researchers have used indirect measures, such as the metabolites of brain neurotransmitters found in blood, urine, or cerebrospinal fluid. Less invasive physiological measures, such as Gunnar's (chapter 7 in this book) measurement of salivary cortisol, can be used even with children to inquire about nervous system response to stress. Neuroimaging techniques such as positron emission tomography scans or magnetic resonance imaging are being used increasingly more often and are contributing to the understanding of brain maturation, as well as providing support for correlations between biology and temperament–personality (Nelson, chapter 3). Although Zuckerman argues that neuroimaging techniques are too expensive for use in experiments and too limited in definition of structure to be of much use in personality research, the research of Haier, Sokolski, Katz, and Buchsbaum (1987) suggests that personality studies can be added onto ongoing neuroimaging projects to minimize costs. Lastly, the use of psychophysiological techniques such as the EEG (Calkins & Fox, chapter 8) cannot be overlooked for use in temperament research, especially because this type of measurement is both more cost effective and relatively risk free.

In formulating theoretical models of the biology of temperament, any and all resources of information should be used, but with three (at least) caveats in mind (Gale & Edwards, 1986): (a) Selection of physiological measures should be theory driven, rather than because certain measures happen to be available; (b) researchers should be alerted to when their particular research designs may be influenced by the effects of range or the law of initial values (the degree of change in a physiological measure following stimulation is a function of the initial level of the measure; for detailed discussion of this point see Stemler & Fahrenberg, 1989; Gunnar, 1989); and (c) researchers must keep in mind that using only one physiological index in an experiment raises the probability of Type II error because it neglects the possibility of individual response stereotypy. One advantage to the use of multiple techniques is that it allows the researcher to explore multiple links between levels of phenomena; that is, using behavioral as well as physiological and psychophysical measures provides more usable information than does any one measure obtained in isolation. Using multiple measures also allows the researcher to link individual differences in physiology and individual differences in behavior (Calkins & Fox, chapter 8).

Possible Future Directions in Biotemperament Research

In reviewing the contributions of biology to an understanding of temperament at the behavioral level, it is important to emphasize what is known as well as what is not known. Two obvious omissions in this book are

(a) an elaboration on evolutionary influences on the biological basis of temperament differences and (b) the role of nutrition in the development of temperament. The tracing of evolutionary influences may prove to be an even more difficult task than the search for the biological bases of a behavior, but at the very least, researchers need to acknowledge and appreciate the fact that they are attempting to map loosely defined behavioral constructs onto a physiological system that has been evolving for tens of thousands of years. Variability in nutritional status has been related not only to CNS development and function (Georgieff, in press; Wurtman & Wurtman, 1990), but also to variability in temperament-related dimensions such as activity (Pollitt & Amante, 1984). However, up to now, there have been few studies illustrating the nature of linkages between nutritional status and temperament.

The just-discussed omissions suggest future directions for biologically oriented temperament researchers. As promised earlier, we now turn to the main theme of this chapter, namely future directions for the behaviorally oriented temperament researcher.

Biological Roots of What?

In searching for biological roots of temperament, the behavioral scientist is likely to assume that the search process resembles the fabled search for the source of the Nile. The assumption that a single biological process underlies temperament, although parsimonious, does not reflect the complexities of the biological processes involved in temperament. Although there may be common physically linked CNS structures that are influential for multiple domains of temperament—because temperament is a rubric and not a monolith—there is not one single biological process that is the source of temperament (Bates, 1989). Rather, as described earlier, there appear to be multiple neural and biochemical systems that differentially relate to different domains of temperament.

For example, the operation of the neural structures that are involved in temperament will be moderated by the actions of both neurotransmitters and hormones (e.g., Rothbart et al., chapter 4; Zuckerman, chapter 9). Similarly, the relation of a central trait of temperament, such as arousal, to other domains of temperament will be moderated via the simultaneous operation of multiple biological systems (Strelau, chapter 5). Not only are there linkages between systems subserving traits of temperament, but these circuits serve many other functions (e.g., learning and memory; Steinmetz, chapter 2). At a more molecular level, although single-gene behavior relations do exist, for the most part, complex behavioral patterns such as temperament are influenced by systems of multiple genes (Plomin & Saudino, chapter 6). In addition, the contribution of nonbiological factors to biology–temperament relations is a central theme of many chapters in this book (e.g., Calkins & Fox, Gunnar, Rothbart et al., Steinmetz). Thus, in understanding the relation of biology to temperament, it is essential to keep in mind that researchers are dealing with the operation of multiple neural subsystems, which are embedded in the operation of other nonneural, biological processes, as well as in the operation of nonbiological influences.

The complexity of this process is seen not only at a biological level but also at a functional level. Given that multiple systems are involved, it is obvious that different behavioral patterns may well have different biological roots. However, because multiple systems are involved, there is also the possibility that highly similar behavioral patterns may well have different biological roots. For example, two children may be equally low in approach behavior. For the first child, low approach may be either a function of the combination of low activation of the behavioral approach system and moderate activation of the behavioral inhibition system, or a function of moderate left frontal activity and high right frontal activation. For the second child, low approach may be either a function of moderate activation of the behavioral approach system and high activation of the behavioral inhibition system, or a function of low left frontal activation and moderate right frontal activation (see Calkins & Fox, chapter 8, or Rothbart et al., chapter 4).

If biological contributions to temperament involve sets of multilevel–multidimensional biological systems, then a critical issue involves understanding exactly what these biological systems are mapping onto. At the behavioral level, not only are there multiple definitions of the overall concept of temperament coexisting in the literature (Bates, 1989; Goldsmith et al., 1987), but there are also continued disagreements about the underlying structure of those domains that researchers assign to the construct of temperament (Strelau & Angleitner, 1991). Is temperament best understood as a single core construct, similar to a latent variable with multiple indicators (e.g., arousal [Strelau, chapter 5]; impulsive unsocialized sensation seeking [Zuckerman, chapter 9])? Alternatively, is temperament best viewed as a series of hierarchically organized independent dimensions, akin to the Big Five of personality theory (Digman, 1990, Rothbart et al., chapter 4), or is temperament best understood as a set of independent unidimensional traits, as seen in the original Thomas and Chess (1977) conceptualization? How behavioral researchers ultimately define the structure of temperament is critical for those biologically oriented researchers who wish to map structure onto function. Mapping of precise biological systems onto imprecise, vague behavioral systems is, at best, an exercise in futility (as is the reverse). This book provides ample evidence that one biological system does not fit all. As the behavioral referents change, different biological systems come into play. Hence, if researchers are to understand the biological roots of temperament, then it is essential that behavioral researchers give biological researchers a relatively stable target to shoot at.

Rather then trying to map one or two traits onto a brain system, one promising venture for future research in this area may involve delineating behaviors (temperament or otherwise) that tend to covary and then attempting to pinpoint the biological systems that are involved. To take an example from the previous chapter on clinical implications, difficultness is said to involve the convergence of negative emotionality and impulsive sensation seeking. To ask what brain systems then subserve difficultness, one must see what structures and interconnections exist that are likely to produce this cluster of behavior. Mapping covariance among traits of temperament in this way can serve as an aid to understanding the psychobiology of temperament.

The importance of a more precise understanding of the nature of temperament is not limited just to the conceptualization of this construct. Some instruments, such as the Infant Behavior Questionnaire (Rothbart, 1981), are based on items defined by relatively specific child behaviors in specific situations. Other questionnaires, such as the Emotionality–Activity–Sociability Scale (EAS; Buss & Plomin, 1984), are based on more comprehensive, overall judgments. It could be argued that the former class of measures assesses relatively specific states, whereas the latter class of measures assesses more general traits (a similar distinction can be made with regard to laboratory measures as well, Bates, 1989). As Nelson suggests in chapter 3, different biological processes may underlie states versus traits; for example, amygdaloid activation may underlie trait processes, whereas frontal activation may reflect state processes. If different classes of instruments are used in the behavioral assessment of temperament, then the understanding of biological processes underlying temperament may be instrument specific rather than construct specific. Taking this possibility into the realm of speculation, Infant Behavior Questionnaire emotionality (state) could be governed by frontal processes, whereas EAS emotionality (trait) could be influenced by the amygdala. Obviously this is not a very desirable state of affairs for researchers who are attempting to understand the biology of temperament.

Although understanding of the measurement and behavioral structure of temperament will ultimately come from the efforts of behaviorally oriented researchers, the efforts of biologically oriented researchers can definitely be of help. The study of genetic correlations (Plomin & Saudino, chapter 6) offers one example of how biological research can help behavioral researchers study the structure of temperament. Traditionally, one strategy that behaviorally oriented researchers use to determine whether a group of different traits share common variance is through statistical techniques such as factor analysis. Looking for genetic correlations among different traits may offer a very useful alternative to factor analysis. Traits that share a common genetic core can be viewed as a composite, in the same way that traits loading on the same factor can be viewed as a composite. Of particular interest to both behavioral and genetic researchers would be comparisons of temperament factor structures with structures derived from genetic correlations.

Although biological research can help, behavioral researchers must be careful about borrowing too deeply from biology. A number of chapters in this book discussed only certain dimensions of temperament, primarily emotionality, approach, and withdrawal. This restriction is presumably because these are the behavioral dimensions for which there is the best biological knowledge. Focusing only on traits for which there is biological knowledge leaves in limbo other recognized traits of temperament, such as activity, persistence, and rhythmicity, for which there is less knowledge on the biological underpinnings. The place of these traits in the structure of temperament is a question that cannot be answered by focusing only on traits for which there is biological knowledge. Although focusing on known biological systems is a good starting point, researchers may be losing valuable information about temperament if they restrict their studies only to those traits of temperament that map easily onto these biological systems.[2]

In considering the contributions of biological and behavioral research to understanding the nature of temperament, a useful analogy may be the systems theory concept of rate-limiting control parameters (Fogel & Thelan, 1987). In systems in which multiple determinants must operate simultaneously if change is to occur, change only occurs when the contributions of the slowest developing determinant process become available. By viewing the study of biological roots of temperament in this way—no matter how rapid the contributions from the biological side—progress in this area will be rate-limited by the extent of the contributions from the behavioral side. That is, no matter how sophisticated the biological technology, a clear understanding of the biology of temperament will occur only when behaviorally oriented researchers begin to get closure on such fundamental issues as the structure of temperament and how best to measure this structure. In the brave new world of neuroscience, one way in which behavioral researchers can play an essential role is by offering more precise measurement approaches and conceptual schemes of what it is that biology is mapping onto.

---

[2]The same point also applies when temperament researchers attempt to borrow from other behavioral domains, as in attempts to link temperament traits to the "Big Five." Although it may be very useful to look for temperament traits that resemble the traits subsumed under the Big-Five categories, it is equally important to also study the development of temperament traits that do not neatly fit into these categories (for an extensive discussion on this question see Halverson, Kohnstamm, & Martin, in press).

Biological Roots of Temperament: Necessary but Not Sufficient

Although there are multiple definitions of temperament, the most commonly evoked working definition encompasses the idea that temperament consists of early appearing biologically based behavioral patterns (Bates, 1989). Although nonbiological factors such as environment may act to influence the course of temperament over time, the role of nonbiological factors on the development and course of temperament is generally viewed as a secondary influence. It is therefore rather surprising in a book dedicated to the biological roots of temperament to find so many chapter authors stressing either the importance of environment (Calkins & Fox, Gunnar, Plomin & Saudino, Rothbart et al.) or environmental processes such as learning (Steinmetz). How are nonbiological parameters, such as environment, important in understanding links between biology and the causes and consequences of individual differences in temperament?

Contributions From the Study of Learning and Memory

One unique area, as delineated by both Steinmetz (chapter 2) and Nelson (chapter 3), is the potential role that learning and memory play in the operation of temperament. Parental responses to temperament questionnaires are obviously based on parents' memories of their children's behavior across time. However, more critically, both Nelson and Steinmetz illustrate that potential linkages between temperament, learning, and memory occur, in part, through functional linkages between areas of the CNS that are involved in emotion and areas that are involved in cognitive functioning. Furthermore, both Nelson and Steinmetz argue that fundamental processes underlying temperament involve the comparison of incoming stimuli with experiences that have already been learned and stored. On the basis of this "comparator" process, the organism may exhibit approach, fight–flight, or inhibition behavior.

Steinmetz further suggests that the relations between learning, memory, and temperament are not unidirectional. Just as learning and memory can influence the expression of biologically based temperament processes, temperament can also influence learning and memory. For the most part, evidence on the role of temperament in learning and memory processes has primarily involved the study of infrahuman species (Steinmetz, chapter 2); supportive evidence is also shown in studies of personality and learning (Gray, 1991), as well as in concepts such as state-dependent learning (Bower, 1987; Overton, 1991). In terms of the study of relations between human temperament and learning–memory, the available evidence is rather scarce. Variability in temperament has been related to variability in classroom achievement (Martin, 1989), infant operant learning (Dunst & Langerfelt, 1985; Worobey & Butler, 1988), intrainfant variability on visual recognition memory performance (Wachs, Morrow, & Slabach, 1990), and interindividual variability on transfer of training (Skuy, 1989). However, temperament has also been related to the child's "testability" (Bathurst & Gottfried, 1987), ability to complete laboratory learning procedures (Fagen, Ohr, Singer, & Fleckenstein, 1987; Wachs & Smitherman, 1985), and quality of the child's behavior in the classroom (Martin, 1989). Hence, it is unclear whether the observed results are a function of direct relations between temperament and learning–memory, or whether they are a function of differences in temperament resulting in child behavior patterns that influence the child's reactions to the learning environment.

For the behavioral researcher, two issues need further investigation. The first, which is less tied into biological processes, is the question of whether the relations between temperament and learning at the human level are based on a direct link between temperament and learning, or whether these relations are indirect, that is, mediated by the role temperament plays on children's behavior in learning situations. The second question, which has much more relevance to biologically based theories of temperament, is the development of the comparator process, which is described as underlying the contributions of learning and memory to temperament (Steinmetz, chapter 2). If comparisons between past and present experience trigger children's biologically based expressions of temperament, then from a behavioral point of view, there are two predictions that can be made. First, children with higher levels of recognition memory should show earlier stability of temperament because these are children who should be better able to compare past and present stimuli and thus organize a systematic, appropriate response such as approach or inhibition (in this case, there may also be higher levels of interparent agreement). Second, children who are exposed to learning experiences that involve repeated reexposure to previously learned emotional cues (e.g., the reinstatement paradigm; Rovee-Collier, 1984) should also show earlier stability of temperament. Children with histories of reinstatements would be more likely to retain learned emotional conditioning cues, which would thus facilitate the comparator process, again leading to greater stabilization. This discussion offers clear examples of how behavioral researchers can build on insights from neuroscience to design research that has direct implications for biological models of temperament.

Context as a Moderator of Links Between Biology and Behavior

A common theme that has emerged across a number of chapters in this book is that the behavioral consequences of biologically based temperament differences cannot be understood without reference to the context within which the child functions. Theoretically, the role of context in temperament–behavior relations occurs in two ways.

Reactive covariance

In chapter 4, Rothbart et al. illustrate the operation of what has been called *reactive covariance*. Reactive covariance refers to situations in which children with certain behavioral patterns have a higher probability of eliciting certain types of behaviors from caregivers in their environment (Plomin, DeFries, & Loehlin, 1977). For example, Rothbart et al. predict that infants with a biological predisposition to exhibit distress will be more likely to experience punishment from their caregivers. This increased punishment, in turn, results in the easily distressed child being more likely to develop conditioned fear reactions. Although it is logical to expect that variability in child behavior (temperament) should relate to variability in rearing environment, reviews of the available evidence relating child temperament to caregiver behavioral patterns in the first 2 years of life have not been generally supportive of strong consistent linkages (Crockenberg, 1986; Slabach et al., 1991). The reasons for the inability to find consistent relations between early temperament and caregiver behavioral patterns have included the possibility of inadequate measures of either temperament or caregiver behaviors (Slabach et al., 1991), or a lack of statistical power (Crockenberg, 1986). On the basis of the evidence presented in this book, we argue for two other possible causes. First, as noted earlier in this chapter, developmental changes in the CNS may influence the consistency of children's responses to the environment. Caregivers may well be unable to organize consistent patterns of response to a child whose behavior is essentially situation specific. If this view is correct, then one should be able to detect systematic changes in caregiver behavior toward infants as a function of changes in the operation of the biological systems underlying temperament, such as the behavioral inhibition system. At present, such studies will have to be based on behavioral changes in children's inhibition patterns. However, given the rate of progress in developmental neuroscience (Nelson, chapter 3), researchers may ultimately be able to measure the actual functioning of the CNS processes that are related to the expression of critical variables of temperament, such as inhibition. At this time, collaborative research between neuroscientists (measuring the maturation of temperament-related biological systems) and behavioral researchers (assessing the nature of the behavioral patterns shown by caregivers toward their infant) would be an obvious way of testing hypothesized relations between rearing environment and biological contributions to the stability of temperament.

The second probable cause of inconsistent relations between infant temperament and caregiver behaviors comes from suggestions that temperament–behavior linkages may be moderated by contextual factors such as environmental chaos or cultural attitudes about the desirability of specific child behavior patterns (Gunnar, chapter 7; Wachs, 1992). Support for both these possibilities exists in the literature. Measures of environmental chaos (e.g., noise and crowding) have been repeatedly shown to influence the nature of caregiving patterns (Wachs, 1992) and have also been related to variability in toddler temperament (Matheny, Wilson, & Thoben, 1987; Wachs, 1988). In perhaps the strongest demonstration of how higher order contextual factors can moderate the role of temperament, DeVries (1984) reported that temperamentally difficult Kenyan infants were more likely to survive famine conditions than were temperamentally easy Kenyan infants. DeVries attributed differential survival to culturally based caregiver preferences for difficult babies, who were viewed as potential "warriors" and who were more likely to be fed by the mother. A similar pattern has also been shown in caregiver preferences for nonplacid infants in areas of endemic high infant mortality in Brazil (Schepher-Hughes, 1987). If links between biologically based patterns of temperament and caregiver behaviors are moderated by micro- and macrocontextual factors, then again, the role of the behavioral researcher is clear, namely to measure the nature and extent of specific micro- and macromoderating variables.

Active covariance

A second moderating contextual link between biologically based temperament and behavioral outcomes involves the concept of *active covariance*. Active covariance refers to children with certain biological predispositions having a higher probability of selecting specific environmental "niches" (Plomin et al., 1977). The data presented by Gunnar (chapter 7) clearly illustrate how inhibited shy children in new situations are more likely to engage in familiar solitary activities and use familiar teachers as a resource, whereas uninhibited children are more likely to attempt new and unfamiliar activities or activities with other children. Both examples demonstrate how children with different temperament characteristics select preferred environmental niches (active covariance). Although Gunnar's data are clear cut and intuitively compelling, other data suggest that processes other than active covariance also are involved. Working within the same conceptual framework, Calkins and Fox (chapter 8) report that EEG patterns at 9 months of age that reflect biological inhibition appear not to predict measures of behavioral inhibition at 14 months of age. Calkins and Fox suggest a number of factors that may moderate whether inhibited children end up in preferred niches. Potential moderating factors include internal nonbiological processes, such as attachment history, and the degree to which caregivers facilitate or impede the child's attempts to select an appropriate niche. Ample existing evidence indicates that caregivers actively attempt to shape their children's behaviors in directions that are consistent with the caregivers' own pref-erences (Bell & Chapman, 1986). However, the existing evidence also indicates that different caregivers have different preferences for the types of temperament-related child behaviors that they can accept or reject (Hubert & Wachs, 1985). On the basis of individual preferences, parents may act to either facilitate or inhibit their child's attempts to find preferred environmental niches.

In terms of future research in this area, obviously much more needs to be known about the processes wherein children select their own en-vironmental niches, perhaps using paradigms such as those described by Gunnar (chapter 7). Another alternative research direction lies in the area of clinical research, in terms of training appropriate parental reactivity to children's attempts at niche selection. Extending the position of Calkins and Fox (chapter 8), it could be hypothesized that parents who intensively support the highly inhibited child may be reducing this child's ability to develop strategies that will, ultimately, overcome the potential conse-quences of too much behavioral inhibition. Following this hypothesis, we argue that it may be important to encourage parents to use "emotional scaffolding" strategies. By emotional scaffolding, we refer to caregivers who expose their children to alternative niches as these children become ready to deal effectively with these niches (akin to inhibited children in Gunnar's study, who, over time, began to venture out into the larger classroom environment). A critical question is how to detect when chil-dren are ready to explore new niches. Although looking at children's behavior is one approach, it seems clear that linkages between inhibited behavior and internal stress reactions are not totally isomorphic (Lewis & Kawakami, 1992). Combining the use of biochemical markers, such as cortisol, with behavioral observations of children's behaviors in new sit-uations offers a further avenue of collaboration between biologically and behaviorally oriented researchers, in terms of answering the question of when parents should be encouraged to push their child into new niches versus holding the child back.

Interactions Between Biology and Environment

The concept of organism–environment interaction refers to differential reactivity to objectively similar environmental input by different individuals (Wachs & Plomin, 1991). A number of authors in this book describe processes that sound very much like the operation of organism–environment interaction. For example, on the basis of anatomical linkages between the amygdala and attentional processing areas of the cortex, Rothbart et al. (chapter 4) postulate that more anxious children may perceive more potential threats in their environment than do nonanxious children. As a result, the subjective experience of the anxious child may be very different from the subjective experience of the nonanxious child, even in highly similar environmental settings. A similar interactional process is seen in the hypothesis by Calkins and Fox (chapter 8) that the salience of the environment may be moderated by the strength of individual characteristics such as temperamental dispositions (also see Buss & Plomin, 1984). The potential operation of interaction is also seen in the argument by Strelau (chapter 5), in which he states that there may be stable individual differences in the degree of arousal that is associated with given levels of stimulation.

As has been argued previously, the study of organism–environment interaction offers a natural bridge for collaborative research between biologically and behaviorally oriented researchers (Wachs & Plomin, 1991). This is particularly true if advances in neuroscience give researchers more precise ways of measuring individual contributions to the organismic portion of the interaction. For the most part, researchers who are interested in interaction have had to use less precise demographic (e.g., diagnostic group) or questionnaire measures (e.g., temperament scales) to assess organismic contributions. Neuroscience researchers will hopefully be able to provide precise measures of the degree of CNS activity or of the biochemical processes underlying individual traits like anxiety or inhibition (Nelson, chapter 3). These measures can then be combined with detailed observations of the environment as a means of answering the question of how individual differences in reactivity interact with specific environmental characteristics to shape the course of development.

Biological and Nonbiological Contributions: The Question of Directionality

From the evidence presented in this book, there can be no doubt that biological factors can influence variability in behavioral patterns that are called temperament. However, running through much of the evidence presented in this book is a common theme: that in analyzing temperament, researchers are not dealing with single biological–behavioral relations operating in isolation. Rather, what researchers are dealing with are multilevel–multidimensional biological and behavioral systems. A common feature of these types of complex systems is bidirectionality: mutual influences across different levels (Gottlieb, 1991). Evidence for bidirectional influences has been noted at various points in this book. For example, experience, learning, and memory have been repeatedly shown to moderate the behavioral consequences of biologically based patterns of temperament (Calkins & Fox, Gunnar, Rothbart et al., Steinmetz). Evidence also indicates that contextual characteristics can influence short-term biological processes. In chapter 7, Gunnar demonstrated that sensitive and responsive care and secure emotional relations may reduce or prevent a hypothalamic–pituitary–adrenal cortisol stress response (also see Cacioppo & Berntson, 1992). What has not been clearly delineated in this book is whether nonbiological processes can also influence the development and operation of the more "hard-wired" biological processes, such as enzyme production or CNS development. Although some chapter authors may well draw the line at this form of bidirectionality (e.g., Zuckerman), we argue that on both empirical and conceptual grounds nonbiological factors may have a role to play in the development and function of more fundamental biological processes.

Empirically, there is ample evidence that environmental factors can influence various aspects of CNS development that are involved in cognitive processing (Diamond, 1988; Greenough & Black, 1992). Can the same be said for those biological processes involving temperament? Conceptually, we argue that a tie-in is possible, to the extent that temperament-related neural processes are governed by *experience-dependent development.* Experience-dependent development refers to those neural processes that are involved in the storage of information that is unique to the individual (Greenough & Black, 1992). Experience-dependent development is manifest in the production and strengthening of new synaptic connections, which can occur across the life span in response to unique information. This is distinct from *experience-expectant development,* which involves selective retention of existing neural synapses as a function of exposure to stimulation that is commonly available to most members of a species, and which occurs within a relatively limited time span (sensitive period).

A number of the points made in various chapters suggest the potential operation of experience-dependent development processes in regard to temperament. The relation of learning and memory to temperament (Nelson, Steinmetz) certainly suggests that specific learning experiences could result in the production of specific experience-dependent synaptic connections, which could influence variability in patterns of temperament. Furthermore, if fearful or inhibited children are more vigilant in surveying their environments for threats (Gunnar), or are more likely to interpret neutral stimuli as threatening (Rothbart et al.), then synaptic connections involving threat and anxiety may be developed and strengthened by a process of interaction and active covariance. That is, children who are more prone to detect threats in their environment, and who set up environmental niches based on the perception of environmental threats, may be producing self-generating experiences that both initiate and strengthen the specific neural connections that are involved in processing fear and inhibition (experience-dependent development).

The just-presented discussion is obviously very speculative, especially because there is little evidence for the operation of experience-dependent development either at the human level or for noncognitive traits. However, if experience-dependent development can be shown to operate at the human level in regard to noncognitive traits such as temperament, then there are major opportunities for collaboration between behavioral and biological researchers. If the technology of neuroscience advances to the point that researchers can actually measure the operation of experience-dependent biological processes, such as formation of specific synapses or the speed of transmission across specific synaptic connections, then among the critical questions that would need to be answered would be (a) what types of experiences are associated with the production or functioning of specific synaptic connections, (b) what part does repeated experience (reinstatement) play in this process, and (c) how much of experience-dependent development is a function of the child's own actions or interpretation of his or her own objective environment? These types of questions can only be answered by direct ongoing collaboration between developmental neuroscientists and behaviorally oriented researchers who have expertise in the nature and measurement of nonbiological influences on development.

Conclusion

It is clear from the chapters contained in this book that researchers have learned a substantial amount about the role of biological processes underlying temperament. Confirming Bates's (1989) original insight on the structure of temperament, it is clear that temperament is a multilevel phenomenon, functioning at both the behavioral and the biological level. Similarly, Rothbart et al.'s statement (chapter 4) that an anxious child may build up representations emphasizing the threatening aspects of his or her environment, leading the child to develop within a threatening world "to some extent apart from the environment as experienced by others" should reiterate that our subjects are not "stimulus–response lumps in the laboratory" (Gale & Edwards, 1986, p. 498). In studying the developmental psychobiology of temperament, as in any discipline, researchers should remind themselves that not only can individual psychology create an ever-changing individual reality but that physiology, as the basis for psychology, is also dynamic.

It is also clear that further progress in understanding the nature, development, and consequences of individual differences in temperament will depend on the degree to which researchers recognize and build on this multilevel dynamic phenomenon. Clearly, there are many biological and behavioral questions that remain to be answered, some of which can best be answered by researchers functioning within their own domains. Ultimately, however, progress will be governed by the degree to which behavioral and biological researchers can collaborate on questions of common interest, some of which have been delineated in this chapter. As suggested by the title of this book, temperament is clearly a phenomena that is at the interface of both biology and behavior. As such, biological and behavioral researchers have the unique opportunity to do both within-

and cross-domain temperament research. Collaborative research of the types suggested here have the potential of leading to advances in the theory of temperament, at both the biological and nonbiological levels. In turn, advances in the theory of temperament can only lead to greater understanding of the role played by temperament in both normal development and deviations from normal development.

References

Anokhin, P. (1964). Systemogenesis as a general regulation of brain development. In W. Himwich (Ed.), *The developing brain: Progress in brain research* (Vol. 9, pp. 58–86). Amsterdam: Elsevier.

Bates, J. E. (1989). Concepts and measures of temperament. In G. A. Kohnstamm, J. E. Bates, & M. K. Rothbart (Eds.), *Temperament in childhood* (pp. 3–27). New York: Wiley.

Bathurst, K., & Gottfried, A. (1987). Untestable subjects in child development research. *Child Development, 58,* 1135–1144.

Bell, R., & Chapman, M. (1986). Child effects in studies using experimental or brief longitudinal approaches to socialization. *Developmental Psychology, 22,* 595–603.

Bower, G. (1987). Commentary on mood and memory. *Behavioral Research and Therapy, 25,* 443–454.

Buss, A., & Plomin, R. (1984). *Temperament: Early developing personality traits.* Hillsdale, NJ: Erlbaum.

Cacioppo, J., & Berntson, G. (1992). Social psychological contributions to the decade of the brain. *American Psychologist, 47,* 1019–1028.

Clarke-Stewart, K. (1978). And daddy makes three: The father's impact on mother and young child. *Child Development, 49,* 446–478.

Crockenberg, S. (1986). Are temperamental differences in babies associated with predictable differences in caregiving? In J. Lerner & R. Lerner (Eds.), *Temperament and psychosocial interaction in children* (pp. 53–74). San Francisco: Jossey-Bass.

DeVries, M. (1984). Temperament and infant mortality among the Masai of East Africa. *American Journal of Psychiatry, 141,* 1189–1994.

Diamond, M. (1988). *Enriching heredity: The impact of the environment on the anatomy of the brain.* New York: Free Press.

Digman, J. (1990). Personality structure: Emergence of the five factor model. *Annual Review of Psychology, 41,* 417–440.

Dunst, C., & Langerfelt, B. (1985). Maternal ratings of temperament and operant learning in two to three month old infants. *Child Development, 56,* 555–563.

Emde, R. N. (1989). The infant's relationship experience: Developmental and affective aspects. In A. J. Sameroff & R. N. Emde (Eds.), *Relationship disturbances in early childhood* (pp. 33–51). New York: Basic Books.

Fagen, J., Ohr, P., Singer, J., & Fleckenstein, L. (1987). Infant temperament and subject loss due to crying during parent conditioning. *Child Development, 58,* 497–504.

Fogel, A., & Thelan, E. (1987). Development of early expressive and communicative action: Reinterpreting evidence from a dynamics system perspective. *Developmental Psychology, 23,* 747–761.

Gale, A., & Edwards, J. A. (1986). Individual differences. In M. G. H. Coles, E. Donchin, & S. W. Porges (Eds.), *Psychophysiology: Systems, processes, and applications* (pp. 431–507). New York: Guilford Press.

Georgieff, M. (in press). Nutritional deficiencies as developmental risk factors. In C. A. Nelson (Ed.), *Threats to optimal development: Integrating biological, psychological and social risk factors.* Hillsdale, NJ: Erlbaum.

Goldsmith, H., Buss, A., Plomin, R., Rothbart, M., Thomas, A., Chess, S., Hinde, R., & McCall, R. (1987). Roundtable: What is temperament? Four approaches. *Child Development, 58,* 505–529.

Goodwin, D. (1989). *A dictionary of neuropsychology.* New York: Springer-Verlag.

Gottlieb, G. (1991). Experiential canalization of behavioral development. *Developmental Psychology, 27,* 4–13.

Gray, J. (1991). The neuropsychology of temperament. In J. Strelau & A. Angleitner (Eds.), *Explorations in temperament* (pp. 105–127). New York: Plenum.

Greenough, W., & Black, J. (1992). Induction of brain structure by experience: Substrates for cognitive development. In M. Gunnar & C. Nelson (Eds.), *Developmental behavioral neuroscience* (pp. 153–232). Hillsdale, NJ: Erlbaum.

Gunnar, M. (1989). Studies of the human infant's adrenocortical response to potentially stressful events. *New Directions for Child Development, 45,* 3–10.

Haier, R. J., Sokolski, K., Katz, M., & Buchsbaum, M. S. (1987). The study of personality with positron emission topography. In J. Strelau & H. J. Eysenck (Eds.), *Personality dimensions and arousal* (pp. 251–267). New York: Plenum.

Halverson, C., Kohnstamm, G., & Martin, R. (in press). *The developing structure of temperament and personality from infancy to adulthood.* Hillsdale, NJ: Erlbaum.

Hubert, N., & Wachs, T. D. (1985). Parental perceptions of the behavioral components of infant easiness–difficultness. *Child Development, 56,* 1525–1537.

Levine, S., & Wiener, S. (1988). Psychoendocrine aspects of mother–infant relationships in nonhuman primates. *Psychoneuroendocrinology, 13,* 143–154.

Lewis, M., & Kawakami, K. (1992, May). *Affectivity and cortisol response differences between Japanese and American infants.* Paper presented at the International Conference on Infant Studies, Miami, FL.

Lindsley, D. B. (1939). A longitudinal study of the occipital alpha rhythm in normal children: Frequency and amplitude standards. *Journal of Genetic Psychology*, *55*, 197–213.

MacDonald, K., & Parke, R. (1984). Bridging the gap: Parent–child interaction and peer interactive competence. *Child Development*, *55*, 1265–1277.

Martin, R. P. (1989). Temperament and education. In W. B. Carey & S. W. McDevitt (Eds.), *Clinical and educational applications of temperament research* (pp. 37–52). Berwyn, PA: Swets North America.

Matheny, A. P., Jr., Wilson, R. S., & Thoben, A. S. (1987). Home and mother: Relation of infant temperament. *Developmental Psychology*, *21*, 486–494.

Overton, D. (1991). Historical context of state dependent learning and discriminative drug effects. *Behavioral Pharmacology*, *2*, 253–264.

Papez, J. (1937). A proposed mechanism of emotion. *Archives of Neurology and Psychiatry*, *38*, 725–743.

Plomin, R., DeFries, J., & Loehlin, J. (1977). Genotype environment interaction and correlation in the analysis of human development. *Psychological Bulletin*, *84*, 309–322.

Pollitt, E., & Amante, P. (1984). *Energy intake and activity*. New York: Alan R. Liss.

Rothbart, M. (1981). The measurement of temperament in infancy. *Child Development*, *52*, 569–578.

Rovee-Collier, C. (1984). The ontogeny of learning and memory in human infancy. In R. Kail & N. Spear (Eds.), *Comparative perspectives on the development of memory* (pp. 103–134). Hillsdale, NJ: Erlbaum.

Schepher-Hughes, N. (1987). Basic strangeness: Maternal estrangement and infant death— A critique of bonding theory. In C. Super (Ed.), *The role of culture in developmental disorders* (pp. 131–153). San Diego, CA: Academic Press.

Skuy, M. (1989). Pertinence of temperament for learning even in highly disadvantaged youth. In W. B. Carey & S. W. McDevitt (Eds.), *Clinical and educational applications of temperament research* (pp. 87–90). Berwyn, PA: Swets North America.

Slabach, E., Morrow, J., & Wachs, T. D. (1991). Questionnaire measurement of infant and child temperament. In J. Strelau & A. Angleitner (Eds.), *Explorations in temperament* (pp. 205–234). New York: Plenum.

Stemler, G., & Fahrenberg, J. (1989). Psychophysiological assessment. In G. Turpin (Ed.), *Handbook of clinical psychophysiology* (pp. 71–104). New York: Wiley.

Strelau, J., & Angleitner, A. (1991). Introduction. In J. Strelau & A. Angleitner (Eds.), *Explorations in temperament* (pp. 1–14). New York: Plenum.

Thomas, A., & Chess, S. (1977). *Temperament and development*. New York: Brunner/Mazel.

Wachs, T. D. (1988). Relevance of physical environment influences for toddler temperament. *Infant Behavior and Development*, *11*, 431–446.

Wachs, T. D. (1992). *The nature of nurture*. Newbury Park, CA: Sage.

Wachs, T. D., Morrow, J., & Slabach, E. (1990). Intra-individual variability in infant visual recognition performance. *Infant Behavior and Development*, *13*, 401–407.

Wachs, T. D., & Plomin, R. (1991). *Conceptualization and measurement of organism–environment interaction.* Washington, DC: American Psychological Association.

Wachs, T. D., & Smitherman, C. (1985). Infant temperament and subject loss in an habituation procedure. *Child Development, 56,* 861–867.

Worobey, J., & Butler, J. (1988, April). *Memory, learning and temperament in early infancy.* Paper presented at the International Congress on Infant Studies, Washington, DC.

Wurtman, R., & Wurtman, J. (1990). *Nutrition and the brain.* New York: Raven Press.

Author Index

Biederman, J., 296, *301*, *304*
Birch, H. G., 85, *115*, 201, *217*, 276, 279, *305*
Birns, B., 85, *110*
Black, J., 224, *254*, 330, *334*
Black, J. E., 49, *79*
Blackburn, R., 226, *249*
Blehar, M. C., 188, *196*
Bliss, E., 240, *250*
Block, J., 109, *110*, 223, *249*
Block, J. H., 109, *110*, 223, *249*
Boerwinkle, E. A., 163, *171*
Bohlin, G., 85, *111*, 289, *303*
Bolduc, E. A., 296, *301*
Bortner, M., 134, *137*
Borysenko, J., 176, *196*
Bouchard, T. J., Jr., 244, 245, *249*, *252*
Bourgeois, J. P., 69, *81*
Bower, G., 94, *111*, 324, *333*
Brandt, M. E., 232, *249*
Braungart, J. M., 119, *137*, 147, 149, *167*, *170*, 277, 295, *304*
Brazelton, T. B., 288, *301*
Brickson, M., 66, 68, *77*
Bridger, W., 85, *110*
Brodersen, L., 180, 181, 182, 184, 195, *197*
Brooks, C., 182, 183, 184, 185, 186, *196*
Brown, G. L., 238, *252*
Brown, M. M., 283, *301*
Brown, R., 36, *43*
Buchsbaum, M. S., 121, 133, 136, *137*, 222, 231, 233, 234, *249*, *251*, *254*, 317, *334*
Buck, R., 102, *111*
Bucy, P. C., 25, *44*
Bungener, C., 227, *250*
Burgess, C., 100, *111*
Burke, J. D., 225, *253*
Buss, A., 2, 3, 4, *13*, 200, *214*, 319, 320, 321, 329, *333*, *334*

Buss, A. H., 49, *77*, 85, *111*, 117, 118, 119, 126, 132, *137*, *138*, 200, 201, *216*
Buss, K., 188, 189, 194, 195, *196*
Butler, F. K., 59, *81*
Butler, J., 324, *336*

Cacioppo, J., 330, *333*
Cador, M., 88, 89, *114*
Calhoon, L., 238, *249*
Calkins, S. D., 74, *77*, 200, 202, 203, 204, 205, 206, 209, 211, 212, 213, *214*, *215*
Camac, C., 33, *46*, 223, *255*
Cameron, J. R., 284, 286, 287, *301*, *302*
Campbell, B. A., 269, *272*
Campos, B. E., 180, *196*
Campos, J., 72, *77*, 149, *170*, 277, 295, *304*
Campos, J. J., 4, *13*, 72, *77*, *79*, 200, 204, *216*
Candland, D. K., 188, *197*
Cannon, W. B., 122, *137*
Capella, J. N., 224, *249*
Carey, G., 147, *169*
Carey, W. B., 200, *214*, 278, 279, 286, 288, *302*
Carmichael, S. T., 59, 60, *78*
Carton, S., 227, *250*
Caspi, A., 281, 284, *302*
Chapman, J. P., 201, *214*
Chapman, L. J., 201, *214*
Chapman, M., 328, *333*
Cherner, M., 148, *171*
Chess, S., 2, 3, 4, 5, *14*, 85, *115*, 117, 118, 134, *138*, *140*, 200, 201, *216*, *217*, 276, 277, 278, 279, 282, 286, 290, *302*, *305*, 319, 320, *334*, *335*
Chipuer, H. M., 144, *169*
Chorney, M., 152, 161, *171*
Christal, R. E., 265, *273*

Subject Index

About the Editors

John E. Bates is a professor of psychology at Indiana University. He received his PhD in clinical psychology in 1973 from the University of California, Los Angeles. His research focuses on the origins of behavioral adjustment in children and adolescents, with special emphasis on the roles of temperament and parent–child relationships. He has coedited a book and written numerous articles on these topics.

Theodore D. Wachs is a professor on psychological sciences at Purdue University. He received his PhD in child clinical psychology in 1968 from George Peabody College. He his a member of the editorial boards of leading developmental psychology journals and is a fellow of the American Psychological Association. His current research concerns the relationships between development and young children's environmental and nutritional influences. He has authored or edited four books and has written numerous articles on developmental psychology.